AF605976

MESSIANIC BELIEFS AND IMPERIAL POLITICS IN MEDIEVAL ISLAM

Studies in Comparative Religion
Frederick M. Denny, Series Editor

Messianic Beliefs and Imperial Politics in Medieval Islam

The ʻAbbāsid Caliphate in the Early Ninth Century

Hayrettin Yücesoy

THE UNIVERSITY OF SOUTH CAROLINA PRESS

Published by the University of South Carolina Press
Columbia, South Carolina 29208

www.sc.edu/uscpress

Manufactured in the United States of America

18 17 16 15 14 13 12 11 10 09   10 9 8 7 6 5 4 3 2 1

Library of Congress Cataloging-in-Publication Data

Yücesoy, Hayrettin.
Messianic beliefs and imperial politics in medieval Islam : the ‘Abbasid caliphate in the early ninth century / Hayrettin Yücesoy.
p. cm. — (Studies in comparative religion)
Includes bibliographical references and index.
ISBN 978-1-57003-819-8 (cloth : alk. paper)
1. ‘Abbasids. 2. Islamic Empire—History—750–1258 3. Caliphate—History. 4. Mahdism—History. 5. Eschatology, Islamic. I. Title.
DS76.4.Y77 2009
956'.013—dc22
2008049200

This book was printed on Glatfelter Natures, a recycled paper with 30 percent postconsumer waste content.

To Mukadder, Ahmet, and Can

Contents

Series Editor's Preface

The 'Abbasid Caliphate in Baghdad, beginning in 749 A.D., ushered in the Golden Age of Islamic civilization in its eastern regions and exerted considerable influence from the Mediterranean basin to the Far East until the Mongol destruction of its capital in 1258. The period of the actual 'Abbasid dynasty's greatest political power and influence was in the eighth and ninth centuries, ending with the Caliph al-Ma'mūn (r. 813–33), who is the principal figure in this absorbing study of the roles that messianic beliefs and apocalyptic expectations played in "harmonizing his religious views and political ambitions," as the author writes. Although historians from 'Abbasid times have recorded the existence of such religiously based influences, Yücesoy's discourse brings the subject to a new level of analysis and understanding, showing not only the strong influence of the new religion of Islam's messianic and apocalyptic propensities—based in part on the Qur'an's message about judgment and the end of the world—but also detailing how the neighboring older religions of Zoroastrianism, Judaism, and Christianity held parallel beliefs along similar lines, although obviously with differing aims and outcomes.

This important new contribution to scholarship on the Abbasid Caliphate is one in an increasingly productive body of recent studies of this vast subject, which may be compared in scope and fateful effects with the Roman Empire centuries earlier. Of particular interest is the author's refreshing consideration and coherent explication of messianic beliefs and apocalyptic expectations as spiritually powerful motivators for political, social, and personal action and not simply realpolitik.

Frederick M. Denny

Preface

Tradition holds that the prophet Muḥammad told his community: "There will be four truces between you and the Romans. The fourth one will be at the hands of a man from the family of Hārūn and will last seven years. The prophet was asked, 'O messenger of God, who will be the imam of the people on that day?' He said, '[He will be] from my progeny, [his age will be] forty years old, as if his face were a planet of pearl. There will be a black mole on his right cheek, and [he will be clothed with] a cloak fashioned for youth. He will resemble a man from the children of Israel (*Banū Isrā'īl*) and he will rule twenty years. He will find treasures and conquer the cities of unbelief'" (quoted from Al-Hindī, *Kanz al-'Ummāl,* 14:268.

Implicit in this prophecy is the major theme of this book. *Messianic Beliefs and Imperial Politics in Medieval Islam* deals with the early 'Abbāsid caliphate and focuses on the tumultuous period immediately after the death in 809 of Hārūn al-Rashīd, whose two sons engaged in a bitter civil war that resulted in the murder of the designated caliph al-Amīn (r. 809–13) and the eventual ascension of al-Ma'mūn (r. 813–33) to the throne. A decade-long (ca. 809–19) civil war caused a great deal of destruction of agricultural lands, shook up the military and administrative structure of the caliphate, created a renewed tension among the landed and bureaucratic nobility in Baghdad and the provinces, and damaged the legitimacy of the caliphate. Against such extraordinary circumstances, I attempt to explain an often overlooked aspect of the civil war and the remarkable policies of al-Ma'mūn from the perspective of Muslim and non-Muslim prophecies circulating at the same time.

Although I examine more closely the period between 809 and 833, my goal is to shed light on the role of messianic and apocalyptic beliefs in shaping 'Abbāsid political behavior as one of the major dominant ideologies that the caliphs used to craft, support, and justify their religio-political agendas. One line of thinking holds that messianic beliefs served only as a rallying cry for protesters in social and political movements against the established order or, worse yet, as a convenient ideological tool for rulers to combat opposition and pacify the masses. Yet this is not only overtly dismissive but also no longer convincing. Clearly messianic beliefs had more substantial and positive roles to play in bringing about political and institutional changes. I hope that specialists and general readers who are interested in ʿAbbāsid history, the political role of messianism in any culture, and the thorny methodological issue of dealing with religion or messianism in historical interpretation will engage the argument and the narrative of this book.

To that end, I have divided the present study into an introduction and six chapters followed by a conclusion. In the introduction, I discuss the pivotal importance of messianic beliefs in medieval Islamic politics. I evaluate historiographical and apocalyptic sources, engage modern scholarship on early Islamic messianism and al-Ma'mūn, and explain the contribution of this work to scholarship on ʿAbbāsid history. Chapter 1 traces the role of messianic beliefs and movements during Umayyad and early ʿAbbāsid caliphates. In this chapter I show how the shift between, or the succession of, messianic charisma and its routinization in early Islamic politics resulted in both sociopolitical unrest and institutional changes in the central government during the Umayyad and early ʿAbbāsid periods. Observing the fact that messianic and apocalyptic anxiety permeated Muslim and non-Muslim communities alike, I also discuss some of the ways in which non-Muslim apocalyptic anxieties contributed to Muslim sensibilities during the first two centuries of Islam.

Chapter 2 explores prophecies as a discourse, as evidence of a political mentality and a normative moral and ideological prescription in ʿAbbāsid history. It illuminates the connections between anxieties associated with the dawn of a new century and political changes. I begin by probing how Qur'ānic discourse of the end of the world might have contributed to the proliferation of apocalyptic ideas in early Islamic history. I then discuss how the image of the Mahdī, the Muslim messianic figure, as a model for renewing and transforming the caliphate emerged as a political ideology of militant piety during the first century of Islam and continued to evolve in diverse directions in the following centuries. By drawing on prophecies focusing on the turn of the third Islamic century, 200 A.H./A.D. 800, whose approach and occurrence provoked a flood of prophecies on the fate of the ʿAbbāsids, I demonstrate the dual role of prophecies as both depicting and potentially influencing the events of the civil war.

Chapter 3 examines the ʿAbbāsid civil war after the death of the caliph Hārūn al-Rashīd in 809 as an example of *fitna*, that is, apocalyptic tribulation. It illustrates how the sharp political divide in ʿAbbāsid society justified radically differing visions concerning the future of the caliphate. Whether the political divide occurred because of the conflict between the center of political power and the provinces—Khurāsān in particular—or between the Shīʿī opposition and the ʿAbbāsid dynasty, it was imagined as an apocalyptic confrontation. Prophecies show that the observers of the civil war imagined it to be either an apocalyptic battle causing the destruction of the ʿAbbāsids or a rite of passage leading to the awaited millennium and the rise of the Mahdī.

Chapter 4 points out the messianic dimensions of al-Ma'mūn's move against his brother during the civil war. Within the context of anxieties about the collapse of the 'Abbāsids and the rise of the Mahdī at the beginning of the third Islamic century, such as the Shī'ī and non-Shī'ī revolts, al-Ma'mūn projected the image of a messianic contender and ruler. By referring to apocalyptic sources and other relevant material, I clarify how anxieties during the civil war might have informed al-Ma'mūn's decision to adopt a strategy responsive to messianic expectations, name his movement the suggestive "second summons" (*al-da'wa al-thāniya*) and designate an 'Alid as heir apparent to overcome the traditional 'Abbāsid ideological obstacles before him.

Chapter 5 provides an account of al-Ma'mūn's return to Baghdad at the turn of the third Islamic century. Al-Ma'mūn struggled throughout his reign to undo the damage of the civil war and reposition the caliphate as a dominant force in the imperial and religious competition of late antiquity. I examine al-Ma'mūn's domestic policies and his activities abroad, in particular his missionary activity in Central Asia and military offensive against Byzantium, to clarify the reasons for the caliph's renewed political vigor. I argue that some of his major domestic policies and activities abroad demonstrate a constructive engagement with messianic beliefs in imperial politics.

Chapter 6 looks into the caliph's two far-reaching policies—the support of the translation movement and the Miḥna policy—to illuminate how the early-ninth-century ideological and intellectual context enabled the caliph to pursue such seemingly incompatible policies. Finally, the conclusion sums up the argument of the book and reiterates the need to approach prophecies with new questions.

Acknowledgments

I have benefited from individuals and institutions without whose contributions this book would have been very different, indeed. I am enormously indebted to all of them. My graduate school mentors Fred Donner, Cornell Fleischer, and John Woods at the University of Chicago guided, with admirable insight and patience, the first incarnation of this work. I am also indebted to Michael Cooperson and John Nawas for their incisive and sound suggestions. The anonymous readers of my manuscript deserve a special expression of gratitude for selflessly reading and commenting on it. I must also single out a number of individuals whose support and contributions were essential: M. ʿAdnān al-Bakhīt, ʿAbd al-ʿAzīz al-Dūrī, Ahmet T. Karamustafa, and John Renard.

I am also indebted to Asma Afsaruddin, John Carroll, Lawrence Conrad, Bruce Craig, Don Critchlow, Robert Dankoff, İsmail Erünsal, Nūfān Rajā al-Ḥammūd, Ekmeleddin İhsanoğlu, Mücteba İlgürel, Wadad Kadi, Walter Kaegi, Hayreddin Karaman, Mahmut Kaya, Fatemeh Keshavarz, Burhan Köroğlu, Scott Lucas, Thomas Madden, Elaine Marschik, Farouk Mustafa, Zuhair Nubani, Hal Parker, Jamil Ragep, Abdulaziz Sachedina, Daniel Schlaffly, Fuat Sezgin, Damien Smith, Nargis Virani, and Paul Walker for their contributions in various ways. The University of Chicago Library, the Center for Documents and Manuscripts at the University of Jordan, the Center for Islamic Studies, ISAM in Istanbul, the Mellon Foundation–University of Chicago, the Mellon Foundation–Saint Louis University, and the Department of History at Saint Louis University provided the support necessary to do the research. I also would like to remember the individual who made this book possible in the first place, ʿAbdallāh al-Ma'mūn. I hope that this study offers something along the lines of his last wish—that we say good things about him, if we know any. *ʿAfā Allāhu ʿan Dhunūbihi*. Inevitably I will realize I have inadvertently left out some individuals whom I should have acknowledged. I can only say to them that their help is much appreciated and will never be forgotten.

I cannot pay my debt to my parents, whose care, love, and patience I constantly tried. I am grateful to my wife and two boys. They had to share a substantial portion of their life with a ghost. No apology can make up for their suffering, and no words can be meaningful enough to express my indebtedness and my love to them. I hope that the outcome offers some excuse for my absence.

A Note on Transliteration

For the transliteration of Arabic and Persian words, I adopted the system used in the *International Journal of Middle East Studies* (*IJMES*) and have spelled out elisions (for example, *fī al-sharq* rather than *fī 'l-sharq*). For Ottoman Turkish words, I followed modern Turkish usage. For other non-Latin languages, I followed the method used by the Library of Congress. Common Anglicized words are given in their common English spelling (for example, Baghdad rather than Baghdād) unless intended otherwise. In references, the transliteration conventions are observed fully. References are abbreviated in footnotes for economy of space. Either the first or the most common usage of any given name or title is used (for example, al-Balādhurī, *Ansāb*). Normally the dates are given in Common Era (C.E.). The Hijrī calendar is indicated with A.H., the Christian calendar with A.D. When A.H. and A.D. dates appear together, they are separated by a slash, with the A.H. date preceding the A.D. date.

Genealogical Chart of the ʻAbbāsid Family

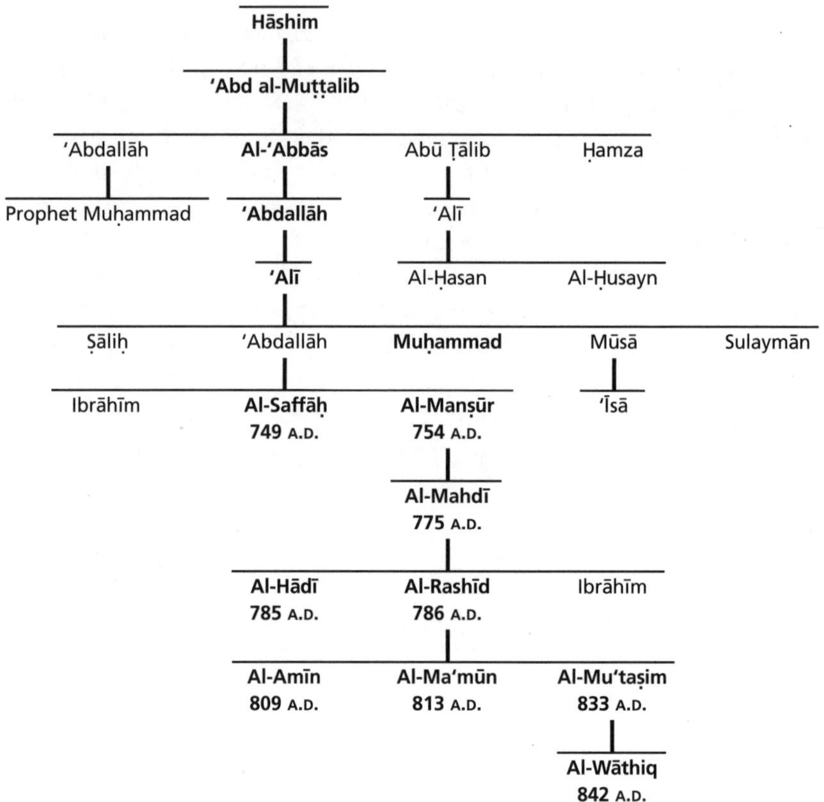

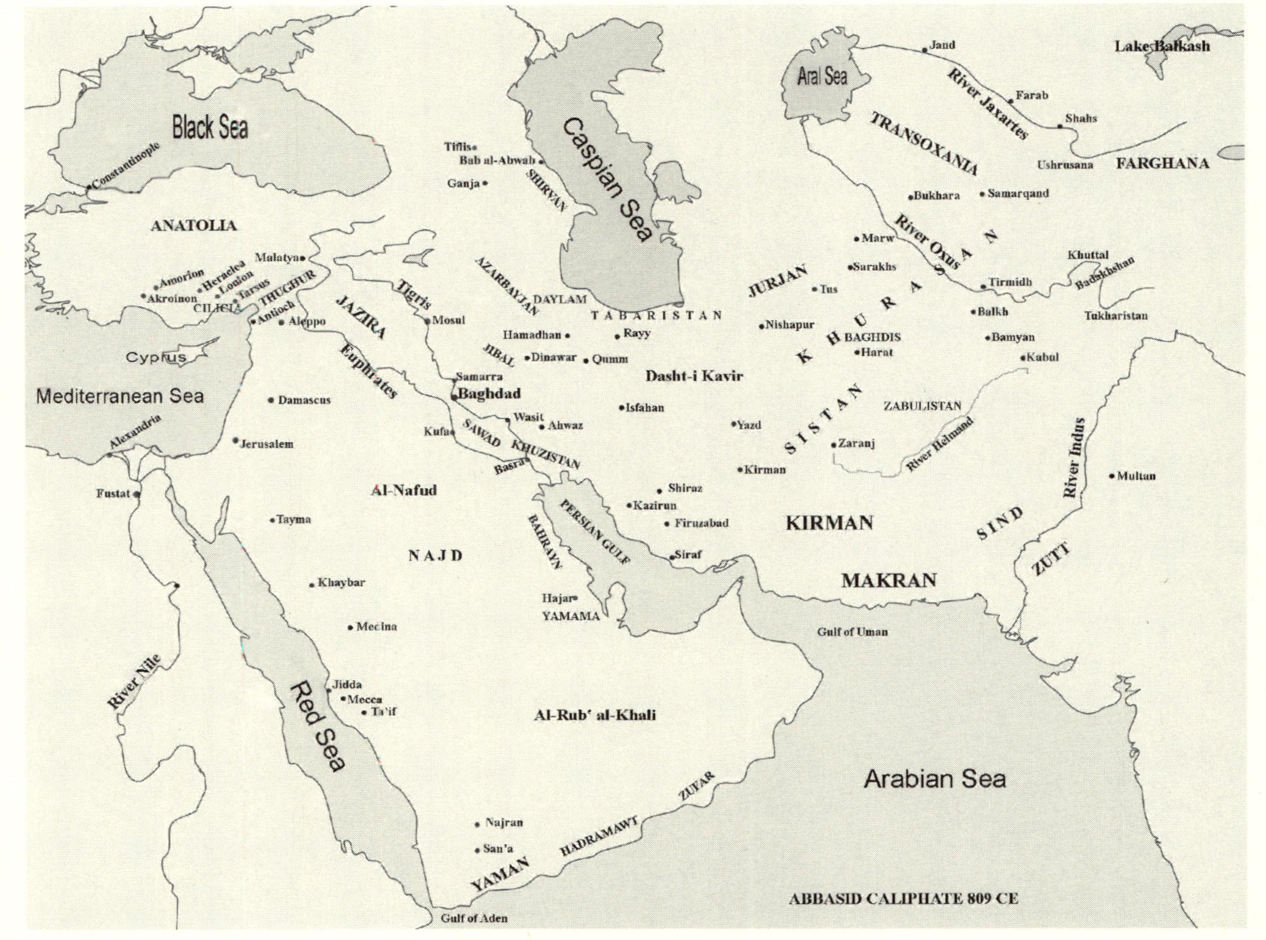

ABBASID CALIPHATE 809 CE

Introduction

Messianic and apocalyptic aspects of Islam date back to its rise in the seventh century. During the early period of Islam, messianic beliefs emerged as a resilient form of thought that affected the religious and political evolution of Muslim society. These beliefs repeatedly interrupted political life and administrative routine and provoked, on popular as well as institutional levels, renewed demands for social and political change. This tension between institutionalization and charismatic leadership remained strong in public life throughout the medieval centuries, receding at times and advancing at others.

Main Question

Since the beginning of the twentieth century, scholars have been interested in the origins of Islam, but have reached differing conclusions. While Casanova proposed that Islam arose originally as a Christian apocalyptic movement, Crone and Cook placed Islam within a Jewish messianic tradition. Recently a number of scholars have argued that Islam could have emerged as an apocalyptic movement regardless whether it derived this concept from the Christian tradition or the Judaic tradition.[1] Controversy regarding the origins of Islam notwithstanding, it is certain that when Islam appeared in the world of late antiquity, many of the inhabitants of western Asia saw in it a portent of the end of time. In the eyes of the followers of the monotheistic faiths, the birth of Islam was a response to their expectations, although soon it became clear to them that Islam did not perfectly fit the trajectory of traditional prophecies. The fact that the Qur'ān itself echoed a vision of the end of time only heightened the anxiety among the observers of this rising faith. Thus as much as Islam grew in, and was a response to, the messianic context of western Asia, it also contributed reciprocally to the proliferation of prophetic expectations in the seventh and eighth centuries. As a community believing in a monotheistic faith, early Muslims could not have been immune from the effects of their environment, especially the biblical tradition. Soon after they encountered native cultures, Muslims began adding biblical apocalyptic and messianic lore to their own culture, intertwining the future of monotheistic communities under the caliphate and opening new channels of communication.

The belief in the end of time and the Mahdī (literally, the rightly guided one) became fairly widespread, although it did not always disrupt the general flow of life along its mundane course. Not everyone held a messianic or apocalyptic belief, and of those who did, most did not always maintain the intensity of their beliefs. Some individuals seem to have even ridiculed belief in prophecies,[2] and others recognized only the Second Coming of Jesus. As one tradition put it, there would be "no Mahdī except Jesus, the son of Mary."[3] While such individuals seem to have shared a historical vision common to many prophecies in seeing a perpetual decline shortly after the death of the Prophet Muḥammad, they openly rejected the idea of a Mahdī figure. To them, life appeared to increase only in hardship, the people in greed, and the world in backward movement until the Hour would befall "the worst of people." Nevertheless, for those who believed in prophecies, portents shaped destiny, provoked ambitions, and called for action, especially at times of actual or perceived crises.

Having been engulfed by the appeal of messianic beliefs, the caliphs liked to project themselves as messiahs since the Umayyad period.[4] Medieval sources suggest that the caliphs used prophecies effectively in their speeches and actions, and were familiar with many prophecies from their ancestors and from the people around them. The early 'Abbāsid period demonstrates a poignant example of the cycle of messianic charisma and its institutionalization. Similar to their Umayyad predecessors, the 'Abbāsids projected an image of themselves, largely successfully, as divinely mandated rulers, the last of whom would submit his authority to Jesus himself at the end of time. They based their claims on sectarian beliefs, alleged scriptures, secret knowledge, prophetic sayings, divine inspiration, and pious wisdom. The 'Abbāsids and their supporters propagated these claims across generations in prophecies and through clandestine dynastic revelations such as the Hāshimid *Yellow Script* and the 'Abbāsid *Book of the Reign*.

When the 'Abbāsids became the rulers of the caliphate, they faced complicated provincial, tribal, and sectarian problems, most notably Shī'ī movements in moderate and extremist forms. The 'Abbāsids did not have a clear agenda for rule apart from a commitment to general principles of justice and upholding religious ordinances and acting piously, but they did attend to mundane administrative needs by building a military institution, a centralized administrative organization, and eventually a judicial hierarchy.

However, the religio-political ambiguity unleashed by the 'Abbāsid revolt and its ideological engine, the extremist Shī'ī movement of al-Kaysāniyya and its subbranches, hindered the institutionalization of military and administrative structures and stalled the nonviolent political continuity. While the caliphs sought stability to achieve their objectives, their supporters and affiliated extremist groups displayed their revolutionary fervor, especially in the province of Khurāsān, frequently rebelling throughout the reign of al-Manṣūr. Even though the ʿAbbāsids realized that messianic rhetoric of social justice and claims to piety alone fell short of overcoming the political, economic, and social challenges they faced and for which the revolt had sought remedy, they could not easily discard messianic beliefs, which were part of their identity. Instead of shedding these beliefs, the caliphs opted for other solutions that were responsive to their ideological inclinations. Since the final years of al-Manṣūr, the caliphs incorporated the messianic and revolutionary fervor as a broad inspiration or rationale for their policies and agendas. The mundane needs of the empire and the meeting of these needs provided a social context in which ʿAbbāsid messianic claims had to function. In a way this was a compromise reflecting the ʿAbbāsid effort to institutionalize the messianic charisma associated with their dynasty.

Nonetheless this compromise was far from a one-time-only transition from charisma to routinized authority, to use Weber's terminology. The ʿAbbāsids, their supporters, and the opposition invoked and reinvoked messianic beliefs at different times, leading to frequent messianic interruptions in the early ʿAbbāsid period. A case in point can be found in the early ninth century, a period of such interruptions that displayed an exemplary sensitivity to social and political circumstances during and after the fourth civil war between al-Amīn and al-Ma'mūn. At the moment when messianic expectations gathered momentum due to the approaching new century, al-Ma'mūn initiated and shaped his movement from the province of Khurāsān against his brother and the ʿAbbāsids in Baghdad. The circumstances of the civil war enabled al-Ma'mūn to claim divine sanction and messianic mission, as exemplified in his *nom de guerre,* the leader of guidance, *imām al-hudā*. Later as a ruler claiming also to be God's caliph, he adopted messianic beliefs to advance his imperial ambitions. Rather than ignore or dampen circulating messianic beliefs, he embraced them for inspiration, support, and the justification of his major religious and secular policies. Al-Ma'mūn's political and religious ideology and actions suggest that he acted like a reformer, *mujaddid*. It is significant that the milieu of the turn of the third Islamic century produced one of the most significant ideas of reform, *tajdīd*, in medieval Islamic history.[5]

Making the caliphate the champion of monotheism and a true successor of the great empires of the past necessitated a particular, but not unique, political posture to conciliate religious claims and imperial ambitions. While neither of the two were new for the ʿAbbāsids, the context of the expanding intellectual and ideological horizon of the ʿAbbāsids in the early ninth century was. The increase of knowledge in almost all aspects of intellectual and cultural life offered singularly fresh perspectives on identity, culture, and politics. For example, it is no coincidence that during this time al-Ma'mūn patronized the drawing of the first *mappo mundi*, known as *al-Ṣūra al-Ma'mūniyya*, in Islamic history.[6] Within this awareness, messianic beliefs came into a sharper focus for the ʿAbbāsids as a religio-political discourse that could articulate imperial demands. Of course messianic expectations were a fundamental dimension of the ʿAbbāsid revolt in the middle of the eighth century, as abundantly documented in modern scholarship. However, being more conscious of his environment, al-Ma'mūn seems to have placed a greater emphasis on the imperial aspects of messianic beliefs and on the imperial competition in late antiquity.

Looking at the early ninth century from this vantage point allows us to better understand how al-Ma'mūn struggled to create an imperial culture by energetically supporting the translation of the ancient scientific and philosophical literature into Arabic, executing a religious policy that emphasized the puritanical version of Islamic monotheism, and tirelessly conducting military raids against Byzantium. The dynamism of al-Ma'mūn in the translation activities reflects his intention to acclimatize foreign sciences to Islamic sensibilities so that they could become a part of the culture of his empire. It stands to reason that al-Ma'mūn, as the leader of guidance and God's caliph, might have aspired for a share in the recovery and dissemination of prophetic wisdom out of his messianic concerns. He might have been convinced that the world "was growing nearer to the Hour," as he remarked on an occasion of his appointment of 'Alī al-Riḍā to be his successor.[7]

Al-Ma'mūn's policy of religious persecution, known as the Miḥna, was conceived as an attempt not only to expand the religious authority of the caliph over a particular group of religious scholars and, as Marshall Hodgson suggested, to create a religious establishment more amenable to his absolutist demands, but also to implement a policy motivated by messianic ideas of reform, renewal, and restoration that would purify faith from social and historical residues through the promotion of a strict notion of monotheism. Launched from the frontier where the caliph was preparing for a major assault on the Byzantines, the Miḥna revealed that his religious policies were intimately related to the caliph's expansionist ambitions. It may also be useful to remember the broader Mediterranean context in which imperial demands expanded into reforming religious doctrine. The Miḥna coincided with the later stages of the Iconoclast controversy in the Byzantine Empire and the reforms of Louis the Pious in the Frankish Kingdom.

Unfortunately modern scholarship has not given enough attention to the role of messianic beliefs in historical events, despite the fact that the field of early ʿAbbāsid history has a distinguished record of scholarship dating back to the nineteenth century. Our perception of the ideas, events, and individuals of the early ʿAbbāsid period have developed following a set of intellectual and ideological premises that were popular in the nineteenth and early twentieth centuries.[8] Scholars had thought that the "national" ambitions of Arabs and Persians played a major role in generating the ʿAbbāsid revolt and, later, the civil war. Having observed the relative clarity of divisions among Islamic sects in later periods and having been convinced by the arguments of later heresiographical works, which paid little attention to change over time, other scholars focused on the relationship among religio-political sects, particularly the Shīʿī, Sunnī, and Muʿtazilī trends, to explain the development of ʿAbbāsid society and polity. Even today this sectarian and nationalistic outlook permeates the thoughts of many scholars in regions where nation- and community-building efforts are under way. Furthermore the legacy of historical positivism, which claims the ability to find facts and sort subjective claims from objective reality, still lingers in scholarship in various manifestations, arriving in many cases at normative conclusions about the entirety of Islamic religion and culture.

Since the 1950s the conceptual parameters of scholarship in academic circles have taken new directions, following developments in the social sciences and historical studies. The binary of religion-politics, in which religion represents the opposition, and the disregard of religiosity as an ephemeral phenomenon have risen as the primary assumption in much of contemporary scholarship dealing with the politics of the ʿAbbāsid caliphate. More often than not, scholarship assumes a paradigmatic Machiavellian political pragmatism, and perhaps more recently a version of rational-actor behavior, and a notion of realpolitik to explain the dynamics of ʿAbbāsid political life.[9] A substantial number of recent studies perceive one major problem affecting the reign of al-Maʾmūn: the preparation of an Islamic-religious establishment more amenable to the religious demands of an absolute monarchy. This view postulates that the reign of al-Maʾmūn was a continuous struggle with religious scholars in an attempt to undermine their power and a calculated modus operandi to gain, or regain, the comprehensive authority of the caliph.[10] Impressive in its description of the mechanics and modalities of relationships, which remain essential for any study of the early ʿAbbāsid period, this view lacks life, temper, and a fuller appreciation of context.[11]

Not unexpectedly, therefore, messianism has been poorly treated in contemporary ʿAbbāsid scholarship until recently, as an anomaly not fitting the institutional organization of the caliphate and the modes of relationship. Lewis illustrates this point well: "The new imperial dynasty was firmly in control; the revolutionary leaders were safely dead; the charisma, in Max Weber's phrase, was routinized. The ʿAbbāsids, like other successful revolutionaries before and after them, chose the path of orthodoxy and empire. . . . Of the revolutionary and messianic origins of the ʿAbbāsid movement, only the outward forms remained. The radical beliefs gave way to pious conformity; the black emblems of revolution became a dynastic livery; the messianic war-cries became part of the style and titles of imperial protocol."[12]

When messianism receives attention, it is usually associated with the Shīʿīs, extremist movements, and popular uprisings.[13] This begs the question of how scholarship handles the role of messianic beliefs in historical interpretation. A brief evaluation of the broader theoretical context might be in order here. The classics of messianic studies in the middle of the twentieth century regard messianism as a collective madness, a paranoid fantasy, an outlet for an extreme anxiety, and, in short, a disruptive and destructive mental illness.[14] Guided by Mannheim's *Ideology and Utopia*,[15] Weber's analysis in his *Economy and Society*,[16] and Cohn's popularly known work, *The Pursuit of the Millennium*, modern studies imagine messianism as a religion of deprived groups, including lower social classes and oppressed and persecuted minorities. When Cohn was criticized for being unjustifiably categorical, he responded to his critics, in the later editions of his seminal work, by clarifying that he accepted the existence of both extreme and mild types of millenarianism, which varied in their social composition and function, and that he was simply interested in the millenarianism that flourished among the rootless poor of western Europe.[17] Such later modifications did little to alter the overall association of messianism with either factual or perceived deprivation and with the imbalance between expectations and the means of their satisfaction, which leaves hopes unfulfilled. Cohn's work continued to enjoy a wide circulation among sociologists, anthropologists, and historians, including those dealing with the history of the Middle East.

Perhaps convinced in part by the discouraging consequences of movements leading to catastrophic failure and by the ideologies of disintegrating movements, this perspective could not envision a constructive role for messianic movements.[18] Granted, many messianic movements had a destructive trajectory, yet many others did aim to maintain social, political, and economic order in a new form.[19] As McGinn has pointed out, the Cohnian approach ignores those practices of messianic traditions that intended to support established institutions rather than to serve as a critique, whether mild or violent.[20] The supporters of messianic movements were certainly displeased with the present and wanted to change it, but they were not necessarily fanatical individuals, underprivileged poor, or marginalized groups. Although most people, even during the time of crises, often went about their daily lives without such preoccupations, messianic beliefs remained for many a frequent means of not only coping with sociopolitical reality but also of changing the status quo. Like any other current of thought, messianic beliefs belonged to a certain social and cultural context within which they took form and operated. Representing the views of a cross section of society in which popular mores mixed with high culture, these beliefs appealed in many cases to the learned elite, including scholars, scribes, rulers, and administrators, as either visionaries or activists. At times even rulers assumed messianic roles to shape and change the political and social institutions of their realms, which gives credence to the idea that messianic movements could support political institutions and even encourage institutional change.[21]

In general ʿAbbāsid studies seem to have taken a path similar to that of western European scholarship on messianism. Following the Christian Church's tendency to exclude messianism from theology by labeling it as error and fantasy, this bias arising from traditional scholarship appears also in Middle Eastern studies.[22] Historians have been particularly successful in reconstructing the relationship between the caliphate and messianic movements, and the history of individual movements.[23] We are indebted to Aguadé, Madelung, and El-Hibri for examining apocalyptic and messianic expectations in relation to the ʿAbbāsid civil war and the reign of al-Ma'mūn.[24] Aguadé examined the life of Nuʿaym b. Ḥammād and the depiction of the early ʿAbbāsids in his *Kitāb al-Fitan*. Because Aguadé concerns himself simply with matching prophecies with particular historical incidents in the early ʿAbbāsid period (that is, histories written in the future tense), he does not seek a historical study of the period at hand, nor does he speculate on how prophecies might have affected the worldview of the ʿAbbāsids.

Madelung's article deals with a letter attributed to al-Ma'mūn that addresses the ʿAbbāsids, their clients, and the people of Baghdad regarding their opposition to his appointment of ʿAlī al-Riḍā. A curious passage in the letter discusses the destruction of the ʿAbbāsids and the coming of the Mahdī, which leads Madelung to argue that al-Ma'mūn might have pessimistically believed that the inevitable end of the ʿAbbāsids would soon come, and therefore he lost hope in the future of the ʿAbbāsids. As sensible as it is, Madelung's suggestion rests on a single reference with a clear Shīʿī agenda and, as we shall see later, a forgery inserted into an otherwise probably authentic letter. Moreover his research remains, unfortunately, too brief for a fair treatment of this subject.

El-Hibri's biography of al-Ma'mūn offers an analysis of the dialectic between messianic expectations and al-Ma'mūn's policy directions. His framing of messianic beliefs as merely battle cries to rally popular support around al-Ma'mūn in his bid for power (a Cohnian position) notwithstanding, El-Hibri engages messianism as a theoretical matter in historical interpretation. The main limitation of his work seems to be the neglect of the relevant literature, except in passing. Cook's short introductory article on the "Apocalyptic Year 200 A.H." concerns itself exclusively with prophecies focusing on the year 200 A.H. but unfortunately lacks any analytical dimension.

After the appearance of Paul Alexander's "Medieval Apocalypses as Historical Sources" in 1968, scholars tended to focus on identifying the factual background of prophecies and to use them as "chronicles written in the future tense," as he suggests.[25] Such a perspective takes us another step away from the mistaken attitude of dismissing messianic beliefs in political life. However, prophecies contribute to historical research as more than mere chronicles of their immediate circumstances. What is missing from this approach is the attention to the function of prophecies as normative foundations upon which social and political action may be based, for prophecies do not merely describe, they also prescribe. Even though each prophecy belongs to a certain historical circumstance, its reproduction and circulation outside of its initial context indicate its continued relevance to sociopolitical life and to its normative or prescriptive power. Prophecies were created and perpetuated by a particular mindset and outlook—an ideological illusion that served as a lens through which historical actors saw political realities and projected action. Unfortunately too little has been written about the 'Abbāsids from this angle, even though several other scholars have offered notable and welcome arguments integrating various dimensions of social and cultural contexts. For instance, Zaman has pointed out and made evident the occurrence of cooperation, and not dichotomy, between religion and politics and between the caliphs and the proto-Sunnī scholars (in particular of *fiqh* and *ḥadīth*) in early 'Abbāsid period.[26] Cooperson examined the intellectual and cultural context of the caliph al-Ma'mūn to better understand his conduct, which helps us see the caliph as a human being rather than as a political machine.[27] Concerned with the fundamental issue of the relationship between the human psyche and behavior, Nawas attempted to show how the personal background of the caliph might have affected his conduct.[28] More studies of this kind are needed to improve current understanding of the intellectual, spiritual, and cultural context of 'Abbāsid rulers and their realms.

In a remarkably apt aphorism, the caliph al-Ma'mūn brings into sharp relief this moral, sociocultural, and human dimension of political power. He is quoted as saying, "kingship is desired for the execution of orders, and the execution of orders is wanted to gain the material world, and the material world is gained to be given to those who are entitled to it. Otherwise, how much pleasure can you gain from it?"[29] This remark, whether or not it is indeed al-Ma'mūn's, reveals how a medieval ruler was expected to respond on a personal level to a fundamental existential question about the meaning of life and of responsibility. It is hard to imagine that al-Ma'mūn managed to remain above the intellectual and ideological beliefs of his society while at the same time skillfully using them for his own self-interests. Rather, like any other member of his society, al-Ma'mūn made an effort to strike a working balance between the concerns of his milieu and his political ambitions.[30] The goal here is to see whether prophecies can provide us enough information to delineate a context in which al-Ma'mūn initiated his movement and reigned over his domain.

Before further elaboration, we should acknowledge a stark reality—the limitation of sources. In general historians need to consult literary sources, historiography in particular, if they hope to write a history of early Islam. Accordingly the skeleton of the historical events in this study comes from an analytical reading of these sources in cognizance of the fact that, given the scarcity of contemporary evidence, we are dealing with narratives constructed with afterthought. As El-Hibri demonstrated in his analysis of the 'Abbāsid civil war narratives,[31] historiography transmits certain messages through its storyline, as any writing does, and intends to shape the direction of social transformation. Because historiography addresses the concerns of its time and society, it also reflects the aspirations, fears, and achievements of the society within which it is born.

Does this fact make history a fiction that invents data for the purpose of teaching a lesson or disseminating a moral point? Let us examine a report. At the end of his narrative of the events of the year 203/819, al-Ṭabarī notes the occurrence of a solar eclipse: "In this year, there was an eclipse of the sun on Sunday, the twenty-eighth of Dhū al-Ḥijja [203/26 June 819], to the extent that the sun's light faded away and over two-thirds of its orb disappeared. The eclipse began when the sun was getting high and continued till it was nearly noon; then it cleared away."[32] As it turns out, a history of lunar and solar eclipses confirms that on that day there was indeed an eclipse. It was visible from Baghdad exactly as al-Ṭabarī described it. Viewed from Baghdad, this eclipse reached the width of 75 percent of the solar disc covered by the moon. In this particular eclipse, the zone of annularity started in northwestern Africa (4°W, 9°N), crossed that continent to the Red Sea, then traversed the Arabian Peninsula and the Persian Gulf, and went on along the coast of the Arabian Sea to India. It crossed that subcontinent, went on through the Gulf of Bengal, reached Sumatra, and ended east of Java (118°E, 7°S).[33]

It cannot be concluded that all records of eclipses were correctly reported or that other, more contentious matters would or could be described with the same accuracy. However, it is reasonable to suggest that transmitting historical reports meant, at least for the transmitter of this account, reporting as accurately as possible an event that actually happened. Medieval historians evaluated reports of earlier times for credibility and utility and inquired as to whether they made sense from their own standpoint so that they could record those subjects that provoked interest in them as historians and individuals living in a society. They had their own ideological or methodological priorities according to which they accepted or discredited evidence and placed some events, but not others, in a certain interpretive frame while still remaining faithful to the principles of accuracy.[34]

These remarks do not discount the importance of taking into account the political, moral, or sectarian concerns of the historians or the problem of conflicting accounts, frequently recurring topoi, or the use of literary tropes to fashion a lucid narrative.[35] Similar to what Cooperson argued about biographical sources of the early ʿAbbāsid period, what is suggested here is that historians did not seem eager to invent facts. Rather they attempted to make sense, through the currents of thought available to them, of what they had received either orally or in writing. Historians, therefore, could only provide their versions of historical facts, their perceptions of what happened, and their interpretations of those facts. Their writings reflect a construction of the past from certain moral, ideological, or intellectual perspectives.[36] One of the sources closest to the period, Khalīfa b. Khayyāṭ (d. ca. 240–41/854–55), for instance, offers a concise and pro-Ma'mūn chronicle. The writer's bias is revealed through his discrediting al-Amīn (r. 809–13) as the Deposed One, *al-Makhlū'*, and his calling al-Ma'mūn the commander of the faithful, *amīr al-mu'minīn*, in anticipation of al-Ma'mūn's future status. Khalīfa b. Khayyāṭ mentions the 'Alid revolts, the nomination of 'Alī al-Riḍā, the appointment of Ibrāhīm b. al-Mahdī in Baghdad as caliph, the "murder" of al-Faḍl b. Sahl, the "death" of 'Alī al-Riḍā, and the return of al-Ma'mūn to Baghdad. Curiously neither the Miḥna nor the raids on Byzantium appear in the annals. In later sources a similar sentimental sympathy for al-Ma'mūn might also be observed. Problems of prejudice and authenticity are also true for other narrative sources and are now the subjects of heated debate in historical scholarship.

Fortunately this is not all we have. Historiographical sources do contain alternative or competing views. Ibn A'tham al-Kūfī's *al-Futūḥ* offers a multi-sided narrative. Ibn A'tham al-Kūfī makes it clear that al-Amīn and al-Ma'mūn conspired to eliminate each other, a point that al-Ṭabarī also repeats in some of his accounts. Recently El-Hibri and Cooperson have shown that the historiography of the period contains both open and subtle criticism of al-Ma'mūn, as well as veneration of the memory of al-Amīn. An examination of the sources indicates that both minor and major accounts contain critical views of al-Ma'mūn in a number of significant incidents.[37] The civil war, the murder of al-Amīn, and the Miḥna are among the chief topics in which such explicit or implicit criticism of al-Ma'mūn can be seen. The question, therefore, is not so much how we penetrate the thick layer of a monolithic narrative but what we do with the numerous alternative narratives.

Despite their limitations, historiographical sources remain essential for any study that attempts to present a comprehensible account of the early 'Abbāsid caliphate. Material evidence can be useful in corroborating these sources. Whether al-Ma'mūn used the title *al-imām*, religio-political leader, and when he did so, and whether 'Alī al-Riḍā was appointed as successor can be ascertained by consulting numismatic evidence.[38] However, material evidence is not without its own problems and often raises more questions than it answers. As far as material evidence establishes dates, names, and localities with a relative degree of certainty, it satisfies curiosity. At the same time, explaining the meaning of material evidence in its larger context cannot be done without reference to literary sources, particularly historiographical ones. We know that al-Ma'mūn used the title *al-imām*, but what did the title mean when he used it? Material evidence rarely provides an answer to such questions. The truth of the matter is that to provide a satisfactory reconstruction of the early 'Abbāsid history, historians are bound to consult any shred of evidence that they can find. Accordingly it may be prudent to pay attention to what prophecies have to say.

Prophecies as Text

Considering the squarely historical and political nature of prophecies, apocalyptic sources offer considerably more intimate perspectives on events. Without aiming to replace historiographical narratives with prophecies—as much as prophecies deal with social and political life, they cannot offer a coherent view without historiography—it seems apparent that prophecies offer a unique perspective on the mentalities and overriding concerns of those involved in the events of the early ʿAbbāsid period and on how the creators and transmitters of prophecies perceived their sociopolitical realities. By the early third/ninth century, prophecies already circulated widely in written form in the massive works of Abdallāh b. al-Mubārak, Abdallāh b. Lahīʿa, ʿAbd al-Razzāq al-Ṣanʿānī, Ibn Abī Shayba, and Nuʿaym b. Ḥammād. Shortly afterward prophecies concerning the Mahdī, the end of time, and apocalyptic turmoil became important enough to merit a chapter in the compendia of *ḥadīth*, traditions attributed to the Prophet Muḥammad. This means that we have contemporary or near contemporary literary sources for the period under consideration.

Even with their limitations, prophecies yield enough information and details about historical events to be taken seriously. They were intimately linked to political life because they were produced by and for the leading classes of society. Unlike some of the medieval European popular millenarian prophecies, parallels of which we observe in the history of the Middle East as well, early Islamic prophecies do not come from or represent the vulgar, the poor, and the uneducated. Ultimately these prophecies represent a body of thought produced by urban elite who had access to information and power. This group's urban roots appear clearly in the social background of the transmitters, whose prophecies come across with only a dim view of the agricultural hinterland and disfranchised classes. In matters dealing with imperial politics, sociopolitical changes in urban centers, religious controversies, and other matters relevant to the urban and ruling elite, the prophecies are strikingly insightful. Because the carriers of knowledge belonged to the learned class of their societies, messianic beliefs remained influential on and relevant to the social, intellectual, and cultural life of the Umayyad and ʿAbbāsid societies.

Nuʿaym b. Ḥammād's *Kitāb al-Fitan* (Book of Apocalyptic Turmoil) is a good example. As Aguadé has noted, Nuʿaym b. Ḥammād himself presents not the views of the lower classes but of the learned religious class, of which he was one.[39] Nuʿaym b. Ḥammād represents in many ways a sad coincidence as a reference in any matter dealing with al-Ma'mūn, as he died in an ʿAbbāsid prison during the Miḥna on the charge of heresy for not acknowledging that the Qur'ān was created. He was originally from Marw in Khurāsān. He studied and resided in Ḥijāz and Iraq before he migrated to Egypt. Antagonistic to Ḥanafī circles and to their use of rational opinion, *ra'y*, in jurisprudence, Nuʿaym b.

Ḥammād did not share the ideological and religious loyalties of al-Ma'mūn. Perhaps because of the pressures in Baghdad, Nu'aym b. Ḥammād resettled in Egypt, becoming a longtime resident and eventually one of the prominent *ḥadīth* scholars there. Like al-Ash'arī a century later, Nu'aym b. Ḥammād might have been a Mu'tazilī before he adopted a *ḥadīth*-transmitter (*muḥaddīth*) perspective on faith. It seems that Nu'aym b. Ḥammād's troubles began with the arrival of a new, energetic Miḥna officer in Egypt in 226/841 during the caliphate of al-Mu'taṣim. The officer had Kūfī views on jurisprudence and Mu'tazilī leanings. He immediately began questioning and transporting scholars to Iraq on charges of noncompliance. Refusing to acknowledge that the Qur'ān was created, Nu'aym b. Ḥammād was chained and transported to Baghdad or Samarra, where he was placed in jail until his death in 228/843 during the caliphate of al-Wāthiq. He asked to be buried with his chains so he could continue his fight with the 'Abbāsids in the hereafter, and sources tell us that his friends complied with his request.[40] Obviously his trials and his death in an 'Abbāsid prison on charges of heresy raise methodological concerns about the impartiality of his work.

Nu'aym b. Ḥammād's *Kitāb al-Fitan*, most likely compiled between 216 and 228/831 and 844,[41] contains about two thousand accounts condensed into ten chapters, covering the period from the early Islamic decades up to the third Islamic century. It presents prophecies in a broad chronological order that start with what had been prophesied to happen from the time of the Prophet Muḥammad onward and detail accounts that pertain, in order of their appearance in the work, to the Patriarchal Caliphate, the Umayyads, and the 'Abbāsids. The work ends with a lengthy discussion of the Mahdī and the circumstances of his rise and other related events. Nu'aym b. Ḥammād seems to have collected material not only from Egypt and Syria but also from Khurāsān, Ḥijāz, and Yemen. His work contains accounts reflecting the concerns of urban and learned elite and popular imagination. It also comprises stories, genuine prophecies, and historical events cast as future predictions, political claims and aspirations, social commentaries, and warnings from someone who felt responsible for informing coreligionists of imminent momentous happenings.[42] There is no scholarly distance between the reports, their transmitters, and their final editor—all seem to share a belief in what the prophecies suggest. Many accounts have a historical ring to them and can be safely dated to a period, or even matched with an individual, while others are genuine predictions. Because of the process of redaction and because many of the accounts in this work are unique, it should be made clear that without *Kitāb al-Fitan*, the majority of prophecies that it contains would have been lost, and many of the details of the civil war would have been unknown to the modern reader. It is the only extant work that contains substantial information about the civil war and the events surrounding it from a messianic and apocalyptic perspective.

Medieval evaluation of Nuʿaym b. Ḥammād as *muḥaddith* varies from considering him an outright liar to trustworthy, although he was quoted on many occasions in canonical *ḥadīth* collections. Chronology may have something to do with it because as we get closer to his time, his reputation seems to improve, perhaps due to the anti-Miḥna solidarity of the *muḥaddiths*. Accordingly his work was received with some reluctance, although no one seems to have discounted it entirely. His compendium contains many prophecies openly antagonistic to the ʿAbbāsids, although numerous others reflect multiple perspectives, including pro-ʿAbbāsid ones. Because of either simple editorial negligence or intellectual honesty, *Kitāb al-Fitan* rises above being a monolithic partisan monograph against the ʿAbbāsids. It brings together diverse and often contradictory accounts from various individuals with dissimilar concerns and perspectives.

The issue for us is not so much Nuʿaym b. Ḥammād's political and doctrinal positions, which more often than not were clearly indicated in various accounts, but rather the broader scholarly methodological problem of constructing a historical narrative by relying on sources not strictly historiographical, such as Nuʿaym b. Ḥammād's *Kitāb al-Fitan* or *Muṣannafs* of al-Ṣanʿānī and Ibn Abī Shayba. Apocalyptic and historiographical sources pose problems of both interpretation and perception, and, by their nature, they can only offer an image of historical reality. However, while the historiography of the early ʿAbbāsid period appears chronologically further removed from the events, prophecies seem to come out of the milieu itself. They are produced, circulated, and recorded in the same period in which events took place. Even the reductions, deletions, and supplements intended to extend the life of a prophecy often leave a trail of time and space, making the amended prophecy historically more valuable than its original form.

Prophecies dealing with the ʿAbbāsid dynasty were sparked by a number of developments in the late second Islamic century. The first was the anxiety associated with the approach of the year 200 A.H. The second was the start of the civil war. Prophecies emphasizing the civil war took issue with the conflict between brothers and the surrounding events to predict the collapse of the ʿAbbāsid caliphate. At the same time, sectarian and political claims (the Sufyānī, the Shīʿī uprisings), reaction to existing political and social order (Bābāk al-Khurramī), interconfessional contacts (non-Muslim prophecies), and unexpected natural events in various parts of the caliphate (eclipses, fires, earthquakes) can be considered motivating forces behind the creation and dissemination of prophecies. Most of the time prophecies were provoked by certain historical or natural crises on which prophecies have something factual to say or imply—hence the view that apocalypses are histories written in the future tense. On other occasions the historical link is weak, or even absent, which makes the prediction genuine but perhaps less useful in determining time-space coordinates. Yet even such predictions serve historical research as an indicator of the mentality of their transmitters in a given context.

Unlike some historiographical reports, prophecies may be accurately assigned to certain locations and periods based on internal evidence. Thus in a tradition on the rise of the Sufyānī, illuminating details about the uprising of Abū al-'Amayṭir appear: "Buqayya and 'Abd al-Quddūs narrated to us on the authority of Abū Bakr from elderly individuals saying, 'The Sufyānī will come forth from the valley of Yābis. The governor of Syria will come out against him to fight him, but as soon as he looks at his banner he [the governor] will be defeated.' 'Abd al-Quddūs said, 'the governor of Damascus will be a governor of the 'Abbāsids at the time.'"[43] Abū al-'Amayṭir did indeed revolt in Damascus; he defeated the 'Abbāsid governor and controlled Damascus and its surrounding countryside for a brief time. What the prophecy does not tell—the fall of the Sufyānī—reveals the date of its composition as 195–98/811–14, during which his revolt was still successful.

However, there are also certain limitations to the use of prophecies, as the Sufyānī prophecy shows. Prophecies are often sketchy. Rarely do they provide a fuller picture of events to which they allude. As may be inferred by now, prophecies are generally not lengthy narratives. They usually consist of short reports that are preceded by a chain of authorities (for example, "I have heard from x, he heard from y") that reaches back by attribution to discrete authorities, including the Prophet Muḥammad, his companions, pious individuals, Jewish and Christian sages, and ancient scriptures. Whether the chain of authorities has any credibility is hotly debated in relevant biographical dictionaries, and in the eyes of the later canonical *ḥadīth* critics, many transmitters of apocalyptic accounts appeared suspicious. Given their format, prophecies can only offer bits and pieces of information and rely on the audience's familiarity with the intended events to connect the dots and make inferences. Thus a better understanding of the prophecies in a particular historical context, and the related ability to more fully incorporate them into modern scholarship, requires historical and historiographical information.

Even then prophecies can remain vague and worse yet for a number of reasons. Sometimes a lack of information about the incident or the society in which prophecies were produced might make inferences difficult. At other times editorial discretions or unintended mistakes can prohibit our grasp of the meaning or the references of prophecies. On other occasions the creator or the transmitter knowingly obscures the prophecy to increase its effect, which makes willful ambiguity a common feature of predictions. Some prophecies, for instance, talk about a postmessianic time, a second messianic round, during which chaos, disorder, tribal dissension, and apocalyptic battles prevail until the appearance of the Antichrist, while others predict the coming of a righteous man who will restore peace to the people.[44] A group of prophecies warns of dissension among prominent tribes and tribal subbranches. One tradition anticipates the rise of the southern Arabian messianic figure, the Qaḥṭānī, after the Mahdī.[45] Another predicts that the Yemenite messianic deliverer, the Yamanī, would massacre Quraysh and usher in the apocalyptic battles, or *malāḥim*.[46] Another prophecy speaks of an outbreak of dissension between Quraysh and Ḥimyar after the Mahdī, which would lead to the transfer of the caliphate to Ḥimyar.[47]

Perhaps the puzzling second round of messianic time results from the effects of oral transmission in which several prophecies are mixed together or broken into separate pieces, creating a bundle of confused predictions. Examining the textual trails of such a process reveals that even the compilers of prophecies, regularly from the class of scholars of *ḥadīth*, were too reluctant to discard such reports, frequently opting instead to edit and recycle them. Adding to this inevitable mutation is the fact that, as Richard Lerner points out, prophecies were not always meant to be clear and intelligible in the first place.[48] On the contrary, the transmitters usually preferred to increase the prophetic tone and mystery of their claims by leaving certain aspects of the report ambiguous and therefore more flexible. As a result prophecies became intentionally or unintentionally on the part of the transmitter more resistant to refutation, and thus they continued to influence the outlook of diverse groups of people on social and political life.[49]

Willful or mistaken, the lack of clarity multiplies the narrative impact of a prophecy, gives it a predictive tone, and helps it remain relevant despite changes in time and space. Most of the time in such situations, the scholar's options are either leaving the accounts in question aside or perhaps making a minimal prosopographical use of them based on any names or any linguistic or cultural references that they may offer. For instance, though al-Ma'mūn is identified as the seventh of the 'Abbāsids in several reports and his name is even sometimes spelled out, the text in these prophecies is so obscured with imaginary events and editorial mismatches and discretions that their use in a specific context becomes problematic, if not impossible. The following tradition refers to al-Ma'mūn's efforts to rally support to himself against his brother, but annoyingly presents confusing details about the events involving the governor of al-Ṭabariyya: "On the authority of Abū Umayya al-Kalbī, who said, 'while the bearers of the black banners fight with each other, when the seventh of the seven will appear. He will send to the people of villages asking their support but they will deny him that. The 'Abbāsid governor of al-Ṭabariyya will find out about his appearance and send a great number of people against him. When they encounter him they will all join him, except their colleague who led them, and he will return to his companion [governor of al-Ṭabariyya] to inform him.'"[50] While abundant information is given about al-Ma'mūn, it is unclear who the governor is and why his troops are first going against but later joining al-Ma'mūn.

Another account of Nu'aym b. Ḥammād, which is recorded in the section dealing with the first portent of the conclusion of 'Abbāsid reign, poses a similar problem: "From Rishdīn from Ibn Lahī'a on Khālid b. Abī 'Imrān, 'Alī said, you will be ruled by imams, the worst of imams. If they split into three banners know that it is their demise."[51] The fact that this prophecy is placed in the section on the demise of the 'Abbāsids shows, with a certain degree of assurance, its relevance to the 'Abbāsid civil war. At the same time, the prophecy itself is too vague to enable any inferences to be made. It mentions three banners, which are too general to be identified readily. The use of the term imams outside a Shī'ī context to mean caliph is another interesting point, which prompts the question about possible uses of the term in the early third Islamic century.

We may be able to work with the chain of authorities to understand the text and to approximate a chronological framework for the composition of the prophecy. However, this task is complicated because the names in the chain of authorities are too common to yield a particular detail about the report itself; even if it does, the chain of authorities will not yield enough information to clarify the "three banners." Yet one aspect of the prophecy is clear: it is not particularly sympathetic to the 'Abbāsids, which brings into consideration another important aspect of prophecies. Being a reflection of a person's position on social and political matters, prophecies offer information about the speaker's mind with little mediation. Unlike historiography, which usually shies away from openly revealing its biases and prejudices, prophecies offer a one-sided view. They are clearly for or against something. The following prophecy cannot be said to be antagonistic to the 'Abbāsids: "By God, then there will be from our family, the Saffāḥ, the Manṣūr, and the Mahdī who will hand it [the caliphate] over to Jesus the son of Mary."[52] Such partisanship is in itself an obstacle that confronts the researcher, but knowing the attitude and position of the prophecy enables the audience to contextualize the report.

The clarity of prophecies on sectarian and political positions is balanced by silence on certain issues. We infer this from instances of a significant editorial process that is occasionally evident. The silence itself is significant, especially if it is about a phenomenon important enough to be covered by prophecies. A case in point is the adoption of the color green by al-Ma'mūn. Numerous prophecies refer to the 'Abbāsids as the holders of black banners and to al-Ma'mūn as the holder of the second (in some instances "small" or "another") black banners. A reference to al-Ma'mūn's use of green, however, is nowhere to be found. The only reference about the color green in messianic context comes in what appears to be a partial prophecy from Ismā'īl b. Abbān (d. between 207 and 216/822 and 831): "the seventh of the sons of al-'Abbās will wear the green."[53] Al-Ma'mūn's adoption of the color green was not secret, as historiography abundantly records its use. Why do prophecies pass over it in silence?

It is certainly possible that prophecies dealing with the matter fell through due to oral transmission and are thus lost. Another possibility is editorial censure. The absence of this prophecy from Nu'aym b. Ḥammād's otherwise extraordinarily rich collection of accounts shows the process of weeding out certain reports. We have to go all the way to the biographical dictionaries of the traditionists to come across this account. This tradition is contained in late sources and is mentioned for criticizing Ibn Abbān.[54] Yet given its descriptive and sterile tone, why did this tradition cause such a stir among the traditionists?

Ibn Abbān hailed from al-Kūfa, apparently served as a judge in Wāsiṭ, and had mild Shī'ī leanings. The traditionists received him with suspicion because some of his credentials were debatable. His contemporaries such as Yaḥyā b. Ma'īn, Aḥmad b. Ḥanbal, and others accused him of outright forgery. Aḥmad b. Ḥanbal, who justified his position that he used to accept traditions from Ibn Abbān but then stopped after noticing forgeries, sided particularly hard against him. The only substantial example given for such acccusations is the above report on the authority of Fiṭr from Abū Ṭufayl on 'Alī. Aḥmad b. Ḥanbal knew very well some of the circulating prophecies concerning the 'Abbāsid civil war. In fact, he was a transmitter of at least one of them. However, Aḥmad b. Ḥanbal and his circle were no friends of al-Ma'mūn and probably dismissed any account about his merits. The report likely contained additional information, which we no longer have, that was not acceptable by the *muḥaddiths*, leading to its elimination from their work. It is possible that we have a case of censorship, and a largely successful one, to erase any record in which al-Ma'mūn might have been portrayed as some kind of messianic figure.

Such problems notwithstanding, the information and the insight that may be acquired from prophecies make them a primary source for the religious, social, and political history of early Islam. Despite the relatively abstract, ambiguous, and even silent Qur'ānic text, Muslim messianic and apocalyptic sensibility developed a discourse through supplementing and interpreting the Qur'ān in light of the political and sociocultural transformation in the two centuries after the death of Muḥammad. Prophecies relied on the authority of sages, scriptures, and the Prophet Muḥammad and his early companions. They were spread both orally and through some of the most prestigious written sources (exegesis, *ḥadīth*). Because of this, they communicated an ideology that appears to have exercised both descriptive and prescriptive power in political life, as we will see in the following chapters.

CHAPTER 1

Messianic Claims and Institutionalization

Making better sense of the messianic discourse and movements of the early Islamic period requires looking at the political context—the groundbreaking rise and impact of the caliphate—in which both the discourse and the movements unfolded. With relentless missionary and, later, military activity starting from his hometown of Mecca, the Prophet Muḥammad (ca. 570–632) spread his message and authority throughout the western Arabian Peninsula and organized his followers into a political community. It was at this time that the Byzantines became aware of an ambitious political and military entity that had not existed only a decade earlier. The Byzantines faced the Muslim armies in the Battles of Mu'ta in the autumn of 629 and Tabūk in 630 in the Ghassān territory on the Syrian border. Muḥammad's greatest impact on his community resulted from the revelations recorded in the Qur'ān and from his life as a prophet. His followers embarked, after a fateful debate immediately after his death, on a mission to bring into their fold new nations and territories before the final Hour.

The Legacy of the Early Caliphate

It is often taken for granted that the followers of Muḥammad established the caliphate seamlessly after his death and went on to conquer territories. This was certainly not the case for his immediate followers. The famous story of his two leading companions, Abū Bakr and 'Umar (who later become the first two caliphs), and their reaction to Muḥammad's death shows an ambivalent state of mind. Upon hearing of the death of Muḥammad, 'Umar exclaimed that the Prophet Muḥammad did not die but went to his Lord in the same way that Moses did and that Muḥammad would be back. It appears that 'Umar maintained this view until Abū Bakr made his famous remark, in which he reiterated the humanity of Muḥammad as noted in the Qur'ān and reassured the community that Muḥammad had indeed died but that God was ever living and eternal.[1] Although medieval sources tend to maintain that everyone realized 'Umar's mistake after Abū Bakr's intervention, the break of the wars of apostasy and the conquest movement suggest otherwise. In this circumstance the caliphate came about as a by-product of the unexpected success of the conquests, and the resulting responsibility of attending to the needs of administration in the short and long term required predictability in governance. Yet anxieties continued to clash with institutionalization. It is within this context the politics of early Islamic history unfolded.

Four major civil wars shook the caliphate in the first two hundred years of its existence. Two of the civil wars led to drastic dynastic changes (from the Patriarchal Caliphate to the Umayyads in 661 and from the Umayyads to the ʿAbbāsids in 750), and the other two overwhelmed the center of political power and the provinces for more than a decade each. In each of these civil wars, messianic and apocalyptic expectations played a large role. After a chain of disturbances in the provinces and with the assassination of the third caliph, ʿUthmān b. ʿAffān, in 656, the door was opened for the first civil war (called, reproachfully, *fitna*). This conflict eventually led to the demise of the Patriarchal Caliphate and the rise of Umayyad rule. Several prophecies pointed to the coming of the final day in the year 35/656, projecting the first civil war as a truly apocalyptic battle.[2]

As a result of these conflicts, the sectarian diversification of the Muslim community also began. The relatively homogeneous community of the Prophet Muḥammad, at least in terms of dogma, broke into diverse subgroups and classes. The golden era of unity, as it would be remembered and invoked in sociopolitical struggles of later times, was gone. From the first to the third civil war, the Muslim community witnessed the emergence of the Khārijī sect and the galvanization and eventual mobilization of the supporters of the family of ʿAlī around a Shīʿī cause. Both of these movements sheltered extremist subsects whose influence on the social and political life in Islamic history can hardly be overestimated. By the time of the ʿAbbāsid revolt in the middle of the eighth century, both sects had been firmly established in religio-political life. These were the most visible sects, but a myriad of other groups also appeared, defining and redefining themselves in relation to other sectarian movements, the caliphate, and increasingly non-Muslim cultural and religious influences.

In the context of confessional and sectarian disputes and of political rivalry in the first Islamic century, the initial use of the concept of the Mahdī appeared. It seems that perhaps during the first civil war, ʿUthmān and ʿAlī, and shortly afterward the latter's younger son, al-Ḥusayn, were venerated as Mahdīs by their supporters, who coined probably one of the most enduring epithets in Islamic history.[3] The use of the title Mahdī soon proliferated. How religio-political factions decided to articulate their claims using messianic vocabulary and attribute to their messianic figures eschatological qualities (for example, concealment, the idea of return) can best be studied within the political and sociocultural context of the first Islamic century. It is quite possible that the title initially meant a rightly guided caliph who would restore Islam to its original perfection, as Madelung suggested, gradually picking up an eschatological dimension.[4] However, the sudden proliferation of the title with eschatological aspects (as early as the movement of al-Mukhtār, for instance) and its clear redemptive meaning during middle Umayyad times suggest otherwise. Yet if it is assumed that the figure of the messiah was in place from the beginning, how can its absence from the Qur'ān be explained?[5] The title seems to have increasingly acquired a redemptive nuance in a short period of time, as the end-of-time prophecies coincided with its use.

Though an investigation into the origins of the title Mahdī is outside the scope of this book, suffice it to say that in the turbulent period after the death of the Umayyad caliph Yazīd I (r. 680–83), Umayyad opposition did use messianic concepts to articulate their claims. The Shī'ī al-Mukhtār, the Meccan Ibn al-Zubayr, and even the Umayyad caliphs themselves expressed their claims and ambitions using messianic vocabulary. In the movement of al-Mukhtār, the title Mahdī became associated with an eschatological redeemer.[6] If previous proto-Shī'ī movements had inspired al-Mukhtār's followers to use the title Mahdī, in the Ḥijāz region Ibn al-Zubayr promoted the legacy of the Patriarchal Caliphate in Medina against the Umayyads and used messianic language to articulate his claims, perhaps shaping the image of messiah for the following generations.[7] Provoked by the heated confrontation between the Umayyad troops and the forces of Ibn al-Zubayr, a number of curious predictions anticipated the end of time in and around 70/689–90.[8]

The use of the title Mahdī by a diverse group of people shows that it was not perceived to be the prerogative of any single individual, family, or tribe. Even groups or individuals outside the Quraysh tribe developed messianic aspirations of their own, perhaps motivated by tribal competition, which made the claims to messianic status widely accessible. The emergence and spread of prophecies regarding the coming of a south Arabian deliverer, the Qaḥṭānī, demonstrate not only the flexibility of messianic ideas to accommodate a range of aspirations but also their currency during Umayyad times.[9] One such prophecy makes the coming of the south Arabian deliverer a portent of the end of time: "The Hour will not come until a man from Qaḥṭān will come forth leading the people with his staff."[10] Apparently prophecies of this sort encouraged Ibn al-Ash'ath, whose uprising against the Umayyads garnered the support of a large number of jurists, to identify himself with the titles of al-Manṣūr and al-Qaḥṭānī during his revolt in 80/699.[11] In the final decade of the Umayyad caliphate, al-Ḥārith b. Surayj also claimed the title of al-Manṣūr for himself in his uprising against the Umayyad governor Naṣr b. Sayyār. It appears reasonable to conclude that since the end of the first Islamic century, the idea of Mahdī (or an analogous figure) was both widespread and politically meaningful.

It is no surprise, then, that the Umayyad caliphs also relied on prophecies to back their own political claims. The title Mahdī often connoted the rule of justice under the caliph as a title of respect, but not always. With regard to Sulaymān b. 'Abd al-Malik and 'Umar II, it referred to their redemptive and eschatological roles.[12] Some prophecies depicted even the Umayyad court and the city of Damascus as refuges for those running away from apocalyptic battles or as gathering points for people of goodwill and saintly vicars, *abādila*.[13] The prime example of Umayyad messianic aspirations is the legend of the Sufyānī. The legend seems to have appeared on the historical scene only after the demise of the Sufyānī branch of the Umayyad family in the second civil war. While its initial use as an Umayyad savior and the Shī'ī use of it as an anathema still require further investigation,[14] it seems that the Sufyānī prophecies already circulated during Umayyad times, although they proliferated after the establishment of the 'Abbāsid caliphate.[15] As early as the reign of the first 'Abbāsid caliph, 'Abdallāh Abū al-'Abbās al-Saffāḥ (r. 132–36/749–54), Abū Muḥammad Ziyād b. 'Abdallāh, one of the grandsons of the second Umayyad caliph, Yazīd b. Mu'āwiya, claimed the title of al-Sufyānī during his revolt against al-Saffāḥ as the expected savior who would return the caliphate and the fortune, or *dawla*, of the Umayyads to the Sufyānids.[16]

The claims of the Umayyads were kept in check by the counterclaims of the opposition.[17] The decades leading to the 'Abbāsid revolution in 132/750 unleashed a rich array of messianic movements, including that of the 'Abbāsids, which was born of a Shī'ī religio-political sect, the Kaysāniyya, whose members were fervent with messianic ideas. The messianic claims of the 'Abbāsids contrast starkly with the pessimistic tone of Umayyad and anti-'Abbāsid prophecies. As the revolt raged in Khurāsān, prophecies for the cause of the 'Abbāsids foretold the collapse of the Umayyads and the dawn of a new era of justice.[18] Although the majority of the prophecies concerning the black banners and the 'Abbāsids date back to the final decade of the Umayyad caliphate, 'Abbāsid historiographical memory would like to date the movement to the end of the first Islamic century, the year 100 A.H. In fact, such a date might be plausible because the year 100 A.H. marked a unique moment of apocalyptic anxiety and messianic expectations in the early Islamic period.[19] Prophecies about the Umayyad downfall are sufficiently numerous (even though the overwhelming majority of them come down to us in later sources) to suggest their widespread circulation among the Umayyads and their opposition.[20] The disruption of social life and the resulting anxiety concerning the future instilled terror in the minds of many observers as prophecies predicted "excessive killing and speedy death and horrifying hunger" befalling the Bedouin Arabs (*al-'arab*) after the year 125/743.[21] Even the survival of the community up to the year 125/743 seemed uncertain in the circulating prophecies. Even if the community survived that date, there still would be apocalyptic battles, "all of which mentioned in the [prophecies of] the end of times."[22] Indeed the ongoing political and military strife often called to mind total annihilation around the year 125/743 and shortly afterward.

Intra-Umayyad conflicts and the ascension of Marwān b. al-Ḥakam to the caliphal seat certainly gave the impression to many observers that after the year

129/747 the Umayyads were doomed. The emergence of the 'Abbāsid revolutionary movement increased the troubles for the Umayyad dynasty. The 'Abbāsid revolt cut across sectarian and confessional lines and was suffused with messianic expectations. A wealth of prophecies recorded the appearance of people with "strange garments" advancing from the East and the ransack of Damascus by the holders of black banners as a portent signaling the end of the world.[23] The 'Abbāsid revolutionary militia, decorated with black banners, seemed to have no mercy for the Umayyads: "The black banners will rise in 129/747 and the leader [Abū Muslim?][24] will appear with a group of insignificant people, whose hearts are like [pieces of] iron, their hair reaching their shoulders; they have neither mercy nor compassion for their enemies." The prophecy offers a detailed account of the rebels, yielding insight into the social origins of the revolutionary army: "They bear nicknames, and their tribes are villages. They wear garments like a dark night's color, he [the Akbash] will lead them to the 'Abbāsids, and that is their fortune."[25] Iranian-Zoroastrian apocalyptic prophecies in the eastern parts of the caliphate also seem to be informed by the emergence of the 'Abbāsids, as Pāzand speaks of "black banners and black garments."[26]

Eventually the Umayyad caliphate collapsed under the weight of mounting problems of questionable legitimacy, tribal and provincial discontent, and pious opposition. Unable to cope with socioeconomic transformations that they themselves largely had shaped and the attendant political complications, and failing to establish political institutions around which they could rally popular support, the Umayyads vanished under the impact of a popular uprising. The remnants of the Umayyad family fled to North Africa and Spain to establish the celebrated Umayyad Emirate there.

The 'Abbāsid revolution of 750 in Khurāsān was born out of the growing sectarian, particularly Shī'ī, opposition against the Umayyads and out of the social and political expectations of converts to Islam, who were called *Mawālī*, clients, and were considered inferior to the Arab Muslims. Certainly the sociopolitical rift between the center of political power and the periphery, in particular the Iranian provinces, played a large role in the revolt. The revolt was organized by nobility belonging to the 'Abbāsid family—the descendants of al-'Abbās, the paternal uncle of Muḥammad—and was structured so as to shore up as much support as possible from the ranks of the opposition to the Umayyads. The 'Abbāsids operated from the town of Ḥumayma in today's southern Jordan at the beginning of the second/eighth century, but the propaganda centered in Khurāsān, the region east of the Caspian Sea, with Marw as its hub. The armed rebellion toward the middle of the eighth century, the bulk of whose participants came from converts to Islam in Khurāsān, sealed the fate of the Umayyads. It also eliminated other contenders for the caliphate—most notably the ʿAlids, the descendants of the paternal cousin of the Prophet Muḥammad and his son-in-law, the fourth caliph, ʿAlī—from within the ranks of the revolt.

The ʿAbbāsid revolution championed the family of the Prophet and called for an acceptable leader among his family, *al-riḍā min āl Muḥammad,* the Hāshimites. The Zoroastrian text *Jāmāsp Namak* clearly refers to the ʿAbbāsids as the descendents of Hāshim: "Afterwards there come up Ṭājiks who bring up their seeds from the branch of Hāshim."[27] The ʿAbbāsids made the black banners their symbol and kept black as their royal color even after they succeeded in overthrowing the Umayyads. Leaving aside the discussion of when exactly ʿAbbāsid political claims began[28] and whether the color black as a symbol of rightful resistance originated in Khurāsān among the non-Arab supporters of the ʿAbbāsids, the use of black banners as a symbol of political resistance certainly proliferated in the later Umayyad period.[29]

The enthronement of the first caliph, al-Saffāḥ, in 132/749 fulfilled prophecies that promised that the leadership would be transferred from one family to another and opened a new caliphal phase based in the small Iraqi town of Hāshimiyya near the city of al-Kūfā, which was known as a center of Shīʿī opposition. The capital eventually was moved to a new city near a small village known as Baghdad. Named the City of Peace, *Madinat al-Salām,* Baghdad was founded by the caliph al-Manṣūr in 762 on the west bank of the Tigris River, leaving Damascus a discontented provincial town in the ʿAbbāsid era. It seems certain that the title al-Mahdī was chosen to honor the first ʿAbbāsid caliph. He was addressed not only as al-Mahdī but also as the Qā'im, he who would rise.[30] Other traditions making the Mahdī a descendant of al-ʿAbbās ("the Mahdī will be from the progeny of al-ʿAbbās")[31] and identifying him as ʿAbdallāh date most probably from the later stages of the ʿAbbāsid revolt,[32] even though a few accounts place such prophecies at earlier times.[33] A piece of epigraphic evidence found on the walls of the al-Saffāḥ mosque in Yemen strongly supports the idea that he was presented as the Mahdī.[34]

The messianic aspects of the ʿAbbāsid revolt were not a recently cultivated ideology. The ʿAbbāsids were intimately involved with the Kaysāniyya sect and other extremist movements, *ghulāt,* especially in Iran. The origin of the ʿAbbāsid revolt is outside the purview of this book, but the manner in which the ʿAbbāsids became a part of various sectarian formations of the Kaysāniyya sect and its subbranches merits a brief discussion. The Kaysāniyya was both the cradle of the ʿAbbāsid claims and a powerful religio-political movement during the time of the Umayyads and the early ʿAbbāsids.[35] During the Umayyad period, the Kaysāniyya in its various branches constituted the bulk of the radical wing of the Shīʿa. Although the movement appeared to be disintegrating after the middle of the second/eighth century,[36] it left a permanent mark on the ʿAbbāsid identity.

Since the movement of al-Mukhtār, who claimed to have operated on behalf of Muḥammad b. al-Ḥanafiyya (d. 81/701), the younger son of the fourth caliph, ʿAlī, the opposition to the Umayyads, most particularly the ʿAlids and the ʿAbbāsids, harbored messianic beliefs. In fact al-Mukhtār designated Muḥammad b. al-Ḥanafiyya the Mahdī.[37] The supporters of Ibn al-Ḥanafiyya continued to believe that he was the Mahdī even after the defeat of al-Mukhtār. Some of his ardent supporters, who gave birth to the Kaysāniyya movement, began to claim soon after his death that Ibn al-Ḥanafiyya was not dead but was in hiding and that they expected his return.[38] A poem attributed to Kuthayyir ʿAzza, (d. 105/723) illustrates this belief: "Behold the imams from the Quraysh, possessors of the truth. . . . [Muḥammad b. al-Ḥanafiyya] shall not taste death until he advances at the head of his cavalry with his banner before him. He has gone into concealment at Raḍwa, where he lives on honey and water."[39] After the death of Ibn al-Ḥanafiyya, his supporters split into several subsects, because they disagreed on the identity of the imam after him.[40]

Among the most prominent of such supporters was Ibn al-Ḥanafiyya's son Abū Hāshim, who died childless (d. ca. 98/717–18). His party, known as the Hāshimiyya,[41] split into several groups after his death. One group claimed that Abū Hāshim was the Mahdī and that he was alive, hiding in the mountains of Raḍwa. Another group maintained that the imamate had passed to the ʿAbbāsid Muḥammad b. ʿAlī b. ʿAbdallāh b. al-ʿAbbās.[42] According to the ʿAbbāsid historical memory, the ʿAbbāsid family held not only the imamate but also the knowledge of future events. For instance, the ʿAbbāsids maintained that Abū Hāshim gave Muḥammad b. ʿAlī the prophetic *Yellow Script, al-ṣaḥīfa al-ṣafrā'*, which foretold the rise of the black banners of Khurāsān. According to ʿAbbāsid apologetics, the script passed from one person to another through a prominent line of the Hāshimites all the way from ʿAlī to the founder of the ʿAbbāsid revolutionary movement, Muḥammad b. ʿAlī.[43] Though the legend of the *Yellow Script* must be seen in light of the competition over legitimacy between the ʿAlids and the ʿAbbāsids, it nevertheless shows the occultist and messianic concerns of the dynasty.[44]

The followers of Bayān b. Samʿān (d. 119/736), known as the Bayāniyya, believed that Abū Hāshim would return as the Mahdī.[45] ʿAbdallāh b. ʿAmr b. Ḥarb, one of the Hāshimiyya, claimed that the imamate had passed to him after Abū Hāshim. After Ibn Ḥarb died, he was believed to be still alive and was expected to return.[46] The Khidāshiyya were the followers of ʿAmmār b. Yazīd, nicknamed Khidāsh, who was an ʿAbbāsid propagandist active in the area of Nishapur and Marw.[47] After Muḥammad b. ʿAlī and Khidāsh had a falling out over doctrinal differences, the supporters of Khidāsh announced that Muḥammad b. ʿAlī had given up the imamate and that it had passed to Khidāsh. After the execution of Khidāsh in 118/736, his supporters claimed that he was alive and had been raised to heaven by God.[48]

Consisting mainly of the former Ḥarbiyya, the Janāḥiyya sect supported the imamate of ʿAbdallāh b. Muʿāwiya.[49] ʿAbdallāh b. Muʿāwiya is reported to have encouraged their extremist beliefs, claiming that the Divine Spirit had been transferred through the prophets and imams to him and that he was able to resurrect the dead. After he died in 131/748–49 in the prison of Abū Muslim, who was a Khurāsānī and the head of the ʿAbbāsid revolutionary army, a group of ʿAbdallāh b. Muʿāwiya's followers claimed that he was alive and hiding in the mountains of Iṣfahān.[50] Some said that he would return as the Mahdī, while others held that he would surrender the leadership to a descendant of ʿAlī before his death.[51]

Abū Muslimiyya was a subgroup of the Kaysāniyya and maintained that the imamate had passed from the first ʿAbbāsid caliph, al-Saffāḥ, to Abū Muslim, whom the group considered its leader.[52] After the execution of Abū Muslim by the caliph al-Manṣūr in 137/755, some of the supporters of Abū Muslim maintained that the imamate had been transferred from al-Saffāḥ to Abū Muslim and that Abū Muslim was still alive.[53] This group, called the (Abū) Muslimiyya, believed that al-Manṣūr had killed not Abū Muslim but a person who only resembled him and that Abū Muslim had gone into hiding. Opposed to them were the Riẓāmiyya, named after their chief, Riẓām b. Sābiq, probably one of the Rawandī extremists who upheld the succession of al-Manṣūr to the imamate. Though they refused to repudiate Abū Muslim, they affirmed that the imamate would remain in the ʿAbbāsid family until the resurrection, when a descendant of al-ʿAbbās would be the Mahdī.[54]

Khurāsān and Transoxiana, the centers of ʿAbbāsid political and military might, continued to be hotbeds of numerous religio-political movements with messianic overtones. The ideas behind some of these movements were mixed with local beliefs and traditions that fell outside the limits of either Shīʿī or proto-Sunnī orthodoxy. Among the leaders of such movements, one may note Sunbād, a wealthy Zoroastrian from Nishapur and an associate of Abū Muslim. Believing that Abū Muslim was not killed and would return to rule, Sunbād revolted only two months after Abū Muslim's murder in 755 to avenge his death, but was defeated.[55] Another revolt in Transoxiana in the name of Abū Muslim was led by al-Muqannaʿ, the Veiled One, in Marw in 777. His was an ideology of incarnation and transmigration of souls, as he claimed to be divine and an incarnation of Adam, whom God created in his image. He claimed to have been incarnated in Noah and reincarnated in Moses, Jesus, Muḥammad, and finally Abū Muslim. His movement began in his native Marw and spread to Samarqand and Bukhārā before ending in a spectacular suicide in fire with all the members of his family and the most loyal of his followers.[56]

The ʿAbbāsids developed their messianic ideology in part vis-à-vis the ʿAlids, who had their own messianic claims in orthodox and extremist forms both inside and outside the Kaysāniyya movement. The followers of Mughīra b. Saʿīd al-Bajalī, a blind old man who practiced magic and jugglery, supported the belief that the Ḥasanid Muḥammad b. ʿAbdallāh, the Pure Soul, would come forth as the Mahdī. When Muḥammad b. ʿAbdallāh vanished from the authorities' sight, the Mughīriyya claimed that he was alive, hiding in Mount al-Tamiyya, which was located east of the route from al-Ḥajīr to Mecca. In his doctrine, Mughīra b. Saʿīd al-Bajalī elevated the ʿAlid imams to the rank of divinity. Nevertheless, until the appearance of the Pure Soul as the Mahdī, al-Mughīra taught that he himself was the imam, the imamate of the ʿAlids having elapsed.[57] He claimed to be a prophet and taught that Muḥammad b. ʿAbdallāh had given him from his mouth the Holy Spirit, with which he was able to bring the dead to life and to heal those who are blind or have leprosy. After the failure of the revolt of Muḥammad b. ʿAbdallāh and his death in 145/762, some of the Mughīriyya claimed that a devil had taken the shape of Muḥammad and that the real Muḥammad still would rise and rule the world.[58]

The Pure Soul's fame among the more moderate Shīʿīs as the expected Mahdī in Medina was also widespread. His popularity increased to the degree that no one, if we believe al-Iṣfahānī, had any doubt that he was the Mahdī. In fact he honored himself with this name in one of his addresses to his supporters: "You have no doubt that I am the Mahdī, I am indeed he."[59] After him, his brother Ibrāhīm, who adopted the title al-Hādī, led an unsuccessful uprising against al-Manṣūr.[60] After Ibrāhīm's death, some of his supporters claimed that he was the expected one. In the Ḥusaynid branch of the ʿAlids, some of the followers of Jaʿfar al-Ṣādiq and his father, Muḥammad al-Bāqir, saw them as Mahdīs.[61] Later the followers of the Ḥusaynid Mūsā al-Kāẓim (d. 799) declared him to be the messianic Qāʾim. When he died, they awaited his return from concealment.[62] These were known as the Wāqifa, who circulated among Shīʿī groups a tradition, attributed to Jaʿfar al-Ṣādiq, that stated, "your seventh imam is your Qāʾim." The Wāqifa thus stopped the imamate with the seventh Shīʿī imam, Mūsā al-Kāẓim.[63]

In this context the ʿAbbāsid family found it necessary to justify their rule by referring to prophecies of the most eschatological kind: "By God, then there will be [rulers] from our family, the Saffāḥ, the Manṣūr, and the Mahdī who will hand it [the caliphate] over to Jesus the son of Mary."[64] When the court poet Abū Dulāma praised the second ʿAbbāsid caliph, al-Manṣūr, as the Mahdī, or when al-Manṣūr claimed to have a vision in which he saw the Prophet entrusting him with a banner until he fought against the Antichrist, *al-Dajjāl*, they were reacting to the claims of their opponents and responding to the ideological context of their time.[65] Although the second ʿAbbāsid caliph seems to have gradually distanced himself from the extremism of the Riẓāmiyya, he assumed the title al-Manṣūr immediately after he defeated Muḥammad b. ʿAbdallāh, the Pure Soul, in 145/762, implying that he was the forerunner who would pave the way for the Mahdī.[66] As his actions indicate, al-Manṣūr honored his son, Muḥammad b. ʿAbdallāh, as the Mahdī around the year 143/760–61, even before his victory over the Pure Soul and before adopting his own title, al-Manṣūr, and made a concerted effort to publicize this.[67] He did not shy away from publicly arguing that the Mahdī was indeed his son, not the Pure Soul.[68] In the succession dispute within the ʿAbbāsid family, the caliph al-Manṣūr forced the heir apparent in line, ʿĪsā b. Mūsā, to cede his place to his son Muḥammad because, al-Manṣūr argued, "he was the expected Mahdī."[69] Al-Mahdī himself, while still an heir apparent, used for the first time in ʿAbbāsid history the title *al-imām* on a coin minted in Bukhārā in 151/768. The issue was minted when al-Manṣūr was still the ruling caliph. Bates quite reasonably concludes that such an anomaly resulted from "revolutionary enthusiasm" in Khurāsān rather than from deliberate manipulation for political gains.[70]

After his accession, al-Mahdī sought to live up to messianic expectations by releasing political prisoners and handing out gifts, especially in the holy cities.[71] Al-Hādī and al-Rashīd also preferred to see themselves not as ordinary rulers but as caliphs who were commissioned to bring about divine justice, religious purity, and military victories.[72]

The messianic dimension of the ʿAbbāsid rule should not stand in the way of recognizing the difficult realities of administering a far-flung empire on a day-to-day basis. How well did messianic rhetoric mesh with the mundane tasks of ruling? Perhaps the most relevant response to this question comes from Ibn al-Muqaffaʿ, who served the Umayyads and briefly the ʿAbbāsids as secretary until his execution under orders from the caliph al-Manṣūr.

Ibn al-Muqaffaʿ's diagnosis of the seriousness of the clash between ʿAbbāsid revolutionary charisma and the institutional need for predictability is a telling account of the ambivalence of ʿAbbāsid politics, dynastic identity, and imperial culture. Having observed the severity and disruptive nature of the veneration of ʿAbbāsid caliphs among the members of the military and administration, he wrote to advise the caliph how to place the caliphate on an institutional military and administrative track. His treatise addresses significant questions regarding the ʿAbbāsid army and administration, and, more important, the image and perception of the ʿAbbāsid caliphs among their followers. Ibn al-Muqaffaʿ warns the caliph that his followers went too far in bestowing semidivine attributes upon him. He informs the caliph that many of the generals claim that if the caliph orders the mountains to move, they will move, and if he demands that the *qibla*, the direction of prayer, be turned around, it will be done. He therefore advises the caliph to curb this potentially dangerous mood of veneration and devotion among the Khurāsānī army and put a system of duties and rights in place for the civil and military bureaucracy to follow.[73]

Ibn al-Muqaffaʿ had an incisive observation. Though he perhaps committed a mistake that cost him his life by downplaying the salvific nature of the caliph, which al-Manṣūr seems to have maintained, he brought into sharp focus the struggle of the caliphs since the time of al-Manṣūr to find a way to balance stability and revolutionary zeal, which the successors of the caliph al-Manṣūr seem to have managed only until the outbreak of the fourth civil war at the end of the second Islamic century. The civil war proved not only that the ʿAbbāsids were reluctant to abandon their messianic claims but also that messianic beliefs could emerge again as a meaningful religio-political ideology. An argument can be made that the ʿAbbāsids merely employed messianic beliefs for their own pragmatic interests or attempted to forge an anti-ideology for the purposes of dampening anti-ʿAbbāsid propaganda;[74] however, such an argument has to explain how the ʿAbbāsids themselves managed to stay immune to the effects of such beliefs and justify why a rich messianic and apocalyptic tradition among Muslims and non-Muslims should be dismissed as inconsequential. Looking into how non-Muslims and Muslims dealt with each other through the prism of prophecies will better clarify the context in which the ʿAbbāsids operated.

Muslims and Others: A Process of Conflict and Confluence

Having been united under a single political umbrella, Muslim and non-Muslim communities shared similar experiences and eventually developed striking similarities in their expectations and visions. A two-century-long interaction contributed significantly to the ideas and expectations during the early ʿAbbāsid period and made possible for the observers among diverse confessions to imagine political developments in a messianic or apocalyptic light. Many remarkable prophecies dating back to the first Islamic century vividly illustrate a process of coexistence. Initially the immediate reaction of Jewish, Zoroastrian, and Christian communities to the rise of Islam was apocalyptic. While apocalyptic prophecies had already been circulating within the respective confessional communities independent of the rise of Islam, new ones clearly arose in response to this and to the Muslim expansion.[75] The emerging faith fed Jewish messianic hopes, reminded Christians of the proximity of the end of time, and pushed the Zoroastrian communities into despair. Muslim expansion compelled all to revisit their end-of-time scenarios. Defensive in nature, non-Muslim prophecies reflected the need of those communities to explain adverse developments that they had faced, to reassure themselves of their legitimacy as communities of faith, and to interpret both their past and their future in ways that confirmed their beliefs.[76]

Numerous Christian apocalyptic prophecies throughout the first Islamic century exposed a persistent sense of apprehension and anxiety, fluctuating from self-blame as in the sermons of Sophronius Patriarch of Jerusalem (d. ca. 639)[77] to a sense of disappointment and hopelessness in the face of Muslim military conquests. Soon the caliphate replaced the Roman Empire as the fourth beast in numerous Danielic prophecies.[78] The rapid advance of the Muslim military and the new administrative organization of the conquered territories gave the impression of Muslim permanence in the provinces. Pseudo Ephraem's apocalypse, written probably around the middle of the seventh century C.E.,[79] Ps. Shenute's apocalypse (644?) in Egypt,[80] and Ps. Methodius's apocalypse reflect the feelings of pessimism and coming to terms with Muslim expansion.

Iranian-Zoroastrian apocalypses, which were reworked extensively in the ninth century C.E., offer another window into the role of apocalyptic expectations in early Islamic society. Zoroastrian texts reflect the social and religious chaos that the Zoroastrian community experienced after losing its prominence as a result of the Muslim conquests.[81] The vision of the *Zand-ī Vohūman Yasn* communicated an image of a tree with seven branches, the last of which was mixed with iron and seems to describe the Muslim rule.[82] The *Jāmāsp Namak* and the *Dīnkard* also echo the core millenarian vision of the *Zand-ī Vohūman Yasn*.[83] Their millenarian visions involving the Muslims underline the Zoroastrian community's struggle to come to terms with Muslim dominance and with the resulting social and cultural dissolution of the traditional order. Various Zoroastrian communities seem to have harbored a strong messianic hope for a savior who would come at the end of time and restore the order of the old days of Iran and reinstitute justice.[84]

In many respects the conquerors were no different. The rise of multiple dissident prophets immediately after Muḥammad, the blazing speed of the conquests, and the dramatic onset of the civil war only two decades after the death of the Prophet Muḥammad suggest that the Muslim community struggled to cope with social and political challenges. Apocalyptic anxiety was one symptom. Exhausted by constant mobilization, plagued by internal strife, and stretched too thin across vast territories in which they remained a tiny minority until the third/ninth century, the conquerors, too, had their own fears of annihilation as a result of their own civil wars or at the hands of their enemies, including the Byzantines, the Turks, and the Ethiopians.[85] Thus numerous prophecies warn of how the Ethiopians would destroy the Kaʿba and the Turks would be unleashed upon Muslims.[86] The revelations of John the Little (ca. 700) in Edessa (today's Urfa in Turkey) show a consciousness of intra-Muslim conflicts and even predict an imminent destruction of Muslim rule as the frequency of natural disasters reminds the author of the approaching end of time.[87]

It would be a miscalculation, however, to reduce the nature of the interactions among the communities inside and outside the caliphate to antagonism and fear. After the dust of the initial conquests settled, a large portion of Eurasia came under a single polity, fostering an increased and more regular and diversified flow of materials and, eventually, ideas and culture.[88] Although Pirenne argues otherwise, the interactions among the eastern and western shores of the Mediterranean and the Near East gradually picked up speed.[89] Even the pattern of the spread of epidemics suggests sustained relations.[90] Trade flourished, the flow of ideas became easier, and the exchange of skilled labor and social interaction and assimilation increased not only in the frontiers but also in the hinterland.[91] The relationship did not remain limited to a coexistence that was necessitated by trade and diplomatic contacts; it penetrated into culture and worldviews, which made possible the construction of a Byzantine palace in Constantinople in the early ninth century modeled on 'Abbāsid palaces.[92] The flow of ideas and culture, facilitated by military expansion and commercial contact, drastically affected the traditional course of life across cultural frontiers and encouraged similarity and cooperation in much of the social, cultural, and economic life of the expanding Muslim empire. As Vryonis notes, "these similarities [were] so definite that they seem to mock the linguistic, religious, and political differences."[93]

Even the expressions of defense and accusation reflected knowledge derived from the cross-cultural exchange of information, which stripped societies of their traditional isolation.[94] In the Iconoclast debate, intriguing clues regarding Muslim-Christian relations and Byzantine perception of and knowledge about Muslim religiosity show the intensity of this interaction. *Vita Stephani*, a contemporary hagiographic work, explicitly accuses the Hellenes (pagans), the Jews, and the Syrians (Muslims) as those responsible for the Iconoclasm.[95] Literary and popular reactions pointed to "Saracen-minded," "Arab-born" emperors and to "infidels" as the culprits of Iconoclasm. John of Damascus wrote his famous treatises while living in Palestine under the Umayyads.[96] While some of the accusations against the Iconoclasts had no historical validity, in the mind of many Byzantines, including the church fathers the Second Council of Nicea of 787, a relationship did exist between Islamic faith, Jewish religiosity, and Byzantine Iconoclasm, as Papadakis maintains.[97] Of course, the interactions, especially the intellectual exchange, were competitive and involved bitter disputes. However, the simple fact that there existed a ground for the learned elite to dispute their differences led to a better understanding of each other and the creation of a shared intellectual platform. Islam was configured into the religious setting of the Near East, where it became a major part of the religiosity of the region. In fact prophetic and apocalyptic literature regarding the Muslims' ascendancy and the perceived decline of the non-Muslim communities helped bridge the differences among the inhabitants of the caliphate.[98]

As it became clear to non-Muslims that the conquerors were there to stay, they looked deeper into the Muslim faith to find common ground, because the exigencies of social life required cooperation. The interaction between religious communities that resulted in conversion, as well as social and economic affiliation, worked to form a greater commonality than was allowed in the literature of religious polemics and heresiography. Non-Muslims gradually realized that they shared a common history with their Muslim neighbors and developed a peculiar similarity in understanding the social and political realities of their time. To an extent, apocalyptic and messianic ideologies, which cast social and political realities in a certain light, played a large role in developing similarities. Thus the apocalypse of John Bar Penkāyē's *Rīs Mellē,* completed shortly before 693 in northern Mesopotamia, appears to be at peace with the Muslim conquests. The author expected the end of time in the near future and referred to Muḥammad as the instructor who brought monotheism to the inhabitants of the Arabian Peninsula in order to hold "to the worship of the one God in accordance with the customs of ancient law."[99] According to Bar Penkāyē, their faith instructed the Muslims to respect and honor the Christians. He acknowledged that the inhabitants of the conquered lands remained free to pursue whatever faith they wished as long as they paid tribute to the caliphate. Though he seems personally uncomfortable with such developments, the atmosphere of peace and tolerance fostered by flourishing commerce and urban life stands out in his writing: "Justice flourished in his [Mu'āwiya's] time and there was great peace in the regions under his control; he allowed everyone to live as they wanted." So much so that "there was no distinction between pagan and Christian and the faithful was not known from a Jew."[100]

As *Doctrina Jacobi* in the middle of the seventh century suggests, at least some people perceived Muḥammad to be a messianic forerunner "coming with the Saracens, and that he was proclaiming the advent of the anointed one, the Christ who was to come."[101] Jewish communities, which numerically were significantly smaller and scattered but still constituted a major faith community according to the Qur'ān, seem to have welcomed the Muslim conquerors as deliverers and made Muslim rule an instrument of the redemption of the Jewish people from Byzantine persecution and a portent of the arrival of the Messiah.[102] Even when prophecies failed to materialize, hopes of peaceful life under Muslim rulers continued to appear in many of the Jewish prophecies in the eighth and early ninth centuries.[103] A good illustration of increased social, cultural, and intellectual interaction is found in the movement of Abū 'Īsā al-Iṣfahānī, whose beliefs represented a popular fusion of Islam, Christianity, and Judaism. Abū 'Īsā, an illiterate tailor who claimed to be the fifth and the last messenger of the Messiah during the last years of the Umayyad caliphate and shortly after the 'Abbāsid revolution, saw the religions of Jesus and Muḥammad as true for their communities and advised his followers to study the three sacred books and their interpretations. He appealed to his supporters even by his name, which included Muslim, Christian, and Jewish references: Abū 'Īsā Isḥāq b. Ya'qūb al-Iṣfahānī, 'Uwayda 'Abīd Allāh.[104] His teachings did indeed resemble the doctrines of some Muslim movements, such as the extremist proto-Shī'īs, the Manṣūriyya in particular.[105] It is very likely that there were also Christianizing aspects to his followers' movement, the 'Īsāwiyya, especially because Abū 'Īsā acknowledged the prophethood of Jesus and Muḥammad. Thus the 'Īsāwiyya might have indeed stemmed from Jewish Christians (that is, from a community that believed in the validity of Mosaic law and considered Jesus a prophet).[106]

The rapprochement among faith communities posed challenges for the more conservative sensibilities on all sides. To the dismay of the clergy, many Christians preferred arbitrating their disputes outside the Church and intermarried with non-Christians. Native Christians were employed in local administration and tax collection, which not only accelerated the pace of interaction but also provoked intraconfessional tensions and divisions over identity.[107] Conversion soon followed among the Christian population, as the apocalypse of Ps. Athanasius, an Egyptian, complains.[108] In Spain, Paulus Alvaris Cordubensis lamented in the middle of the ninth century that Christian youths and men of education preferred Arabic costumes and excelled in speaking, reading, and writing Arabic, while Christian traditions and the study of Latin were abandoned.[109] On the Muslim side, a widespread tradition attributed to the Prophet Muḥammad discloses the irritation of stricter groups among Muslims: "Abū Hurayra said that the Prophet said, 'you will follow the path of those who went before you . . . so that even if they enter the hole of a lizard you will enter it.' They said, 'O Prophet of God, are they the Jews and Christians?' He replied, 'who else?'"[110] Such conservative voices were rampant, especially when social integration worked against sectarian and confessional divisions, but did little to keep the inhabitants of the Umayyad and 'Abbāsid caliphates within strict confessional limits.

As Muslims struggled to find meaning in what was happening around them and to construct a self-image during the conquest, they drew on biblical tradition, messianic or otherwise, and developed a sense of a shared past.[111] The formation of stricter confessional barriers in the second Islamic century only to a limited extent hindered this sense of belonging to a larger faith tradition. A case in point is the poet al-Farazdaq (d. 110/728 or 112/730). In his praise of the Umayyad caliph Sulaymān b. 'Abd al-Malik (r. 96–99/715–17), al-Farazdaq echoes a vision of an eschatological messiah—evidently popular in his milieu—that transcends religious boundaries, resembling a holy man or shrine venerated by all faiths: "You are the one who is described for us in the book and told of in the Torah and Psalms / How many priests or rabbis have been informing us of the caliphate of the Mahdī?"[112] The emphasis on monotheistic scriptures and on the predictive authority of the biblical clergy as a legitimate source of admissible prophecy speaks volumes about the amount of interaction between faith-based communities as early as the first Islamic century.

In a source as sober as the *Biography of the Prophet Muḥammad*, by Ibn Isḥāq, available today through the recension of Ibn Hishām (d. 218/833), the Muslim learned elite struggled to deal with the ancient practice of numerical symbolism and the duration of time allocated for the survival of the Muslim community.[113] Ibn Isḥāq's report depicts Abū Yāsir b. Akhṭab, a Jew from Khaybar, passing by the Prophet Muḥammad as the Prophet was reciting the opening verse of the chapter "The Cow": "*Alif Lām Mīm*. That is the book about which there is no doubt." The report continues that Abū Yāsir went to his brother, who was with some other Jews, and said to him:

> Do you know that I have heard Muḥammad reciting in what has been sent down to him, *Alif, Lām, Mīm,* etc. After expressing surprise, Ḥuyay and these men went to the apostle and told him what had been reported to them and asked if Gabriel had brought the message from God. When he said that he had, he said: God sent prophets before you, but we do not know of any one of them being told how long his kingdom would survive and how long his community would last. Ḥuyay went up to his men and said to them: *Alif* is 1; *Lām* is 30; and *Mīm* is 40, i.e. 71 years. Are you going to adopt a religion whose kingdom and community would last for only 71 years? Then he went to the apostle and said, "Have you anything else, Muḥammad?" He replied, "Yes, *Alif, Lām, Mīm, Ṣād*." Ḥuyay replied, "This, by God, is more weighty and longer: *Alif* is 1; *Lām* is 30; *Mīm* 40; *Ṣād* 90, i.e. 161 years." Similar questions were asked and answered in respect to *Alif, Lām, Rā* 231; *Alif, Lām, Mīm, Rā* 271; then Ḥuyay said, "Your situation seems obscure to us, Muḥammad, so that we do not know whether you will have a short or long duration." Then they left him. Abū Yāsir said to his brother Ḥuyay and the others, "How do you know that all these totals should not be added together to make a grand total of 734 years?" They answered, "His affair is obscure to us."[114]

Disagreement over the value of numbers and over the conclusion notwithstanding, this account projects the numerical symbolism (*abjad*) as an acceptable way of interpreting the Qur'ānic text. It also reveals an ongoing discussion among the Muslim community, at the latest during the lifetime of Ibn Isḥāq, about the duration of the Muslim community, which the transmitter attempts to dispel.

The work of Nu'aym b. Ḥammād, *Kitāb al-Fitan*, represents one among many other examples that mirror the efforts of several generations of Muslims to cling to the idea of shared heritage from as early as the first decades of Islam. In one of his traditions, Nu'aym b. Ḥammād relates how a small group of Muslim soldiers came upon a script, which they thought was the book of Daniel, during the conquest of Tustar (Shustar in contemporary Iran) during the reign of the second caliph, 'Umar (r. 12–22/634–44).

> On the authority of Muḥammad b. Yazīd on Abū Khilda on Abū al-'Āliyā, who said, "When Tustar was conquered we discovered a manuscript next to the head of a dead person lying on a bed in the treasury of al-Hurmuzān [a Sasanian commander]." He [Abū al-'Āliyā] said, "It was Daniel as

we reckoned." He [Abū al-ʿĀliyā] continued, "then we took it to ʿUmar. I was the first Arabic speaker [ʿArab] to have read it. It was [then] sent to Kaʿb, who translated it into Arabic. It contained what was going to happen, meaning the *fitan*."[115]

Nuʿaym b. Ḥammād's position is a good illustration of the dialogue with biblical material. As noted at the beginning of this book, he belonged to an unlikely ideological camp. He was a *ḥadīth* scholar of the stricter kind. Yet not only did he not object to including a wealth of information from biblical sources into his work, but he also defended his action. Despite the fact that many doubted and even ridiculed the authority of monotheistic scriptures in matters of future knowledge, the cross-confessional borrowing continued in large volume during the seventh and eighth centuries.

Although the process of adaptation and adoption was gradual, unsystematic, and mostly oral, it quickly produced results because it responded to individual and social anxieties and involved the faith communities intimately. It is no wonder that Muslim prophecies circulated among Jewish and Christian communities and non-Muslim prophecies witnessed a renaissance in the Muslim apocalyptic tradition.[116] The apocalypse of Ps. Methodius, which was most likely written in northern Mesopotamia at the end of the seventh century, exhibits noticeable similarities in its themes to some of the Muslim apocalyptic prophecies. The speed by which this apocalypse spread through Byzantium and the Latin West is indicative of the interest in prophecies in vast regions and diverse cultures.[117] By the early eighth century, it was available in Greek, Slavonic, and Latin translations,[118] and there is evidence of its spread to Egypt and Ethiopia as well.[119]

As Choksy rightly points out, a greater appreciation of the other appears to have slowly made its way through the whole region, especially because the conquests maintained constant contact and thereby awareness of the other among Zoroastrian, Jewish, Christian, and Muslim communities.[120] Even wall inscriptions echoed the spread of a culture of coexistence, as demonstrated in the wall inscriptions of the Syrian Church of Saint Sergius in Ehnesh, today's Gümüşgün of Maraş, where the name of the caliph al-Mahdī (r. 775–85) is appended with the honorific title, the commander of the faithful. This reference was not unique nor was it simply a vulgar attempt to please the caliph. The long period of Muslim rule might have caused these local Christians to internalize Muslim supremacy and identify their community with Muslim rule.[121] In Baghdad, the Patriarch of the East, Timothy I, whose stature and impact on the early ʿAbbāsid milieu is well documented, also referred to al-Mahdī as the commander of the faithful and prayed for the success and universality of his and his progeny's rule ("may God extend the authority of his kingdom").[122] ʿAbd al-Masīḥ al-Kindī (259/873) similarly addressed al-Ma'mūn as the commander of the faithful. He praised his just and impartial rule and prayed for the longevity of the caliphate in his apology.[123] Eventually interactions over the course of two centuries resulted in a shared perspective and language and led to Christian, Jewish, and Muslim observers developing messianic or apocalyptic anxieties and attitudes in facing sociopolitical realities, which will be examined next in greater detail.

CHAPTER 2

Shaping up a Messianic Discourse

For an audience in the early-ninth-century ʻAbbāsid world, the Qur'ānic references to the end of time were understandable against the background of the intellectual discussions, sectarian controversies, and political experiences of the preceding two centuries. Whether the Qur'ānic text itself justified an apocalyptic vision and whether there would be a messianic figure were discussed in other literary sources, particularly *ḥadīth* and exegesis. However, no specific chapter in the Qur'ān is devoted to matters dealing with the end of time. References to it are scattered in various places, and many of them are inconclusive, which made the Qur'ān secondary in importance to *ḥadīth* in formulating prophecies. The result was the increased reliance on extra-Qur'ānic knowledge for prophecies and for an interpretation of the Qur'ān to accommodate the evolving messianic and apocalyptic thought. To better understand this, a brief look at the Qur'ānic text from a messianic perspective is in order.

Qur'ānic Views on the End of Time

The Qur'ān names the end of time the Hour, *al-Sāʻah*, when earthly life ends in the Resurrection, *al-Qiyāma*, which, in turn, ushers in the Day of Judgment, *Yawm al-Ḥisāb*. The end of time in the Qur'ān appears certain, imminent, and catastrophic. The sense of certainty and imminence is communicated in a sharp, direct, and clear tone: "And because the Hour is coming, no doubt of it."[1] The following verse describes the proximity of the Hour: "Nigh unto men has drawn their reckoning, while they in heedlessness are yet turning away."[2] In some instances the verses describe it as if it had already happened: "And when it was said, 'God's promise is true, and the Hour, there is no doubt of it,' you said, 'We know not what the Hour may be; we have only a surmise, and are by no means certain.'"[3] Yet the exact time is never specified, and the possibility of anyone but God knowing it is denied: "They will question thee concerning the Hour, when it shall berth. Say: 'The knowledge of it is only with my Lord; none shall reveal it at its proper time, but He.'"[4]

The Hour is not only imminent but will also be sudden: "Are they looking for aught but the Hour, that it shall come upon them suddenly? Already its tokens have come; so, when it has come to them, how shall they have their Reminder?"[5] Clearly the Qur'ānic text feeds a state of alertness in the minds of its audience by stressing the Hour's imminence, without revealing its exact time. Moreover the following verse reminds the audience of the swiftness with which the Hour will be initiated: "To God belongs the Unseen in the heavens and in the earth. And the matter of the Hour is as a twinkling of the eye, or nearer. Surely God is powerful over everything."[6] However, the consequences of this effortless action will be catastrophic: "O men, fear your Lord! Surely the earthquake of the Hour is a mighty thing."[7]

The Hour is associated with the Resurrection and the Day of Judgment. A sounding trumpet and blowing horn signal the arrival of the Hour: "On the day the Trumpet is blown, and terrified is whosoever is in the heavens and earth, excepting whom God wills, and every one shall come to Him, all utterly abject."[8] The beast is another element associated with the end of time: "When the word falls on them, We shall bring forth for them out of the earth a beast that shall speak unto them. Mankind had no faith in Our signs."[9] The references to Gog and Magog reinforce the sense of the proximity and certainty of the end of time. Gog and Magog have been locked behind an iron wall by a prophetic character, Dhū al-Qarnayn, the Two-Horned One, largely associated with Alexander the Great in Muslim tradition. The wall will remain standing until the Hour arrives and the apocalyptic trumpet is blown, freeing Gog and Magog from their incarceration.[10]

One of the most frequently mentioned portents of the end of time in Muslim prophecies is civil disorder, *fitna*. Yet contrary to what one might expect, in none of the many instances in which the term *fitna* (civil disorder) is mentioned in the Qur'ān is it connected to end-of-time events. In the Qur'ānic text, *fitna* refers to a sort of trial: "And know that your wealth and your children are a trial [*fitna*], and that with God is a mighty wage."[11] In other verses, the term connotes discord, controversy, and dissension: "As for those in whose hearts is swerving, they follow the ambiguous part, desiring dissension [*fitna*], and seeking to explain it; and none knows its meaning, save only God."[12] *Fitna* may also mean seduction: "Children of Adam! Let not Satan tempt, [v. *yaftatin*], you as he brought your parents out of the Garden, stripping them of their garments to show them their shameful parts."[13] On other occasions, it describes chaos and civil disorder: "As for the unbelievers, they are friends one of another. Unless you do this, there will be strife [*fitna*] in the land and great corruption."[14] Finally it refers to plotting and acts of conspiracy: "Had they gone forth among you, they would only have increased you in trouble, and run to and fro in your midst, seeking to stir up sedition [*fitna*] between you; and some of you would listen to them; and God knows the evildoers."[15] A similar meaning is given in the following verses, where conspiracy against the community and its social and religious status quo is condemned: Persecution [*fitna*] is more grievous than slaying. But fight them not by the Holy Mosque until they should fight you there; then, if they fight you, slay them—such is the recompense of unbelievers."[16] Even the ban on fighting during the holy months is lifted in cases of the greater danger of persecution: "They will question thee concerning the holy month, and fighting in it. Say: 'Fighting in it is a heinous thing, but to bar from God's way, and disbelief in Him, and the Holy Mosque, and to expel its people from it—that is more heinous in God's sight; and persecution [*fitna*] is more heinous than slaying.'"[17]

Given the absence of any apocalyptic meaning attached to the term *fitna* in the Qur'ān, its apocalyptic connotations must therefore be ascribed to the civil war generation in the decades following the death of Muḥammad. It is certain that the term acquired its apocalyptic meaning very quickly, even perhaps during the first civil war. It seems plausible that the readers of the Qur'ān sufficiently appreciated the religious and rhetorical value of the term to use it in end-of-time prophecies, particularly because it captured the image of multiple layers of anarchy. As illustrated in Nuʿaym b. Ḥammād's work, by the early ninth century the term appeared inextricably associated with apocalyptic thinking, with or without end-of-time scenarios.

Similar to the absence of the concept of apocalyptic disorder, *fitna,* in the Qur'ān, the striking fact is that there is also no mention of a messianic figure, a Mahdī, as a part of eschatological ideology. While the Prophet Muḥammad is certainly presented as "the seal of the prophets," no one is suggested as the expected messianic figure. In a sense, this ambiguity implies Muḥammad as the forerunner.[18] It seems that medieval scholars associated the finality of prophecy to the Qur'ānic discourse of the end of time since the early eighth century.[19] The early Islamic exegetical interpretations emphasize the Qur'ānic mention of a Christian prophecy in respect to Muḥammad's arrival as a sign of the end of time: "And remember, Jesus the son of Mary said, 'O Children of Israel! I am the messenger of God [sent] to you, confirming the law [which came] before me, and giving glad tidings of a messenger to come after me, whose name shall be Aḥmad.' But when he came to them with clear signs they said, 'this is evident sorcery!'"[20]

While classical and modern assessments concur that this verse refers to Muḥammad's prophetic role, it is important to note that the designation of Muḥammad as Aḥmad appears to be associated with the belief in the end of time in one of the circulating traditions among prominent scholars. Mālik b. Anas (d. 179/796) transmitted a report that placed this verse in such a context: "[It is related] on the authority of Muḥammad b. Jubayr b. Muṭʿim (d. after 100/718), who said that the Prophet, peace be upon him, said, 'I have five names, I am Muḥammad and I am Aḥmad. I am the eraser [*al-māḥī*] by whom God erases unbelief. I am the resurrector [*al-ḥāshir*] upon whose advent the people will be resurrected. And I am the final one [*al-ʿāqib*].'"[21] In a relatively prolonged discussion on the matter, al-Ṭabarī, too, cites similar epithets and relates numerous reports to supplement the aforementioned tradition with a yet more ominous epithet: "the prophet of the apocalyptic battle, *malḥama*."[22]

What appears to be an early tradition that is cited in later sources gives a different account of eschatological time. It is related on the authority of the Prophet's wife, 'Ā'isha: "Say [that Muḥammad is] the seal of the prophets and do not say that there is no prophet after him."[23] The apparent discrepancy between the two views was justified by identifying the prophet after Muḥammad. Although a discussion of the finality of prophecy is beyond the scope of this work, suffice it to say that exegetical literature does not deny the credibility of this report but tends to associate the phrase "prophet after him," as early as the eighth century, with the advent of Jesus, therefore making Jesus one of the portents of the Hour. The Qur'ānic references to the second advent of Jesus, upon whose arrival life on earth would be concluded, reinforced the expectation that the end of time was near and that Muḥammad was the forerunner of Jesus's Second Coming.[24] In one of the much discussed verses in medieval exegetical literature, Jews and Christians believe in Jesus before his death: "There is not one of the People of the Book but will assuredly believe in him before his death, and on the Resurrection Day he will be a witness against them."[25] Another verse refers to Jesus as one of the portents of the end of time, leaving little possibility for other interpretations: "He [*innahu*][26] is knowledge of the Hour; doubt not concerning it, and follow me. This is a straight path."[27]

The context in which both verses appear suggests that the pronouns *him* and *he* refer to Jesus. This is what scholars inferred from the verses, according to the earliest evidence from the Umayyad period. By the early ninth century, Jesus's messianic persona became a major component of any messianic and apocalyptic discussion. Setting aside early Muslims' view for the moment, the rise of Jesus to heaven was already well known by Christians of the time to be a Muslim belief. Jacob of Edessa (d. 89/708) unambiguously notes that "the Muslims, too, although they do not know nor wish to say that this true Messiah who came and is acknowledged by the Christians, is God and the son of God, they nevertheless confess firmly that he is the true Messiah, who was to come and was foretold by the prophets, on this they have no dispute with us."[28] In a similar sense, John of Damascus (wrote ca. 111/730) emphatically expresses that "they [Muslims] say, [Jesus] was not crucified nor did he die; for God took him up to himself into heaven because he loved him."[29]

As early as the first/seventh century, the notion that Jesus would return seems to have been a common belief among Muslims. Mujāhid b. Jabr (d. ca. 102/720), for instance, interprets the aforementioned verses within the context of the Second Coming of Jesus as signaling the arrival of the end of time.[30] Only a half-century later, Muqātil b. Sulaymān (d. 150/767) reiterates that the messianic interpretation of Jesus's return had already been established among

Muslims. Muqātil b. Sulaymān restricts the People of the Book, *ahl al-kitāb*, to the Jews and identifies the pronoun *he* in the verse with Jesus, who is to appear on mount Afīq near Jerusalem[31] and kill the Antichrist, *al-Dajjāl*.[32] In a prophecy most probably dating before or around the end of the first Islamic century, Abū Hurayra (d. 679), a companion of the Prophet Muḥammad, urges the community to restore and refine the mosques for the descent of Jesus, the son of Mary. To indicate the imminence of his coming, Abū Hurayra looks around and identifies the youngest of the crowd to tell him, "O my nephew, if you meet him, give him my greetings."[33] Thus, although the Qur'ān retained its ambiguity about any messianic figure, it became possible for the readers of the Qur'ān as early as the first Islamic century to conflate the image of Jesus with the Mahdī and present both as the primary protagonists of the messianic era—a process that contributed to an increased controversy surrounding the identity of the Mahdī.

Messianic Beliefs as Political Ideology

What made the 'Abbāsid messianic claims feasible and viable was the flexibility of messianic discourse. Diverse opinions abounded in the first two centuries of Islam concerning not only the identity of the Mahdī but also the very existence of such a redeemer. This is also reflected in early-ninth-century literature. Whatever the point of departure of such traditions, it remains clear that prophecies motivated a wide range of claimants, including the 'Abbāsids. Though many of the prophecies were born out of a particular historical context—such as those provoked by the movement of 'Abdallāh b. al-Zubayr in the seventh century and by the 'Abbāsid revolt in the middle of the eighth century—later memory erased the historical link but elaborated on or left the message intact, partly because of the symbolic nature of prophecies and partly because the predictions were recycled in the process of oral and textual transmission. Ultimately even traditions announcing specific times and individuals came to accommodate broader messianic aspirations.[34]

Obviously opinions that were reflected in early-ninth-century apocalyptic literature are too diverse to be outlined here. For one, the very idea of the Mahdī was so contested that, in sharp contrast to predictions describing the Mahdī and his characteristics, many recognized no Mahdī except Jesus—"the Mahdī is Jesus the son of Mary"[35]—as the sole eschatological redeemer. The rise of Jesus would put an end to worldly rule, *imāra*, and conclude historical time by disrupting the mundane flow of history.[36] One of the most explicit critiques of the belief in the Mahdī appears in *Kitāb al-Fitan*. 'Abdallāh b. 'Umar is depicted debating Ibn al-Ḥanafiyya about the Mahdī: "'What is this Mahdī you are speaking of?' He [Ibn al-Ḥanafiyya] said, '[Another way of] saying a good person. If a person is righteous, *ṣāliḥ*, we call him Mahdī.' ['Abdallāh] Ibn 'Umar [comments], 'May God curse the stupidity.' It is as if he did not like his [Ibn al-Ḥanafiyya's] opinion."[37] Perhaps to avoid controversy, individuals articulated their views in a suggestive manner. Instead of denying the idea of the Mahdī openly, they emphasized the messianic role of Jesus, such as 'Abdallāh b. Lahī'a's prophecy predicting no hope until Jesus, the son of Mary, appears.[38]

Even when the assumption was the endorsement of the idea of the Mahdī, many prophecies still retained a measure of ambiguity. Given the controversy among multiple claimants about the Mahdī's identity and the meaning of the Mahdī—as a description of either a fair ruler or an eschatological figure who was associated with the end of time and, broadly speaking, a messianic era—prophecies accommodated and even encouraged ambiguity. Not revealing the whole point, being suggestive rather than straightforward, and leaving an element of uncertainty in both the wording of the prophecy and characterization of events were major features of many prophecies.

A dialogue between a rebel and an Umayyad governor illustrates this point. During his socially and politically important revolt in Khurāsān (127–28/745–46), al-Ḥārith b. Surayj al-Murji'ī announced to his supporters that he might indeed be the expected savior who would rescue the oppressed from the Umayyad tyranny.[39] He was serious enough about his claim to use the messianic battle cry O *Manṣūr* during his confrontation with the Umayyad governor, Naṣr b. Sayyār.[40] This is corroborated by numismatic evidence that presents Ibn Surayj as al-Manṣūr and his revolt as a call for justice.[41] Naṣr challenged Ibn Surayj to attack Damascus, as predictions foretold, if indeed he was the holder of the black banners. Ibn Surayj responded by acknowledging his claims that he was "he of the black banners." Naṣr replied that if Ibn Surayj was who he claimed to be, then he himself would tear down the walls of Damascus and end the rule of the Umayyads: "So take five hundred men from me and two hundred camels, and load up with whatever wealth and weapons you will, and go! By my life, if you are the one you mention, then I am indeed in your hands; but if you are not that one, then you have destroyed your tribe." Ibn Surayj's response was less than certain: "I have learned that this [claim] is true, but none of my followers have given me an oath of allegiance on that basis."[42]

Surely in the end Ibn Surayj destroyed his tribe. However, the exchange remains as evidence showing that none of the leaders doubted the validity of the prophecy that the two of them apparently knew and shared, though they disagreed on its true protagonist. Neither Ibn Surayj nor his supporters were certain of his messianic identity, as he openly acknowledged to the Umayyad governor. His claims were flexible enough to serve as a provisional ideological support, whose validity could only be verified by its fulfillment. This point is important because such flexibility made prophecies and their content durable, pervasive, and amenable enough to retain their prescriptive and normative value for diverse claimants.

Predictions usually assume the Mahdī's awareness of his identity, although the community may not be able to recognize him at first. Many other prophecies envision the Mahdī embarking on his mission after a moment of awakening to his identity, of which he had not been aware previously. In medieval Muslim political morality, this nuance is symbolized in the reluctance to demand leadership openly or aggressively for oneself. This is an important detail for two reasons. It allows for the possibility of a sudden transformation of an individual with hitherto ordinary qualities into a hero (like prophethood), and it suggests that the Mahdī might not disclose his identity in full. One such tradition predicts that God will prepare the Mahdī in one night for this mission.[43] Another prophecy has the Mahdī unwilling to acknowledge himself as the Mahdī even when his supporters single him out in their midst and pledge allegiance to him.[44] In a variant of this tradition, the Mahdī runs away from those who tell him that he is indeed the Mahdī, until he eventually gives in and assumes his messianic identity.[45]

Furthermore, while common wisdom suggests that the Mahdī hails from the family of the Prophet Muḥammad, many predictions do not make the expected Mahdī a member of a particular family or clan. Numerous traditions suggest that the Mahdī is a male member of the community of believers, without any further qualification. In a tradition attributed to the Prophet Muḥammad, the narrator simply indicates a general religious affiliation: "He is a man from my community."[46] Along the same lines, Jesus praying behind the Mahdī is a common theme in many prophecies: "The Mahdī is from this community. He is the one who will lead the prayer in front of Jesus the son of Mary."[47] Sometimes further details of the Mahdī's mission are given, as in the following tradition: "There will be the Mahdī from my community, who will rule seven, eight, or nine years, regardless of whether his life will be short or long. He will fill the earth with justice and righteousness just as it has been filled with injustice and oppression. The sky will pour down its rain, and the earth will give forth its bounty. My community will live in his time a life which has been never experienced before."[48] Other traditions specify the name of the Mahdī but leave his family ties unclear: "His name will resemble my name and his father's name that of my father's."[49]

Alternatively, other prophecies offer more specific details: "His [the Mahdī's] name is the name of your prophet."[50] While certain prophecies do not even mention the community, others provide minute details about the Mahdī, including his physical features,[51] age,[52] and the duration of his rule, and discuss them at some length.[53] Still other prophecies identify a limited group of candidates from which the Mahdī will arise. Some prophecies, for example, predict that the Mahdī will be from the Quraysh tribe,[54] from a specific branch of the Quraysh tribe,[55] and even from a family in the Quraysh tribe with ties to the tribal federation of Yemen.[56]

Circulated by diverse individuals and groups with varying intentions in mind, conflicting prophecies increased the ambiguity surrounding the identity of the Mahdī. To allay the confusion, other prophecies with more specific details were spread, but for the most part to no avail, as they only increased the confusion and further multiplied messianic expectations. One tradition predicts that after a prolonged *fitna*, a "voice from the sky," unmistakable in its reference, will identify the Mahdī.[57] Other prophecies add a pointing hand to the voice. In a vivid description of the encounter between the Mahdī and the Sufyānī, the "voice from the sky" is cited as pointing out the Mahdī.[58] The following tradition shows how multiple layers of insertions, presumably intended to clarify the content of the prophecy or give it a certain character, did little but further confuse the text, but perhaps ironically also preserved its credibility under changing circumstances:

> A person from the family of Abū Sufyān the second (?) will be appointed to [oversee the Ḥajj] season. He will be accompanied by a delegation. When they witness the season, they will hear a voice from the sky who will say "the ruler is this one." Another voice from the earth will say "he lied." Another voice from the sky will say "he told the truth." This will go on [for a while] and people will not know which one to follow. However, the first voice from the sky is the trustworthy one. If you hear something like that, know that the word of God is the higher one and the word of the Devil is the one from the bottom.[59]

Perhaps a more widespread view of the Mahdī was that the Mahdī would be from the family of the Prophet Muḥammad, which makes both the 'Alid and 'Abbāsid families a source of eligible candidates for Mahdīship because both boasted relation to the Prophet. The Mahdī from the family of the Prophet would appear when the oppression upon the Muslim community became unbearable. He "will fill the earth with justice as it has been filled with injustice."[60] Alternatively, the Mahdī would rise after a civil disturbance, *fitna*, to restore peace and security among the Muslim community.[61] In other cases the Mahdī, identified as "a man from the family of the prophet," would appear during the fourth civil war, *fitna*: "'Alī b. Abī Ṭālib said, 'there are four civil wars': the *fitna* of well-being, the *fitna* of distress and a *fitna* in which people will be put to a test of purification just as gold is extracted from the mine. They [the community] will remain in this situation until a man from the family of the prophet appears and straightens out their affairs, God willing. Twelve or fifteen thousand men will accompany him. He will bring fear, and no one among his enemies will escape defeat, God permitting. [His soldiers'] cry will be kill, kill."[62]

Even the phrase "the family of the prophet" leaves much room for interpretation. Competing claims to the title echoed persistent attempts at narrowing it down to a particular house, including the two houses of Hāshim, 'Alī and al-ʿAbbās.[63] It is important to note that while some traditions exposed an awareness of the rift between the ʿAlid and the ʿAbbāsid families, others revealed the still evolving self-consciousness of both families vis-à-vis each other, as in the following prophecy:

> We were with the Prophet of God when a group of youth from Banū Hāshim approached us. When the Prophet, peace be upon him, saw them . . . he said, "We are the *Ahl al-Bayt*, God has chosen the hereafter for us instead of this world. My family will suffer hardship, exile and oppression until a group [of men] comes from the direction of the East carrying black banners and demanding what is right. However, it will not be given to them. They will fight and cause damage. Then, they will be given what they wanted, but they will not accept it until it is given to a man from my family who will fill it with justice as they [those who fight against the black banners?] have filled it with injustice. Whoever remains alive until then let him set out towards them even if it is as difficult as crawling on snow." [64]

This prediction—plausibly dating to later phases of the ʿAbbāsid revolt itself, when the final shape of the new regime was still unclear—describes the ʿAbbāsid revolutionary army as from the "family of the Prophet" and asserts the right of the family of the Prophet to rule.

As is evident from numerous traditions, prophecies appealed to aspirants from various families among the Quraysh, including the ʿAlids and the ʿAbbāsids. Prophecies stimulated the competition between and the messianic aspirations of these two prominent families in early Islam: "A Herald in the sky will announce 'verily right [of leadership] belongs to the family of the prophet.' A Herald on the earth will announce, 'right [of leadership] belongs to the family of Jesus,' or, he said, 'of al-ʿAbbās.' 'I suspect that the voice from below comes from the Devil so that he can confuse people,' Abū ʿAbdallāh Nuʿaym suspected."[65]

Despite Nuʿaym b. Ḥammād's antagonistic comment, the idea of an ʿAbbāsid Mahdī was not marginal at the time. The messianic image of the ʿAbbāsids was propagated in numerous prophecies inside and outside ʿAbbāsid circles. One prediction foretells of a man of outstanding ability who is compared with one of the foremost companions of the prophet: "When Zayd b. Thābit died, Abū Hurayra remarked: 'The best of the Arabs died tonight, and there will be someone from among the sons of al-ʿAbbās who will be successor to him.'"[66] Religious purity and restoration of rule were attributed to the ʿAbbāsids: "The days and nights will not end until a young man from our family, who is not touched by the *fitnas*, rules. We said, 'O Abū al-ʿAbbās do mature people among you fall short of it but youth achieve it?' He said, 'It is God's. He gives it to whomever he wishes.'"[67] A better-known tradition listed early ʿAbbāsid caliphs in a chain of rulers ending with the Mahdī: "There will be the Saffāḥ and the Manṣūr, and the Mahdī from among us."[68] The ʿAbbāsid Mahdī would rise at the end of time and hand over the supreme political leadership, imamate, to Jesus.[69]

This and numerous similar prophecies leave little doubt that the idea of an ʿAbbāsid messiah persisted as a viable belief in the early ʿAbbāsid period. What is more important, perhaps, is whether ʿAbbāsid or ʿAlid in inclination, prophecies also propagated a particular moral and political ideology that was attractive not only to mass movements, sectarian opposition, or pious literati but also to rulers. Included in the rich compendium of Nuʿaym b. Ḥammād is a prophecy that outlines some of the major aspects of the early ʿAbbāsid messianic beliefs. The prophecy describes three Mahdīs: the Mahdī of welfare, *khayr* (who is identified in the prophecy as ʿUmar b. ʿAbd al-ʿAzīz); the Mahdī of blood, who will put an end to bloodshed; and the Mahdī of faith, who is Jesus, whose community (in another version, "all nations") will become Muslim during his time.[70] The metaphor of three Mahdīs corresponds to three important dimensions of messianic beliefs in early Islam. The first dimension noted in the prophecy was the demand for political and social justice. Although it was not articulated in any specific institutional or legal form, justice certainly connoted welfare, abundance, prosperity, safety, and peace. The second dimension involved the call for establishing the awaited righteous kingdom by putting an end to bloodshed. The final dimension announced the triumph of God's original message through religious renewal, reform, and conversion.[71]

Expressions of the demand for justice and the hope for prosperity and peace appeared frequently in early-ninth-century apocalyptic literature. Although the call for justice was not new (as monotheistic messianic traditions also viewed the messianic redeemer as the bringer of justice), Muslim messianism made its own contributions while also adopting existing currents of thought. The demand for justice often recalled the era of the Prophet Muḥammad and his immediate two successors as a model to be imitated or replayed, making the legitimacy of current historical experience at once precarious and temporal. Thus the Mahdī was compared with the first two caliphs, Abū Bakr and ʿUmar, and even to the Prophet himself.[72]

To expect a systematic exposition or even a relatively fuller description of what exactly justice meant in prophecies is futile. However, there is an implicit and sometimes explicit recognition of the broad customary order, within which messianic beliefs originated and operated. This peculiar stance vis-à-vis the established sociopolitical order enhanced the moral value of messianic beliefs as ideologies of reform without challenging the broad lifestyle of ʿAbbāsid society. Messianic beliefs sought to redistribute and reorganize the political, economic, and moral assets of society, but generally avoided a radical challenge to the caliphate as an institution or to the existing social structure. Contrary to antinomian and renunciatory movements, and in manifest dissimilarity to mass movements targeting disenfranchised groups or classes, messianic beliefs under consideration came from groups and individuals who were already participating in the social and political life of the early ʿAbbāsid society. Revealing its fundamentally urban and learned nature, the messianic demand for justice entailed a change in the administration of justice and its application, which failed to uphold the higher social norms and aspirations.

Thus the Mahdī was portrayed as so extraordinarily just that even minute details of injustice would not escape his attention. He would constantly supervise his administrators for any wrongdoing;[73] he would be generous,[74] bringing wealth and prosperity to his domain.[75] As numerous prophecies assert, the commanders of the Mahdī would be the best of the people from among his supporters and those who pledged allegiance to him from among the people of the two Kūfas, Yemen, and the saintly vicars, *abādila,* of Damascus. God would extinguish the civil discord with him, and the earth would become so safe that women would set out for pilgrimage without a man accompanying them for protection. They would not fear anything other than God on their journey. The earth would give forth its share and the sky its bounty.[76] Under his rule, "the lamb would live happily with the lion."[77] The Mahdī would, in fact, become the embodiment of the tranquillity of his reign—an earthly paradise where all blessings come forth unstintingly.[78]

The ideas of justice and renewal were closely related to missionary and military activities, as well as to universal political ambitions. Many prophecies in the extant apocalyptic sources from the early ninth century unmistakably demand spreading the authority of Islam through peaceful and military means, and, more important, eliminating any rivals of the caliphate.[79] One such remarkable prophecy aspires to world conquest under the banner of the Mahdī. In the course of discussing the rule of the Umayyads, the transmitter of the following prophecy, Ḥudhayfa, explains the spread of Muslim rule: "How will it be when the Muslims go, bearing pickaxes and iron bars, until they reach Constantinople, the city of the king Heraclius, and they take it apart, stone by stone, according to the [prophecy] by the tongue of Muḥammad." His audience asks whether this event will happen under the Umayyads, to which he responds, "No, at the hands of the youth from Banū Hāshim." The narrator continues to predict how Muslims will march "to the city of China, and take it apart stone by stone . . . at the hands of the youth from Banū Hāshim." Perhaps to increase its effect, the transmitter refers to the authority of one of the most distinguished transmitters of biblical material into Arabic, Kaʿb al-Aḥbār. The transmitter of the Ḥudhayfa prophecy notes, "I mentioned this to Kaʿb [al-Aḥbār], and he said: 'There is no army greater in reward than the army going to China. Then they will bring the kings of China and the kings of al-ʿAqaba back in chains, and when they bring them they will find that [Jesus] the son of Mary has already descended in Syria.'"[80]

Such messianic hopes calling for universal rule that is both righteous and potent are best exemplified in a rich tradition of prophecies focusing on the conquest of Rome and Constantinople. By the time Islam claimed its role in the world, Constantinople had already been recognized as an eschatological city in Christian and Jewish apocalyptic thought—as the New Jerusalem where the Messiah would reign.[81] Soon after the rise of Islam, the city of Constantinople secured a similar place in Muslim apocalyptic imagination. Perhaps in a reciprocal relation with Muslim military advances against Byzantium and Constantinople, many prophecies tie the end of history to the apocalyptic battle, *malḥama*, against Byzantium,[82] echoing universal ambitions and the reworking of biblical apocalyptic material to reflect the new role that was assigned to Muslims in fulfilling ancient prophecies.[83] Muslim predictions depict the Mahdī and his followers as the conquerors of Byzantium and Constantinople.[84] Numerous prophecies see the conquest of Constantinople as the culmination of a series of apocalyptic battles, revealing an awareness of the potential for expansion.[85] In one prediction, for instance, the narrator foretells how the end of time will unfold following the conquests of the Arabian Peninsula, Persia, and Byzantium, leading to the final battle against the Antichrist.[86] The following prophecy incorporates historical information to emphasize the inevitability of the imminent apocalyptic battle that will terminate Byzantium: "It is at the hands of the fifth of the family of Heraclius, Hirāql, that the apocalyptic wars, *malāḥim*, will occur. Heraclius has reigned (*tamallaka*)[87] then after him his son Constans, son of Heraclius, Qusta b. Hirāql; then his son Constantine, son of Constans; then his son Justinian, son of Constantine (Iṣṭafān,[88] Ustinān);[89] then the kingship of the Romans will move from the family of Heraclius to Leon and his son after him. The rule will return to the fifth of the family of Heraclius, at whose hands the *malāḥim* will be."[90]

The conquest would fulfill the mission of the Mahdī and bring about the supremacy of the authentic monotheism, the unification of the world under a righteous ruler, and the correction of Judaism and Christianity through the rediscovery of the authentic religious scriptures. The Mahdī would advance against the Romans, conquer Constantinople,[91] and discover the treasures and the feast of Solomon, before returning to Jerusalem to usher in the coming forth of the Antichrist and of Jesus, the son of Mary.[92] The obliteration of the Sasanian kingship already fulfilled a promise. Byzantium would suffer the same end, and there would be no other Byzantine emperor afterward. Muslims would then be in charge of distributing the treasures fairly.[93] The Mahdī, or Jesus, would rule supreme. He would smash the cross, kill the swine, institute a poll tax, and abolish the Muslim obligation to give alms as an affirmation of the validity and superiority of God's final revelation. A variant mentions missionary activity and voluntary submission as vehicles to realize a universal messianic order. The Mahdī would march to Jerusalem, and the treasures would be carried to him. Arabs, Persians, Romans, people of the Abode of War, and others would submit to his authority without warfare, and mosques would be built in Constantinople and in other places.[94]

In tandem with some Muslim prophecies, non-Muslim apocalypses echo a messianic imperial competition. *Visions of Daniel* shows how widespread the spectacular competition over Constantinople and over universal hegemony was across confessional boundaries. Inspired by the tradition started by Ps. Methodius, perhaps through its lost Greek translation, *Visions of Daniel*, written sometime between 821 and 829 in Sicily, portrays Muslims as instruments of an apocalyptic wrath, destined to capture and destroy Constantinople in an apocalyptic battle. With striking similarity in content and details to Muslim prophecies of the period, *Visions of Daniel* predicts an Ishmaelite invasion of Iran and Rome and an eventual defeat by a man rising from the "Rebel City" and anointed as emperor in Akroion, contemporary Afyon in Turkey. This emperor will tame the "Blond Beards," *Banū Aṣfar* (the yellow people of Muslim prophecies?),[95] expel the children of Israel, defeat the Ishmaelites in a bloody battle, and fulfill the prophecy. He will then march to Rome and finally arrive at Constantinople, where he will rule peacefully for thirty-two years. The apocalypse describes an eruption of unclean people under a subsequent ruler, when order will be disrupted with fear and terror until an archangel destroys those unclean people and the last emperor takes up residence in Jerusalem, placing his crown on the cross and submitting his kingdom to God.[96]

What is remarkable is that prophecies anticipated that groundbreaking events would happen imminently. In one of ʿAbdallāh b. Lahīʿa's reports, the transmitter warned his audience not to discard their possessions after the battles because the people would love living afterward.[97] In fact some predictions conveyed the sense that the apocalyptic drama had already been unfolding. Upon hearing a prediction describing how the final apocalyptic war will be fought with the Byzantines, ʿAbdallāh b. Sallām (d. 43/664), one of the companions of the Prophet Muḥammad, is said to have made the following remark: "If this [apocalyptic] war should happen in my lifetime while I am sick, carry me on my bed until you have placed me between the two armies."[98]

The appeal for the purification of religion also played a central role in early Islamic messianic discourse. If the call for justice did not necessarily upset the overall sociopolitical status quo, the demands for religious purity did require a change in customary religiosity within Islam and vis-à-vis other faiths. Prophecies of the early ʿAbbāsid period called for renewal to bring about a religion that was closely associated with its pristine form in the past and that looked forward to its ultimate universal victory at the end of time. As expected, the Mahdī or Jesus, or both, appear as the primary instruments for the realization of such demands. In a widely circulated prophecy, Jesus is depicted as not only the bringer of justice and wealth but also as a religious puritan.[99] The noteworthy combination of temporal and religious authority in the person of the messianic figure situated religious reforms squarely within the authority of the ruler, provoking an expectation that could only be addressed and satisfied by political action. In a variant of the aforementioned tradition, religious purification is realized through the unification of diverse monotheistic confessions under a single supreme faith and through the implementation of universal messianic justice so that "the lion would join the cattle and the wolf would join the lamb" in a peaceful harmony.[100]

Even though the purification or restoration of faith and the unification of diverse confessions were often sought under the rubric of Islam as the final revelation of God,[101] religious revival was not seen as restricted to Islam. On the contrary, prophecies addressed ancient scriptures positively as an integral part of messianic religious reform, identifying monotheistic religions as manifestations of God's message throughout history. As one of the prophecies suggested, the Mahdī would discover the original forms of older scriptures and grant the People of the Book, *ahl al-kitāb*, the right to live according to the ordinances of their scriptures.[102] Unearthing the monotheistic *Ur* texts, the Torah and the Gospel in particular,[103] to find a permanent, unifying solution to historical disagreements among the monotheistic faiths communicated a powerful religio-political message to rulers. One prophecy describes a treasure map of Rome, *Rūmīyya*, or Constantinople, to assist the conquerers in the discovery of ancient oracles upon their entrance to the city.[104] Al-Mahdī's quest for the hidden[105] extends to finding not only older scriptures but also sacred relics: "At the hands of the Mahdī the Ark of the Covenant (*tābūt al-sakīna*, the ark of the divine spirit)[106] will be unearthed from the Lake Galilee, and handed to him in Jerusalem. When the Jews see it, they will accept Islam, except a few; then the Mahdī will die."[107] The emphasis on ancient scriptures, for their value in end-of-time scenarios and as a source of Muslim religious imagination, helped create a shared religious and cultural space, or at least the sense of it, among Muslims and non-Muslims. While prophecies asserted the primacy of Islamic faith as the final revelation under whose aegis all other religions would gather, they nevertheless granted legitimacy to older traditions, making the religious landscape of late antiquity a subject of interest for rulers.

Although prophecies were circulated by diverse groups with varying agendas and views and were not equally available everywhere, the demand for justice, for military and missionary activity, and for renewal and restoration, *tajdīd*, of faith under one divinely guided ruler appeared as a common element in circulating predictions. Despite the challenges posed by more restrictive theological and legal views, the ideas of reform and change were maintained through a messianic discourse, which spurred the caliphs to claim additional prerogatives and initiate radical changes by falling back on prophecies, particularly when circumstances favored a new dynamism in prophetic activity. Once in circulation, prophecies assumed lives of their own, which sometimes led to interpretations and meanings that were not originally intended.

A New Millennium: The Year 200/800

A new orientation of prophecies on the dawn of the third Islamic century focused on the cosmic significance of ʿAbbāsid sociopolitical life. This phenomenon was motivated both by a particular calculation of the age of the world based on the biblical idea of millennium and by the messianic reading of contemporary events. The former appears more closely linked to genuine millenarian computations that were associated with the age of the world, often informed by biblical references, the book of Daniel in particular. Only in part is it related to an apocalyptic reading of the immediate past or contemporary political and social circumstances, such as the events of the late second Islamic century. When we consider the following computations, we notice only a weak link to immediate events: "Al-Walīd said, 'I have read in [the book of] Daniel that the conclusion of this community after its prophet Muḥammad until [the rise of] Jesus is 274 years.'"[108] Another prophecy fixes the duration of the Muslim community at a span of three hundred years in an analogical reasoning, with no specific reference to any historical event: "The duration of Muḥammad's community is 300 years, like that of the children of Israel."[109] Because the prophecies had been transmitted in a source—Nuʿaym b. Ḥammād's *Kitāb al-Fitan*—dated earlier than the projected date, these prophecies appear to be genuine predictions that were based on some sort of biblical source and operated on the assumption that one day equals a millennium and that historical time would last only seven millennia.

Not unexpectedly, the millennium-day equation appears as a frequent matrix in such computations. An explicit reference to this idea is seen, for instance, in the following prediction: "I hope that God will not make my community incapable of lasting half a day. Saʿd said half a day is 500 years."[110] The following tradition suggests that a system of calculation based on the number seven was used as a measure in computation and that chronological calculations were merged with and used in apocalyptic prophecies:

> From al-Ḥakam b. Nāfiʿ on the authority of Jarrāḥ b. Arṭāt b. al-Mundhir who said, "We have been informed that Nāth was a prophet and that he mentioned the time and said, 'the time is seven weeks (*sawābīʿ*) and the week (*sābūʿ*) is seven thousand years and the day (*ʿidān*) a thousand years.' He then described the past ages clarifying what their closure was until he arrived at the final age, and said, 'when the first four days (*ʿidānāt*) of the last week (*sābūʿ*) are complete the Virgin [Mary] will give birth [to Jesus who] will come with signs.[111] He [Jesus][112] will resurrect the dead;

then he will be raised into the Heavens. False beliefs (*ahwā'*) will diverge after him.'"[113]

The prediction continues to foretell what will happen through the ages up to the ninth century, shortly after the conquest of Amorium (838), when the completion of the seventh millennium is expected. The erratic calculation of numbers notwithstanding, this prophecy merges the computation of the age of the world with an apocalyptic scenario, yielding a socially or politically relevant message for the audience.

A discussion of chronology, the age of the world, and messianic expectations also takes place in historiography. An instructive illustration of the interest of historians in the age of the world and messianic beliefs is found in al-Ṭabarī's compendium. Al-Ṭabarī deals with the problem at the outset of his work.[114] He announces that he will mention whatever information has reached him about kings throughout the ages, from the creation to the end of the world. He notes that he will discuss the meaning of time, the total duration of it, and its beginning and end. He then elaborates on the total duration of earthly time, relying on previous authorities dating back to the early ninth century: "The early scholars before us differed in this respect. Some said that the total extent of time is seven thousand years. . . . Others said that the total extent of time is six thousand years. . . . The correct statement here is the one whose soundness is proved by information having come from the Messenger of God." In an attempt to arrive at an accurate total, he discusses the duration of the Muslim community: "Thus, (the evidence permitting) a conclusion is as follows: The beginning of the day is the rise of dawn, and its end is the setting of the sun. . . . The messenger of God said, 'indeed, God will not make this nation incapable of (lasting) half a day—referring to the day of a thousand years.'"[115]

We have seen that the notion of "half a day" was already circulating in the early 'Abbāsid period. Al-Ṭabarī thus maintains that the total historical time from Adam to the end of the world should be seven millennia, six and a half of which had already passed by the time of the prophecy of Muḥammad: "The world is one of the weeks of the other world—seven thousand years. Consequently, because it is so and the report on the authority of the Messenger of God is sound—namely, that he reported that what remained of the time of this world during his life was half a day, or five hundred years, since five hundred years are half a day of the days, of which one is a thousand years—the conclusion is that the time of this world that had elapsed to the moment of the Prophet's statement corresponds to what we have transmitted on the authority of Abū Tha'laba al-Khūsānī from the Prophet, and is 6,500 years or approximately 6,500 years. God knows best!" Notably Al-Ṭabarī also cites the views of his authorities, in effect corroborating the sustained interest in this subject across generations of scholars from the eighth through the ninth century.[116] In addition to citing his authorities, al-Ṭabarī discusses the views of the Christians, the Jews, and the Magis on the subject to underline the validity of Islam as the religion of the final episode of historical time.[117] By engaging biblical and Zoroastrian traditions, al-Ṭabarī exemplifies how Muslim scholars embraced the idea of the millennium and the assumptions about the computation of time, and how they ultimately situated Islam within the context of a shared monotheistic heritage.

In medieval Europe a comparable and even more vigorous concern with chronology and messianic expectations focused on a period between the last decades of the eighth century and the first decade of the ninth century as the seventh millennium. Richard Landes convincingly argues that the overwhelming majority of computations made between the third and eighth centuries point to the late eighth and early ninth centuries as the beginning of the seventh millennium anno mundi, unleashing millenarian visions that were associated with the turn of the ninth century.[118] Substantiated by unusual prodigies and popular anxiety, millenarian hopes made the coronation of Charlemagne on Christmas Eve 799 a timely response to such expectations.[119] The work of Beatus of Liebena (d. after 798) exemplifies well the attempts to link the idea of the age of the world with millenarian visions. An Asturian monk and the author of the *Commentarius Apocalypsin*,[120] a commentary on the book of Revelation possibly written around 776 but enjoying great popularity in ninth-century Spain,[121] Beatus was concerned with the duration of the world and the projected time for its demise. Like some of his Muslim counterparts, Beatus followed a cautious approach as to the credibility of such calculations and their relevance to apocalyptic expectations. Therefore, like his Muslim peers, he preferred to base his opinion on the probability, but not the certainty, of his computation: "The time remaining to the world is uncertain to human investigation. . . . You should know in truth that the world will end in 6,000 years; but whether these years are to be completed or to be shortened is known only to God."[122] He nevertheless proceeds to compute the time from Adam to Christ to be 5,227 years, and from the coming of Jesus to the Spanish era of 824 as 786 years. Finally, when he calculates the time from Adam to the Spanish era, he arrives at 5,986, leaving only 14 years to the conclusion of the sixth millennium in the Spanish year of 838 (800 C.E.), which would usher in the era in which the "Kingdom of Christ" will be established.[123]

Although Beatus did not mention Islam or Muslims in his commentary, it is inconceivable that he was unaware of the Muslims. As Ruggles observes, the silence of the *Commentarius* on Islam and Muslims does not indicate unawareness of the Muslims. Ruggles points to the artistic reproduction of the ninth- and tenth-century copies of the *Commentarius*, which do depict Muslims, reflecting a selective cultural and artistic interaction between the Christian north and the Muslim south.[124] Both Beatus's later ninth-century copiers and his

Muslim contemporaries were clearly concerned with similar subjects from a comparable perspective within their own chronological frameworks.

In itself this interest in calculation shows not only the widespread concern with the idea of millennium in the early ninth century but also the intellectual cross-pollination among the followers of monotheistic faiths. ʿAbd al-Malik b. Ḥabīb's *Kitāb al-Tārīkh* is a good example of this. Ibn Ḥabīb (ca. 180–238/796–53) was a scholar from Islamic Spain who had wide-ranging interests in numerous subjects and a high degree of credibility in scholarship.[125] The fact that he was an Andalusian scholar who had strong ties with the Near East reveals an important dimension of the intellectual exchange within the ʿAbbāsid world.

Although his information on the period after the death of Hārūn al-Rashīd is sparse, the content of his work shows the impact of messianic beliefs on his milieu. ʿAbd al-Malik b. Ḥabīb contends that the life of the world would be only seven millennia and that he lived at the very end of the seventh millennium. After a careful calculation of the time from Adam up to his own day, he predicted that the world would end soon. He then set out to count down the time remaining and to create a chronicle based on a millenarian vision. The introduction to his chronicle opens with the following remarks:

> God the exalted said: "A day in the sight of your Lord is like a thousand years of your reckoning" [Qur'ān 47:22]. The whole world from its beginning, when God created Adam, was created on Friday. He created Adam on Friday, he was sent down to the earth on Friday, and the resurrection will take place on Friday. It is the first day of the world, and it will be the last day. It started with Friday and it will end with it. God has made each one of these days a thousand years, and made the world as a whole until its end, seven thousand years. I will start from Adam, arranging the time in thousand year units. I will mention each millennium of the world's age, as well as the prophets and kings and their affairs and stories, God permitting. . . . Relying on transmissions and portents [I will mention] what will happen after its [Andalus's] ruin until the arrival of the final hour, God permitting.[126]

ʿAbd al-Malik b. Ḥabīb was certainly not alone in viewing history from this perspective and in his expectation that the remaining days of the world were numbered. He and his contemporaries were inspired by biblical universal histories and millennial and theological concerns of late antiquity, which influenced the way chronology was constructed and revised. He concurred with his *muḥaddith* authorities that the world in its totality, from the day God created Adam until its end, was seven millennia. However, ʿAbd al-Malik b. Ḥabīb acknowledges that scholars disagreed on the portion that had already passed in the current millennium, which was the consummation of the seven millennia.[127] He backs his claims by a discussion of the sacredness of the number seven.

According to ʿAbd al-Malik b. Ḥabīb, the number seven represents the symbol of the order of things. He notes that God created the universe in seven days, the week has seven days, there are seven heavens and seven regions, the circumambulation of the Kaʿba is seven times, and finally the rite of running, *saʿy*, between the hills of Ṣāfā and Marwā in the Muslim pilgrimage, Ḥajj, is performed seven times.[128]

Thus ʿAbd al-Malik b. Ḥabīb's vision of universal history not only equates a creation day with a millennium but also predicts an imminent end to history. The idea that the age of the world corresponded to the days of creation and that historical time would end on the sixth day—ushering in the seventh millennium or day—was an early and persistent one.[129] Throughout history, many scholars made strenuous efforts to explain previous out-of-date calculations and to establish a starting point for new computations. The dawn of the third Islamic century presented an opportune moment for such calculations to converge with apocalyptic and messianic thought.

If the aforementioned prophecies derive inspiration from long-term computations that were turned into messianic and apocalyptic predictions at times of crises, then concrete political realities and social circumstances surrounding the transmitters provoked new and decidedly expedient prophecies. Alarmed by the speed of conquests, ensuing civil wars, and social upheaval as the countdown to the year 100 A.H. began, prophecies had been quick to depict the dawn of the second Islamic century as a watershed in the history of the Muslim community. In a tradition attributed to the Prophet Muḥammad, the Muslim community had been given only one hundred years: "I [the companion Mustawrid b. Shaddād] heard the Messenger of God, peace be upon him, saying, each community has an appointed time, and my community has a hundred years. If my community lasts a hundred years, the promise of God will befall them."[130]

Although the prophecy does not—most likely consciously—clarify what the promise is, the subtext certainly implies a disaster. In what appears to be a variant of this tradition, the Prophet Muḥammad is said to have commented just one month before his death on the duration of his community: "By God there is no single soul on earth today that will witness a hundred years."[131] Ibn Abī Shayba even dates another variant of this tradition to sometime around the Prophet Muḥammad's return from his expedition against Tabūk in 630, in which Muḥammad specifically remarks, "no one alive today will remain [alive] when the year hundred dawns."[132]

That prophecies circulated, were disputed, and debated before the turn of the second Islamic century is certain. In a prophecy that is included in *al-Muṣannaf* of al-Ṣanʿānī (211/827)—on the authority of Maʿmar b. Rāshid (154/771)—al-ʿUryān b. Haytham narrates a story of himself with the caliph Muʿāwiya at the caliph's residence in the presence of ʿAbdallāh b. ʿAmr b. al-ʿĀṣ. Having heard that ʿAbdallāh b. ʿAmr circulated a prophecy concerning the end of the world, al-ʻUryān b. Haytham complains to Muʻāwiya: "Is this the one who says, 'the people will not be alive after the year 100?' He ['Abdallāh] approached me and said, 'Have I said that? [While] you find them [people] alive a long time after one hundred. But [the end of] this community has been postponed for 130 years.'"[133]

Debates on the accuracy of such predictions only modified, but did not eliminate, expectations. On the contrary, as the year 100 A.H. drew closer, the sentiment spread even beyond the Muslim community to the degree that it became a rationale for military action against the caliphate. A unique and independent confirmation of the apocalyptic significance of the Hijrī year 100 and the apprehension it caused among the Muslim community comes from Ghurek, the Lord of Samarqand (r. 710–38). Tired of the raids and overlordship of the Umayyads, Ghurek seems to have sent a letter to the Tang emperor Xuanzong in 718, which is the year 99 A.H., asking him for military support against the Muslim armies. The striking confidence that his troops, if supported by Chinese soldiers, would certainly crush the Muslim forces this time is explained in these words: "My humble request from the Imperial benevolence, being informed [about the situation], is to send here a certain number of Chinese soldiers for me to help in the difficulties. As for these Ta-che [that is, Muslims], they are not to remain potent for a total of [more than] one hundred years; it is this year that the total of one hundred years is exhausted. If Chinese soldiers come here, I and you together we will certainly succeed in destroying the Ta-che."[134] Ghurek's intentions did not materialize, and for all those who waited, the deadline disappointingly passed without the expected results. However, the predictions lingered in later sources, reminding us of the apocalyptic anxiety surrounding the year 100 A.H.[135]

Putting into circulation such specific predictions carried the danger of making the transmitter vulnerable to accusations of forgery and the loss of credibility when the prophecies failed. However, it appears that even this setback only stalled, but did not stop, the emergence of new prophecies, some of which were reborn from the ashes of the older ones. As Leon Festinger demonstrated in another context, once the messianic or apocalyptic vision becomes a lens through which believers see reality, the failure of any given prophecy does not deter its followers from modifying it or spreading new ones. This is exactly what happened to the prophecies of 100 A.H., as well as to the prophecies that arose one hundred years later.

Since the turn of the second Islamic century, prophecies focusing on the arrival of new centuries showed a marked increase.[136] Prophecies, both new and modified, emerged to offer hope by predicting the Mahdī's rise in future years. In a way, messianic and apocalyptic anxiety associated with the year 200 A.H. echoed the anxieties that accompanied the year 100 A.H. As the second Islamic century came to a close, the religio-political movements among the ranks of the

Shī'īs and the Jamā'ī-Sunnīs circulated prophecies predicting the year 200 A.H. as the deadline for the rise of the Mahdī, the end of the world, or the occurrence of great calamities.[137] In the following text, for example, the transmitter offers a chronology of the 'Abbāsid period to justify a final prediction: "In a few years after your prophet there will be disagreement; but in 133[138] the person of forbearance will not rejoice with his progeny. In the year 150, the heretics will rise;[139] in the year 160, reserve food for two years;[140] in 166, escape, escape; in 190 [it should be 170 as the variant of this tradition attests], the kings will be deprived of their kingdom until [1]80; until [1]90, the ordeal will befall sinners; in 172 [probably 192], covering up with rocks and swallowing up and transformation and the advent of great sins; and in 200, the judgment. Chastisement will find the people while in the market places."[141] The prophecy seems to have been composed several years before 200/816 in the circumstances of the civil war, although it shows only a dim awareness of the conflict. If we exclude the first three dates, apparently associated with actual events, the text that describes the remaining dates could very well be a genuine prediction intended to set the stage for and magnify the approach of the year 200 A.H.

The year 200 A.H. is given special attention in prophecies. One tradition divides the first two centuries of Islam into five consecutive generations, the last of which will witness apocalyptic calamities after the era of the fifth generation. The Prophet Muḥammad predicts: "My community is five generations [ṭabaqāt]. Each generation is forty years. The first generation is I and those who are with me, the people of knowledge and certainty [*yaqīn*]. The second generation is the people of piety and faith. The third generation is the people of attainment and compassion. The fourth generation is the people of division and dissimilarity. The fifth generation is the people[142] of . . . turmoil and bloodshed. In 210 fornication, swallowing up, and metamorphosis will befall the people."[143] Evidently each generation is thought to last forty years. The prediction allows the survival of the community, if we take the Hijrī dating as a measure, only up to the year 200 A.H. The reason why the last generation, the fifth, seems to have been divided into two qualitative phases leading up to the calamities of the year 210/826 could very well be that the original tradition predicted only up to the year 200 and that a later transmitter amended, as often happens, the prophecy to salvage it after the passage of the year 200 A.H.[144] In fact another version of the same prophecy, recorded in Ibn Māja, predicts the year 200 as the culmination of calamities.[145]

Instead of offering abstract numbers, some prophecies from this time predict the duration of the 'Abbāsid caliphate. These prophecies also seem to focus on the 'Abbāsid civil war and the year 200 A.H. In one prophecy, the 'Abbāsid caliphate, described as "their kingdom," was to last nine multiplied by seven years (that is, sixty-three years) from the first appearance of the black banners, which brings the demise of the 'Abbāsids to the beginning of the fourth civil war, the year 195/811.[146] Although the prophecy then goes on to predict an additional ten years, extending the life of the caliphate to 205/821,[147] it cannot be assumed that the transmitter gave two separate numbers for a single computation. It is more likely that the two dates belong to two separate traditions amalgamated together, perhaps in order to bring the prophecy up-to-date.

It is not coincidental that the prophecies summarized so far are pessimistic about the future of the ʿAbbāsids, as well as the future of the whole community. However, concurrent with doomsday prophecies, the approach of a new century fed the anticipation that the Mahdī would rise in 200 A.H. to put an end to suffering and restore justice to the faithful. The political implications of this expectation will be examined later, but such prophecies clearly show that ʿAbbāsid society was not consumed by the fear of destruction and calamity. Rather many people expected and encouraged change in the hope of overcoming the impasse in political and social life, albeit relying on the rise of the Mahdī to guide this change with the dawn of the third Islamic century. In some instances prophecies predict "the Mahdī will rise in the year two hundred," regardless of whether preceded by portents.[148] Careful attention to the generic nature of the Mahdī in this prophecy—no note of family association, no specific individual characteristics—shows the potential in it to inspire diverse individuals to lay claims to Mahdīship, which is what happened in early Islamic history, as noted earlier.

Many individuals circulated prophecies with signposts pointing to calamities leading up to the rise of the Mahdī in 200 A.H.: "The affair of the ʿAbbāsids will disintegrate in the year 197/813 (or, he said, 199/815), and the Mahdī will rise in the year 200."[149] A more detailed prophecy with historically identifiable specific signs sees four portents before the appearance of the Mahdī around 200/816. According to the prophecy, there will be four events before the rise of the Qā'im, three of which have already occurred and one that remains. "We said, 'May we be your ransom, what has already passed?' [He said,] 'in Rajab, he deposed the ruler of Khurāsān; and in Rajab, Ibn Zubayda was attacked; and in Rajab, Muḥammad b. Ibrāhīm rebelled in al-Kūfa.' We said to him, 'is the fourth Rajab next to it?' He said, 'Thus spoke Abū Jaʿfar.'"[150] Clearly the portents refer to well-known events of the ʿAbbāsid civil war. The first Rajab is about al-Amīn's dismissal of al-Ma'mūn; the second one about is the siege of Baghdad; the third one is about the uprising of the Shīʿī Muḥammad b. Ibrāhīm al-Ṭabāṭabā in al-Kūfa in 199/815. The logic follows, as implied in the tradition itself, that the Mahdī will rise in the year 200 A.H. The obvious Shīʿī bend of the prophecy suggests that the expectations of the rise of the Mahdī around the turn of the third Islamic century cut across sectarian lines, and therefore are shared by the Jamāʿī-Sunnīs and the Shīʿīs.

The ʿAbbāsid society displayed widespread interest in messianic beliefs as a framework to explain the nature and direction of sociopolitical changes in the last decade of the second Islamic century. New and already circulating prophecies, accelerated by political problems and military conflicts, intensified anxiety among diverse groups and classes, although messianic visions never remained homogenous and were not generally accepted. The events of the early ninth century, in particular the approach and dawn of the year 200/800, inaugurated a new historical era of cosmic proportions. In particular, the fourth civil war foregrounded, signaled, and provoked a radical change in the lives of the inhabitants of the ʻAbbāsid caliphate. While many prophecies propagated the downfall of the ʻAbbāsids and destruction without any hope of recovery, many others demanded action to reform society. As ʻAbbāsid religio-political life unfolded in this ideological atmosphere, al-Maʼmūn found messianic beliefs to be an effective means of harmonizing his religious views and political ambitions.

CHAPTER 3

Prophecies and the Fourth Civil War

The caliphal succession proved to be a formidable hurdle for the 'Abbāsids. For one thing, even before the 'Abbāsids from the time of the first caliph, Abū Bakr, the method of succession to the caliphate remained uncertain, leading to tensions during the transfer of power following the death of a caliph. Procedures for succession fluctuated from election (Patriarchal Caliphs) to hereditary (from father to son) or lateral succession (between brothers and even cousins), and sometimes crude force (civil wars, military coups) decided the outcome. To prevent instability and to block fraternal strife, many caliphs resorted to designating more than one heir apparent in case of the unexpected death of either the caliph or his designee. Ironically, more than once, multiple designations led to civil wars. However, dynastic rivalry was not simply a clash of interests within the ruling tribe, although all four of the civil wars involved competition among Qurashite contenders. Rather the unrest mirrored a much larger conflict in a polity torn apart by ideological ambivalence and rapid social transformation.

Crisis after Hārūn al-Rashīd

It was evident from the beginning that the 'Abbāsids sought to keep the caliphate in the house of al-'Abbās (the paternal uncle of Muḥammad) to the exclusion of the 'Alids. The 'Abbāsids faced a practical and moral dilemma, however, when they insisted on keeping the caliphate in their house. Their own successful revolt had been organized around the call for the leadership of *al-riḍā min āl Muhḥammad,* which did not give the 'Abbāsids exclusive right to the caliphate but also included the 'Alids. The ideological justification that the 'Abbāsids had inherited the imamate from Abū Hāshim (d. 716), the grandson of Muḥammad b. al-Ḥanafiyya, did little to convince the 'Alids, who, starting from the reign of the second caliph, Abū Ja'far al-Manṣūr, joined the ranks of opposition to the 'Abbāsids. When al-Saffāḥ designated two prominent individuals among the 'Abbāsid family, Abū Ja'far, who would be known by his honorific al-Manṣūr, and 'Īsā b. Mūsā, to succeed him, it became evident that the 'Alids had been pushed aside. Abū Ja'far al-Manṣūr himself went even a step further to free the 'Abbāsids from the notion of an inherited imamate through delegation by Abū Hāshim. He abandoned this claim altogether, basing his family's claims instead on their direct descent from al-ʿAbbās, the uncle of the Prophet Muḥammad, thus bypassing the ʿAlids.

The ʿAbbāsids and the ʿAlids parted ways in a manner that left no option for some of the ʿAlids except revolt or complete withdrawal from the political scene. Even without having to take the ʿAlids into account, the ʿAbbāsid family still struggled to maintain a problem-free succession procedure. For instance, ʿĪsā b. Mūsā had been designated the heir apparent after the caliph al-Manṣūr, but the caliph al-Manṣūr forced ʿĪsā b. Mūsā to yield to his own son Muḥammad (who would be given the honorific al-Mahdī), on the promise that ʿĪsā b. Mūsā would remain second in line of succession after Muḥammad.

When Muḥammad al-Mahdī, in turn, wanted to appoint his own sons (who would be given the honorifics al-Hādī and al-Rashīd), he incited the army to pressure ʿĪsā b. Mūsā to give up his right to the succession. The caliph's maneuvers succeed in forcing ʿĪsā b. Mūsā out of his office, but using military force for intimidation set a bad precedent in dynastic politics. Al-Hādī himself tried without success—perhaps because of the army's reluctance—to depose his brother Hārūn al-Rashīd and appoint his own son Jaʿfar as successor. The most violent succession crisis erupted between the sons of al-Rashīd himself, al-Amīn and al-Ma'mūn, in the end leaving the ruling caliph dead (198/813) and the ʿAbbāsid legitimacy greatly undermined.

During the last three years of al-Rashīd's reign, Khurāsān was torn by a major revolt led by Rāfiʿ b. Layth, an Umayyad notable with strong family ties in Khurāsān, against the caliphate, which prompted the caliph himself to lead a campaign in person to pacify the revolt in 192/808. By the time al-Rashīd, accompanied by his son ʿAbdallāh (al-Ma'mūn), al-Faḍl b. Sahl, and al-Faḍl b. al-Rabīʿ, the head of the central administration, set out against Rāfiʿ b. Layth in 192/808, the succession provisions were in place.[1] When al-Rashīd died at Ṭūs on 3 Jumādā II 193/24 March 809 before encountering Ibn Layth, al-Ma'mūn had already preceded him to Marw with a part of the army. Having been declared caliph at Baghdad, al-Amīn aborted the campaign and ordered the return of the army and of the treasury to the capital. The caliph al-Amīn took charge of the central administration, while al-Ma'mūn stayed in Khurāsān.[2] On the surface, everything seemed to be running smoothly. Soon after the death of al-Rashīd, however, clear signs of tension between Baghdad and Khurāsān emerged. Under still unclear circumstances, al-Ma'mūn's post in Khurāsān, his status as heir apparent, and the legitimacy of the caliph in Baghdad became a matter of dissension between the two brothers.[3]

Since the Umayyad period, Khurāsān had been a province with distinct concerns that defied the attempts of the central authority to exercise control over the region. Although Khurāsān had been conquered during the caliphate of ʿUthmān in the 30s/650s, a stronger grip on the province was achieved only with the appointment of Ziyād b. Abīhi in 45/665 as governor of al-Baṣra and the East under the Umayyads. Khurāsān was a large province with territories to the east of the Oxus River, including such distant regions as Farghāna, eastern Afghanistan, Makrān, and Sind. As such, the pacification of the region was a long and often violent process. Local potentates frequently rebelled against Umayyad control and appealed to outside powers like the Hephtalites (White Huns), Western Turks, Soghdians, and even Chinese emperors. Marw had become the military base of the conquerors where Muslims began to settle down permanently by the end of the first Islamic century. Even under firm Muslim rule, social and political problems persisted.

On the one hand, there was a social chasm between Arab tribal nobility and common tribesmen as well as tribal conflicts among Arab Muslims in the satellite communities (mostly from the North Arab or Qaysī tribes of Tamīm and Bakr, and to lesser extent the Yamanī Azd tribes) in a vast sea of non-Muslim peoples. New converts to Islam who were attached to particular tribes or a particular individual through the process of alliance, *walā'*, were also pulled into tribal dispute. Since confession was a primary marker of identity, a policy that was based on religious beliefs eventually created a social divide in the province between Arab Muslims and converts over social privileges as the latter demanded equal status. On the other hand, there were issues between the Arab Muslims of Khurāsān and the central government in Damascus. Still holding on to their tribal structure, these communities competed bitterly among themselves, between the Qaysī and less prominent Yamanī tribes, and against the central government, pulling in the non-Arab Muslims as allies. The central government tried in vain to assert its authority and calm the region, which finally exploded in the middle of the eighth century in the 'Abbāsīd revolt, which ended the Umayyad caliphate.

Thus the close ties between Khurāsān and the 'Abbāsīd caliphate dated back to the revolt in the middle of the eighth century. The 'Abbāsīd revolt owed much of its success to the efforts of the *abnā' al-dawla*, the sons of the reign, mixed Arabo-Persian groups. The new ruling family intensified its links with Khurāsān through marriage and by appointing 'Abbāsīd princes, heirs apparent, and local notables as governors of the province, as well as by filling the central administration and army ranks with the *abnā'* and Khurāsānī troops. While these measures tied Khurāsān closer to the center, the relations with the province were worsened because the new caliphate created its own privileged elite who paid less and less attention to the socioeconomic and political grievances of the province, and hence became increasingly alienated from the general population. The *abnā'*, based now mostly in Baghdad and al-Raqqa, severed the links with the general body of supporters in the region, provoking growing unrest led by local landowners and semi-independent princes of the frontier and mountain areas.

It seems that the competition over social status and privileges between the *abnā'* in the central government and local nobility, as well as disagreement whether tax revenues should be used locally or sent to the center, an old issue plaguing the relations between the region and the center since the caliphate of 'Uthmān (r. 644–56), played a major role in escalating the tension in Khurāsān. Various attempts to relieve the tension, most notably by the Barmakīds, a family from the region, when Faḍl b. Yaḥyā al-Barmakī was appointed governor to Khurāsān in 177/793–94, failed because of the discontent of the *abnā'* in the capital. The reversal of policy by al-Rashīd marked by the appointment of a leading member the *abnā'*, 'Alī b. 'Isā b. Māhān, as governor in 180/796 rekindled resentment in Khurāsān, leading to the Khārijī and other uprisings.[4]

Standard historiographical sources maintain that in 177/794 al-Rashīd announced his intention to appoint Muḥammad (al-Amīn) as his first successor and only a few years later, in 183/799, declared 'Abdallāh (al-Ma'mūn) second heir, following his brother Muḥammad. In 186/802 al-Rashīd formally announced the succession provisions before 'Abbāsid dignitaries in a pilgrimage in Mecca. According to historiographical sources, Muḥammad was designated the first heir to assume the caliphate after the death of al-Rashīd. His brother al-Ma'mūn was given the exclusive governorship of greater Khurāsān, including Transoxiana. The third successor, al-Qāsim (al-Mu'tamin), was later assigned to the governorship of al-Jazīra and northern Syria, and his position was conditional on the consent of the ruling caliph at the time.[5]

After El-Hibri's work on the topic, this traditional explanation appears all too convenient to accept. It is perfectly plausible that the provisions stipulating al-Ma'mūn's exclusive sovereignty over Khurāsān represent later modifications put forth by al-Ma'mūn's camp, and perhaps even later by his overzealous sympathizers.[6] El-Hibri has already demonstrated the tendentiousness of the succession narratives; there is no need to repeat those arguments here. From the vantage point of this book, the original designation protocol seems to have contained no stipulations concerning al-Ma'mūn for two reasons. First, in the civil war rhetoric, al-Ma'mūn and his allies frequently referred to God as being the arbitrator in the conflict—hence the victory would serve as God's endorsement of al-Ma'mūn. God arbitrating in a political conflict had often meant in early Islamic history the rejection of the status quo. Arguing from this line of reasoning rather meant nullifying the succession stipulations even if they had been in place. Second, prophecies from the civil war era support only the argument of the designation of two sons and their disagreement, but say nothing about succession provisions and certainly nothing at all about the amendment.

An example is the following prophecy on the authority of Abū Qabīl: "Their ['Abbāsids] affair will remain successful until the pledge of allegiance is given to two boys among them. When these two boys mature, they will disagree among themselves and their disagreement will last a long time until three banners are raised in Syria. If they [three banners] are raised, it will be the cause of the destruction of their rule."[7] Here the only commonly known references are the pledge of allegiance to al-Amīn and al-Ma'mūn when they were young princes and their disagreement when they mature. Despite the fact that the prophecy is recorded in Nu'aym b. Ḥammād's work, it does not favor either of the heirs apparent; rather it displays a sense of dissatisfaction with the 'Abbāsid caliphate in general. This lack of details concerning the double designation is noteworthy in light of the fact that al-Ma'mūn's designation of 'Alī al-Riḍā receives more attention from prophecies than does al-Rashīd's designation of al-Amīn and al-Ma'mūn. It seems plausible that the succession arrangement of Hārūn al-Rashīd became a subject of speculation in prophecies only after the start of the civil war, unlike that of al-Ma'mūn's designation of 'Alī al-Riḍā.

There is a relevant and suggestive poem full of messianic imagery, which appears to have been composed during the civil war by the blind poet 'Alī b. Abī Ṭālib. It claims that treachery and betrayal of truth by the enemies of al-Ma'mūn were the reasons why al-Ma'mūn rose against his brother: "They have betrayed the truth and al-Ma'mūn with treachery / The deceiver will never succeed / He [al-Ma'mūn] is justice, the pure one, the pious one among us / His love won our hearts / The end of things is known to him / The Sharī'a and Zabūr verify him / He will rule forty years until they are completed / Upon [the completion of his reign] the new moons,[8] and months will come to an end."[9] Obviously this is a panegyric, intently propagandistic, and genuinely predictive poem. It is nevertheless of historiographical value in terms of what it reveals about the early stages of the civil war. First, the poem has an unequivocal messianic tone. It reveals a keen awareness of some of the major aspects of the early 'Abbāsid messianic mentality: the Mahdī in the poem is an eschatological one, knows the hidden, is foretold in both Islamic and biblical scriptures, will rule for forty years, and will usher in the end of the world. Second, it was clearly written during the civil war, as it only anticipates victory but has no knowledge of it, nor does it predict correctly the duration of al-Ma'mūn's rule. The line "the deceiver will never succeed" suggests that the poem was composed probably before the murder of al-Amīn but after the victory of Ṭāhir. Third, it reveals an awareness of the nature of the conflict between the two brothers, a violation of justice, without quite disclosing what it is. In that sense the poem only goes a step further than other prophecies dealing with the same subject. Thus it is apparent that prophetic sources differ from mainstream historiography about the issue, which is significant enough to note.

Historiographical claims notwithstanding, Umayyad and 'Abbāsid practice dictated that al-Amīn administer his realm as he saw best. It seems that in this case an effective control of Khurāsān was at stake, hence the need to pressure al-Ma'mūn into complying to his demands. However, the dispute between Baghdad and Khurāsān escalated in a short period of time, resulting in the removal of al-Ma'mūn from the line of succession in favor of al-Amīn's son Mūsā.[10] Al-Ma'mūn's refusal to acknowledge this change of succession put in motion one of the succession crises that marked Umayyad and 'Abbāsid history. As in the past, the designated successor refused to yield and rose in rebellion against the caliph, in this case al-Amīn. In a span of approximately only one year, the rift between brothers passed the point of reconciliation, as al-Ma'mūn was designated *al-imām* on coins struck in Khurāsān in late 194/810. Al-Amīn's name was removed from the coinage and from the royal attire, signaling an open confrontation. Although al-Ma'mūn refrained from using the title caliph, the title *al-imām* was certainly a strong enough signal to provoke a discussion of *fitna*. Whether it was competition over the throne resulting from al-Ma'mūn's discontent with al-Rashīd's succession provisions, or al-Ma'mūn's reaction to al-Amīn's political maneuvering, or even a plot on the part of the factions in Baghdad (the *abnā'*) and Khurāsān (Khurāsānī nobility) motivated by gaining more privileges and regional interests, this was an open revolt, a civil war, a *fitna*.

Realpolitik could not tolerate two rulers, one ruling in Baghdad and another in Marw. The mental catalog to accommodate two contenders as legitimate, even if they were brothers, had limited resources in the early ninth century. In general the norm was one caliph for the Muslim community. Even the Umayyads in Spain had to content themselves with the title of emir until the caliphate of 'Abd al-Raḥmān III (r. 300–350/912–61). The idea of a single imamate, perceived as a safeguard against revolt and civil strife, persisted during the early 'Abbāsid period in tandem with the development of the caliphal institution. In his celebrated book *Kitāb al-Kharāj*, written for al-Rashīd, Abū Yūsuf (d. 182/798) thus finds it appropriate to warn his audience, in a tradition attributed to the Prophet Muḥammad, that after a person pledges allegiance to an imam, that person is as loyal to him as possible. If another contender challenges the imam, the person is permitted to execute this contender.[11] The idea of one imam for the community acquired an additional legal sanction among jurists when an eminent jurist such as al-Shāfi'ī (d. 205/820) came to regard it as a principle established by the consensus of the community: "That which the Muslims have concurred upon is that there should be one caliph, one judge, one *amīr*, and one imam."[12] It was therefore inconceivable to expect an outcome accommodating both al-Ma'mūn and al-Amīn. Either one conceded to the other, or war would decide the outcome.

It was obvious in 195/811 that the brothers were inching closer to military confrontation than they were to agreement. The months leading up to the military confrontation with al-Amīn seemed so grim that even after al-Ma'mūn adopted the title *al-imām* for himself, he was still contemplating concession. According to al-Dīnawarī, in one such moment just before the armies of Ṭāhir and 'Alī b. 'Īsā met, al-Ma'mūn consulted al-Faḍl b. Sahl, who then asked his patron for some time to think about the matter. Astrological calculations that al-Faḍl b. Sahl himself had made convinced him that his patron would win, which he told al-Ma'mūn the next day. Assured by these astrological predictions, al-Ma'mūn decided to resist his brother.[13]

Before we dismiss this report as merely propaganda, we should take into consideration that both al-Faḍl b. Sahl and al-Dīnawarī were experts in astrology and that astrology, particularly political astrology, was studied and highly respected in the 'Abbāsid court since the time of al-Manṣūr.[14] Astrology/astronomy was one of the first sciences to enter the 'Abbāsid world. From the day that al-Manṣūr (d. 775)—on the recommendation of his court astrologer, al-Nawbakht, and his colleagues, including the famous Māshā'allāh (d. 199/815)—picked 30 July 762 as the day to lay the foundations of Baghdad, interest in the occult occupied an increasingly central position in the public and private lives of the 'Abbāsid rulers.[15] Al-Faḍl b. Sahl himself hailed from the al-Nawbakht family, who had long service to the 'Abbāsid caliphs. Al-Ya'qūbī, another historian known for his fascination with astrology, confirms that al-Ma'mūn had been very interested in astrology while he resided in Khurāsān.[16] Even though al-Ya'qūbī claims that al-Ma'mūn abandoned this habit after he returned to Baghdad and began to sit with legal scholars and theologians, the activities of the caliph in Baghdad and testimonies of others strongly suggest otherwise.[17] In fact, a circle of well-respected astrologers worked in al-Ma'mūn's court, including the ancestor of the Banū Munajjims and Abū 'Alī Yaḥya b. Manṣūr, who was an astronomer and astrologer and is said to have underwent his conversion to Islam in the presence of al-Ma'mūn.[18]

The flourishing political astrology was associated above all with two names: Māshā'allāh and Abū Ma'shar. Māshā'allāh (d. 199/815) and his astrological casts exemplify the prominence of astrology in the 'Abbāsid court. Particularly relevant among his extensive writings are works that deal with history, religion, and politics[19] and attempt to explain major changes in human history by way of astral conjunctions, particularly of Jupiter and Saturn, based on the Sasanian astrological millennial theory.[20] In his *Fī Qiyām al-Khulafā' wa Ma'rifat Qiyām Kull Malik*[21] (*On the Accession of Caliphs and Knowledge of the Accession of Each King*), he calculated the accession of the Prophet Muḥammad and eighteen caliphs up to al-Rashīd. Abū Ma'shar Muḥammad b. Mūsā (d. 273/886), who gained widespread fame in medieval Middle East and Europe, studied not only astronomy and mathematics but also astrology. Due to the longevity of his life, he appears to have served multiple caliphs through and after the caliphate of al-Ma'mūn.[22] The title of his now lost work, *Kitāb al-Tārīkh* (*The Book of History*), which apparently provided an astrological explanation of history, is a testimony to the relevance of astrological prognostications to historical and political matters in the early ninth century.[23]

It is certain therefore that al-Faḍl b. Sahl knew his colleagues and their work. He was likely aware of the astral conjunction of 809, as calculated by Māshā'allāh, that the 'Abbāsid caliphate would break down in 195/811, "and the rulership [would] be transferred from one house to another in the fourth year of the conjunction [of 809]." This change, according to Māshā'allāh, was only second in significance to the rise of the Prophet Muḥammad two centuries earlier.[24] Available prophecies do not provide any further help in the specific case of al-Ma'mūn, but this much is certain: messianic and apocalyptic prophecies, which might have been available to al-Ma'mūn and his court, did see a correspondence between astrology and prophetic prediction.[25]

Ultimately prognostications proved correct. To take control of the province, al-Amīn appointed 'Alī b. 'Īsā b. Māhān, the former governor of Khurāsān, as governor of Jibāl (the provinces of Qum, Nihāwand, Hamadān and Iṣfahān) and supplied him with a substantial army composed of the people of Baghdad,[26] *ahl Baghdād*, whose military core included the Sons, *al-abnā'*.[27] Al-Ma'mūn placed his confidence in Ṭāhir b. al-Ḥusayn, who was one of Al-Ma'mūn's foremost commanders and administrators and came from a Khurāsānī family with a distinguished service record since the 'Abbāsid revolution.[28] Al-Ma'mūn appointed Ṭāhir the governor of Jibāl and dispatched him to Rayy with a small army composed of soldiers from Khurāsān, Transoxiana, and perhaps even beyond[29] to confront the army sent by the caliph.[30] To the astonishment of most observers, in the ensuing battle Ṭāhir defeated and killed 'Alī b. 'Īsā b. Māhān near Rayy (7 Shawwāl 195/3 July 811).[31]

The outcome of the battle verified that God was on al-Ma'mūn's side. This was a groundbreaking victory—a new basis of legitimacy. Ṭāhir's exhortations to his troops convey how convinced he was that the direction of the divine support would emerge clearly at the end of the battle: "Fight for your religion against tempters to civil strife and lords of hellfire! Repel their falsehood by your truth, for it is but a single hour until God will judge between you—and He is the best of Judges!"[32] The fact that al-Ma'mūn adopted the title *imām al-hudā* immediately after his victory shows that in al-Ma'mūn's mind the title, the victory, and the astrological information that he was given were all connected.

Honored with a new title, the Ambidextrous, *Dhū al-Yamīnanyn*, after his victory, Ṭāhir occupied Qazwīn and marched against Hamadān. Al-Amīn's reinforcements, which were commanded by 'Abd al-Raḥmān b. Jabala and sent against Ṭāhir, were defeated, and Ibn Jabala was killed (196/812). By this point the entire province of Jibāl had fallen, opening the road to Baghdad. Preparation and commission of a third army by the caliph in Baghdad came to naught, while the troops of al-Amīn were expelled from Khurāsān.[33]

In Baghdad itself, the authority of the caliph continued to deteriorate. Al-Ḥusayn b. 'Alī organized a coup d'etat in Baghdad in Rajab 196/March 812.[34] Al-Amīn was arrested, and al-Ma'mūn was proclaimed caliph. Although the attempt was short-lived and al-Amīn was restored to his position two days later, the mere fact of this incident further eroded the authority of the caliph and accelerated the political chaos in Baghdad. During this incident, the leader of the coup, al-Ḥusayn b. ʿAlī, referred to al-Ma'mūn as "O Ma'mūn, O Manṣūr,[35] revealing the charged messianic anxiety during the conflict. An interesting prophecy that matches the circumstance of the early stages of the civil war points to the continued degeneration of al-Amīn's image. This prophecy speaks of the death of a caliph who liked amassing wealth, the appointment of another one after him whom the prophecy describes as "weak" and who is deposed after only two years, the attack of the people of North Africa on Egypt, and the rule of the Sufyānī in Damascus. If one considers this to belong to the civil war era, it suggests that the notion that al-Amīn was a weak caliph must have circulated concurrently with the civil war.[36]

Soon after al-Ma'mūn was proclaimed caliph in Khurāsān, he ordered Ṭāhir b. al-Ḥusayn to march on Khūzistān and from there on Baghdad, which Ṭāhir did, subduing al-Ahwāz and Wāsiṭ on his way.[37] By the end of 196/812 Ṭāhir had reached the outskirts of Baghdad, having obtained pledges of allegiance from a number of governors from the ʿAbbāsid family itself, in addition to the submission of the provinces of Ḥijāz and Yemen.[38] The pilgrimage of 196/812 was performed in al-Ma'mūn's name for the first time, announcing his legitimacy from the pulpit in Mecca.[39] When Ṭāhir finally arrived west of Baghdad, a second Khurāsānī army, commanded by Harthama b. Aʿyan—another Khurāsānī and one of the leading military chiefs under al-Rashīd who joined al-Ma'mūn in Khurāsān immediately after the conflict started[40]—had already been sent by al-Ma'mūn to blockade the capital from the east (Dhū al-Ḥijja 196/August 812). The provinces situated to the west of Iraq—Ḥijāz, Egypt, North Africa, northern Syria and al-Jazīra, Āzarbayjān, and Armenia—had already recognized the authority of al-Ma'mūn. For the next thirteen months, al-Amīn was a virtual prisoner in Baghdad, with his defense perimeter gradually shrinking.

The siege finally ended when Ṭāhir captured al-Amīn and ordered his execution on the night and early morning of 24–25 Muḥarram 198/24–25 September 813. Al-Faḍl b. Sahl's brother al-Ḥasan was put in charge of Baghdad, while Ṭāhir b. al-Ḥusayn was appointed to the Byzantine frontier.[41] The caliph was eliminated, the legitimacy of the ʿAbbāsids was greatly damaged, and the territories were far from being under complete control. The fall of Baghdad is of course sufficiently, but for the most part vaguely, reflected in the prophecies: "There will be a city between the Tigris and the Euphrates in which the sons of al-ʿAbbās will rule. It is al-Zawrā' [the winding city].[42] There will be in it a destructive war in which women will be taken as slaves and men slaughtered like sheep." When the prophet was asked why it was named al-Zawrā' he responded, "because the war will rage around it until it destroys it."[43] There are more explicit references as well. An example of this, an ʿAlid prophecy, refers to "the dismissal of the ruler of Khurāsān" and "the attack on Ibn Zubayda," who is al-Amīn.[44]

Divided between al-Ma'mūn loyalists and the reactionary 'Abbāsid family and its supporters, Baghdad was virtually left to the commoners, *ghawghā'*, and the riffraff. Since the murder of al-Amīn, the people of Baghdad and some of the Hāshimites looked desperately for a source of authority around which they could rally. When criminals took over the city—robbing, pillaging, attacking, and kidnapping people—what appears to be spontaneous civil resistance emerged in Baghdad. Neighborhoods looked for men of good conduct, *ṣulaḥā*, and volunteers to resist the banditry and to bring a measure of security to the city. These *ṣulaḥā'* gathered in groups and started forming defense units against the brigands in the city. Two eminent leaders, Khālid b. Daryūsh in the Ṭarīq al-Anbār quarter of Baghdad and Sahl b. Salāma in al-Ḥarbiyya, gathered supporters independently around the slogan "Command the good and forbid the evil."[45]

Khālid b. Daryūsh seems to have done no more than help the authorities in Baghdad fight the gangs, while Sahl b. Salāma, signaling broader political ambitions, registered his followers in a *dīwān*-list and demanded the application of the Qur'ān and the *Sunna* of the Prophet. As leader of Ahl Khurāsān, he spread the motto "There is no obedience due to a creature in disobeying God." Sahl b. Salāma refused to submit to the authority of Ibrāhīm b. al-Mahdī, who was appointed caliph by the 'Abbāsids in Baghdad after the murder of al-Amīn and continued his activities.[46] In an effort to prevent some of the banditry in the city, Ibrāhīm b. al-Mahdī took action against Sahl b. Salāma and even imprisoned him. The punishment was so mild, however, that he was allowed to preach during the day and return to his cell in the prison at night, until he was set free completely by al-Ma'mūn after his entry into Baghdad.[47]

Two major theories have been advanced concerning the movement of Sahl b. Salāma. In his article on the separation of state and religion in Islam, Lapidus argues that the political activism of Ahl Khurāsān in Baghdad after the murder of al-Amīn emerged as an ad hoc resistance to banditry, but was eventually transformed into an opposition to the caliphate. Sahl b. Salāma, as the leader of this faction, preached a political ideology that would undermine caliphal authority and promote obedience to the Qur'ān and the Prophetic practice, *Sunna*.[48] Although his movement did not last long, it succeeded in turning an ad hoc formation into a proto-Ḥanbalī sentiment, which would later oppose al-Ma'mūn in the Miḥna. Lapidus sees Sahl b. Salāma's activity as an echo of both social identity and the ideology of the Abnā'. Sahl b. Salāma's movement, according to Lapidus, represented more than a struggle for power in a period of political turmoil; it revived the religiously inspired political activism of the Abnā', which had already replaced one dynasty with another.[49]

Madelung rejected Lapidus's proposition and pointed out that Sahl b. Salāma was associated with Mu'tazilī circles rather than proto-Ḥanbalīs. In fact his movement opposed directly, and sought protection against, such a group of proto-Ḥanbalīs, which consisted of unruly soldiers and allied bandits. Madelung further argues that Sahl b. Salāma and his supporters wanted to ensure public safety and the restoration of order in a time of political turmoil and that they were quick to be satisfied as soon as al-Ma'mūn entered Baghdad and restored his rule. The group against which Sahl b. Salāma and his movement fought was one in which most of the proto-Ḥanbalīs were found. The 'Abbāsids of Baghdad relied on this group in their war against al-Ḥasan b. Sahl and al-Ma'mūn. Madelung contends that this group of proto-Ḥanbalīs had resisted al-Ma'mūn ever since the outbreak of his conflict with his brother al-Amīn and that al-Ma'mūn wanted to curb it later in the Miḥna.[50]

Both scholars seem to give too much credit to Sahl b. Salāma's role during and after the civil war. It is perhaps too optimistic to attribute proto-Sunnism and anti-al-Ma'mūn and anti-Miḥna resistance in Baghdad to his followers. Although he became a moderately popular leader among a portion of the masses in Baghdad, Sahl b. Salāma was not influential enough to bring about major changes. In the absence of authority in the city, he tried to bring a measure of security and moral standards to Baghdad in order to stave off further deterioration. His distance from the 'Alids, from the 'Abbāsids in Baghdad, and from al-Ma'mūn in Khurāsān testifies to such a provisional civic task more than it does to political ambitions. In the circumstances of the civil war, alliances definitely shifted, but Sahl b. Salāma's activities do not reveal an 'Alid inclination nor did they radically oppose the authority of the 'Abbāsids. Sahl b. Salāma's assertion that his movement supported the 'Abbāsids, in broad ideological and religious terms, also seems sincere, because there is no indication of any ideological anti-'Abbāsid sentiment in his movement. Sahl b. Salāma did not actively support the 'Abbāsids in Baghdad, but neither did he support any other candidate. When he was arrested, the main allegation against him was that he had incited people against the 'Abbāsids and impugned the validity of their authority.[51] Similarly, although he did not favor al-Ma'mūn, he did not oppose him either. The fact that he was released by al-Ma'mūn upon his return to Baghdad suggests that Sahl b. Salāma might have been a marginal popular figure with no specific political aims and intentions in this episode of Baghdad's history.

Although there remains the possibility that Sahl b. Salāma negotiated with the Zaydī 'Abdallāh b. Mūsā, the particular political circumstances of Baghdad and the fact that the 'Alids had few supporters in the city make the 'Alids unlikely allies for Sahl b. Salāma. If nothing else, the resistance displayed against the appointment of 'Alī al-Riḍā would have given him enough reason to look for other allies, especially when contemporary 'Alid uprisings in lower Iraq and Ḥijāz proved to be eventually unsuccessful. His was an ad hoc movement that lacked a detailed religious and political vision. As an ordinary individual with little political experience, Sahl b. Salāma probably could not control his movement once it had grown too large. His swift fall and the absence of any trace of later resistance on his behalf show the fundamental weakness of his movement. That the opposition to al-Ma'mūn came from Baghdad is true—perhaps even some came from Sahl b. Salāma's supporters—but it can hardly be attributed to him or to his movement.[52]

The capture of Baghdad by Ṭāhir and the collapse of order in the city shortly afterward coincided with similar troubles in a number of other places. Al-Ḥasan al-Hirsh revolted in central Iraq in 198/814, calling for the one agreed upon, *al-Riḍā*, from among the family of the Prophet.[53] Abū al-Sarāyā revolted in al-Kūfa in 199/815,[54] and a number of other Fāṭimid uprisings occurred in the regions of Ḥijāz[55] and Yemen.[56] Although the 'Alid uprisings gradually faded away without much success, they seem to have contributed to the drastic decision of al-Ma'mūn to appoint an 'Alid as his successor. In the uprising of Abū al-Sarāyā, proclaimed on behalf of the Fāṭimid Muḥammad b. Ibrāhīm Ṭabāṭabā, the rallying slogan was "Command the good and forbid the evil." Like Al-Ḥasan al-Hirsh, Abū al-Sarāyā also called for *al-Riḍā*,[57] referring to the current political parlance as well as invoking the past, not the least of which was the 'Abbāsid revolt itself.[58] Abū al-Sarāyā initially succeeded; he designated some of his followers to offices and spread his authority as far south as al-Baṣra and as far east as al-Ahwāz, but eventually was forced out of al-Kūfa by the forces of Harthama b. A'yan. Shortly after this, he was captured in Khurāsān and executed upon the orders of Ḥasan b. al-Sahl.[59]

In 200/816 another 'Alid and the uncle of 'Alī al-Riḍā, Muḥammad al-Dībāj b. Ja'far, claimed the title commander of the faithful in Mecca for a short while, until he abandoned his claims in al-Ma'mūn's favor.[60] A remarkable report in al-Iṣfahānī's *Maqātil* leaves no doubt that messianic expectations motivated his uprising. Muḥammad b. Ja'far hoped that he was the expected Mahdī and al-Qā'im. Al-Iṣfahānī states that one of Muḥammad b. Ja'far's eyes was stricken with something that affected its function. Muḥammad b. Ja'far was delighted that he had a disabled eye because he took it to be a sign of his Mahdīship. He used to say, "I hope I am the Mahdī, the Qā'im. I have been informed that the Mahdī has something in one of his eyes and that he embarks upon this affair despite his dislike [of it]."[61]

In the end he was not successful. In his remarkable concession speech, a reflection of his and some of his supporters' attitude in respect to the leadership of al-Ma'mūn, he renounced the title commander of the faithful in favor of al-Ma'mūn. He began by announcing his name, Muḥammad b. Ja'far b. Muḥammad b. 'Alī b. al-Ḥusayn b. 'Alī b. Abī Ṭālib, and his original voluntary pledge of allegiance to al-Ma'mūn, whom he called, among other things, the imam, the commander of the faithful. Then he mentioned the civil war and how he had heard that al-Ma'mūn was dead. He explained how he deemed it appropriate to accept the pledge of allegiance for himself. Now, having been informed that al-Ma'mūn was alive and well, he announced his intention to become an ordinary individual and withdraw from claiming leadership.[62] This and other 'Alid uprisings unambiguously show how the 'Alids energetically made their bids for the caliphate at this fateful juncture of 'Abbāsid history.

With unrest present in the center and in the provinces since 809, the conflict took on a much larger meaning. For many the civil war became a conflict striking at the core of their religio-political convictions. It was a *fitna,* and it was far from clear if one should participate in it. As the Islamic calendar was approaching the closure of the second Islamic century, the civil war itself, and the events it mobilized, appeared to those who looked for portents as an ominous and unwelcome social disorder, nonetheless preordained to occur. For others, it meant a rite of passage ushering in the awaited millennium.

The Civil War as an Apocalyptic *Fitna*

As is known from relevant jurisprudential and political opinions in early Islamic history, civil disorder caused a major concern for pious intellectuals. This also held true for believers in prophecies. A rich array of prophecies foretold the occurrence and recurrence of civil discord (*fitan*) and apocalyptic battles (*malāḥim*). An example of such prophecies include: "I warn you of seven civil wars taking place after me: One will approach from Medina, one in Mecca, one from Yemen, one from Damascus, one from the East, one from the West, and one in the Center of Damascus, which is the *fitna* of the Sufyānī. Ibn Mas'ūd added, 'some of you will witness its beginning and others among this community will see its last part.'"[63] Many of these prophecies urged witnesses to avoid civil disorder by not participating in armed rebellions.[64] As might be expected, many such prophecies were produced by those fearing the collapse of the established sociopolitical order and were motivated either by partisanship or a more general concern with maintaining common welfare. On the one hand, the originators of the prophecies hoped to defend the caliphate against its enemies and to curtail the opposition. On the other hand, they had a distinct desire, as documented abundantly in apocalyptic writings, to protect the Muslim community from disintegration as a result of civil wars, irrespective of their view on the legitimacy of any given caliph—a view common within the mainstream Jamā'ī-Sunni group.

The two-century-long accumulation and circulation of prophecies helped the early 'Abbāsid pious learned elite and their supporters see sociopolitical and military conflicts as a part of a cosmic drama that had begun sometime in the past and would conclude in the future—a future that now appeared imminent. This ideology communicated two powerful messages. First, history was nothing but a perpetual moral and social decline after the Prophet Muḥammad or, at best, after his immediate two successors—imagined as the Golden Age. The passage of time, as 'Abdallāh b. 'Umar (d. 73/693) remarked in a prophecy attributed to him, was nothing but escalating hardship, calamity, and *fitna*.[65]

Second, history was imminently approaching its end. Thus a prophecy attributed to the Prophet Muḥammad compared the remaining time of the world with the very last portion of a day. The Prophet is said to have commented while watching a sunset that the world was also living its final hour before the end of times. Similar to the passage of a day, the world was already at its sunset, having consumed most of its time.[66] This sense of urgency stands out in another account about the impending day of reckoning:

> Qasama b. Zuhayr said, "I have heard that the prophet said: My situation and yours with the Hour is like a group of people fearing an attack of their enemy. They sent a watcher to a nearby location [to monitor the enemy]. When the watcher saw [the enemy] attacking, he was worried that, if he descended from his location to inform his people, the attack would strike his people before he reached them. He, then, stayed in his place, rolled up his clothes and called out to his people: 'Awake!'"[67]

Such prophecies were too alarmist. Perhaps to challenge their universal validity or to curb the sense of anxiety, alternative prophecies were put into circulation without eliminating apocalyptic expectations altogether. One way that was done was by postponing the end of time as far into the future as possible by linking it to formulaic numbers of portents;[68] unlikely social, religious, or political circumstances; the occurrence of supernatural events, such as the dislocation of mountains; or other miraculous and unprecedented happenings.[69] Predicting a set of portents, commonly anywhere from three to ten, was a frequent means to postpone the end of time.[70] Another way was to refer to the testimony of prophets, "ancient scriptures," "books," and simply "texts." In a prophecy of this sort, Jesus asks Gabriel about the Hour and its appointed time, to which Gabriel responds, "The one who is being asked is no more knowledgeable [in this matter] than is the one asking."[71] The Qur'ān, too, seems to have served as a way to keep apocalyptic anxiety in check. A number of prophecies refer to the ambiguity of Qur'ānic verses about the Hour. In a tradition attributed to 'Urwa b. al-Zubayr, he appears to have commented that "the prophet was still being asked about the Hour until [this verse] was revealed: 'Wherein are you with the declaration thereof. With your Lord is the final end of it.'"[72]

Near or far, however, the fear of *fitna* continued to provoke anxiety, especially when there was unrest. As soon as the news of strife between al-Amīn and al-Ma'mūn became known outside the palace, the civil war brought into the open old and new fears of annihilation and destruction. Al-Ma'mūn's adoption of the title of imam for himself recalled the devastating consequences of past civil wars, as the 'Abbāsids now had two rulers, one in Khurāsān and one in Baghdad, pitted against each other. Aḥmad b. Ḥanbal, a contemporary eyewitness and a victim of al-Ma'mūn's Miḥna policy two decades later, transmits a prediction attributed to Ibn 'Abbās and casts the 'Abbāsid civil war in an apocalyptic light: "I was with the prophet one night. He said to me, 'See if you [can] spot a star in the sky.' I said, 'Yes.' He said, 'What do you see?' I said, 'I see the Pleiades.' He said, 'Well, there will reign in this community as many rulers from among your progeny as there are stars in this Pleiades; two of them will be in *fitna*.'"[73] The civil war fulfilled this prophecy, which incidentally illustrates editorial discretions done most probably by Aḥmad b. Ḥanbal himself, owing to his survival after the reign of al-Ma'mūn, to present the civil war as merely *a fitna*, civil disorder, unlike numerous others that link the civil war to the destruction of the 'Abbāsids.

Not only did the bystanders producing prophecies see the civil war as an apocalyptic battle, but so also did the parties involved in the conflict themselves. Both sides resorted to projecting their identities with messianic jargon, and both donned epithets, al-Amīn and al-Ma'mūn, and had names, Muḥammad and 'Abdallāh, with messianic overtones.[74] Abū Nuwās used the title al-Qā'im for al-Amīn during his coronation: "The Qā'im, al-Amīn, moves us to joyous mirthfulness, whilst the death of the imam just recently makes us weep."[75] Some of the supporters of al-Amīn called him "Yā Manṣūr,"[76] and even depicted him as the Mahdī. In a poem lamenting al-Amīn, al-Ḥusayn b. Daqqāq al-Ashqar, a client of Bahīla, who was one of Muḥammad's confidants, claimed that al-Amīn had not been killed and expected him to return.[77] This was perhaps more than a lone voice, as we see a poet loyal to al-Ma'mūn refuting the exact same sentiment in his poem deriding al-Amīn: "They have alleged that you are alive and recruiting / anyone who has said this has lied."[78] It is important to remember that these claims, whether they were intended as messianic or merely hoped that al-Amīn was not killed, were produced in a milieu in which ideas of a second coming and concealment were powerful among various sectarian movements, including the Shī'īs of the late eighth century.

However, when the civil war appeared to tilt in favor of al-Ma'mūn, al-Amīn's reputation as a messianic figure diminished. Instead the advance of al-Ma'mūn and the ongoing battles created a fear of imminent destruction in Iraq and Syria,[79] as the execution of al-Amīn heightened the sense of defeat among the 'Abbāsid family and their allies in Baghdad. Even before al-Amīn's execution and the capture of Baghdad, prophecies foresaw a fraternal disagreement leading to the demise of the 'Abbāsids.[80] As has been mentioned, the conventional view suggesting the removal of al-Ma'mūn from his post as the cause of conflict does not find much resonance in apocalyptic scenarios. Prophecies refer only to a "conflict" or "disagreement" between the two brothers. Even when prophecies do not show any awareness of active war, but rather a disagreement whose actual outcome appeared still uncertain, they nonetheless predict the destruction of 'Abbāsid authority. Not the result of al-Rashīd's succession policy, it seems, but the conflict itself—the actual birth of the civil war—became the focus of many predictions. For example, Al-Azdī, a provincial historian, relates a prediction in his *Book of History* that the 'Abbāsid rule will split in 195/811. The prediction anticipates a period of chaos that can only be averted by not participating in the civil war. "Hide yourself," the prediction admonishes, "even underneath the stone of a scorpion, because there will be a long period of evil."[81]

The actual conflict between al-Amīn and al-Ma'mūn and other events in the 'Abbāsid caliphate became portents of an apocalyptic and imminent collapse of 'Abbāsid authority. One such prediction mentions three 'Abbāsid rulers, whose names will be the names of prophets and who will rule for forty years. "If you see them disagreeing among themselves and a group of people from the sons of Hāshim gathering between the two rivers, and the governorship of a man from the sons of al-'Abbās in the proximity of the Maghrib, and the battle between the black banners and yellow banners in the navel of Syria, the murder of the governor of Egypt, and the withholding of its land tax, that is a sign of their end."[82] As Madelung noted, although the murder of the governor of Egypt does not seem to correspond to an actual incident, the rest of this account agrees with the events of the civil war, including the names of the preceding caliphs, al-Mahdī, al-Hādī, and al-Rashīd.

Messianic hopes and apocalyptic fears ignited by the civil war show up also in prophecies discussing the deeds of Abū al-'Amayṭir al-Sufyānī (active 195–98/811–14), abstracted in apocalyptic literature as the Sufyānī. These prophecies, which reveal both activist and pacifist inclinations in medieval Islamic messianic and apocalyptic tradition, display vividly the competing claims on the caliphate and the expectation of a calamitous destruction of the 'Abbāsids. The Sufyānī is a curious figure, reminding us of the die-hard Umayyad aspirants to the caliphate. As previously noted, the legend most likely originated during Umayyad times and proliferated during the uprising of Abū al-'Amayṭir at the end of the second Islamic century.[83] Messianic aspects of his uprising enhanced the political relevance of earlier Sufyānī prophecies to the 'Abbāsid civil war and contributed to the messianic dimension of al-Ma'mūn's movement. Although a number of scholars have already examined the uprising of Abū al-'Amayṭir al-Sufyānī from historical and apocalyptic perspectives, the importance of his movement and the apocalyptic lore accompanying it for al-Ma'mūn's biography warrant an additional look.

Abū al-'Amayṭir 'Alī b. 'Abdallāh b. Khālid b. Yazīd b. Mu'āwiya, who declared himself the expected Sufyānī who would restore the Umayyad rule, revolted in Damascus in Dhū al-Ḥijja 195 / August–September 811. In doing so, he was clearly attempting to fulfill earlier prophecies.[84] An aged (in his nineties) Umayyad notable and scholar with no extraordinary previous fame,[85] Abū al-'Amayṭir was a Hāshimī from his mother's side and an Umayyad from his father's. Thus he had enough reason to see himself all at once the Sufyānī, the Mahdī, the commander of the faithful, and *al-riḍā min āl Muḥammad*.[86] Abū al-'Amayṭir defeated the 'Abbāsid governor, Sulaymān b. Abī Ja'far, and drove him out of Damascus, benefiting from the support and unrest caused by the Zawāqīl, brigands, in the countryside. The second army, sent by al-Amīn under the command of al-Ḥusayn b. 'Alī b. 'Īsā b. Mahān, advanced no farther than al-Raqqa.[87] Despite the hesitation of al-Ṭabarī to provide additional information, Abū al-'Amayṭir appears to have been briefly successful. Some Umayyads and their supporters, including some learned elite in Syria, saw Abū al-'Amayṭir credible enough to support. A leading scholar in Damascus at the time, Abū Mushir (d. ca. 218/833), who was later interrogated in the Miḥna, not only supported Abū al-'Amayṭir but also transmitted some of the Sufyānī prophecies that are still in existence today.[88] As 'Abbās and Cobb point out, Abū al-'Amayṭir expanded the area under his control and was probably recognized as caliph around Damascus, the coastal districts, Ḥimṣ, and Qinnasrīn.[89] However, tribal factionalism in Damascus between the Qaysīs and Yamānīs prevented Abū al-'Amayṭir from going any farther. He was opposed by the Qaysīs and even imprisoned for a while, only to escape and flee Damascus in 198/814, dying shortly thereafter.

The Sufyānī is identified in prophecies as a descendant of Abū Sufyān, who would rise from the city of Damascus.[90] He "will come forth from the valley of al-Yābis.[91] The governor of Syria will come out against him to fight him, but as soon as he looks at his banner [the governor] will be defeated. 'Abd al-Quddūs said, 'the governor of Damascus will be a governor of the 'Abbāsids at the time.'"[92] Prophecies foretell the duration of the Sufyānī's reign as well. The predictions, varying from seven months up to three-and-one-half years, fit the actual duration of Abū al-'Amayṭir's uprising.[93] The details of some of these prophecies reveal illuminating and curious information about the civil war and al-Ma'mūn. According to the prophecies, the Sufyānī is to appear when the seventh of the 'Abbāsids, unmistakably al-Ma'mūn, matures[94] and during a conflict among the 'Abbāsids, identified as *Banū Fulān*, over the caliphate.[95] The vague and indefinite tone of some of the prophecies is sharply contrasted in a detailed account about Hārūn al-Rashīd's last years. The prophecy describes a ruler among the descendants of al-'Abbās who will reside in al-Raqqa and stay there for two years. He will raid the lands of the Byzantines (Rūm) and then return from his campaign to al-Raqqa, only to go again to the East upon receiving unfavorable news. He will die in the East and will be succeeded by his son, during whose rule the Sufyānī will appear and the 'Abbāsids' reign will end.[96]

As noted by Nagel and Madelung, this prediction refers to Hārūn al-Rashīd's campaign against the Khārijī rebel Rāf'i b. al-Layth in 192–93/809. It was, indeed, during this campaign in that same year that al-Rashīd died in Ṭūs and was succeeded by al-Amīn. Clearly this prophecy was composed during the civil war and before the fall of the Sufyānī. The silence of the prophecy about al-Ma'mūn is a cause for pause, but the casual mention of the ascension of al-Amīn to the throne is more important.[97] It is possible that the prophecy is intended primarily to highlight the uprising of the Sufyānī, similar to other prophecies that also depict the Sufyānī as a portent of 'Abbāsid demise. In one such Sufyānī prophecy, the transmitter anticipates two disagreements, leading to the dynasty's annihilation: "On the authority of Ka'b, who said, 'if two men from the 'Abbāsids, who are the two branches [of the family] are deposed, the first disagreement will affect these two. Then it will be followed by the final disagreement, in which the annihilation will occur. The coming forth of the Sufyānī will [happen] during their second disagreement."[98] While the historical reference to the first disagreement is difficult to identify (it can be any of the succession disputes within the 'Abbāsid family), the second disagreement clearly refers to the civil war and the rise of Abū al-'Amayṭir in Syria, and therefore dates to shortly after 195/811.

The Sufyānī prophecies offer a remarkable insight into the interlocking relations between the Sufyānī and the Mahdī. The Mahdī and the Sufyānī would come forth concurrently to fulfill their missions. In one such tradition the Mahdī and the Sufyānī are described as coming forth like two racehorses. Each one of them subdues the region in which he arrives or the people whom he encounters.[99] Madelung sees this account as pre-'Abbāsid, which is entirely possible. However, these prophecies are very susceptible to reincarnation and recycling. Thus in *Biḥār al-Anwār* there is a significant new detail that juxtaposes Abū al-'Amayṭir and al-Khurāsānī: "The 'Abbāsids will certainly rule. When they rule and disagree and their authority collapses, the Khurāsānī and the Sufyānī will come forth against them. This one [will come] from the east and the other one from the west. They will race to al-Kūfa like racehorses, this one from here and the other one from there until their ['Abbāsids'] end comes at their hands. They will leave not even one of them [alive]."[100]

Because this tradition indicates no knowledge of the Sufyānī's troubles shortly after 196/812, it must have been put into circulation around this time. There is much ambiguity in the account concerning the identity of the Khurāsānī. If he will rise after "they rule and disagree and their authority collapses," how can he then be identified with al-Ma'mūn? If he is not al-Ma'mūn, who is he? There is a possible candidate within the estimated dates of the prophecy (195–96) who fits this description: Al-Ma'mūn's commander in chief, Ṭāhir. The period seems to reflect his circumstances after the defeat of al-Amīn's army. That the 'Abbāsids would be destroyed as a result of the concurrent advance of the Sufyānī and the Khurāsānī echoes again Ṭāhir's march toward Baghdad. The advance of Ṭāhir would indeed appear calamitous to any observer. In the end the prophecy proved to be only partially correct. While Ṭāhir captured Baghdad, Abū al-'Amayṭir's movement disintegrated, leaving an ideological legacy far more significant than its political impact.[101] That is perhaps why medieval historiography generally shows little interest in Abū al-'Amayṭir's movement, while apocalyptic sources pay it a great deal of attention.[102]

Prophecies seem to address the developments surrounding the 'Alids, the 'Abbāsids, and perhaps the chaos in Baghdad after its capture by Ṭāhir. The following prophecy mentions three parties:

> On the authority of Abū Umayya al-Kalbī who said, "an old man whose eyebrows fell on his eyes [because of old age] who witnessed [the days of] Jāhiliyya [Arabian pre-Islamic past] narrated to us saying "the holders of the black banners will remain standing firmly until they fall into disagreement among themselves opposing one another. [When that happens] they will break up into three parties. One party will call for the sons of Fāṭima, one party will call for the sons of al-'Abbās, and another party will call for themselves." I said, 'who are themselves?' He said, 'I do not know; this is what I heard.'"[103]

The prophecy seems to talk about the 'Abbāsids, specifically, and about new controversies and groupings that the civil war created rather than the succession controversy prominent in other prophecies. It is possible that the party calling for the sons of Fāṭima is al-Ma'mūn, which places the account sometime after the designation of al-Riḍā as heir apparent. If this is the case, the other party fits Ibrāhīm b. al-Mahdī's position in Baghdad. However, the third party is certainly problematic, and the wording does not allow for more than a hazardous guess. Given the circumstances in Iraq after the appointment of al-Riḍā, a good guess might be Sahl b. Salāma, who seemed to operate independently of the previous two parties, but lacked a clear purpose—a very candid observation indeed as modern scholars still grapple to understand his movement.

The turmoil surrounding the 'Abbāsids was not a concern limited only to Muslim observers. A comment on the civil war between the two sons of al-Rashīd in the Greek *A Short Chronology ad Annum 818* leaves no doubt that anticipation of the 'Abbāsid disintegration around 200 A.H. was widespread enough to appear in non-Muslim historiography: "Anarchy and war [raged] among the latter's [al-Rashīd's] sons for seven years up until the present eleventh indiction. Presently (*nyn*) God will curtail the years of their rule and will raise the horn of the Christian empire against them."[104]

This sentiment, which is apparent in the brief comment of the chronographer, is echoed by a sibylline prophecy that offers some intriguing details on the civil war. The prophecy narrates a dream in which one hundred judges saw in one night nine suns, each with a different appearance. According to the prophecy, the news of the dream eventually reached a Roman emperor, who became curious about its meaning—so curious that he searched for an interpreter to explain it to him. Eventually the Sibyl heard the news and, upon the request of the emperor, agreed to interpret the dream for him.

The Sibyl's interpretation of the dream is based on the notion of nine suns corresponding to the ages of the world, the last of which is the apocalyptic one. The ninth sun is the period when the "Lion Cub" will rule and fill the earth with peace, abundance, and security for forty years, at the end of which the Antichrist will be revealed, only to be thrown into hell, and "God shall rejoice with his son." The passage dealing with Hārūn al-Rashīd and the following developments describes Syria and Baghdad (the great city that lies in the East) in ruins. Under a king the region would prosper for twenty-three years, and gifts would pour down from the islands of the Mediterranean and from the countries of the Franks. Syria would flourish during this king's rule but would be ruined upon his decease. "He shall leave as his successors two sons, the name of one being the same as the name of the one who shall come from the south. Syria shall weep over the one who is called Amīn.[105] Then the coast shall be ruined, and the churches also and all the people shall walk in falsehood and injustice."[106] The prophecy goes on to narrate what will happen in the "eighth age" before the millennium. "In this fashion horror and fear shall grow upon the whole earth, to such an extent that it shall take the people's breath from their bodies through its severity. At that time Mesopotamia will be ruined, and some of Egypt will be set on fire. Great ships shall be wrecked at sea, and blood shall be spilled, and killing and plunder shall take place upon it. The people shall be pillaged and shall be in great distress, and they shall envy those who are dead."[107]

The Sibylline apocalypse raises a number of important issues. The originator of the prophecy places himself in a pre-Islamic era and narrates everything related to Muslims as happening in the future.[108] The eyewitness' narrative of the civil war aside, the prophecy contains no historical information beyond the civil war, but rather a genuine prediction of an imminent millennium followed by the coming of Gog and Magog and the Antichrist. The king with two sons is, of course, Hārūn al-Rashīd. The one coming from the South is most likely the Prophet Muḥammad, as al-Amīn's first name is Muḥammad. The intriguing mention (without detail similar to Muslim prophecies) of Hārūn al-Rashīd, the appointment of his two sons, the caliphate of al-Amīn, and the civil war make the prophecy particularly noteworthy. It suggests that al-Rashīd designated two successors, that al-Amīn was not popular in Syria,[109] and that there was widespread fear and confusion among both the Muslim and the Christian communities because of war and instability. Nevertheless the prophecy remains hopeful that an era of justice will erase the injustice, repair the ruins, purify the faith, and restore it to its supreme place during the ninth age, which is the millennium.

Another Syrian prophecy, the Baḥīra legend, predicts, similar to many Muslim prophecies, the end of the ʿAbbāsids at the conclusion of the civil war. The prophecy seems to be composed of several layers incorporated into each other from different periods.[110] The passage in question describes the civil war in a coded language:

> Then will Hāshim bear seven kings: two will be called [by one name], one will be called with two names; the names of two are mentioned in the Law; one has a name of three letters, and one of seven letters.[111] When these have ruled and will be dead, know that the kingdom of the sons of Hāshim is at an end. Then the sons of Ishmael will awake, as if from a sleep. They will fight among themselves. Everyone will say of himself, "I am the king." God will permit them to do this; for he will incite them against each other, so that their end and their destruction will be brought about by themselves.[112]

Without trying to guess the meaning of what is meant to be obscure, we know that seven 'Abbāsid caliphs are mentioned. The text "they will fight among themselves" and that which follows makes clear that the civil war is being discussed. The prophecy perhaps is genuine in predicting the death of the seventh caliph, as it does not show an awareness of the period after the civil war. The section beginning with the sentence "Then the sons of Ishmael will awake, as if from a sleep" breaks the logical flow of the passage, but this could be a later addition, misplacement, or mistranslation. The section can also be interpreted as speaking about the Muslims as a community, because the previous sentences seem to describe the 'Abbāsids. For the moment, if we read the passage as painting a picture of the civil war and the destruction of the 'Abbāsids, which would also tally well with numerous Muslim predictions, we can make more sense of the following passage: "Then there will come from the East a man, a merciful king clothed in [green] garments.[113] In his days, there will be quiet and peace in the whole world. Churches and monasteries will be renewed and rebuilt. The truth will be proclaimed. He is the last king, who will come at the end of the kingdom of the sons of Ishmael, who will collect the sons of Hagar and bring them to the wilderness of Yathrib, will punish them and will take vengeance for the former sins of their ancestors."[114]

This passage mentions the East and the color green and fits with al-Ma'mūn's situation on his way to Baghdad. Could the prophecy of Baḥīra's "merciful king clothed in green garments" refer to al-Ma'mūn? That is a possibility, for the Baḥīra prophecy has been ascribed to the reign of al-Ma'mūn by Abel, whose dating has so far not been challenged.[115] As already noted, Muslim prophecies are next to silent on al-Ma'mūn's adoption of the color green. Even though the text of the prophecy cannot be taken, as Griffith notes, as a unit representing one original copy because of later editions and editorial corrections, the passage in question could still be a favorable description of his reign. It must be conceded, however, that the remainder of the prophecy—beginning with the sentence "The truth will be proclaimed"—goes on to narrate the mission of the messianic Christian king, the last Roman emperor, and bears no further information on the civil war.

Whether the warnings against participating in the *fitna* stopped anyone from taking political action may be debated, but they were certainly counterbalanced by alternative prophecies and pious and legal opinions justifying opposition to unjust authorities. *Fitna*, whether it meant apocalyptic battle or relatively mundane civil disorder, had a contested definition and applicability. Foremost among alternative views were of course the coming of the Mahdī and his rise against injustice. Although we tend to associate political dissent with Shīʿī and Khārijī opposition to the caliphate, apocalyptic material provides ample evidence of voices of dissent within the Jamāʿī-Sunni religiosity. One of the illustrative examples of this position spells out exactly when one cannot call dissent *fitna*: "If the people of righteousness, *ahl al-ḥaqq*, prevail over the people of falsehood, *ahl al-bāṭil*, that is not *fitna*."[116] Therefore one person's *fitna* is another's legitimate resistance. As indicated in a prophecy, at least a portion of the concerned pious thought that the end of time would happen only after a young man from the family of the Prophet, specifically an ʿAbbāsid, ruled.[117] Within this messianic and apocalyptic context, which justified and offered a rationale for religio-political action, the caliph al-Ma'mūn led his movement.

CHAPTER 4

Second Black Banners from the East

Al-Ma'mūn could not have been unaware of the implications of messianic expectations focusing on his person. Among other things, he was the foremost member of a family known for its spiritual and religious claims and whose history was imbued with messianic beliefs and movements; a prince whose education and personal traits exemplified piety, moral conduct, and personal refinement; a rebel against his brother; a leader in a region saturated with messianic expectations; and the subject of affection of a population that was ready to see him as a remedy for its grievances. Before we examine the occasions on which al-Ma'mūn's image intersected with messianic expectations, some background information about him is in order.[1]

Making a Messianic Contender

'Abdallāh b. Hārūn al-Rashīd, al-Ma'mūn, was born on 15 Rabī' I 170 / 14 September 786 in Baghdad, the eldest of the eleven sons of al-Rashīd. His mother, Marājil, was a concubine who might have been the daughter of the famous Khurāsānī rebel Ustādhsīs, who revolted against al-Manṣūr. Ustādhsīs had been defeated and captured together with his daughter, who was probably given to al-Rashīd.[2] Whether or not Marājil was the daughter of Ustādhsīs, she died soon after 'Abdallāh's birth, and he was brought up by Zubayda, the granddaughter of al-Manṣūr, wife of al-Rashīd, and mother of Muḥammad al-Amīn, who was born in Shawwāl 170 / April 787. Unlike al-Ma'mūn, al-Amīn had a distinguished lineage as the son of a mother from the 'Abbāsid royal family. The two brothers were the same age, received a similar education often from identical mentors, and spent their childhood and teenage years together.[3] Al-Ma'mūn's education benefited him greatly during and after the civil war.

Al-Ma'mūn received his early education in Arabic and the Qur'ān from the famous grammarian al-Kisā'ī (d. 189/805).[4] By the time both boys were ready for education, the Arabic language had become a scholarly discipline under the patronage of the 'Abbāsid caliphs. Pioneering figures such as al-Sibawayhi (d. 183/799), originally from Shīrāz, who came to study law and then became a first-rate linguist, had laid down the foundational work for Arabic grammar and lexicography. Another pioneer, al-Kisā'ī, was not only considered to be the leading grammarian of his time but also was credited with one of the seven authoritative readings, *qirā'a*, of the Qur'ān.[5] Al-Ma'mūn was trained in language by al-Kisā'ī's pupil Yaḥyā b. Ziyād al-Farrā' (d. 207/822), who rivaled the talents of his teacher and was a scholar of language of the stature of his earlier colleague al-Sibawayh. Later, under the patronage of al-Ma'mūn, al-Farrā' would compose *Ma'ānī al-Qur'ān* (*Connotations of the Qur'ān*), a treatise arguing for the grammatical perfection of the Qur'ān. The caliph, whose reputation largely derived from his arguments about the nature of the Qur'ān, must have considered such a work a significant contribution to Qur'ānic scholarship and argumentation.[6] Royal etiquette, as well as music and poetry, was taught by Abū Muḥammad al-Yazīdī (d. 202/817), who was a member of a small group of poets and grammarians associated with the 'Abbāsid court.[7]

In jurisprudence, al-Ma'mūn was educated by Abū Ḥanīfa's student al-Ḥasan b. Ziyād al-Lu'lu'ī (d. 204/819), and in *ḥadīth* by a group of scholars, some of whom were members of Abū Ḥanīfa's circle, such as 'Abbād b. al-'Awwām and Abū Mu'āwiya al-Ḍarīr. Al-Ma'mūn was reported to have excelled in both subjects.[8] The colleagues of Abū Ḥanīfa (d. 182/798) had a distinguished place in al-Rashīd's court. In fact, Abū Yūsuf, a student of Abū Ḥanīfa and the author of the celebrated *Kitāb al-Kharāj*, (*Book of Taxation*), became the Chief Judge of al-Rashīd and structured the administration of the judicial system of the caliphate. Abū Yūsuf was given the title of Chief Judge, *Qāḍī al-Quḍāt*, and his successors were put in charge of appointing and monitoring the provincial judges, thus making the judicial hierarchy more centralized. The efficient administration of the judiciary in this far-flung empire seems to have justified the 'Abbāsids to designate their judge as the Chief Judge of the World, *Qaḍī Quḍāt al-Dunyā*. During the reign of al-Ma'mūn, the Chief Judge came to occupy an exceptional position of influence, as exemplified in highly influential figures such as Yaḥyā b. Aktham, who was a close adviser of the caliph and accompanied al-Ma'mūn on his expeditions to Egypt, Damascus, and the Byzantine frontier in the 830s,[9] and Aḥmad b. Abī Du'ād, who was one of the mentors of the caliphs during the Miḥna.[10]

Al-Ma'mūn's education in *ḥadīth* enabled him to transmit traditions from the Prophet Muḥammad on the authority of a number of teachers, including members of the 'Abbāsid family. It is noteworthy that he came to embrace a view of *ḥadīth* that was not exactly in line with that of the *ḥadīth*-transmitters (*muḥaddithūn*), some of whom later contributed to laying the foundations of the Sunni paradigm of *ḥadīth*. The caliph gradually came to question the method of verifying the authenticity of a report attributed to the Prophet Muḥammad by evaluating the credibility of transmitters in a chain of transmission, *isnād*, rather than the content. This view was not in line with the *isnād*, as criticism had become hugely popular among *hadīh* transmitters.[11]

Al-Ma'mūn might have been associated more with the students of Abū Ḥanīfa. Kâtip Çelebi reports an account on the authority of al-Khawārizmī attributed to al-Ma'mūn himself that reveals the association of al-Ma'mūn with Ḥanafite circles. According to this report, the reason that 'Īsā b. Abbān wrote his book *al-Ḥujja al-Ṣaghīra* was actually to dispel rumors and criticism that the associates of Abū Ḥanīfa did not know about *ḥadīth* and its transmission. Al-Ma'mūn had earlier been presented with a work on *ḥadīth* apparently by a transmitter of *ḥadīth* with a tongue-in-cheek remark that although the followers of Abū Ḥanīfa did not understand *ḥadīth*, they were still favored in the caliph's court. Evidently this remark disturbed al-Ma'mūn, until 'Īsā b. Abbān wrote his work and explained in detail the issues of *ḥadīth*. After al-Ma'mūn read it, the caliph wished blessings upon Abū Ḥanīfa.[12]

Al-Ma'mūn was only in his early twenties when the civil war broke out—an age at which he could entertain new ideas and act on them. When the confrontation came into the open, al-Ma'mūn apparently faced a hard choice between resistance and submission. Significant in this regard are the coins of 194/810 and 195/811. They show that al-Ma'mūn was still willing to concede to al-Amīn, had he been allowed to remain in his position in Khurāsān.[13] It follows that the initial years after the death of al-Rashīd must have been decisive for the emergence and evolution of al-Ma'mūn's purpose and his political strategy. His decision to go against al-Amīn shows his determination to respond to the immediate situation created by his father's death. He was there as an heir apparent prince and governor, with a loyal adviser, in a province torn by discontent and anxiety.[14]

His adviser al-Faḍl b. Sahl contacted the notables in Khurāsān, including the descendants of the *abnā'* and the 'Abbāsid governors, to shore up support for his patron, perhaps initially without much success, but thereby unequivocally announcing al-Ma'mūn's intentions. The Khurāsānīs eventually found an answer to their grievances in al-Ma'mūn and were drawn to his emerging religio-political image.[15] While al-Amīn's popularity faded in Khurāsān, al-Ma'mūn won sympathy and support.[16] From the beginning, al-Ma'mūn identified his movement with piety, puritanical revival of faith, and justice. If we trust al-Ṭabarī, al-Faḍl b. Sahl advised al-Ma'mūn to send for jurists, *fuqahā'*, in his entourage, summoning them to the truth, *al-ḥaqq*, and its realization and to the revival of the prophetic example, *Sunna*. He advised al-Ma'mūn to hear cases of injustices, *maẓālim*, which, it is said, al-Ma'mūn did.[17] When possible, he ordered a reduction of taxes in Khurāsān.[18] The support that al-Ma'mūn attracted in Khurāsān spread to other regions in the following years.[19]

There has been a tradition of attributing the conduct of al-Ma'mūn to his vizier al-Faḍl b. Sahl's influence. This line of argument is ultimately connected with nationalist historiography and personality cult in vogue in the nineteenth and early twentieth centuries. For instance, Gabrieli's two important surveys maintained that the civil war was a confrontation between the supporters of the Persianism of al-Ma'mūn and of the Arabism of al-Amīn and that the two viziers, al-Faḍl b. Sahl and al-Faḍl b. al-Rabīʿ, played central roles in influencing both brothers.[20] Al-Dūrī sees al-Amīn as the representative of the Hāshimī Arab faction and al-Ma'mūn as that of the Persian group, which included al-Faḍl b. Sahl, who promoted pro-Persian policy in form and content. In reaction to this policy, al-Dūrī argues, the ʿAlid and other revolts had a certain "Arab" character that resisted Persian influence.[21] ʿUmar also holds that the ʿAbbāsid court, which harbored rival tendencies, had political factions and personal fortune seekers who inflamed the conflict in the succession disagreement between al-Amīn and al-Ma'mūn. ʿUmar repeats the view that the resistance of the population of Baghdad to al-Ma'mūn reflected regional and national tensions and a reaction to al-Ma'mūn's Khurāsānī policy and to Faḍl b. Sahl's strategy.[22] Hodgson sees the succession agreement as a policy that was based on al-Rashīd's personal whim and executed in the absence of a social element that would prevent a dynastic quarrel and avert political dismemberment. Because there was no institutional and social body to devise a transition of power, the events leading up to the civil war were shaped by the personalities of al-Amīn and al-Ma'mūn, and of their close advisers. Hodgson believes that al-Amīn, who was open to manipulation by his mother and his vizier, violated the agreement and appointed his son as successor. Thus he deprived al-Ma'mūn, who was more likely to be independent, of his position and effectively paved the way for the civil war.[23]

In general modern scholarship concerning al-Ma'mūn's revolt against his brother places the agency with his vizier al-Faḍl b. Sahl, the Khurāsānī nobility, the disenfranchised families, and their regional privileges.[24] There is ample evidence in historiography to support this view, and it appears reasonable that al-Ma'mūn allied with the Khurāsānīs as they had a common interest in opposing Baghdad. Al-Ma'mūn was tutored by the Barmakid family and their successors, the foremost of whom was al-Faḍl b. Sahl. Recently converted to Islam (probably upon the encouragement of al-Ma'mūn himself), al-Faḍl b. Sahl occupied an influential position in al-Ma'mūn's court in Khurāsān until his assassination in 202/818. A number of sources, some plausibly dating back to the civil war era, suggest and even plainly state that al-Faḍl b. Sahl had a direct influence on al-Ma'mūn's actions. Many people had good reasons to depict him that way, especially if they were opposed to al-Faḍl b. Sahl.

Such an explanation, however, is not without its own problems: Making al-Ma'mūn an amenable proxy of al-Faḍl b. Sahl is one. Another problem relates to al-Faḍl b. Sahl's circumstances. In addition to being a recent convert, which likely placed some limitation on his influence on al-Ma'mūn, at least in matters related to the religio-political discourse al-Ma'mūn crafted for his movement, al-Faḍl b. Sahl was only an emerging administrative figure until the military victory against al-Amīn. Another important factor that would have dampened al-Faḍl b. Sahl's ambitions was the fall of the Barmakids. As a protégé of the

Barmakids, whose disastrous fate had been recently sealed, al-Faḍl b. Sahl had full knowledge of the wrath the caliphs could inflict on their advisers. He must have been well aware that he was playing with fire, and if the game did not go in the direction that the caliph wanted, he, and not the caliph, would have to answer for it.

It seems unlikely that al-Faḍl b. Sahl could take full responsibility for the decision to resist the caliph in Baghdad. He certainly was instrumental in planning the strategy of the movement and exceedingly helpful to al-Ma'mūn, but perhaps no more than that. As discussed in further detail later, the ideological dimension of al-Ma'mūn's movement became increasingly a reflection of al-Ma'mūn's views. Like any good adviser, al-Faḍl b. Sahl facilitated the means for their execution and implementation. His swift fall later without any noticeable reaction from anyone speaks volumes about this situation; the mastermind's fall should have created wide-ranging visible reverberations, if not in Baghdad then at least in Khurāsān, but this was not the case.

When al-Ma'mūn left Marw for Baghdad in Rajab 202 / January 818 to address the brewing chaos himself and to claim the capital, he had been made aware of the situation in Baghdad and of al-Faḍl b. Sahl's agenda in hiding the chaos in the capital from him by more than one high-ranking court member, including his heir apparent, ʿAlī b. Mūsā al-Riḍā. In the previous attempts to warn al-Ma'mūn, al-Faḍl b. Sahl had apparently won out in court conspiracies, causing Ṭāhir b. al-Ḥusayn to be demoted to a post in al-Raqqa and Harthama b. Aʿyan to be executed.[25] This time, it seems, al-Faḍl b. Sahl lost the contest. At Sarakhs, al-Faḍl b. Sahl was assassinated (Shaʿbān 202 / February 818).

Al-Ma'mūn was implicated in the death of al-Faḍl b. Sahl. The timing and location of his death were too fortuitous for al-Ma'mūn not to be a suspect, as many modern scholars argue. However, the ambiguity and tendentiousness of the sources justify the consideration of other scenarios not necessarily involving al-Ma'mūn. Al-Faḍl b. al-Sahl could have been eliminated because of court conspiracies among al-Ma'mūn's advisers and commanders who had their own reasons for wanting to do so, as Cooperson noted.[26] Al-Faḍl b. Sahl was very, perhaps too much, involved in palace politics, and there were others besides al-Ma'mūn who would have wanted to eliminate Ibn Sahl.

Ultimately the point whether al-Faḍl b. Sahl was too influential on al-Ma'mūn might be inconsequential, but the perspective of prophecies on this matter should be addressed. The fact that prophecies remain utterly silent about al-Faḍl b. Sahl raises questions about the impact of al-Faḍl b. Sahl on al-Ma'mūn. No hint about the role of al-Faḍl b. Sahl or the Khurāsānī nobility surfaces in prophecies. If anything, the prophecies point to al-Ma'mūn himself and to the movement collectively (for example, second black banners, the seventh of the ʿAbbāsids, people from Khurāsān). Even if we account for the metonymic nature of prophecies—that they might focus on the caliph as the symbol of the entire ʿAbbāsid structure regardless of background influences on him—that argument falls short because the identities of other administrators and military commanders are implied and even spelled out in various prophecies. Also the influence of al-Faḍl b. Sahl would have been an excellent point with which to attack al-Ma'mūn. Why would antagonistic transmitters not take advantage of this opportunity?

However, the opposite is the case. In one particular prophecy, al-Ma'mūn is directly found responsible for the civil war: "The seventh of the ʿAbbāsids will call people to unbelief, and they will not respond to him. His family will say to him, 'do you want to deprive us of our income.' He will say, 'I will act among you with the conduct of Abū Bakr and ʿUmar, may God be pleased with them.'"[27] On another occasion, a Khurāsānī poet depicts the confrontation as a struggle between the imam of justice and the people of Iraq and their ruler, placing the agency directly on al-Ma'mūn: "The imam of justice and rightly-guided king / has launched an attack against the people of Iraq and its ruler / the man who, of all who walk upon [the earth], is most resolute in judgment, prudence, / and in devising effective stratagems."[28] Again, the poem seems to date before the murder of al-Amīn, the "ruler" of Baghdad, but not before 194/810, because al-Ma'mūn had already been announced as imam.

As the fraternal disagreement between al-Ma'mūn and al-Amīn transformed into a religio-political rivalry, it took on messianic overtones, similar to how prophecies described it: fraternal disagreement and, depending on a person's point of view, either a *fitna* or a call for justice. How and why it evolved along the lines of a messianic confrontation are questions that shed some light on the contributions of al-Ma'mūn to this process. One of the landmarks of this process is al-Ma'mūn's use of the titles imam and *imām al-hudā*. Available coins prove that al-Ma'mūn began using the title *al-imām* as early as 194/810,[29] though he was not the first of the ʿAbbāsids to use it.[30] In 195/811 the title *al-imām* seems to have become more regular on coins, with the inclusion of the title commander of the faithful on some of them, until the coinage became anonymous from 206/821–22 onward.

As is known, the title imam had a rich religio-political history among a wide range of Muslim sects and political movements. It was primarily associated with legitimate religio-political leadership, divinely sanctioned authority, a call for justice, and legitimate resistance.[31] Al-Ma'mūn himself and his supporters used the term to indicate his rightful resistance against the ruling caliph al-Amīn and the divine support of al-Ma'mūn. It also connoted the notion of holiness and saintliness whereby the physical contact with the protagonist was seen as a source of healing and blessing. This is indicated in an anecdote in which a visitor to al-Ma'mūn was later asked to touch the head of an inquirer for a blessing with the hand that touched al-Ma'mūn.[32] Looking at the title from the perspective of prophecies, the semantics of imam include a divinely guided leader as well. Evidence of such usage in apocalyptic literature is plentiful, even if we exclude the Shīʿī use of it in that sense, which was no doubt known to all parties in the civil war. In the famous prophecy of Jesus's Second Coming as the expected Mahdī, he is called equitable judge and imam, *ḥakam wa imām muqsit*.[33]

Sources suggest that as early as late 194/810, al-Ma'mūn began using the title *al-imām*. A few months later, after hearing that al-Amīn had ordered his governors to drop his name from the Friday sermon, al-Ma'mūn began using an even more suggestive epithet, *imām al-hudā*, to refer to himself.[34] It seems that al-Ma'mūn cast the use of this title widely, as it emerged not only in the writings of his court officials but also in poetry. After al-Ma'mūn's general Ṭāhir defeated al-Amīn's commander in 195/811, one of the poets of Khurāsān addressed al-Ma'mūn as *imām al-hudā* in celebration of his victory: "The community has come to be in a state of happiness regarding its worldly affairs and religion: For it has kept the compact of the imam of right guidance, the best of Eve's sons, its trusted one (*ma'mūniha*)."[35]

The various uses of the title suggest that it connoted multiple meanings, including a messianic one. Of course *al-imām* and *imām al-hudā* are not synonyms. However al-Ma'mūn's use of the title in both forms suggests that not only was he aware of the layers of its meaning[36] but also, and perhaps more important, that he emphasized this particular messianic nuance of it.[37] This ideological armor gave al-Ma'mūn the necessary credentials for legitimate resistance and allowed him to dissociate himself from the ʿAbbāsids in Baghdad, which materialized in two symbolically significant policies: branding his movement the second summons, *al-daʿwa al-thāniya*, and appointing an ʿAlid as heir apparent.

Second Black Banners

The confrontation with his brother afforded al-Ma'mūn an opportunity to reconsider the ideological and political conventions of the ʿAbbāsids, and it also gave him an incentive to replace them. From the early stages of this confrontation, al-Ma'mūn seemed to understand that his resistance had to have an ideological dimension if it was going to mean anything beyond fraternal competition. By adopting a symbolically significant name, the second summons, for his bid for the caliphate, al-Ma'mūn made clear that his movement was genuine, new, and even beyond the initial ʿAbbāsid revolutionary ideology. His religio-political convictions, manifested rather boldly later in his reign, developed not along a conciliatory path, despite Sourdel's assertion, but were marked by a series of departures, aiming at an overhaul. Of course prophecies rarely discuss such issues in detail, but they do have a surprising clarity on agency.

A number of prophecies capture the divide between the ʿAbbāsids in Baghdad and al-Ma'mūn by using the second black banners, *al-rayāt al-sawdā' al-thāniya*, to describe al-Ma'mūn's supporters. As is known, "black banners" was a title of the 'Abbāsid revolutionary militia in Khurāsān in the middle of the eighth century. It continued to be associated with the 'Abbāsid dynasty in apocalyptic and political writing and in popular consciousness. When at the end of the second Islamic century a civil war among the black banners themselves broke out, many prophecies depicted it as a *fitna* of the 'Abbāsids. Yet numerous other prophecies talk about the first and second black banners as if they were distinct parties.[38] A substantial portion of these predictions credit the second black banners and the army of Khurāsān with the collapse of the first black banners, the 'Abbāsids. A prophecy of this sort spells out the fate of the 'Abbāsids clearly: "A black banner from the direction of Khurāsān will come forth and remain victorious until their ['Abbāsids'] destruction comes from Khurāsān where their first victory began."[39] The following prophecy has the second black banner go against the first one and defeat it:

> I have heard 'Amr b. Murra al-Jamālī, the companion of the prophet of God, say, "there will certainly come forth from Khurāsān a black banner until it ties its horses to these olive trees between Bayt Liḥya and Harasta." We said, "between these two olive trees?" He said, "olive trees will be planted around the two trees so that people of that banner arrive at it [this location] and tie their horses there." 'Abdallāh b. Ādam said, "I have narrated this tradition to 'Abd al-Raḥmān b. Salmān who said, 'the holders of the second black banner, who will come forth against the first black banner, will tie [their horses] to it [to its trees]. If they arrive at it [this location], a rebel from among this [people] will rise against them. He will not get hold of any member of the first black banner except in hiding. He will defeat them.'"[40]

The prophecy assumes, like many others, knowledge of geography and events. Bayt Liḥya and Harasta were villages near Damascus. The first black banner refers to the 'Abbāsids, while the second black banner identifies al-Ma'mūn's movement. The rebel who is neither from the first nor the second black banner is most probably Abū al-'Amayṭir al-Sufyānī, as geographical setting (near Damascus) and the time period revealed through the prediction suggest. Because the prophecy assumes the victory of the Sufyānī, it must date from 195–98/811–14 but before the Sufyānī was completely defeated. The main point here, however, is that the events of the civil war and the strategy of al-Ma'mūn during the conflict seem to have given the creators of such prophecies reason enough to see a political and an ideological break between the first and the second black banners and between al-Ma'mūn and the 'Abbāsids in Baghdad.

Similar to what al-Ma'mūn intended to do in adopting the title the second summons for his movement, the prophecies underline the fracture within the 'Abbāsid dynasty and the distinct nature of al-Ma'mūn's call. It is remarkable that prophecies mention the conflict without any background information, but they do offer clues to help the audience make inferences about the events and the identity of the actors. In the following prophecy, the transmitter notes the welfare and then the affliction of the people of Ḥimṣ under the ʿAbbāsids. The prophecy unequivocally distinguishes between the first and second black banners and attributes the doom of the former to the second black banners:

> Ibn Shawdhab said, "I was with al-Ḥasan when we mentioned Ḥimṣ. He said, 'They [the people of Ḥimṣ] are the most felicitous people under the first black [banners] and the most afflicted people under the second black banners.' We said, 'What are the second black banners, O Abū Saʿīd?' He said, 'Abū al-Ṭahawī[41] will rise from the east, accompanied by 80,000 men whose hearts are filled with faith as a pomegranate filled with seed. The doom of the first black banners will be at their hands.'"[42]

It would not be too surprising that prophecies correlate the rise of the second black banners with the Mahdī. If some of the prophecies warn of destruction and calamity, others suggest the dawn of a millennium at the end of turmoil. The following prophecy seems to function in that manner: "There will rise black banners of the ʿAbbāsid from the East. They will stay for as long as God wills. Then there will rise small black banners that will fight a man from the sons of Abū Sufyān and his supporters, from the direction of the East. They will submit in obedience to the Mahdī."[43] In this case the prophecy describes the circumstances of the civil war, the rise of the Sufyānī, and the second black banners (which are all historical) to justify its prediction that all will submit to the Mahdī. The identity of the Mahdī is anybody's guess; however, he is certainly expected to rise immediately after the conflict.

Historiographical sources portray the civil war as a dynastic quarrel. Of course they contrast Baghdad and Marw, al-Amīn and al-Ma'mūn, the Abnā' and the Khurāsānīs, but still continue to depict the conflict as ultimately a family feud and quarrel between two brothers. Some prophecies also depict the civil war as a *fitna* within the ʿAbbāsid family itself. However, the availability of the aforementioned prophecies justifies the suggestion that at least some people perceived the rivalry between the two brothers to be an encounter between two different and incompatible groups. Such prophecies endow a qualitative nuance to the meaning of the civil war and remind the listener in a direct tone of a deeper level of conflict, of competing visions and interests, of a correspondence between second black banners and the second summons of al-Ma'mūn, and of a split in the ʿAbbāsid political ideology and image precipitated by al-Ma'mūn's new call, the second summons.

Prophecies involving the second black banners might, therefore, allow the introduction of an additional layer to the meaning of the second summons. We know that al-Ma'mūn branded his uprising against his brother the second summons. In *Kitāb al-Sharṭ wa al-Hibā*, a letter composed on behalf of al-Ma'mūn and his then heir apparent, ʿAlī al-Riḍā for al-Faḍl b. Sahl, to acknowledge al-Faḍl's good deeds and his service to the caliph, al-Ma'mūn makes certain provisions for al-Faḍl to live comfortably should he retire from his service. In the course of praising al-Faḍl's assistance to him, al-Ma'mūn alludes to, and hence draws parallels between, his second summons and the first summons of the Prophet Muḥammad. Al-Ma'mūn praises al-Faḍl's assistance to him "in instituting religion and the *Sunna*, carrying out the second summons and favoring the first one, along with terminating polytheism, destroying idols, and eliminating the insolent" and for all other good deeds that are known to the provinces.[44] By likening his movement to that of the Prophet in a number of points (instituting religion and *Sunna*, terminating polytheism, destroying idols), al-Ma'mūn blurs the line between Muḥammad's mission, the ʿAbbāsid revolutionary movement, and his second summons.

Similarly in the *Risālat al-Khamīs*, a caliphal address to the Khurāsānīs, al-Ma'mūn explains how his movement fits into the Prophetic model. Like the Prophet Muḥammad himself, al-Ma'mūn delegated the responsibility of executing the mission to twelve deputies and seventy missionaries.[45] Furthermore al-Ma'mūn asserted that God has planted love and affection among the supporters of the caliph, as God did for the companions of the Prophet Muḥammad. By outlining a strategy that was divided into three stages—initial summons, action to realize the mission, and entrusting the mission to those who are entitled to it—al-Ma'mūn mimicked a strategy followed by Muḥammad.[46]

Even though this epistle shows respect to the supporters of the ʿAbbāsid revolutionary movement, al-Ma'mūn does not see his movement as a replica or an imitation of it. The letter implies that his summons actually surpasses the first summons in a number of ways, which makes his movement unique and authentic. In his address to the people of Khurāsān, al-Ma'mūn explains the uniqueness and wide appeal of his movement among the virtuous of the Muslims, who did not have a share in the first *daʿwa*, as a result of God's favor of giving them the opportunity to support it. "So the disciples (*duʿāt*) of the commander of the faithful are composed of people from Mecca and Medina (Ḥaramayn), and al-Baṣra and al-Kūfa (Miṣrayn), the City of Peace (Baghdad), the East and the West."[47] According to al-Ma'mūn, the supporters of the second summons have three qualities that, by the exclusive grace of God, distinguish them from others. First, from the time of their ancestors, they have a distinguished lineage of supporting the house of the Prophet and those who defended his heritage among the ancestors of the caliph; second, they are privileged with supporting God's second summons; and third, they are given clear conscience and the gift of pure counsel. As is plain, all three qualities derive from the association of al-Ma'mūn's supporters with the second summons.[48]

This evidence allows us to modify Arazi and Elad's argument that al-Ma'mūn's second summons was a reenactment of the ʿAbbāsid revolutionary movement a century earlier and aimed to restore its original ideological and political principles.[49] It is quite possible that the caliph might have sought to lead a new movement that was inspired by the initial prophetic message to correct the shortcomings of the initial 'Abbāsid *da'wa* and the caliphate. He introduced this dimension not as a total replacement of the 'Abbāsid *da'wa*, but as an additional element, intended to revise the first one and reinforce the uniqueness of his call. As an heir to Muḥammad, both in lineage and in spirit (as he claimed), the caliph could liken his resistance to the ideological legacy of the previous two foundational missions to bridge the gap between the past and the future, falling into a pattern discernible in many messianic movements across cultures.

Hāshimid versus 'Abbāsid Succession: Designation of 'Alī al-Riḍā

In the succession arrangement of 201/817, the disjuncture between the al-Ma'mūn and the 'Abbāsids in Baghdad came into a sharp focus. Al-Ma'mūn proclaimed the Shī'ī imam 'Alī b. Mūsā al-Kāẓim as his successor on 2 Ramaḍān 201/24 March 817 with the title of *al-riḍā min āl Muḥammad*. At the same time, he also announced his decision to abandon the black regnal color of the 'Abbāsids in favor of green. Al-Ma'mūn's decision to appoint an 'Alid came as a shock to the 'Abbāsid family and plunged the capital into ever deeper chaos. The 'Abbāsids and their supporters, reacting against al-Ma'mūn's decision, offered the pledge of allegiance for the caliphate to al-Manṣūr b. al-Mahdī, and when he refused, they convinced his half-brother, Ibrāhīm b. al-Mahdī, to accept the title (Dhū al-Ḥijja 201 / July 817).[50] It seems that Ibrāhīm b. al-Mahdī took his job seriously enough to act against the political chaos in the city and to extend his authority in Baghdad, then al-Kūfa, from which the 'Alid governor al-'Abbās, brother of 'Alī al-Riḍā, was expelled (Jumādā I 202 / November 817). His authority could do little to help alleviate the chaos in the city, and Baghdad remained volatile until the arrival of al-Ma'mūn in 204/819.

As a matter of historical development, the policy came to a premature end when al-Riḍā died unexpectedly, in very complicated circumstances historically and historiographically, probably through no fault of al-Ma'mūn. As Cooperson convincingly argues, the suspects behind 'Alī al-Riḍā's death quite possibly were the Khurāsānī *abnā'*. The elimination of al-Riḍā would work well for them and their plans of reestablishing a connection with their counterparts in Baghdad.[51] If they killed al-Riḍā, they did it very skillfully. Historiography is, as usual, full of contradictions,[52] and the available non-Shī'ī prophecies are ambivalent about 'Alī al-Riḍā's death.[53]

Appointing an 'Alid successor was a radical break with the 'Abbāsid tradition. A unique practice with such immediate consequences has caused much disagreement among modern scholars trying to understand the reasons for 'Alī al-Riḍā's appointment. On a practical level, the way al-Ma'mūn gained the caliphate and the resulting animosity between al-Ma'mūn and the 'Abbāsids in Baghdad left little incentive for him to remain loyal to the 'Abbāsid family. After his victory over the 'Abbāsids, al-Ma'mūn became not only free and entitled as the winner of the war to appoint someone he personally chose but also perhaps obliged to do so.[54] Nonetheless why did he use his prerogative in this direction? And why only once? Explanations include 'Alid sympathies (Gabrieli), al-Faḍl b. Sahl's and Khurāsānī influence on the caliph (al-Dūrī), a reconciliation of the Shī'ī and nascent Sunnī branches of Islam by a Mu'tazilī-Zaydī-leaning caliph (Sourdel, 'Umar, Hodgson), the establishment of the caliphate as guidance (Nagel), an apocalyptic resolve to relegate the caliphate to the 'Alids out of a belief that the 'Abbāsid caliphate would soon be destroyed (Madelung),[55] a pragmatic reading of political circumstances to manipulate apocalyptic beliefs and 'Alid sympathies (Crone, Tor), an umbrella policy to eliminate the root cause of the animosity between the 'Alids and the 'Abbāsids by returning to the objectives of the original Hāshimite *da'wa* (Arazi-Elad), and a Shī'ī view of the caliphate/imamate to act by divine guidance (Bayhom-Daou).[56]

While the exact reasons why al-Ma'mūn appointed an 'Alid to be his heir apparent are still puzzling, the appointment was made within the context of several interrelated developments. Given that the new type of legitimacy that al-Ma'mūn gained from his victory against the 'Abbāsids in Baghdad and that his proclaimed second summons necessitated the promise of change, the appointment came to be seen as a follow-through on this promise. In the same period, the increased 'Alid uprisings—some openly messianic—in Iraq, Ḥijāz, and Yemen perhaps prompted an early execution of the decision. Finally the *afḍaliyya* (identifying the most excellent candidate for the caliphate) debate that was popular at the time must have informed the formulation and articulation of the decision.

Since the publication of Madelung's "New Documents Concerning al-Faḍl b. Sahl and 'Alī al-Riḍā," scholars have been debating whether al-Ma'mūn's appointment had any relationship to the end-of-time scenarios.[57] To support his argument, Madelung introduces a letter from al-Ma'mūn to the 'Abbāsids in Baghdad. The text is found in Ibn Ṭāwūs's (d. 664/1266) *Kitāb al-Ṭarā'if fī Ma'rifat al-Ṭawā'if* and in al-Majlisī's (d. 1111/1699) *Biḥār al-Anwār*. In the relevant section of the letter, al-Ma'mūn is claimed to have said that he was informed by his father, al-Rashīd, on the authority of his ancestors and of what he found in the Book of the Reign, *Kitāb al-Dawla*,[58] and elsewhere that 'Abbāsid authority would not remain standing. After his death, the 'Abbāsids would be destroyed by the Ḥasanī and the Sufyānī.[59] Partly because of the anti-'Abbāsid apocalyptic traditions, Madelung suggests that al-Ma'mūn believed that the 'Abbāsid caliphate approached its end in the context of an imminent age of apocalyptic turbulence and the coming of the Mahdī. Even in his last days, Madelung argues, al-Ma'mūn did not seem to have much faith in the future of the caliphate. He therefore designated ʿAlī al-Riḍā and, later, al-Muʿtaṣim as his successors, who would have been unlikely choices under normal circumstances, instead of the better-suited al-ʿAbbās, al-Maʾmūn's own son.[60]

There are serious problems with the text in question. As Bayhom-Daou also points out, that passage is a later insertion into the letter by someone other than al-Maʾmūn. However, there is no reason why the insertion could not be contemporaneous to the incident.[61] On the most basic level, there is little incentive for forging a prophecy of this sort after its deadline has already passed. Also the prophecy cited in the letter corresponds to numerous prophecies of similar bent circulating in the early ninth century, some of which have already been examined here. Finally it is certainly not a unique prophecy and is corroborated by another account in *Ithbāt al-Waṣiyya*, which discusses the end of the ʿAbbāsids and the appointment of ʿAlī al-Riḍā. The prophecy has al-Maʾmūn urge ʿAlī al-Riḍā to accept his nomination as heir apparent because the ʿAbbāsid rule will not remain for more than twenty men after the appearance of the Sufyānī.[62] Why the prophecy prefers to begin the list of "men" with the Umayyads is not clear; however, there is no reason to think that the prophecy dates after the death of ʿAlī al-Riḍā. In fact another prophecy hopes that ʿAlī al-Riḍā will become the caliph because he has been appointed the heir apparent of al-Maʾmūn: "From Ayyūb b. Nūḥ, I said to Abū al-Ḥasan al-Riḍā, 'I hope that you are the holder of this affair [caliphate] and that God gives it to you without [a need for] the sword. The allegiance was pledged to you and dirhams were minted in your name.'"[63] Since prophecies predicting an ʿAlid caliph/imam and the destruction of the ʿAbbāsids were quite widespread at the time, it is possible that the addition had been circulating before the account reached Ibn Ṭāwūs.

Although the passage alone cannot justify an argument for the impact of apocalyptic beliefs on al-Maʾmūn in this particular incident, the absence of explicit apocalyptic statements in the letter should not be taken as evidence to rule out their impact, but for reasons that differ from those offered by Madelung. There remains the question of why al-Maʾmūn would bother to implement changes if he believed the end was fast approaching. The question is a valid one, but has its own limitations. As said before, this view presupposes messianic or apocalyptic beliefs to be prima facie limited to either inaction or a destructive course of action, which seems to be Madelung's assumption as well. However, this is not the case. Making an effort to establish a righteous community has been a major aspect of apocalyptic beliefs and a motivation for social and political action. More important, apocalyptic beliefs do not always entail the notion of the end of the world. They can also advocate the closure of an era and the opening of a new one (millennium).[64] Contextual evidence examined so far sufficiently proves that such messianic and apocalyptic beliefs were widely circulating at the turn of the third Islamic century.

Considering the circumstances, it seems too early for the caliph to designate his successor in such a rushed manner, especially given his subsequent long silence about the issue until his death. This leads to the question of whether al-Ma'mūn intended more to define a vision for the caliphate rather than simply to appoint an heir apparent. If setting an example and defining a vision were considerations, the decision aligned well with his broader aspirations in his second summons and certainly with his claims to transform the 'Abbāsid caliphate. At the turn of the third Islamic century, al-Ma'mūn emerged both victorious and vindicated in his war against his brother. God, not the succession provisions of his father, had settled the dispute between the two. In the year 198/814, after the defeat of al-Amīn, the coinage began to display a Qur'ānic verse on the dirhams; no doubt the inclusion of the verse was intended to frame al-Ma'mūn's victory within God's assistance and mandate to rule.[65] For his supporters, this policy was concrete evidence of his aspirations and his will to follow through on his promises.

Ideologically, al-Ma'mūn opposed the 'Abbāsid succession conventions as unjustifiably narrow and wanted to replace them with a more equitable and inclusive policy.[66] As his defense of 'Alī al-Riḍā's appointment indicates, he did not oppose an 'Abbāsid heir apparent in favor of an 'Alid but simply wanted the door of succession left open for candidates from both houses. He considered both the 'Alid and 'Abbāsid families as the house of the Prophet, hence equally qualified for the office. If we trust al-Qalqashandī, 'Alī al-Riḍā acknowledged this point in the letter of acceptance of his nomination. He noted that al-Ma'mūn recognized the right of the 'Alids, established bridges with his relatives, and brought peace and security to souls who hitherto had lived in fear.[67] In his harsh letter to the 'Abbāsids, al-Ma'mūn also emphasized this point. He spoke of the injustices that the 'Abbāsids had inflicted upon the 'Alids and reminded them that both the 'Alids and the 'Abbāsids had been a single party until God decreed power for the 'Abbāsids. He continued, "then we frightened them, harassed them, and killed them more (ruthlessly) than the Banū Umayya had killed them. Woe to you, for the Banū Umayya killed of them only he who drew a sword; but we, the kindred of Banū al-'Abbās, killed them all."[68]

Al-Ma'mūn's comparison of the 'Abbāsids to bygone nations in the Qur'ān shows how al-Ma'mūn perceived his own appointment of 'Alī al-Riḍā and hence how he and the 'Abbāsids should be seen: "In your hands is the Book of God, the Exalted, and the traditions and everything brought to you by the truthful one, Muḥammad, may God bless him. Yet you act as if you belonged to the bygone nations which perished through being swallowed by the earth, through drowning, storm, the cry, and thunderbolt and stoning."[69] Al-Ma'mūn further likened the 'Abbāsids, who accused him of making the views and dreams of their ancestors look foolish, to the Meccan polytheists by citing the Qur'ānic verse, "we observed our fathers upon a community and we are following on their traces."[70]

Several of al-Ma'mūn's other comments spoke of the decadence of the 'Abbāsids and of the ideological principles that had run their course. He argued that he appointed 'Alī al-Riḍā in order to protect the 'Abbāsids and perpetuate the love between them and their cousins. He appeared utterly disappointed with the 'Abbāsids as he accused them of not thinking of mending their way of life, of not seeking to prolong God's favor, of not doing a noble act, and of not achieving a good deed for their records in the hereafter. By designating an 'Alid successor, al-Ma'mūn argued, he in fact put into practice a long-standing promise of his ancestors from the time of the 'Abbāsid revolution to choose "the one agreed upon from the family of the prophet."[71]

As Crone observes in her discussion of the concept of al-Riḍā, this sobriquet referred to a political candidate who is agreed upon, who is selected, and who is the choice of communal agreement among the group in question, the family of Muḥammad or the tribe Quraysh. Al-Ma'mūn's use of this concept, given the debate it generated, emphasized the meritocratic dimension of the term within a Hāshimite context that succession should not follow automatically within any particular Hāshimite house and that qualification should be based on personal merit rather than on exclusive 'Abbāsid or 'Alid lineage.[72] This was not a simple sentimental sympathy for the 'Alids, or an admission that the 'Alids were closer in kinship to the Prophet than were the 'Abbāsids. In selecting a successor among the Hāshimites, al-Ma'mūn hoped to set a precedent that the most qualified and most deserving candidate from among the Hāshimites, not necessarily the closest in kin to the 'Abbāsids or to 'Alī/Fāṭima, should be eligible for inclusion in the line of succession.

The substance of al-Ma'mūn's position is revealed in a report depicting al-Ma'mūn debating 'Alī al-Riḍā on the relative proximity of the 'Alids and the 'Abbāsids to the Prophet Muḥammad. In it al-Ma'mūn not only openly refutes the claim that the 'Alids were closer to the Prophet than the 'Abbāsids and maintains the eligibility of both houses, but he also launches a definite criticism of the Shī'īs by emphasizing that eligibility for the imamate requires more than proximity, *qarāba*, to the Prophet.[73] With the appointment of 'Alī al-Riḍā, al-Ma'mūn attempted to reshape the image of al-Riḍā outside the Shī'ī context of exclusive right to the leadership. Far from recognizing al-Riḍā as a divinely inspired imam, on the coins announcing 'Alī al-Riḍā's appointment al-Ma'mūn styled himself God's caliph and imam, but 'Alī al-Riḍā as simply amīr.[74] Nowhere is al-Ma'mūn seen questioning his own entitlement to the caliphate, despite the acknowledgment of the right of the 'Alids.

If defining a vision were a consideration in the designation, it would also tally well with the current, intense debate on the excellence of the companions of the Prophet Muḥammad. Available textual sources refer to the action of al-Ma'mūn within this context.[75] It might be relevant to remember that since the Umayyad times, the *afḍaliyya* debate was very much current among various religio-sectarian groups,[76] largely because it involved stating one's position on the ordering of the patriarchal caliphs in terms of merit.[77] Because this debate focused on the patriarchal caliphs, whose image was of enormous consequence for the emerging sectarian movements, it encouraged claims to a similar religious and political authority among later caliphs. Therefore the invocation of the *afḍaliyya* was an appropriate discourse if the caliph wanted to frame his appointment of a successor within the authority attributed to the "rightly guided caliphs."

Zaydīs are commonly known to have defended the idea that the caliph be the most excellent, *afḍal*. However, in the early third Islamic century this position was far from an exclusive Zaydī doctrine. It seems that the radical positions taken by Imāmī Shī'īs and Khārijī groups early on drove the mainstream Mu'tazilīs, Zaydīs, legal scholars, and *ḥadīth*-transmitters to close ranks in many respects. It was not until the fourth/tenth century that the ranking of the first four caliphs according to their merit was settled among the mainstream Sunni-Jamā'ī community, even though some *ḥadīth* and legal scholars seem to have ranked the caliphs in merit according to their succession to the caliphate as early as the late Umayyad times.[78] The debate eventually encompassed not only the legitimacy of the first four caliphs and the merits of individual companions of the Prophet but also the qualifications of a legitimate caliph. Thus among the proto-Sunnīs, the Mu'tazilīs, and the Zaydīs were those who preferred the imamate with the most excellent qualifications but were satisfied with a person inferior in merit as an imam. There were also groups, certainly including the proto-Sunnīs, who maintained that only the most meritorious could be the imam. The fact that al-Jāḥiẓ wrote his famous work *al-'Uthmāniyya* in response to the Shī'īs and the preference they gave to 'Alī over Abū Bakr and its refutation by al-Iskāfī, which has not survived except in fragments in *Sharḥ Nahj al-Balāgha*, shows that the debate on this particular subject was passionate at the time.[79] Whatever the motive in 'Alī al-Riḍā's appointment, merely proposing and debating it in this context show al-Ma'mūn's engagement with the intellectual and ideological currents of his milieu.

It must be remembered that the appointment of 'Alī al-Riḍā unfolded at the dawn of the year 200 A.H. The manifestation of divine will in the civil war verified the caliph's political and spiritual legitimacy and entitled the caliph to step outside conventions. This, in turn, allowed him to initiate radical changes to many aspects of governance, including succession appointment. If his policy still seems erratic to modern scholars, it is because it belonged to the context of the revolutionary charisma during the civil war and it reflected all the elements of the unsettled nature of this period.

CHAPTER 5

Al-Ma'mūn in Baghdad

With the entry of al-Ma'mūn into Baghdad, hopeful expectations seem to have gained momentum. Similar to the coronation of Charlemagne on Christmas Eve of 799, al-Ma'mūn's entry into Baghdad at the turn of the century must have had exceptional meaning—for al-Ma'mūn's arrival was not a simple political victory, but a return to a home once hostile to him. By its sheer resemblance to the Prophet Muḥammad's return to Mecca, or his arrival in Medina, al-Ma'mūn's return invoked a symbolism that lifted a mundane military victory into a cosmic drama unfolding in front of its observers. Shortly before al-Ma'mūn entered Baghdad, the city experienced a solar eclipse on Sunday, 28 Dhū al-Ḥijja 203/26 June 819,[1] further heightening the anxiety related to al-Ma'mūn's arrival. On the date of his arrival, the Hāshimites and the citizens of Baghdad already had gathered in advance in the outskirts of al-Nahrawān east of Baghdad to welcome the caliph when he made his appearance.[2]

Healing the Wounds of a Civil War

This moment of great victory stood for no less than the awaited millennium as recorded in one of Nu'aym b. Ḥammād's impressive accounts: "On the authority of Rishdīn from Ibn Lahī'a[3] from Abū Qabīl,[4] who said, 'The people will rally around the Mahdī in the year two hundred and four.'"[5] In the course of ten years of conflict and against all odds, al-Ma'mūn defended his claim to the caliphate, defeated his enemies, and now returned to Baghdad victorious. It was perhaps the expectation of peace and a return to normal life at the beginning of the third Islamic century that Ibn A'tham, al-Dīnawarī, and al-Ṭabarī echoed—they all associated the arrival of al-Ma'mūn into Baghdad with the cessation of civil strife, *fitan*.[6] The progeny of the Medinese companions of the Prophet Muḥammad, *al-Anṣār*, found no better way to describe their feeling than to compare al-Ma'mūn's entry into Baghdad with the Prophet's descent on Medina: "Praise to God who has strengthened the truth by you and returned you victorious to your home, answering our prayers for you. You are like what our cousin Ḥassān b. Thābit said regarding your cousin the Prophet of God, peace be upon him, the day he entered al-Madina: . . . 'By the grace of God when you joined us / with your light we cleared the darkness of misguidance. / You are a blessing which came down to us / on the most felicitous bird and in a good state.'"[7]

The 'Alids were no less enthusiastic about the arrival of a ruler whose deeds had elevated him in the popular imagination to saintly status, radiating justice and spiritual fulfillment. One of the 'Alids welcomed the caliph with the following words: "May God make your arrival, O commander of the faithful, a key of compassion for you and for your subjects to whom you have come. The regions became luminous when you descended on them. And because of you, God privileged their inhabitants with intimacy [with each other]; and the subjects fixed their eyes upon you, and raised their hands to God for you and through you. Thus, from your arrival they obtain justice to rejuvenate them, and from the favor of your hand [they attain] grace to satisfy them."[8]

An eyewitness report of al-Ma'mūn's entry into Baghdad by Aḥmad b. Yaḥyā, known as Abū al-'Abbās al-Tha'lab, the celebrated grammarian, expressed the arresting power of the moment: "Abū al-'Abbās Aḥmad b. Yaḥyā said, 'I saw al-Ma'mūn when he arrived from Khurāsān. That was in the year 204 [819]. He had just exited from the Gate of Iron heading al-Rusāfa Palace, and people were lined up in two rows as far as the mosque. My father was carrying me in his arms, and when al-Ma'mūn came by, he lifted me up and said, "This is al-Ma'mūn and this is the year four [and 200 A.H.]." I still remember him telling me that. I was four years old at the time.'"[9]

Of course al-Ma'mūn knew the political and religious implications of his triumphal return to Baghdad. Similar to the Prophet Muḥammad's benevolent manner toward the inhabitants of Mecca when he triumphed over the city, al-Ma'mūn lived up to his image in the popular imagination. On his way to Baghdad, al-Ma'mūn talked with his companion and chief secretary, Aḥmad b. Abī Khālid al-Aḥwal, a Syrian who had been one of his close associates since his days in Khurāsān.[10] The caliph articulated his views concerning the inhabitants of Baghdad and his intended course of action. Al-Ma'mūn divided the inhabitants of Baghdad into three categories: the oppressors, the oppressed, and those who fell into neither category. Al-Ma'mūn remarked that the oppressor could expect only to be forgiven and to escape punishment; the oppressed, on the other hand, could expect only justice; as for someone who was neither an oppressor nor oppressed, he said that his house was large enough for him.[11]

It seems that al-Ma'mūn, as Ibn al-Ṭiqṭaqā notices, proceeded with determination to bring about the promises of his summons during the civil war.[12] Any step in policy change would have implications for al-Ma'mūn's popular support and image as a ruler; but his reign had to involve change and confrontation. As his conciliatory measures show, al-Ma'mūn considered, but did not oblige himself to continue or reproduce, a tradition against which he reacted. Indeed both as a gesture of goodwill and out of political necessity, al-Ma'mūn restored black as the royal color and pardoned a significant number of his active opponents during and after the civil war. Among others these included al-Faḍl b. al-Rabī', who received a position at the court; the anticaliph Ibrāhīm b. al-Mahdī; the governor of Egypt, 'Ubaydallāh b. al-Sariyy; and the rebel Naṣr b. Shabath.[13] But at the same time, he replaced many administrators, including the members of the 'Abbāsid family and *al-abnā'*, with some of his followers who acquired seniority during the second summons, and his associates, mostly of Khurāsānī origins, during the civil war.[14] He reorganized the army and put in place security measures for Baghdad to neutralize the disorder that he inherited from the civil war.

From the time of the civil war, al-Ma'mūn based his movement on the call for justice. Within a medieval context, the ruler gained his reputation and glory from acting fairly, protecting subjects, and delivering justice as much as from successful conquests. If the promise of justice was to be achieved, according to al-Baghdādī, who cites al-Ma'mūn, the implementation of principles had to begin with the ruler personally and with his close circle of associates, spreading out gradually until it reached the lowest class of society.[15] In this view, there is a noteworthy amalgam of Islamo-Persian traditions. Placing the ruler in the center of social structure and imagining the classes of society as concentric circles echoed the Sasanian political culture. At the same time, parallels were evident between al-Ma'mūn's notion of implementing justice and the Prophet Muḥammad's dictum that one should begin with the closest.[16] Ibn Qutayba remarks that al-Ma'mūn displayed good conduct, inquired about the welfare of his subjects, and presided over court hearings after his return to Baghdad.[17]

Undoubtedly al-Ma'mūn had a charismatic personality and attracted admirers, sympathizers, and enemies down to modern times. Modern scholarship tends to attribute the magnified image of al-Ma'mūn to historians' partisanship rather than emanating from his time. To some extent, this is justified. However, the evidence from apocalyptic literature strongly suggests that the image of the caliph as a divinely sanctioned figure was also contemporaneous to the caliph. His intentions and policies were propagated effectively through a circle of admirers around him, who actually seemed to have been convinced of their patron's spiritual qualities. Marwān b. Abī al-Janūb, in his praise of al-Mamūn's judge Aḥmad b. Abī Du'ād, referred to al-Ma'mūn as the Mahdī showing the way to righteous deeds.[18] Al-Ma'mūn's secretary, Aḥmad b. Yūsuf, in his address to al-Ma'mūn on behalf of al-Ḥasan b. Sahl, ascribed to the caliph titles clearly intended to draw attention to his spiritual qualities and the divine support for him. He praised al-Ma'mūn as the rightly guiding one (*al-hādī*), the pious one (*al-taqī*), the chaste one (*al-ṭāhir*), the pure one (*al-zakī*), abundant rain (*ghiyāth*), the trusted imam (*al-imām al-ma'mūn*), and as the one who follows the prophets and the rightly guided caliphs.[19] The exaggerated praise notwithstanding, choosing these qualities but not others makes it a valuable source for gauging the nature of al-Ma'mūn's image among his associates. This praise reflected more than an imaginative conjuncture of the historians who had a romantic view of the caliph. His image emerged since his days in Khurāsān and continued through his reign.

An 'Alid prophecy referring to the caliph's title, al-Ma'mūn, shows that the caliph won the sympathy of the 'Alids and that, perhaps more important, the title itself had acquired messianic qualities. In this curious account, the Prophet Muḥammad is depicted as saying to 'Alī that there would be twelve imams after him and that 'Alī was the first of those imams. He then continues, "God has named you in the heavens 'Alī and the chosen one, *al-Murtaḍa*, and the commander of the faithful, *amīr al-mu'minīn*, and the Great Endorser, *Ṣiddīq al-Akbar*, and the Great Distinguisher, *al-Fārūq al-A'ẓam*, and *al-Ma'mūn*, and *al-Mahdī*. And these names are not appropriate for anyone but you."[20] There is no doubt that *Ṣiddīq* and *Fārūq* are references to Abū Bakr and 'Umar, respectively, just as *al-Ma'mūn* refers to 'Abdallāh b. Hārūn. The fact that the tradition mentions no other name after al-Ma'mūn, except al-Mahdī, which is not historical, indicates that the report originated in al-Ma'mūn's lifetime, or possibly shortly thereafter. It seems, therefore, that the context in which this prediction circulated must have made this appellation a highly desirable epithet to describe the qualities of the fourth caliph, 'Alī.

There is another peculiar reason why al-Ma'mūn became the subject of messianic speculation: he was the seventh of the 'Abbāsid caliphs. Prophecies and poetry refer to al-Ma'mūn on numerous occasions as the seventh imam or seventh caliph.[21] On the occasion of al-Ma'mūn's pardon of his uncle Ibrāhīm b. al-Mahdī, the former anticaliph, a poet praised his patron in the following lines: "The one who allotted noble characteristics [*-khilāfata*][22] gathered them all up / in the loins of Adam for the seventh imam. / The one who controls people's affairs has gathered together hearts around you / and your cloak has gathered together all goodness which brings [men] together."[23] As noted earlier, the number seven was used since ancient times to explain cosmological theories, astrology, the order of the universe, the days of the creation, the cycle of spiritual and physical phenomena, the notion of time, and the duration of the world.[24] Qur'ānic verses and an abundant amount of material in *ḥadīth* lore prove that early Muslims were equally fascinated with this enigmatic number.[25] By the early ninth century, the number seven had become, as in Christian and Jewish traditions, a symbol of perfection, fullness, completion, and order. Also of importance was the ongoing debate among the Shī'ī Imāmīs of who succeeded the sixth imam, Ja'far al-Ṣādiq, who died in 765. The emergence of the party that later would be called the Seveners (the Ismā'īlīs) claimed that Ja'far al-Ṣādiq's son Ismā'īl, who died before his father, was the seventh imam. Given the significance of the debate for the Imāmīs, many prophecies on the identity and the return of the imam circulated among both the Seveners and other Shī'ī groups, spreading the popularity of the number seven. It seems likely that those who used the number seven to refer to al-Ma'mūn were aware of the symbolism of this number in terms of its larger and more specific connotations.

It is possible that the dynamism of the caliph after his return to Baghdad inspired an observer to circulate the following prophecy: "The seventh of the 'Abbāsids will call people to justice, but they will not follow him in that. He will say, 'I will act among you with the conduct of Abū Bakr and 'Umar, may God be pleased with them, and distribute the revenues equally.' His family will say to him, 'do you want to deprive us of our income?' And they will reject him."[26] Popular pious imagination devotes a great deal of attention even today to the example of these two patriarchs as symbols of the Golden Age, and medieval sources frequently used their images, explicitly or implicitly, as a measure to judge the actions of the subsequent caliphs and their administrators. Similarly a contemporary poet praises policies of the caliph as the materialization of justice: "He does not exact for himself anything above the official rate of taxation / so that the wolf and the ewe can remain under one roof / and the thief and the merchant can lie down together under one coverlet."[27] Although such poetry has to be considered within the tradition of court panegyric and cannot be taken at face value, it nevertheless reflects the popular sentiments of its age.[28]

Against this background, al-Ma'mūn initiated and executed his policies to realize his promises during the civil war. As El-Hibri rightly points out, al-Ma'mūn's reform initiatives in coinage, tax policy, and measures of capacity and weight were part of a series of more general economic and agrarian reforms that were aimed at bringing a degree of stability to social and economic life.[29] The civil war had destroyed considerable farmland and impoverished many peasants. The central treasury also had suffered great losses because of the constant military activity, despite an apparent jump in the revenues of the Iraqi *Sawād* in 204/819.[30] Aware of these problems, al-Ma'mūn initiated a significant tax reform immediately after he arrived in Baghdad to ease the financial burden on the peasants who had suffered losses during the civil war. In the course of his journey from Ṭūs to Baghdad in the year 203/819, al-Ma'mūn made his intentions clear by lowering the tax assessment of Rayy by two million dirhams.[31] This was a public demonstration, on a practical level, that his reign would be one of justice.

In his narrative of the year 204/820, al-Ṭabarī mentions the reduction of the tax burden and an accompanying adjustment to the official measure of capacity in Iraq. The caliph ordered the proportional tax (*muqāsama*) levied on the produce of cultivation in the *Sawād* be reduced from 50 to 40 percent. These steps were, however, more than a gesture of goodwill. They formed part of his efforts to reform the fiscal policies of the caliphate to generate revenues without creating discontent in the provinces. Thus it appears that al-Ma'mūn allowed the Ṭāhirid governors in Khurāsān to spend their revenues internally, in addition to the annual gift of thirteen million dirhams sent from Baghdad.[32]

A similar conciliatory step came in the reform of the measure of capacity. After al-Ma'mūn arrived in Baghdad, he inquired about the condition of the people and was informed that some merchants cheated buyers by using inconsistent measures. In response to this news, al-Ma'mūn ordered that a *qafīz* composed of eight *makkūks*[33] would be the standard measure and called it the bridled, *al-muljam*.[34] He then ordered the merchants to adjust their scales accordingly, which apparently they did.[35] His adoption of the "bridled" *qafīz* (*al-qafīz al-muljam*), made up of eight Hārūnī *makkūks*,[36] as the officially authorized measure of capacity makes it clear that he wanted standard units of calculation and measure for taxation and trade.[37]

Al-Ma'mūn's bold initiatives and new policies continued with groundbreaking reforms in currency. The addition of a verse on the coinage beginning in 198/814 foreshadowed the further changes to come. Al-Ma'mūn's new coins, distinguished by the new style of inscription on the gold dīnār (which shifted from angular Kūfic to curvilinear Kūfic) and by their remarkable fineness,[38] began circulating in 205/821 and came into general use by 215/831. Another change to the currency began in 206/822. It had been customary for the 'Abbāsid caliphs, beginning with al-Mahdī and his governors, to inscribe their names on coins. But beginning in 206/822, al-Ma'mūn began experimenting with minting anonymous coins that had no names in their legends.[39] This constituted a major change in coinage unprecedented since the pioneering reforms of the Umayyad 'Abd al-Malik, and it established the norm for the following centuries until the demise of the 'Abbāsid caliphate in the middle of the seventh/thirteenth century.[40]

In order to implement and sustain his ambitious projects, al-Ma'mūn had to unify his realm. Therefore he needed to bring the provinces back into the fold of the central authority. Thus he addressed the uprisings and contention in Iraq, Egypt, northern Syria, al-Ḥijāz, Ushrusānā, and Ṭabaristān and through military and diplomatic means reinstated the caliphal authority in these regions.[41] In 205/820 a number of incidents occurred in the marshlands of lower Iraq, where the Zuṭṭ intermittently disrupted the routes of communication until 219/834. 'Abdallāh b. Ṭāhir suppressed the revolt of Naṣr b. Shabath in al-Jazīra, who surrendered to Ṭāhir in 210/825. In Yemen, a new 'Alid revolt by 'Abd al-Raḥmān b. Aḥmad broke out in 207/822, but it was contained with his surrender. And uprisings by the citizens of Qum, dissatisfied with the caliph's refusal to reduce their land taxes, *Kharāj*, were suppressed in 210/825 and again in 216/831.[42]

In Āzarbayjān, al-Ma'mūn combated the religio-political movement of Bābāk al-Khurramī,[43] which began in the last two years of Hārūn al-Rashīd's reign[44] and remained a constant problem for al-Ma'mūn from his time in Khurāsān until his death on the Byzantine frontier.[45] Already in 201/817, Bābāk gathered supporters from the Jāwidāniyya movement around him and propagated the belief that the spirit of Jāwidān b. Sahl was incarnated in him.[46] The Khurramiyya movement shows the revitalization of Iranian apocalyptic thought in the early ninth century among the population of the eastern regions of the caliphate.[47] The Khurramiyya embodied an open missionary and apocalyptic message and posed a serious threat to the caliphate. It challenged the power of the caliphate, the local populations and administration, and above all al-Ma'mūn's missionary activity in the eastern frontier. In 204/820 al-Ma'mūn tried in vain to crush Bābāk's movement, which he considered extremely dangerous.[48] 'Īsā b. Abī Khālid put an end to the autonomy of the chieftains in the principal cities but failed to subdue the mountainous region held by Bābāk. The various expeditions entrusted to Ṣadaqa b. 'Alī al-Azdī (in 209/824), then to Muḥammad b. Ḥumayd al-Ṭā'ī or al-Ṭūsī (in 212–14/827–29), failed to curb the uprising of Bābāk, who succeeded in killing Muḥammad b. Ḥumayd (214/829) and repelling his army. This forced al-Ma'mūn to charge Ṭāhir, who commanded the pacification of al-Jazīra and then of Egypt, defeating this movement. However, before being able to intervene against Bābāk, 'Abdallāh b. Ṭāhir was transferred to Khurāsān on the death of his brother Ṭalḥa (214/829). This coincided with the end of the revolt of the Khārijī Ḥamza b. Ādarak, which had lasted for thirty-three years in Kirmān. Despite such efforts, al-Ma'mūn could not purge Bābāk's insurrection and found no better way to deal with it than to instruct, while on his deathbed, his brother al-Mu'taṣim to follow an aggressive policy against Bābāk.[49]

In the western frontier, Egypt had been shaken by intermittent unrest since 196/812. During the civil war, the commanders and the governor of Egypt were divided into factions whose loyalties were split between al-Amīn and al-Ma'mūn. Tribal hostilities between Lakhm and Mudlij complicated the situation, as did the activity of an obscure group called al-Ṣūfiyya, whose leader, 'Abd al-Raḥmān al-Ṣūfī, had been declared the leader in Fusṭāṭ.

The turmoil in Egypt grew with the arrival of a group of outcasts called al-Andalusiyyūn. Al-Azdī mentions that this group landed their ships on the shores of Alexandria, where they thrived through crime during the years 200–12/816–18.[50] This band of approximately three thousand comprised exiles from Cordova, and, owing to the political troubles in Alexandria, they became the masters of the city.[51] In 201/817 Sariyy in Fusṭāṭ controlled upper Egypt, al-Andalusiyyūn controlled Alexandria, and al-Jarawī occupied most of the Delta.

The following years were marked by constant strife among these factions. The sociopolitical chaos ended only when al-Ma'mūn commissioned 'Abdallāh b. Ṭāhir, who personally came to Egypt and used military force to control the province.[52] 'Abdallāh b. Ṭāhir then marched against al-Andalusiyyūn and besieged them in Alexandria in Ṣafar 212 / May 827. After ten days of siege, he forced the city to capitulate. Al-Andalusiyyūn surrendered and agreed to leave Egypt in exchange for ʿAbdallāh b. Ṭāhir's protection until they sailed out of Alexandria, but only on the condition that they took neither slaves nor Egyptians and that they promised not to land in any region under Muslim rule.[53]

Even after the expulsion of al-Andalusiyyūn, Egypt remained a volatile province. Two decades of political and military turmoil resulted in Egypt's irrigation system showing significant signs of neglect, the arable soil steadily shrinking, and the number of Coptic farmers declining.[54] The revolt of ʿAbdūs al-Fihrī in 213/828,[55] partly caused by poor governance and excessive taxation, was, therefore, a symptom of the ongoing unrest in Egypt. The period of violence in this case lasted for only a short time, and peace was restored in 217/832 by ʿAbdallāh b. Ṭāhir and then by al-Ma'mūn personally, who took responsibility for the wrongdoing of his governor in Fusṭāṭ, ʿĪsā b. Manṣūr, and removed him from office upon hearing of his maladministration and abusive taxation.[56]

The Bashmūric Rebellion in the marshlands of the lower Egyptian Delta in 216–17/831–32 became one of the most serious of the local insurrections socially and politically.[57] Like the revolt of ʿAbdūs al-Fihrī, the Bashmūric Rebellion was sparked by excessive taxation and poor governance and required al-Ma'mūn to journey to Egypt to fight the Bashmūric rebels and to pacify the Coptic community. Following a Byzantine expedition, al-Ma'mūn arrived at Egypt in Muḥarram 217 / February–March 832 in the company of al-Muʿtaṣim and the patriarch of Antioch, Dionysius of Tell-Mahre.[58] As soon as he arrived, the caliph commissioned the patriarchs of Egypt and Antioch to negotiate an agreement with the rebels in order to avoid bloodshed.[59] The plan did not succeed, however, as the envoys failed to convince the rebels to lay down their arms, whereupon al-Ma'mūn ordered his commander Afshīn to extinguish the insurrection by military force. In the ensuing crackdown, many of the rebels were killed, while others were carried off to Baghdad.[60] However, the Coptic bishop Severus ibn Muqaffaʿ (d. 978) noted how al-Ma'mūn initially demonstrated goodwill by attempting to solve the conflict through negotiations, promising not to retaliate against the rebels if they ended their insurrection and commissioning the patriarchs of Egypt and Antioch to negotiate an agreement that would comply with the Christian scriptures (Nāmūs). Indeed the caliph's reputation as a ruler wise in his conduct, compassionate for his subjects, curious about religious matters, and tolerant in his attitude won him sympathizers among the non-Muslims.[61]

As the work of the bishop Ibn al-Muqaffaʿ showed, this two-decade-long turmoil in Egypt provoked speculations describing the unrest in the province as messianic portents. A curiosity from a historical perspective, al-Andalusiyyūn's invasion of Alexandria acquired apocalyptic meaning. Before discussing the actual events, Ibn al-Muqaffaʿ related a prophecy that predicts the appearance of a group of people known as Ahl al-Andalus or al-Andalusiyyūn in

Alexandria. The prophecy speaks of an old man called Johannes who, confined to a church in western Alexandria, could see into the future. According to the prophecy, he once revealed to the people of the city that a group from the west would come forth to destroy them and their city without mercy. To Ibn al-Muqaffaʻ, the Cordovan's invasion of Alexandria fulfilled that prophecy.[62]

Al-Ṭabarī, on the other hand, relates that Yūnus b. ʻAbd al-Aʻlā, who lived through Egypt's troubled decades, interpreted ʻAbdallāh b. Ṭāhir's entry into Egypt as a sign of messianic justice.[63] Yūnus b. ʻAbd al-Aʻlā said that ʻAbdallāh b. Ṭāhir came to Egypt from the direction of the east at a time when the region had been plunged into strife and various usurpers had seized power and terrorized the people. When ʻAbdallāh b. Ṭāhir arrived, he put an end to the conflicts and "brought peace and security to the innocent and struck fear into the evil-minded, and the subjects flocked to him tendering their obedience." Yūnus b. ʻAbd al-Aʻlā further links ʻAbdallāh b. Ṭāhir's action to a prophecy on the authority of ʻAbdallāh b. Lahīʻa: "God has an army in the East, and none of His creation has rebelled against Him without His having wrought vengeance on them by means of it (or some other form of words with this meaning)." Another report in the Egyptian al-Kindī's *Wulāt Miṣr* similarly depicts the reign of al-Ma'mūn from the perspective of Egyptians as an era of messianic justice and tranquillity by referring to a prophecy on the authority of ʻAbdallāh b. Lahīʻa. The transmitter, a contemporary of the events in Egypt, relates the prophecy first: "O people of Egypt, what will you do if *fitna* occurs in your town and [when] the lame-one, the yellow-one and then the rebellious one rules? Then there will come a man from among the sons of al-Ḥusayn who will not be defeated and stopped. His banners will reach the Green Sea. He will fill it [Egypt] with justice." He then remarks, addressing ʻAbdallāh b. Ṭāhir, that "this has happened. The *fitna* has occurred, al-Sarīyy was governor and he is the lame-one. The yellow-one is his son Abū Naṣr. The rebellious one is ʻUbayd b. al-Sarīyy. And you are ʻAbdallāh b. Ṭāhir b. al-Ḥusayn."[64] Honoring the governor with a messianic mission tells much about his patron's image in the eyes of his subjects. Certainly al-Ma'mūn's efforts to restore peace to his realm earned him the reputation of a fair ruler as his conduct fit political wisdom in the region since the Sasanians, as well as messianic expectations among his subjects.[65]

After his arrival in Baghdad, the caliph's domestic policies were characterized by a concern for unification of his realm and reform of policies. The unification of the territories and organization of the administration went hand in hand with his push for missionary activities on the Khurāsānī frontier and his military effort against Byzantium. His policies aspired to bring the ancient world under the banner of a single, divinely supported empire proclaiming the last monotheistic message, which meshed rather smoothly with his domestic reform initiatives.

Missionary Activity and Byzantine Raids

When the governor of Ṭabaristān under al-Ma'mūn conquered Larīz and Shirrīz in Daylam and the mountainous parts of Ṭabarīstan and overthrew Shahriyār b. Sharwīn in 201/817, a poet placed al-Ma'mūn's achievements in the context of world conquest: "Indeed, we expect the conquest of Byzantium and of China/at the hands of one who has made us prevail over the royal power of Sharwīn."[66] What inspired the poet's ambitious wish of world conquest was an empire bordering Central Asia in the East and the Atlantic in the West, an empire that succeeded not only the Sasanian Empire in Iran but also a large portion of the Roman Empire, against which the caliphs had waged a relentless campaign throughout the previous two centuries.

It seems that al-Ma'mūn made missionary activity and expansion in the eastern frontier major priorities of his rule. Al-Balādhurī reports that when al-Ma'mūn was proclaimed caliph in Khurāsān, he embarked on military expeditions to the Soghdian border, Ushrūsāna, and Farghāna. At the same time that al-Ma'mūn conducted military raids, he corresponded with the local rulers, encouraging them to accept Islam and remain loyal to the caliphate. He advised his commanders to make propagating Islam a priority by calling and encouraging populations to accept the overlordship of the caliphate.[67] Several local princes in the eastern stretches of the caliphate who rallied to al-Ma'mūn and converted to Islam were honored with the title of clients, *mawālī*, of the commander of the faithful as a reward for their support of his policies. Medieval sources credit al-Ma'mūn with the conversion of the king of Tibet to Islam during his caliphate. As recorded in al-Azraqī, an unnamed king of Tibet sent to the Ka'ba, upon his conversion to Islam, a statue of gold with a crown of gold and jewels set on a baldachin throne of silver, which was covered with a cloth adorned with spherical tassels. This gift was exhibited in the Ka'ba in 200–201/816–17, with an inscription emphasizing that the throne was given to the Ka'ba as a token of the king's submission to Islam.[68]

At approximately the same time, a prince from Afghanistan named Kābūl-Shāh, who converted to Islam around 198–99/814–15, sent gifts to the Ka'ba. His crown was immediately taken to the Ka'ba, as an accompanying inscription makes clear, but the throne was kept for a few years in the treasury of Khurāsān before being moved to Mecca in 200/816 for public display. The inscriptions displayed with these two objects, apparently written by al-Ḥasan b. Sahl, emphasize the victory of the "righteous" caliph al-Ma'mūn, imam from among the rightly guided ones, *mahdīyyīn*, and imams,[69] over his deposed brother and the victory of the commander of the faithful over the unbelievers.[70] In Ṭabaristān, Mazyar the Qārīnid was among the local rulers who converted to Islam, thus becoming a subject of the caliph, and took an active part in extending the caliphate's sphere of influence in the East.[71] After Aḥmad b. Abī

Khālid succeeded in integrating the principality of Ushrusāna into the caliphate in 207/822—thus securing a foothold for the caliphate to engage in further expansion in Farghāna—the caliph received an embassy from a king in India named Dahma around 210/825, which al-Ma'mūn reciprocated. Although the correspondence amounted to no more than an exchange of gifts and letters, it nonetheless shows that the ambitions of the caliph to expand in Transoxiana were recognized by local rulers as far south as India.[72]

His achievements in unifying the empire, pacifying revolts, and forging alliances on the frontiers for further expansion and missionary activity helped al-Ma'mūn foster the image of Muslim superiority and the continuation of the prophetic missionary legacy. His efforts on this front enhanced the religious-moral dimension of his rule and promoted the image, if not the reality, of universal recognition of the caliphate, as prophecies of the early ninth century predicted. Coincidentally Bulliet has shown that the rate of conversion to Islam increased noticeably during the reign of al-Ma'mūn, if for different reasons.[73] Conversion could only have furthered the image of the caliph as missionary, *dā'ī*, and warrior, *ghāzī*.

It is expected that as a *dā'ī*, al-Ma'mūn made efforts to maintain the two sanctuaries, in Mecca and Medina, out of his reverence for them and to heal the wounds of the civil war.[74] But why is his name on the Dome of the Rock? Al-Ma'mūn's name appears three times on the inscriptions of the Dome of the Rock. In one place, his name replaces that of 'Abd al-Malik: "The servant of God, 'Abdallāh, the imām al-Ma'mūn, the commander of the faithful, has built this domed structure."[75] Why does al-Ma'mūn's name replace that of the Umayyad Caliph, 'Abd al-Malik b. Marwān?[76] Rosen-Ayalon writes that this may have been the act of a zealot reflecting an individual's—most probably a governor's—view, with no relevance to al-Ma'mūn personally.[77] Al-Ma'mūn's hostility toward the Umayyads could provide another explanation; but if this were this case, why did he leave the date intact? Or as van Berchem and Creswell have suggested, he might have wanted to participate in the blessing of this sacred place.[78]

It may be appropriate to turn our attention briefly to the monument itself to understand the significance of the monument for al-Ma'mūn and his missionary and expansionist policies. It is possible that when the Dome of the Rock was built, Jerusalem and this particular spot had already been revered as the location from whence Muḥammad ascended into the heavens.[79] By the third Islamic century, at any rate, this belief appeared to be firmly established. Grabar has suggested, beginning with the evidence of the inscriptions and of the mosaics, that the Dome of the Rock represented a monument proclaiming the new faith and empire in the city of the older two religions, Judaism and Christianity. It sanctified anew the Jewish sanctuary and slowly incorporated within itself the memories of Abraham and Joseph, among others. It set up the crowns of Byzantine and Persian kings as an offering around the center of the monument and presented its own image of Christ above the crowns. As Grabar argues, this amounted to a missionary victory monument intended to communicate a message to Muslim and Christian viewers that Islam was the true and final faith.[80] The inscriptions on the Dome of the Rock had, therefore, a double implication. It was a missionary statement that included an invitation to the new and final faith, accepting Christ and the Hebrew prophets among its forerunners, and it declared the superiority and power of the new faith and of the political order embodying it.[81]

Based on her iconographic analysis, Rosen-Ayalon has further proposed that the Dome of the Rock represented a statement by a Muslim to fulfill the prophecies of the Jews, the Christians, and the Muslims, at once symbolizing the cycle of paradise, the Judgment Day, and the Resurrection.[82] If this was the case, the eschatological and apocalyptic importance of the Dome of the Rock in the communal consciousness must still have been alive during al-Ma'mūn's lifetime, for in the late second and early third Islamic centuries, Muslim prophecies unmistakably referred to Jerusalem, the mosque of *al-Aqṣā,* and the Sanctuary, *Ḥarām,* in just such a context. Several prophecies describe the *Bayt al-Maqdis* and the *Masjid al-Aqṣā* as being among the few refuges from the terror of the Antichrist: "Surely the Antichrist will reach every place except four mosques: The mosque of *al-Ḥarām* [in Mecca], the one in Medina, the one in Ṭūr-Sīnā and the Mosque of *al-Aqṣā*."[83] Another prophecy announces the *Bayt al-Maqdis* as the refuge of the Muslims from the Antichrist.[84] The fact that the insertion of al-Ma'mūn's name took place most probably in or around 216/831, when he made his journey to Egypt, makes his Byzantine expeditions all the more relevant to the inscriptions on the monument.

Al-Ma'mūn's campaigns in the West against Byzantium provide another dimension of his expansionist ambitions as a *ghāzī* caliph. The idea of the conquest of Byzantium was not new to al-Ma'mūn. The caliphate, from its inception, made constant efforts to conquer Constantinople.[85] Whether connected with prophecies or not, the conquest of Byzantium remained a primary political goal of the caliphs in the first two centuries of Islam. This also symbolized a popular desire, as abundantly evidenced in a wide range of sources.[86] Al-Ma'mūn seems to have followed the example of his predecessors in pursuing the conquest of Byzantium[87] with a renewed vigor that replaced the calmer mood during early 'Abbāsid times. Al-Ma'mūn intended his conquests to address two main goals. The first was to heal the wounds of the civil war by rallying support around a shared cause, and the second was to eliminate Byzantium as a competitor, so that the caliphate could triumph against its rivals, fulfilling the prophecies of the fall of Rome and Constantinople. On the one hand, the ideology of jihad and the prophecies on the conquest of Rome justified ex post facto the early Islamic military initiatives against Byzantium. On the other hand, the same discourse functioned as a military ideology that motivated Umayyad and 'Abbāsid rulers to continue in this effort. As long as the conquest of Byzantium and Constantinople remained unfulfilled, this dream continued to inspire rulers, including al-Ma'mūn, until it was realized by the Ottoman Mehmet the Conqueror, a sobriquet given to him precisely because of this, in 1453.

A Spanish Umayyad ruler's testimony supports the suggestion that imperial politics unfolded in an atmosphere clouded by apocalyptic and messianic beliefs. The Byzantine emperor Theophilos (r. 829–42) wrote to the Umayyad 'Abd al-Raḥmān al-Awsaṭ shortly after the death al-Ma'mūn to ask for support against al-Mu'taṣim. In his response, the Umayyad ruler has this to say about al-Ma'mūn and al-Mu'taṣim:

> The matter you have mentioned concerning the deeds of the two despicable [individuals], the Son of Marājil and the son of Mārida, his brother after him . . . and the arrival of the time of their reign's demise, and the termination of their kingdom's duration, and the grace of God to recover our rule and the power of our forefathers whom the [sacred] books foretold and prophets spoke of . . . and your encouragement of us to go out against [the 'Abbāsids] and ask revenge from them, and your promise to assist us [in this matter] in the manner a friend assists his friend . . . and all what you have told and narrated to us in your letter, we read and understood.[88]

The emir then continues to reveal what he thinks about Theophilos's proposal:

> Concerning what you have mentioned about the despicable son of Mārida and your encouragement of us to set out to attack him and what you mentioned from the coming near the demise of his and his family's reign and destruction of their power, and the arrival of the time for the return of our reign . . . we have always heard and acknowledged [that] disaster will strike them, and the destructive strike of fortune (*dā'ira*) will reach them from the people of North Africa. God will terminate their line (*dibāruhum*) with us and on our hands.[89]

The correspondence must have taken place shortly after the death of al-Ma'mūn, when the Byzantine emperor still felt the impact of al-Ma'mūn's offensive. The correspondence shows the anxiety that accompanied the imperial competition in the early ninth century and the reverberation of the circulating prophecies in the minds of the early-ninth-century rulers and throughout the territories of the 'Abbāsids caliphate, Byzantine Empire, and Spanish Umayyad Emirate. In fact, as Vasiliev noted, both the 'Abbāsids and the Byzantines saw their competition as an eschatological rivalry ushering in the end of time.[90] In the Abbāsid world, many expected the end of the world to be preceded by the fall of Constantinople. In the Latin and Greek worlds, the legend of the last Roman emperor gained wide currency that he would enter Jerusalem before the end of the world and hand over his crown to the Messiah.[91]

If the Byzantine emperor and the Umayyad emir had reasons to expect an imminent destruction of the ʿAbbāsids, the ʿAbbāsid caliph himself relied on prophecies indicating otherwise—prophecies concerning the conquest of Byzantium. Al-Ma'mūn's conquest efforts must be judged therefore not by their success or failure but by the motivations and intentions of the caliph, and by the psychological and ideological expectations that they created during his reign. We know that while the caliph focused on unifying his realm and reforming its administration, he sought to destabilize Byzantium. Al-Ma'mūn corresponded with Omurtag (r. 814–31), the king of the Bulgars, most probably before or during his unsuccessful raid against Byzantium in 814–15. Although medieval sources briefly mention that the king wrote to al-Ma'mūn inquiring about Islam and the caliph responded with a detailed letter in hopes of his conversion, the correspondence must have included a proposal for alliance against Byzantium.[92] This is highly probable in light of the fact that the caliph sought other alliances against Byzantium as well. For instance, he actively supported the insurrection of Thomas the Slav in Asia Minor against the Emperor Michael II in 821. With al-Ma'mūn's help, Thomas arrived at Antioch and was crowned as Basileus of the Romans by the patriarch of Antioch in 821. Backed by the caliph, Thomas captured the majority of Byzantine themes, or administrative/military regions, in Anatolia and even finally besieged Constantinople. However, he was defeated by the Byzantines with the support of Omurtag, who at that point had a peace treaty with the Byzantines since 815.[93] Although al-Ma'mūn never made Byzantium a vassalage of the caliphate, this incident shows the extent of his hopes and ambitions concerning its conquest. After a hiatus of several years, al-Ma'mūn continued an aggressive policy against the Byzantines, beginning in 213/827. He appointed his son al-ʿAbbās to the governorship of the Byzantine frontier, al-Jazīra, Thughūr, and al-ʿAwāṣim, granting him the sum of 500,000 dinārs for his expenses.[94] From 215/830 onward, al-Ma'mūn continued his attacks on the Byzantine frontier.

A curious prophecy with direct bearing on the ʿAbbāsid Byzantine military encounter under al-Ma'mūn is worth examining in detail. The prophecy reads as follows: "There will be four truces between you and the Romans. The fourth one will be at the hands of a man from the family of Hārūn and will last seven years. The prophet was asked, 'O messenger of God, who will be the imam of the people on that day?' He said, '[He will be] from my progeny, [his age will be] forty years old, as if his face were a planet of pearl. There will be a black mole on his right cheek, and [he will be clothed with] a cloak fashioned for youth. He will resemble a man from the children of Israel, *Banū Isrā'īl*, and he will rule twenty years. He will find treasures and conquer the cities of unbelief.'"[95]

This prophecy is found in a later source, al-Hindī's *Kanz al-ʿUmmāl*, but internal evidence makes it more likely that it dates from the early third century A.H. The description of the ʿAbbāsid ruler seems to fit al-Ma'mūn. He was the son of Hārūn and belonged to the family of the Prophet; he ruled for twenty years, and, as al-Ṭabarī notes, he had a mole on his cheek.[96] The references to the conquest of cities and discovery of treasures must therefore refer to the activities of the caliph on the Byzantine frontier from 830 onward, during which time the prophecy was apparently composed, but before al-Ma'mūn's death. Since al-Ma'mūn was born in Rabī' I 170 / September 786, he would have been forty years old in Jumāda II 211 / September 826; thus the prophecy is reasonably accurate here as well.

The suggestion of a truce with Byzantium is a curious one, as no Muslim source mentions it. However, the absence of it in historiographical sources does not mean it did not happen. Looking at the years of certain events, some possibilities present themselves. Historiographical sources mention al-Ma'mūn's correspondence with Omurtag most probably in 198–99/814–15 in his bid against Byzantium. Al-Ma'mūn also supported the insurrection of Thomas the Slav in Asia Minor against the Emperor Michael II, which ended in failure in December 821, as noted previously. We know that al-Ma'mūn began his offensive against Byzantium in 215/830. He did apparently prepare for the offensive before this date by appointing al-'Abbās to the governorship of the Byzantine frontier, but the actual offensive began in 215/830. Between the insurrection of Thomas the Slav and al-Ma'mūn's Byzantine campaigns, there is a hiatus of activity on the Byzantine frontier from 206–7/822 until 215/830. If we assume that the Byzantine emperor and al-Ma'mūn agreed to a truce shortly after the insurrection of Thomas the Slav, the relative calm on the 'Abbāsid-Byzantine frontier afterward and the duration of the hiatus correspond exactly to what the prophecy suggests.

After the calm the first raid by three major armies—one led by the caliph himself, the other by al-'Abbās, and the final one by the Turkish general Ashinās—came in 215/830. It dealt a significant blow to the Byzantine Empire, as al-Ma'mūn captured the fortress of Mājida (Magida), and shortly afterward Qurra (today's Çorum), both located in Cappadocia (26 Jumādā I 215 / 21 July 830).[97] Al-'Abbās seized Darb al-Ḥadath (Ibn A'tham: al-Ḥarb) on 27 Muḥarram 215 / 26 March 830,[98] while Ashinās succeeded in taking control of Soanda (today's Nevşehir).

Following this expedition, al-Ma'mūn returned to Damascus in September of the same year to spend the winter and prepare for another campaign the following summer. It seems that successes persuaded al-Ma'mūn to adopt a more ambitious strategic objective, which eventually culminated in the annexation of much of Cappadocia with the surrender of Lu'lu'a (Loulon, present-day Ulu Kışla near Adana) in 832.[99] In the meantime, however, the Byzantine emperor Theophilos seized an opportunity to intercept and kill more than one thousand soldiers and take several thousand prisoners, as 'Abbāsid raid forces were campaigning in the Byzantine Armenian theme in the spring of 831.[100] The defeat only spurred al-Ma'mūn to renew the assault on the Byzantine Empire. The caliph hastily regrouped his men. Marching at the head of his army and accompanied by his brother Abū Isḥāq al-Mu'taṣim, al-'Abbās, and his adviser Yaḥyā b. Aktham,[101] al-Ma'mūn and his forces soon reached the outskirts of Hirāqla (Heraclea, now Ereğli), and quickly captured it. Then al-Ma'mūn's army was divided into units and proceeded in different directions for further conquest. During the course of this expedition, al-Mu'taṣim captured thirty forts and subterranean shelters, *maṭāmir*, while al-'Abbās conquered Ṭuwāna (Tyana) and defeated the Byzantine emperor. After these victories in Asia Minor, al-Ma'mūn rejected a proposal for an exchange of prisoners and a five-year truce. Although he initially set off toward Kaysūm for further campaigning, with the approach of winter al-Ma'mūn returned to Damascus.[102]

When al-Ma'mūn arrived in the city in September 831, he met with a Byzantine ambassador, possibly John the Grammarian, who came to negotiate a peace agreement on behalf of the Byzantine emperor.[103] Determined to continue his offensive against the Byzantines, al-Ma'mūn was in no hurry to accept the truce. In the meantime, he personally attended to the pacification of the Bashmūric revolt in Egypt in the winter. After his trip back to Damascus in April 832, he immediately returned to the Byzantine front with the objective of gaining control over the ports of Cilicia beyond the Taurus. In June of the same year, he laid siege to Lu'lu'a (Loulon), but soon departed for Salaghus and, from there, for al-Raqqa, leaving his deputy 'Ujayf to carry on the campaign. In September 'Ujayf negotiated an agreement with the people of Lu'lu'a, who surrendered in return for their safety.[104]

This alarming news prompted the Emperor Theophilos, who perhaps now realized the extent of al-Ma'mūn's ambitions, to send a letter to the caliph asking him for a truce that would benefit both sides. The emperor noted that a peace agreement would promote trade and secure the safety of highways. He also promised to pay a large sum of money, 100,000 nomismata, and to release Muslim captives. This came as a timely, conciliatory, and practical offer that al-Ma'mūn should have had little reason to decline. Nonetheless, the caliph declined the offer, even though the strategic objective of capturing Cappadocia was almost realized, and the Byzantine emperor was eager for peace.[105] In his letter, as quoted in al-Ṭabarī, al-Ma'mūn sent the following response to the emperor:

> But I consider that I should proffer you a warning, with which God establishes clearly for you the decisive proof [of Islam], involving the summoning of you and your supporters to knowledge of the divine unity and the divine law of religion of the *ḥanīfs*. If you refuse [to accept this offer], then you can hand over tribute [literally: a ransom] which will entail the obligation of protection [*dhimma*] and make incumbent a respite [from further warfare].

> But if you choose not to make that [payment or ransom], then you will clearly experience face-to-face our [martial] qualities to an extent which will make any effort [on my part] of eloquent speaking and an exhaustive attempt at description superfluous. Peace be upon him who follows the divine guidance.[106]

Al-Ma'mūn was not bluffing and clearly was not looking for an immediate pragmatic advantage.

The caliph prepared for a greater assault. He ordered his brother al-Mu'taṣim to recruit troops from the regiments of Syria, Jordan, and Palestine, each to supply a contingent of four thousand soldiers, each of whom would be paid one hundred dirhams if a cavalryman or forty dirhams if an infantryman. Al-Ma'mūn also made levies on the army of Egypt, Qinnasrīn, al-Jazīra, and Baghdad, mobilizing them, as well, toward Tuwāna.[107] The caliph also dispatched al-'Abbās to encamp at Tuwāna, commissioning him to embark on a building program there. Al-Ma'mūn had already dispatched workers and detachments for that purpose (1 Jumādā I, 218 / 25 May 833). He himself marched to Ṭarsūs on 16 Jumādā II 218 / 9 July 833, hoping to penetrate further into Byzantine territories.[108] Once again al-Ma'mūn received a truce offer, more generous than the previous one.[109] However, determined to continue his advance, perhaps with the conquest of Byzantium as his ultimate goal, as Ibn A'tham reports, the caliph declined the offer and continued preparations for a major assault.[110] At Ṭarsūs, however, he fell ill and soon died in Rajab 218/August 833 after a short illness, leaving his plans unfulfilled.[111] His sudden death prevented the start of the campaign and forced his successor, al-Mu'taṣim, to withdraw to Baghdad to secure his reign.

In his reply to Theophilos, al-Ma'mūn offered some of the most radical solutions available to the caliph to show his insistence on campaigning. The Byzantine emperor could either accept the laws of the *ḥanīfs*, *al-sharī'a al-ḥanīfiyya*, or pay a poll tax; otherwise al-Ma'mūn would resume warfare.[112] The call for unity under one overarching and authentic monotheism on the model of Abraham as a way to solve imperial competition in the context of al-Ma'mūn's milieu recalls the ultimate messianic dream of realizing a monotheistic empire within the context of *Ur*-monotheism, *ḥanīfiyya*. The term *ḥanīf* has a complicated history, too complicated to delve into here.[113] In the Qur'ānic text, it describes the following ideas and people: adherents of any pure and real religion;[114] the natural religion, *fiṭra*, itself;[115] the faith of Abraham as an adherent of the true religion;[116] the faithful who are neither Jews nor Christians;[117] and the religion of the resurrection.[118] For al-Ma'mūn and his milieu, the term connoted the idea that God had only one message throughout history, which various communities altered at certain points in time. Although the expression of the authentic divine message and the laws accompanying it in history changed over time—hence the laws of the Torah, the Gospel, the Qur'ān—all were thought to be compatible with the final and most complete revelation, Islam, which represented the most recent revelation to set straight for the final time God's only message to humankind.

The idea that one could still discover or uncover this pristine monotheistic faith is attested to in a wealth of scholarly opinions, traditions, and prophecies. The exegetical tradition devotes substantial attention to the unity of religion and *ḥanīfism* under the Second Coming of Jesus. Perhaps reflecting his awareness of the wider religious milieu and representing a more conciliatory perspective that called for unity under one monotheistic religion, al-Ṣan'ānī includes the followers of "all religions" among those who will believe in Jesus after his Second Coming.[119] It may not be anachronistic to refer to al-Ṭabarī, who cites in detail the views of previous authorities on this subject and unambiguously refers to *Ur*-monotheism, *ḥanīfiyya,* as the universal religion of the end of time to elaborate on this concept: "Before his death, meaning before Jesus' death. He [God] declared that all of them will believe in him when he [Jesus] descends to fight the Antichrist, so all religions will be one, and that is the religion of Islam, the *ḥanīfiyya*, religion of Abraham, peace be upon him."[120]

Presenting Islam as the orthodox and latest version of what was essentially considered a single religion, ḥanīfism (from which Jews and Christians were seen to have deviated), has textual traces in the first two centuries of Islam. As early as the Prophet's "Charter of Medina," which embraces those who believe in God and the Last Day and follows the revealed law as a community of believers, this tendency is evident.[121] The Qur'ānic text calls upon the Jews and Christians to assemble on common ground with the new faithful: "Say: 'People of the Book! Come now to a word common between us and you, that we serve none but God, and that we associate not aught with Him, and do not some of us take others as Lords, apart from God.'"[122] Another verse recognizes the legitimacy of older scriptures and thus describes seeking the common ground as behaving righteously, believing in God and the Last Day: "Surely those who believe, and those of Jewry, and the Sabaeans, and those Christians, whosoever believes in God and the Last Day, and works righteousness—no fear shall be on them, neither shall they sorrow."[123]

In prophecies, too, the Mahdī leads to the authentic divine scriptures that were revealed to previous prophets since Adam in order to unlock the divine secrets and unify diverse confessions under the authentic revelation of God. Thus one tradition predicts that after the Sasanian kingship had been permanently obliterated, Byzantium would suffer the same end, and there would be no Byzantine emperor. Muslims would then be in charge of distributing the treasures fairly.[124] Even though religious reform and unification were generally sought under the rubric of Islam as the final and most complete revelation, diverse monotheistic laws were also recognized as legitimate. In one remarkable tradition the legitimacy of ancient laws is clearly acknowledged. The Mahdī will discover the original forms of older scriptures and grant the People of the Book, *ahl al-kitāb*, the right to live according to the ordinances of their scriptures.[125] Missionary activity and voluntary submission will follow to bring about the expected universal messianic order. The Mahdī will march to Jerusalem, and the treasures will be carried to him. The Arabs, Persians, Romans, people of the Abode of War, and others will submit to his authority without warfare.[126] As Bashear has demonstrated, early Islamic prophecies encourage conquests in general and the conquest of Byzantium in particular as one of the final steps before the end of the world.[127] While al-Ma'mūn made his political and military decisions in a concrete historical context, his response to the Byzantine emperor revealed that he was not only aware of the implications of his conquests but also that he consciously aligned his actions with messianic expectations.

CHAPTER 6

God's Caliph as *Mujaddid*

At the same time that the caliph dealt with the unification and expansion of his empire, he promoted interest in Sanskrit, Pahlavī, and Greek cultural and scientific heritages, encouraging the translation of works of astronomy, mathematics, medicine, and philosophy mostly from Greek and Syriac into Arabic. A diverse body of scholars from various confessions—Muslims and non-Muslims from different provinces of the empire, including Khawārizm, Farghāna, Khurāsān, Ṭabaristān, al-Jazīra, and Iraq—were given opportunities and support for their contributions. Some of these activities were obviously done in the House of Wisdom, Bayt al-Ḥikma.[1] The 'Abbāsid interest in ancient knowledge within the context of the increased popular and learned interest in divine wisdom—scripted and inspired, secular and religious—afforded al-Ma'mūn to gear the translation activity toward developing an imperial culture and establishing the caliphate as the inheritor of the great empires of the past and the champion of monotheism.

Translation Activities

What did the poet Khuzayma b. al-Ḥasan mean when he praised al-Ma'mūn as the inheritor of the ancients' knowledge and understanding, *'ilm al-awwalīn wa fahmihim*?[2] On the most basic level, al-Ma'mūn is known for his interest in knowledge and scholarship. The lengthy narratives of his legal, theological, and intra- and interconfessional debates,[3] and his knowledge of theology and the law, enabled him to participate in intellectual and religious discussions[4] and reflect al-Ma'mūn's personal involvement in his milieu's scholarly debate. Out of genuine interest in scholarly matters, he held regular disputations in which literary, religious, sectarian, theological, and philosophical issues were discussed.[5] He not only encouraged research into ancient science and philosophy but also personally pursued research.[6] Al-Dīnawarī noted that al-Ma'mūn excelled among the 'Abbāsids in learning; he acquired a certain degree of knowledge about and had an active interest in every branch of knowledge.[7] For example, he was involved extensively enough in astronomical calculations to verify, while in Damascus, conflicting observational results and to check the functioning of instruments for accurate measurement.[8]

Several contemporary scholars have already discussed the reasons why the 'Abbāsids supported the translation activities,[9] but little has been said about how they internalized and embraced ancient knowledge, and the process by which ancient knowledge became acceptable intellectually, ideologically, and socially to the ruling and learned elite. The argument can be made that the 'Abbāsid learned elite imagined ancient sciences to be a body of knowledge that was ultimately prophetic and divine, reaching as far back as the antediluvian prophetic wisdom. On the one hand, political support for ancient knowledge evolved in the context of the social, political, and cultural needs of a large territorial empire.[10] This is where the efforts of court secretaries and scientists made the most sense from a practical point of view. On the other hand, the translations had to be envisioned and implemented in a milieu in which worldviews produced cognitive categories to define what ancient knowledge meant and entailed. The reconstruction of ancient knowledge in the early 'Abbāsid period involved a process of adoption, adaptation, and mental and cultural negotiation between the 'Abbāsid learned elite and ancient heritage. This process of adoption or orientation of ancient knowledge required the efforts of a generation of courtiers and scholars until the sciences became legitimate subjects of study that were endowed with courtly patronage.

A remarkable example of an early attempt to enter ancient sciences into the 'Abbāsid mental catalog was made by Abū Sahl b. al-Nawbakht (d. 777), who served as the court astrologer of al-Manṣūr after his father, al-Nawbakht. The fragment dealing with the ancient sciences in Ibn al-Nawbakht's *Kitab al-Nahmutān* is preserved in Ibn al-Nadīm's *al-Fihrist*. In it, Ibn al-Nawbakht accuses Alexander the Great of destroying the Persian scientific heritage during his rule in Persia by literally pillaging, scattering, and burning the material after translating whatever he needed into Greek and Coptic and shipping scholars and books on science, medicine, and astronomy away to Egypt.[11] Ibn al-Nawbakht maintained that some remnants of these scattered books, "which the kings of Persia had copied and preserved there when charged to do so by their prophet Zoroaster and Jāmasp the learned," survived in India and China until Ardashīr b. Bābāk and his son Shāpūr the Sasanian attempted to retrieve and reassemble whatever there was left of them from India, China, Byzantium, and Iraq "until all these books had been copied in Persian in the way in which they had been [compiled by] Hermes the Babylonian who ruled over Egypt, Dorotheus the Syrian [of Sidon], Qaydarus the Greek from the city of Athens which is famed for its science, Ptolemy the Alexandrian, and Farmasb the Indian." The Persians continued to promote, improve, and teach people these books "in the same way in which they had learned from all those books which originated in Babylon." After Ardashīr and Shāpūr, Chosroes I Anūshirwān (531–78) "collected these books, put them together [in their proper order], and based his acts on them on account of his desire for knowledge and love for it."[12]

Ibn al-Nawbakht refers to "the earliest people," *awā'il al-khalq*, as the source of scientific and prophetic knowledge to justify the study and support of secular sciences of the antiquity.[13] Why does Ibn al-Nawbakht want to establish a link between ancient sciences and earliest humans?[14] According to Ibn al-Nawbakht, the foundational knowledge originating with the earliest people was forgotten until it was rediscovered and expanded upon during the time of Jam b. Avanjhān.[15] It is remarkable that Jam appears in Ibn al-Nawbakht's account as the son of Avanjhān, who is none other than Hermes or Awanjhān, the grandson of Adam, in Abū Ma'shar's account. In historiographical sources, Jam appears as an early figure both before and after the Flood. Al-Dīnawarī (d. 895–96), whose knowledge of Persian sources is well established, maintains that Jam was a member of the fourth generation after Noah, putting him after the Flood.[16] Al-Ṭabarī, on the other hand, considers Jam an antediluvian figure, the brother of Ṭahmuras b. Awanjhān, who ruled after Hoshank. According to al-Ṭabarī, Hoshank was a contemporary of the biblical Mahalal'el b. Cainan, the grandfather of Enoch, and for some scholars they were one and the same.[17]

Ibn al-Nawbakht understood that if the sciences were to take hold in the 'Abbāsid world, they had to first be deemed acceptable. Ibn al-Nawbakht pointed out that sciences emanated from a singular and ultimately divine origin in Babylon and had been promoted, above all, by the Persians.[18] In an attempt to convince his patron to pay attention to ancient knowledge, Ibn al-Nawbakht correlated the accomplishments of the Persian kings with those of the 'Abbāsid caliphs and specifically noted the conduct of Anushirwān as exemplary. He further encouraged his patron to embrace ancient sciences because "the people of every age and era acquire fresh experiences and have knowledge renewed for them in accordance with the decree of the stars and the signs of the Zodiac, a decree which is in charge of governing time by the command of God Almighty."[19] It was incumbent on the caliph to preserve and promote knowledge both as act of piety and royal magnanimity if he was to be compared with or supersede the great kings of the past.

Ibn al-Nawbakht's explanation shows that the reasoning through which ancient knowledge was legitimized, internalized, and reproduced formed an important facet of the translation activity. Court secretaries, scientists, and scholars made a visible effort to redefine and relocate mundane scientific knowledge within the recognized categories of knowledge in Muslim scholarly sensibilities at a moment when Muslim scholarship itself was producing religious sciences and discovering the relevance of pre-Islamic Arabic cultural heritage and of the Near Eastern practical wisdom. This effort demonstrates a mental adjustment, an effort to make sense of the past to fit an Islamic worldview, through cultural recalibration and the reorientation of its legacy.[20]

This is not to say that all early scientific endeavors had to be justified by similar reasoning. There certainly existed multiple scientific currents in Baghdad with various understandings of the meaning and purpose of science. This difference of opinion emerged partly due to domestic religious and intellectual diversity and partly due to the access to various sources from which knowledge had been acquired.[21] Yet one can make a good case for the fact that there existed a belief in early 'Abbāsid history among scholars close to the 'Abbāsid court that sciences were essentially of single divine origin, although they were preserved in different languages and locations for historical reasons.[22] For the patrons of the translation activity, it was important that this diversity was ultimately reducible to a legitimate source that confirmed their background and aspirations. Therefore it is important to look briefly into the motives of translators and into the context in which ancient sciences made sense to the 'Abbāsids.

As a form of revelation, Qur'ānic passages inform the believers of the existence of previous revelations and scripts (*ṣuḥuf, zubur,* and *kutub*), which contained, like the Qur'ān itself, not only laws for various communities but also the essence of the divine message and occult knowledge. One verse notes the relevance of ancient divine scripts to the message of the Qur'ān: "They say, 'Why does he not bring us a sign from his Lord?' Has there not come to them the clear sign of what is in the former scrolls (*ṣuḥuf*)?"[23] In another place the Qur'ān asserts that what has been revealed to Muḥammad, or a portion of it, was included in the ancient scripts given to previous prophets: "Surely this is in the ancient scrolls, the scrolls of Abraham and Moses."[24] Another verse implies that ancient scriptures contained both hidden knowledge and prophecies: "We have destroyed the likes of you; is there any that will remember? Everything that they have done is in the Scrolls, and everything, great and small, is inscribed (*zubur*)."[25] Yet another verse speaks of exalted scripts containing pure knowledge: "No indeed; it is a Reminder (and whoso wills, shall remember it) upon pages (*ṣuḥuf*) high-honored, uplifted, purified, by the hands of scribes noble, pious."[26] There also exist scripts that can only be disclosed to a privileged few: "Nay, every man of them desires to be given scrolls unrolled (*ṣuḥuf*)."[27]

This brief display of Qur'ānic verses demonstrates that the Qur'ānic discourse provided a justification for scholars to develop a curiosity about ancient scriptures and hidden knowledge, especially among the recently converted learned Jews and Christians. This is exemplified in interesting exegetical opinions. Exegetical literature reveals that at least as early as the eighth century scholars exhibited interest in occult knowledge and in lost books containing divine wisdom. In fact Ibn Sa'd (d. 845) reports that Wahb b. al-Munabbih (d. ca. 728) claimed that he had "read ninety-two books, all of which were sent down from heaven. Seventy-two of which are in the churches and in the hands of the people, and twenty are only known to a few."[28] Wahb b. al-Munabbih's remark about ancient scripts is backed by Ibn al-Nadīm, who relates that he read an ancient manuscript that seemed to be from the treasury of al-Ma'mūn and listed the names and numbers of scriptures (*suḥuf*) and the revealed books (*al-kutub al-munazzala*). According to Ibn al-Nadīm, who said that he quoted the relevant sections of the manuscript in his work, most of the proto-Sunnis (*al-Ḥashwiyya*) and common people (*'Awām*) trusted its content.[29]

Early 'Abbāsid exegetical tradition provides a good example of the mental and cultural context in which ancient knowledge was sought and received, and of the popular interest in its transmission. A case in point is the interpretation of chapter 18 ("The Cave") of the Qur'ān. The Qur'ānic narrative has Moses seek, find, and accompany a saintly figure (popularly known as Khiḍr), who is privileged with occult knowledge. In their quest, Moses finds the sage's conduct to be contrary to common sense—he knowingly makes a ship sink; he kills an individual without an apparent provocation; and he repairs a wall that is about to collapse. This prompts Moses to object, and the sage explains his actions. The last point in the sage's explanation, which involves why he repaired the collapsing wall, sparked an interesting exegetical discussion. The sage explains that he repaired the wall because it belonged to two orphans, and he wanted the wall to remain until the boys came of age and discovered the treasure under it.[30] In the course of elaborating on the details of the story, al-Ṣan'anī cites the opinion of his colleagues that the treasure hidden under the falling wall in the narrative was knowledge (*'ilm*) kept in books and scriptures. In another opinion the treasure was described as the knowledge of scriptures, suggesting a body of knowledge with hermeneutical quality.[31] By the time of al-Ṭabarī, who also cites opinions concerning "treasured scripts containing knowledge," *ṣuḥuf fīhā 'ilm madfūna*, not only is a continuing interest in the buried knowledge apparent but so, too, is an interest in secret knowledge, as indicated in his remark, "golden tablet with script on it."[32]

This curiosity about the content and discovery of ancient scripts that would explain the mysteries of the future and of the universe appears in various kinds of prophecies as well, forming a body of opinions that cannot be ignored in matters dealing with ancient knowledge. Suffice it here to mention some of such prophecies. Nu'aym b. Ḥammād's prophecy discusses, as noted earlier, how a number of soldiers discovered a script during the conquest of Tustar that they thought was the book of Daniel. The script, according to the prophecy, contained knowledge of what would happen in the future.[33] Similarly Ibn 'Abd al-Barr (d. 1071) relates that an early authority on biblical material in Arabic,

Ka'b al-Aḥbār (d. ca. 645–55), a converted Jew, used to say that "there is no foot[-wide portion] of the earth that the Torah, which God sent down to Moses the son of Imran, peace be upon him, does not mention what is going to happen on it until the day of resurrection."[34]

It is remarkable that the title al-Mahdī itself was interpreted in such a way to connote a quest for hidden knowledge. Al-Ṣan'ānī transmits a prophecy on the authority of Ka'b al-Aḥbār explaining why the messianic figure is named Mahdī: "He is named Mahdī because he guides to hidden truth." That hidden truth is, according to al-Ṣan'ānī's prophecy, none other than the Torah and the Gospel: "He will excavate the Torah and the Gospel from a location in Antioch."[35] Another early-ninth-century collector of prophecies, Nu'aym b. Ḥammād, transmits what appears to be a variant on the authority of Ka'b al-Aḥbār: "He is called Mahdī because he will guide to scripts from among the scriptures of the Torah. He will excavate them from the mountains of Syria. The Jews will be summoned to them. Many people will be converted to Islam upon [the discovery of] these books."[36]

Prophecies had a straightforward and noble aim: learning about the mysteries of creation and solving the historical conflicts among monotheistic faiths through unearthing sacred texts and relics so that divergent opinions finally could unite on a common ground based on irrefutable evidence. Thus in a prophecy the Mahdī will march to Rome (Rūmiyya) with his army and conquer it. He will seize the Ornament of Jerusalem, the Ark of the Covenant, the Table of Solomon, the Staff of Moses, and the Garment of Adam. He will then return the relics to Jerusalem and usher in the coming forth of both the Antichrist and Jesus.[37] In another prophecy the Mahdī will receive the Ark of the Covenant in Jerusalem after it has been unearthed from the Lake of Galilee.[38] Prophecies about the location of relics and scriptures can be as specific as a treasure map: "When you conquer Rome enter its great eastern church from its eastern gate and count seven tiles and lift the eighth. There will be under it the staff of Moses, the Gospel and the Ornament of Jerusalem."[39] Although the locations of relics and scriptures change in prophecies, the mission of finding them is persistent. The conquest of Roman territories, associated with the Christian faith, will facilitate this messianic discovery and bring about the supremacy of true monotheism; the unification of the world under a righteous ruler, the Mahdī; and the reformation of Judaism and Christianity to conform to their pristine forms.

The exegetical opinions and prophecies presented so far suggest that 'Abbāsid literati, including court astrologers, *ḥadīth*-transmitters (*muḥaddiths*), exegetes, and transmitters of prophecies sought and justified the use of ancient knowledge within a multidimensional context. It is important, therefore, to keep in mind these exegetical opinions and messianic prophecies, which seem to function as a rehabilitative medium in embracing ancient knowledge as a socially and religiously desirable and even necessary activity for ʿAbbāsid rulers. Granted that the type of knowledge that prophecies and exegetical opinions discussed here is different from what we know today as the sciences. In the minds of ʿAbbāsid literati, however, this difference might not have been as pronounced as it is in our minds, particularly given the traditional attribution of knowledge to antediluvian figures since the middle of the eighth century.

Before the ʿAbbāsids, the cultures of southwest Asia, including the Egyptian, Mesopotamian, Greek, and Jewish traditions, had produced legends concerning the foundation and preservation of knowledge from destruction by flood or fire, and attributed this endeavor to figures who, by the ʿAbbāsid time, came to be identified with Enoch and Hermes. Being the masters of the territories in which these legends circulated, the ʿAbbāsids gravitated toward them. Ibn al-Nawbakht, for instance, attributes the foundational knowledge to ancient sages, including Hermes. Ibn al-Nadīm reports that Ibn al-Nawbakht maintained that Hermes was one of the seven sages who left Babylon to settle in Egypt, where he became king and made its inhabitants prosperous. According to Ibn al-Nadīm, Ibn al-Nawbakht narrated in his *Kitāb al-Nahmutān* that al-Ḍaḥḥāk b. Qay built a city in Mesopotamia (*sawād*) named after Jupiter, because he ruled under the sign of that planet. In this city, he constructed twelve palaces that he named after the twelve signs of the Zodiac, and each palace housed a library filled with books and staffed with numerous scholars. Ibn al-Nawbakht noted also that al-Ḍaḥḥāk b. Qay built seven temples and assigned each one of them to a wise man, one of whom was Hermes. The inhabitants followed the leadership and guidance of these seven wise men until a prophet was sent, people turned their attention to him, and the harmony among the wise men was broken. Hermes—the most thoroughly intelligent, the most strikingly wise, and the most refined in discernment among the seven—abandoned the city and set out for Egypt, where he became king. He brought prosperity to its inhabitants and manifested his wisdom among them.[40] It appears that Ibn al-Nawbakht knew of the work of Dorotheus Sidonius, *Carmen Astrologicum*, in which Hermes figures as the son of the king of Egypt, and honored as Trismegistus.[41]

As early as al-Manṣūr's time, Hermes was therefore known to be one of the ancient patron saints of sciences. Further references to his role in the origin and preservation of sciences catapulted him, in only a few decades, into an even more exalted position. The famous court astrologer Māshā'allāh mentions Hermes in his *Fī al-Qirānāt wa al-Adyān wa al-Milal*, as far as we know from its abridgement by Ibn Ḥibinṭa.[42] A contemporary of Māshā'allāh, al-Fazārī, who worked at the court of al-Manṣūr, also seems to have used books attributed to Hermes, which were partly geographical in content. Al-Bīrūnī relates that al-Fazārī credited Hermes with the geographical division of the inhabited world into seven climes.[43] Shortly after the death of al-Ma'mūn, al-Muʿtaṣim

(r. 833–42) ordered the translation of the *Thesaurus Alexandri*, a work on elixirs and amulets, from Greek and Latin into Arabic. This work was attributed to Hermes and was supposed to have incorporated a prologue and epilogue by Aristotle that was addressed to Alexander the Great.[44] *The Book of Bālīnās* attributed to Appolonius of Tyana, available in Arabic in the early 'Abbāsid period, also refers to Hermes.[45]

It is quite possible that Hermes was, in fact, mentioned at a dinner table of the caliph al-Ma'mūn, as described in the following anecdote: While the guests of the caliph were being served from a table full of various dishes, al-Ma'mūn described to his guests the properties of each dish, one by one. Astonished that the caliph knew so much about the properties of food, the adviser and judge Yaḥya b. Aktham (d. 242/856) commented on his patron's intellectual breadth: "O commander of the faithful! If we take up medicine as our subject, you are Galen incarnate in your familiarity with it; if astrology, you are Hermes [Trismegistos] in your calculations."[46] The interesting fact here is that Yaḥya b. Aktham, a religious scholar, knew Hermes in detail and attributed astrological knowledge to him.

Most intriguing, perhaps, is how 'Abbāsid scholars linked prophetic wisdom to Hermes. So far Hermes appeared as scientist, sage, patron saint of astrology, and king of Egypt whose original domicile was Babylon, with no particular connection to the Deluge. Soon the link between prophetic knowledge and Hermes was made, and Hermes became the antediluvian grandson of Adam. As early as the late eighth and early ninth centuries, Hermes emerged as the common source of wisdom, the inventor of crafts and sciences, who was also given a divine script. First, the connection between the biblical figure of Enoch and the Qur'ān's Idrīs was made, as evidence suggests, by Wahb b. al-Munabbih, who claimed that Idrīs also received a thirty-page script from God.[47] Then Idrīs was identified with Hermes. In his *Kitāb al-Tarbī' wa al-Tadwīr*, al-Jāḥiẓ refers to Hermes in connection with the knowledge of the nature of celestial beings[48] and asks his interlocutor whether Hermes is identical with Idrīs.[49] Thus this passing reference confirms that the identification of Hermes with Idrīs was, in fact, known in the early ninth century among intellectuals close to the 'Abbāsid palace.[50] With this significant shift in his identity, Hermes became the ultimate source of knowledge—secular and religious; Greek, Indian, and Persian.

The most complete account of Hermes as the antediluvian sage of science and wisdom is given by Abū Ma'shar, who perfected the legend of Three Hermeses in Arabic.[51] According to Abū Ma'shar, the name Hermes was an appellation like Caesar or Chosroes. Its first bearer, who lived before the Flood, was he whom the Persians called Awanjhān, the grandson of Gayomarth, the Persian Adam, as well as he whom the Hebrews called Enoch (Ukhnukh), whose name in Arabic was Idrīs; the Harranians mentioned his prophecy. He inspired the emergence of the first revealed religion, Sābi'anism, the religion of the *ḥunafā'*, antedating Abraham.[52] Abū Ma'shar maintained that the antediluvian Hermes "was the first to speak of upper things, such as the motion of the stars, and his grandfather, Adam, taught him the hours of the night and day. He was the first to build sanctuaries and to praise God therein, the first to think and speak of medicine." Hermes wrote numerous books of rhythmic poems about the knowledge of terrestrial and celestial subjects. "He was the first to prophesy the coming of the Flood and saw the heavenly plague by water and fire threatened the earth." He resided in Egypt, which he selected for himself, and built the sanctuaries of the pyramids and the temple towns. "It was because of his fear that wisdom might be lost that he built the temples, namely, the temple known as al-Barbā, the temple of Akhmīm (Panopolis), engraved on their walls drawings of all techniques and their technicians, made pictures of all the working-tools of craftsmen, and by inscriptions indicated the essence of the sciences for the benefit of those who were to come after him. In doing so, he was guided by the desire of preserving science for later generations and by fear that its trace might disappear from the world."[53] The second Hermes lived in Babylon after the Flood, bringing Sābi'anism to Mesopotamia, and, finally, the third Hermes lived in Egypt and had links both to Greece and to the Roman Empire.[54]

Chronologically it seems that Abū Ma'shar reasoned that the antediluvian Hermes came first. He later added the remaining two Hermeses to his explanation.[55] It is likely, therefore, as Pingree suggested, that the legend of the transmission of the sciences from the prophetic *Ur*-wisdom might even have originated during the reign of al-Rashid among scholars of Persian and Harranian origins in the Chamber of Wisdom, *Khizānat al-Ḥikma*.[56] Although this argument still needs to be proven with more concrete evidence, the fact that Abū Ma'shar claimed to have received his information from Hermes and attributed his astrological information to the primordial wisdom in its divinely revealed form is sufficient to show the belief in a singular and ultimately divine fountain of wisdom. By the time of al-Ṭabarī, this view was well established. Al-Ṭabarī mentioned that some scholars even maintained that Idrīs was a universal prophet sent to all humankind, was given previous knowledge in full, and was supplied with a thirty-page script from God. For al-Ṭabarī, the Qur'ānic references to *Ur*-scriptures, *al-suḥuf al-ūlā*, simply mean the revelations given to Idrīs.[57]

This background information might provide an appropriate context to evaluate al-Ma'mūn's conduct in dealing with ancient sciences. Interestingly enough, the path that al-Ma'mūn and his courtiers followed to retrieve ancient wisdom invoked the Hermetic notion of search for knowledge. As numerous examples in medieval sources show, ancient wisdom was associated with manuscripts, concealed libraries, scripts, and magical tablets either lying buried in ruins or kept in palaces, temples, and monasteries until they were discovered by and revealed to the deserving seeker. Two notable medieval sources attribute the translation activities to al-Ma'mūn's dream of Aristotle, two different versions of which exist. According to the dream, al-Ma'mūn, motivated by what he had seen in his dream, wrote to the Byzantine emperor and requested his permission to obtain selected manuscripts that contained ancient knowledge, *al-'ulūm al-qadīma,* and were kept in Byzantine territories. Having obtained the permission, al-Ma'mūn dispatched a group of scholars who selected and eventually brought a number of manuscripts to Baghdad, where they were translated into Arabic on al-Ma'mūn's orders.[58] However, only one version of the dream, as Gutas suggests, seems to have originated during the lifetime of the caliph, although it does not seem to have any direct bearing on the translation activities. As Gutas argues, the dream narrative was a social result not the cause of the translation movement.[59]

Yet given the eminence of dreams in medieval Islamic society and literature, it may be helpful to look at the dream as a form of revelation.[60] If the dream narrative was invented or used to explain the caliph's intellectual and doctrinal activities (in both dreams Aristotle appears as the authoritative sage), the audience of this account must have regarded dreams not only to be a convincing reason to take action but also a privilege given to few people. The primary value of the dream narrative for us here is not the content of the dream but the image of the dreamer himself who was shown a dream, or given a revelation while unconscious, and privileged with divine providence to have access to the sources of wisdom.[61]

Further evidence comes from Miskawayh's (d. 1030) *Jāvidan Khiradh*. In it, al-Ma'mūn's name appears in a fascinating story, which seems to have originated in the court of al-Ma'mūn to justify his support of the translation activities, concerning the recovery of an ancient manuscript reaching as far back as the antediluvian King Hoshank.[62] According to the narrative, when al-Ma'mūn was pronounced caliph, he received gifts from some kings, including the king of Kābūlistān. The king dispatched an old man named Dhubān, who offered his knowledge to the caliph. Dhubān informed al-Ma'mūn of a manuscript written in ancient script, based on ancient wisdom, and kept in a little box of black glass under the floor of a palace courtyard in al-Madā'in (Ctesiphon), which the caliph finally excavated. The story ends with the note that the 'Abbāsid courtier al-Ḥasan b. Sahl (d. 850 or 851) translated a portion of this manuscript into Arabic.[63] The story credits al-Ma'mūn with unearthing or unveiling a portion of the *sophia perennis* that was attributed to Hoshank and entitled the *Book of Eternal Knowledge*. This story, whether fact or fiction,[64] links al-Ma'mūn's name not only to the collection of manuscripts but also to Hermetic mediation by which the mysterious sage under the protection of al-Ma'mūn, the caliph, and the translator collaboratively expose a hidden text and mediate between divine wisdom and the people at large. A valuable hidden source of knowledge finally finds its deserving seeker. This account is only one of the numerous narratives about al-Ma'mūn's role in collecting the sources of ancient sciences.[65]

Perhaps the most curious of al-Ma'mūn's such activities is his excavation of the pyramids in Egypt, which he conducted most probably at the beginning of 832 when he came to Egypt to quell the Bashmūric uprising.[66] During his stay of several weeks in Egypt, he ordered the pyramid of Cheops opened up to find out what it housed. After arduous excavation through the narrow passageways and chambers, al-Ma'mūn succeeded in reaching the gallery and the burial chamber but found nothing except decayed remains. At that point the caliph apparently ordered the project halted.[67] Before leaving for Damascus to prepare his troops for the ongoing offensive against Byzantium and on the recommendation of the sages in Egypt, al-Ma'mūn commissioned Ayyūb b. Maslama, an old sage, to decipher and translate "what was written on the Pyramids, the two obelisks of Heliopolis, a stela found in a village stable near Memphis, another stela from Memphis itself, [as well as writings found] in Bū Sīr and Sammānūd. Everything he translated is in a book called the *Book of Priestly Talismans*."[68]

What was he looking for in the pyramids?[69] Contextual evidence concerning what the pyramids might have meant for al-Ma'mūn and his contemporaries suggests that, as al-Idrīsī maintained, the caliph hoped "to expose the secrets that the pyramids concealed from the people and to learn their true meaning."[70] His comment suggests the possibility that various legends concerning the pyramids were available to al-Ma'mūn, some of which we fortunately know. It seems that al-Idrīsī suspected that inscriptions, knowledge, and relics would be found in the pyramids, which justifies Cooperson's argument that the caliph was looking for libraries from pagan times. Futhermore Ibn al-Nawbakht's and Abū Ma'shar believed, which suggested that the pyramids were structures built to preserve antediluvian knowledge. Fodor also has demonstrated the circulation of legends concerning the pyramids as structures built not only to endure the destructive force of the Flood but also to hide divine and scientific knowledge from the curious and uninitiated until someone with right intention and credentials could retrieve what was hidden.[71] Another legend, whose translation to Arabic seems to have been completed in 225/840–41, shortly after the death of al-Ma'mūn, attributes the construction of the pyramids to the antediluvian king of Egypt, Sūrīd. According to the legend, the king saw in a dream one hundred years before the Deluge the devastation of Egypt by a natural catastrophe. Acting upon his dream, the king ordered the construction of the pyramids to protect and preserve the sciences until new generations came to Egypt and discovered the sciences.[72] Sufficient evidence exists to suggest that the pyramids were known by the time of al-Ma'mūn to preserve sacred knowledge concealed both within their walls and in the symbolic language of the hieroglyphic script.[73]

Given the availability of such legends, van Reeth appears to be justified in suggesting that al-Ma'mūn was looking for the legacy of Adam where he and his five sons—along with the gold, myrrh, and frankincense that Adam carried off from Eden—lay buried. According to this legend, the treasure also contained Adam's prophetic legacy to his son Seth, who is identified with Agathadaimon, the pupil, or master, of Hermes in other places,[74] which revealed the secrets of prophetic knowledge based on Adam's stay in paradise, as well as the mystery of creation.[75] Van Reeth notes that al-Ma'mūn was accompanied to Egypt by Dionysius of Tell Mahre, the Jacobite patriarch of Antioch, who would have been familiar with a sixth-century Syriac text (*Me'arat Gazze*) that described the Cave of Treasures, which was identified with the pyramid of Cheops. According to van Reeth, the patriarch must have informed the caliph of this Syriac legend, prompting the caliph to excavate the pyramid looking for Adam's legacy.[76]

Granted that it is difficult to prove that the caliph looked specifically for either the Tablet of Hermes, of whose existence the caliph had learned from the Greek translation of a Babylonian tale, as Plessner argues,[77] or Adam's legacy to his sons,[78] but it is still possible that his excavations in the pyramids were inspired by the available legends. Later sources report that the Tablet of Hermes, containing his *Risālat al-Sirr* (*The Epistle of Secret Knowledge*), was discovered on a gold tablet in the tomb of the Egyptian princess of Akhmīm (Panopolis) when al-Ma'mūn was in Egypt in 832, positively linking al-Ma'mūn and Hermes to the pyramids. *Risālat al-Sirr* belonged to a field of magical knowledge associated with Jābir b. Ḥayyān and the *Kitāb Sirr al-Khalīqa wa Ṣan'at al-Ṭabī'a* (*The Book of the Secret of Creation and the Art of Nature*), also known as the *Kitāb Bālīnās al-Ḥakīm fī al-'Ilal* (*The Book of Balinas the Wise on the Causes*),[79] which was attributed to Apollonius of Tyana but seems to have been penned by an author during the reign of al-Ma'mūn.[80]

Whether or not the tablet was found, al-Ma'mūn's knowledge of the pyramids was most certainly similar to that of his contemporaries. If he shared a similar view of the pyramids, the mission of his expedition must have been to find the remnants of the antediluvian knowledge housed there so that he would have a share in its recovery and dissemination. Considering the background of the caliph, the context of his support of the translation activities, and the image he projected through his conduct, it seems reasonable that al-Ma'mūn not only was aware of such prophecies and legends but also engaged them as a possible source of justification for dealing with ancient knowledge and its integration into Islamic sensibilities.[81]

Shortly after his excavations in the pyramids, the caliph unleashed the most drastic of his religious policies—the Miḥna—in Rabī' I 218/April 833. While preparing for a major campaign on the Byzantine frontier, the caliph requested that the governor of Baghdad question a number of scholars on the issue of whether the Qur'ān was created. He asked to conduct the interviews of prominent scholars himself and was later personally involved in the resulting persecutions. Al-Ma'mūn's conciliatory posture and restrained response to his political opponents in Baghdad during the civil war stands in sharp contrast to his insistence on aggressive—and divisive—religious policies, which will be examined next.

Religious Purity and the Miḥna

As he grew up, al-Ma'mūn received extensive training in religious sciences, Qur'ān, jurisprudence, *ḥadīth*, and theology from some of the best scholars of his time. In his adulthood and during his caliphate, he continued his enthusiastic interest in learning. He regularly held scholarly discussions on such diverse subjects as jurisprudence, *ḥadīth*, theology, philosophy, and science, enlisting scholars of varying religious backgrounds from far and near. In accord with his image as the leader of guidance and as God's caliph, he saw the prospect to combine his scholarly knowledge with religio-political authority. He therefore appropriated to himself the authority to interpret religion and to act upon his judgments.

However, al-Ma'mūn was not the first caliph or ruler to have such ambitions. In that sense, his claim to religious authority was a recurring problem throughout the late antiquity and the medieval world. Reforming religion was a major concern of early-ninth-century emperors, with each claiming divine mandate. Byzantine emperors were still pursuing, albeit less passionately by this time, their policy of Iconoclasm to enforce a certain religious dogma, while the Carolingians in France embarked on a large-scale reform of the Church under Charlemagne and, particularly, under his son Louis the Pious.[82] In the imperial world of the early ninth century, such reform initiatives sprang from the religio-political competition and struggle among the three territorial empires as much as they did from domestic policies to forge a modus vivendi between imperial policies and religious sentiments.[83]

Al-Ma'mūn's claims to religious authority were therefore neither proclaimed solely for domestic purposes nor unusual in the early-ninth-century imperial context. First, given his adoption of the title the leader of guidance and then God's caliph since the civil war, his religious claims in Baghdad were based on these titles. Second, in the religio-political struggle of the early ninth century, he needed political legitimacy, one that included religious authority as well, to combat his imperial competitors. Third, his claim to religious authority reinforced his fiscal and administrative reforms, as well as his missionary activities. His religious claims were integral to his policies domestically and abroad, and met popular expectations focusing on the dawn of the third Islamic century.

Several years after he arrived at Baghdad, al-Ma'mūn began announcing his controversial religious opinions. Al-Ma'mūn's religious initiatives unfolded in a series of policies of varying religio-political significance over a period of several years. In 212/827 al-Ma'mūn proclaimed that no protection would be given to anyone who mentioned Mu'āwiya favorably and preferred him to the other companions of the Prophet. His action was seen as scandalous and created serious resentment among the masses. Al-Ma'mūn finally gave in to the advice of his judge Yaḥya b. Aktham and rescinded this proclamation, despite the famous Mu'tazilī scholar Thumāma b. Ashras's opinion to the contrary.[84] Following his proclamation regarding Mu'āwiya, al-Ma'mūn took yet another step and proclaimed 'Alī the most virtuous of all the companions of the Prophet Muḥammad.[85]

His 'Alid sympathy is also reflected in a legal matter involving the inheritance of a fief—a palm grove in Fadak, a small town in northern Ḥijāz near Khaybar—which was allocated to the Prophet after his expedition against the Jews of Khaybar. The ownership of this land had been in dispute since the death of the Prophet because of the disagreement between Fāṭima, the Prophet's daughter, and Abū Bakr over its legal status. In the initial discussion of the matter after the death of the Prophet, Fāṭima demanded that she inherit the land as her father's heir, while Abū Bakr claimed that it should be kept as common charity. The Prophet, he maintained, had stated that he would have no heirs; what he left would to go to charity, *ṣadaqa*.[86] Now, in 210/825, al-Ma'mūn reopened the case for judgment and reversed Abū Bakr's ruling, stating that Fadak be given to Fāṭima's heirs.[87] In a letter he wrote to his governor of Medina, he ordered that his ruling be recorded in the administration register.[88] Al-Ma'mūn's letter emphasized the caliph's right to overrule the previous verdict because of his high standing in God's religion and because he was an heir of the Prophet. He noted that by returning the land of Fadak to Fāṭima's heirs, he hoped to come closer to God and to do what was right.[89] Although the controversy over the land was never a matter of great dispute in the early ninth century, al-Ma'mūn's putting himself on an equal footing with Abū Bakr and overruling his verdict certainly was symbolically significant.

If the verdict in the case of Fadak showed that al-Ma'mūn considered himself equal in authority to Abū Bakr, al-Ma'mūn's legal opinion to allow temporary marriage, *mut'a,* in 215/830[90] came as an attempt to assert his religious-legal authority vis-à-vis 'Umar's. For most of the *ahl al-ḥadīth* and jurists in the ranks of broad proto-Sunnī circles, temporary marriage was, following the opinion of 'Umar (the first to ban it), little more than fornication.[91] Both cases not only emphasized the caliph's religious and moral equality with the first two caliphs, but they also made clear the chasm between the caliph and some of the religious scholars among the *faqīh*s and *ḥadīth* folk, who would become the conservative wing of the proto-Sunnīs trumpeting reverence to

Muʿāwiya and defending the ban on temporary marriage. There is an intriguing parallel between al-Ma'mūn's position vis-à-vis Abū Bakr and 'Umar and the circulating prophecies announcing the superiority of the Mahdī to the first two caliphs. One may suspect, therefore, that the subtext of al-Ma'mūn's ruling against the two caliphs, placed in the context of the prophecies, stresses the relative superiority of the caliph to Abū Bakr and 'Umar, without openly expressing this notion, as the following prophecy suggests: "Ibn Sīrīn was asked whether the Mahdī or Abū Bakr and 'Umar were better. He said, 'He is better than they were. He is compared to a prophet.'"[92]

In 216/832, during his campaign against Byzantium, al-Ma'mūn made another proclamation, this time concerning the daily prayer. Al-Ma'mūn ordered his governor of Baghdad, Isḥāq b. Ibrāhīm, to direct the troops to pronounce an extra *takbīr* when they performed the prayer. Al-Ṭabarī reports that the caliph's order was first put into practice in the mosque of Baghdad and at Ruṣāfa on Friday (16 Ramaḍān 216/27 October 832). All worshippers pronounced the *takbīr* three times while standing as soon as they had completed the worship. Subsequently participants in the congregational prayer followed this practice at every prescribed session of worship.[93]

At the same time that al-Ma'mūn declared his views concerning 'Alī and Muʿāwiya, he also announced his view that the Qur'ān was created.[94] Unlike his father, al-Rashīd, al-Ma'mūn believed that God's unity was compromised by the dogma of an uncreated Qur'ān. It was not until 218/833, while on a campaign against the Byzantines, however, that al-Ma'mūn decided to enforce his teaching. He wrote the first letter of the Miḥna (Rabīʿ I, 218/April 833) to the governor of Baghdad instructing him in the steps he should follow and declaring the caliph's intentions and motives for choosing such a path. The Miḥna evolved into a persecution policy in a span of a few months, as seen in several letters exchanged between al-Ma'mūn and his governor. Several judges and scholars were questioned by Isḥāq b. Ibrāhīm in Baghdad, and seven were questioned by al-Ma'mūn personally in al-Raqqa. Those who accepted the caliph's view were released and their opinions made public. In the end, there were only two individuals who still refused to comply with al-Ma'mūn's order, Aḥmad b. Ḥanbal and Muḥammad b. Nūḥ, who were referred to al-Ma'mūn to be questioned by him in person in Ṭarsūs. However, before they arrived at their destination, news reached them that al-Ma'mūn had died. Thus Aḥmad b. Ḥanbal was released and returned to Baghdad, but Muḥammad b. Nūḥ, who also was released, died on his way back.[95]

Because I have examined the subject elsewhere,[96] there is no need to narrate the details of contemporary scholarship on the Miḥna. But a few words are in order. In its broad outlines, modern scholarship is unequivocal about al-Ma'mūn's goal of furthering his religious authority and ultimately combining both spheres of authority, religious and political, in his office.[97] A number of scholars have experimented with the notion of the Mu'tazilī-leaning caliph's predilection to impose the Mu'tazilī view on the Sunnīs, whom he disliked, or to fashion a reconciliation between these two sects that tore his reign apart.[98] Others see the Miḥna as an attempt to formulate a policy of reconciliation and compromise among the autocratic bloc composed of the court secretaries and the constitutionalist bloc represented by the *'ulamā'*.[99] A number of other scholars largely approach the Miḥna as a symptom of state-religion tension. Gibb sees the Miḥna as the breaking point in the conflict between the expansionist character of the central political authority, which attempted to bring the religious institutions under state control, and the religious institution, which pronounced its independence from any external supervision, including the central authority.[100] For Hodgson, the Miḥna had to do more with "shoring up a courtly imperial ideal with an officially recognized religious establishment" in which as many Muslims as possible could unite. Al-Ma'mūn's position was a theological one requiring submission and conformity, as well as an operation against the growing public power of the "*sharī'a*-minded *ḥadīth* folk" and for the preparation of an Islamic institution more amenable to the religious demands of an absolute monarchy.[101]

Crone and Hinds argue that al-Ma'mūn's political strategy aimed to regain for the caliphate its religious authority embedded in the person of the caliph since its inception but which had begun losing ground against the increasing popularity of religious scholars.[102] Several other scholars argue similarly and have unearthed new details of the Miḥna and brought new questions to bear on the extent, execution, and aim of the policy.[103] Zaman offers another perspective altogether. He maintains that the relationship between the caliphs and the proto-Sunni scholars in the pre- and post-Miḥna period may be best defined as an expression of the caliphs' intent to act as patrons of and collaborators with the scholars regarding the regulation of religious life. Collaboration rather than clash or competition being the traditional mood, the Miḥna represented a departure from the already ongoing cooperation between the caliphate and the religious scholars, but not the culmination of a long struggle.[104]

Sourdel and Watt seem to place an undue emphasis on the nature of the Qur'ān and give the mistaken impression that the central issue in the Miḥna involved the determination of the nature of the Qur'ān. Although they argue that the theological problem was advanced as a pseudo-question, as the ultimate aim was actually political, recent research shows that the debate rose rather over the unity of God, *tawḥīd*, as the most fundamental principle of the faith. As a theological question, the argument that the Qur'ān was created went back to Umayyad times and was associated with Ja'd b. Dirham and Jahm b. Ṣafwān, both of whom were executed for heresy (and in the case of Jahm, rebellion) on the orders of the Umayyad caliphs.[105] Arguments on the issue persisted during 'Abbāsid times, and the Mu'tazilīs adopted as one of their doctrines the belief that the Qur'ān was created, although it was not an exclusively Mu'tazilī doctrine. Diverse individuals and religio-political movements adopted this belief, including some of the Ḥanafīs.[106] Even among the Mu'tazilīs, this issue remained unsettled for a while,[107] and there were Mu'tazilīs who did not support the Miḥna.[108]

Whether the Qur'ān was created was, therefore, far from being a pseudo-question. On the contrary, it involved a genuine theological controversy in which the caliph finally participated. The Miḥna essentially involved God's unity, *tawḥīd,* and opposed anthropomorphism, *tashbīh.*[109] The dispute over the Qur'ān raised fundamental religious issues, including the core belief of Islam. Claiming that the Qur'ān was not created meant, for those who argued the opposite, attributing co-eternity to something other than God, which violated the unity of God, and hence bordered on polytheism. In a letter addressed to his governor, Isḥāq b. Ibrāhīm, al-Ma'mūn introduced the problem of anthropomorphism into the discussion, juxtaposing Jesus and the Qur'ān as God's words. He distinguished between God and Jesus, and between God and the Qur'ān, as two separate entities: one the creator and the other created.[110]

The Miḥna does indeed appear to have involved the caliph's push to further his sphere of authority in religious matters. However, the question is about the impetus for and to some extent the manner in which the Miḥna was carried out. In the Crone and Hinds paradigm, religious authority was a prerogative of the caliph from the beginning, and al-Ma'mūn simply wanted to emphasize it. In the Zaman paradigm, the Miḥna came as a surprise, an anomaly in the long-term cooperation between the caliphs and the *'ulamā'* on the production of religious knowledge (*ijtihād*), though he agrees with Crone and Hinds on the nature of anomaly. What strikes the student of the Miḥna is that both arguments assume too much about the institutional and group consciousness of the involved parties and, in the Crone and Hinds case, al-Ma'mūn's reliance on the religio-political tradition of his predecessors.

That al-Ma'mūn reasserted his predecessor's policy of reclaiming his office's religious authority seems to contradict the proliferation of religious ideas during his time. Had the caliphate been self-conscious of its political and religious authority and systematically suppressed independent thought, intellectual output would have been far less and controversy rarer in legal and religious matters. Caliphal pretensions to religious authority were occasional, erratic, and inconclusive. In fact, perhaps because al-Ma'mūn did not think that he reclaimed a traditional right, his references to the past remained vague.[111] He mentioned God's caliphs, imams, and heirs of the Prophet in plural form, but refrained from using names or alluding to actual caliphs.[112] As Zaman demonstrates, the reign of al-Ma'mūn looms as an anomaly in the relationship between proto-

Sunni *'ulamā'* and the 'Abbāsids, who usually collaborated in the production of religious knowledge through *ijtihād*.[113]

Furthermore the religious and educational activities had not yet acquired an institutional embodiment. No institutional church existed that he could reform by asserting his religious authority, nor did he try to establish one. Instead religious scholars in various branches of knowledge operated as a heterogeneous and loosely connected network, a substantial segment of whom were administered by the caliphate in their role as judges. As Nawas has shown, even those interrogated in the Miḥna had little in common that would have provided a reason for al-Ma'mūn's policy. Not only the judges but also other scholars of diverse legal and religious views were questioned and implicated.[114] Therefore there was no central institution, or any one institution, representing the body of scholars with which he could negotiate to settle differences or reform.

On what basis, then, could al-Ma'mūn claim religious authority? The title of the caliph, *imām al-hudā*, and the idea of religious renewal, *tajdīd*, are instructive in this regard. Both suggest the possibility that the Miḥna might have had something to do with ambitions of renewal and purification of faith. The goal of al-Ma'mūn might have been much larger than inserting a new doctrinal principle or contesting scholars on a theological matter to prove the caliph's authority. In what it implies, the idea of renovation and restoration of faith might have been one of the few compelling ideological supports available to the caliph. The idea of *tajdīd*, religious renewal and restoration, emerged as one of the fundamental components of messianic discourse since the second Islamic century and was expressed in one of the politically most influential traditions in medieval Islamic history, the *mujaddid* tradition: "God will raise up for this community at the beginning of every hundred years one who will renovate its religion."[115] Whatever the source of this tradition, the background leading to its appearance at this particular time not only provided legitimate grounds for any claimant to deal with critical religious and political issues as the *corrector et reparator* of religion, but, more important, it established a normative principle for political action.[116] To push for religious authority the caliph had to depend on certain intellectual and ideological premises if his action was going to have any meaningful resonance. Messianic claims appear to be one of the few ways through which the caliph could embark on religious and secular reforms within the mental categories of his opponents and supporters. Messianic beliefs justified secular action with religious premises and bestowed religious authority on secular rulers. The pinnacle of messianic beliefs, the Mahdī, symbolized none other than a political leader endowed with religious authority (*khalīfat allāh al-mahdī*, God's caliph the Mahdī)[117] to realize the secular and religious dreams of his community in this world. He was not a religious sage.[118]

From the vantage point of al-Ma'mūn, messianic beliefs would have been a compelling model to which he could aspire and through which he could embark on secular and religious innovations. If he did so, he was not alone. Al-Ma'mūn's appropriation of this model in his own unique way reflects a fundamental and recurring process in medieval Muslim politics, which linked rulers to messianic beliefs in such a way that beliefs provided a valuable means for rulers to claim religious prerogatives. In his correspondence with his governor in Baghdad during the Miḥna, al-Ma'mūn saw himself primarily as an instrument to restore God's religion, destined to guide his community from ignorance into salvation and from falsehood to truth. The Miḥna letters forcefully reflect this distinctive tone. Acting consciously as God's caliph and the Prophet's heir, the caliph charged himself with a simple obligation: the correction and renovation of the faith to its pristine state; hence the determination of what is Islamic and what is not.[119] As a reflection of his image among the courtly elite in Baghdad, the testimony of his advisers is highly intriguing. The secretary of al-Ma'mūn, Aḥmad b. Yūsuf, promoted his patron as a beacon of salvation when he described the position of the caliph vis-à-vis his subjects: "[People] follow his road of salvation, *hadyihi*, and in their religion are guided through a dark path by his light."[120]

Understood in the context of prophecies of the early third/ninth century, which described the Mahdī as both imam and God's caliph, the titles of the caliph indicate the caliph's perceived authority to intervene in religious matters. Al-Ma'mūn seemed to have seen himself as God's representative and the Miḥna as a necessary act to purify religion and to correct errors. He asserted that God made it incumbent upon the imams and the caliphs to be zealous in five fundamental principles: establishing God's religion and guarding it faithfully; protecting the heritage of prophethood of which they were inheritors; preserving the tradition of knowledge, which God entrusted to their keeping; acting justly with the government of their subjects; and being diligent in obeying God's will in their conduct toward those subjects.[121] Clearly al-Ma'mūn saw himself responsible both for the well-being of his subjects and for their salvation. As the inheritor of the prophecy, he was obliged to guide his subjects in divine unity from erroneous belief and defective faith to the right belief and to show them God as God really is. Once they accepted his guidance and recognized God in the manner that the caliph described God to them, al-Ma'mūn assured his governor, who was instructed to summon the judges, his subjects would be on the path of right guidance and salvation.[122]

> That which God has a right to expect from His representatives on earth . . . [to] guide back to Him the one who has turned aside from Him and bring back the one who has turned his back from His command; trace out for their subjects the way of salvation for them; draw their attention to the limits of

> their faith and the way to their heavenly success and protection from sin; and reveal to them and those of their affairs which are hidden from them and those which are dubious and obscure by means of what will remove doubt from them and bring back illumination and clear knowledge to them all.[123]

According to his letter, he was in fact charged with making God known through the divine learning that had been entrusted to him and the knowledge that God had placed within him.[124]

The letters of the caliph concerning the Miḥna discussed not only the issue of the created Qur'ān but also described a ruler transformed into a gate for salvation for his subjects. It seems that the circle of followers around the caliph echoed back this image ever since the days of the civil war. When al-'Attābī addressed him in the following lines, "certainly there is no faith except in [your path] and no worldly [success] without you,"[125] he referred to qualities reminiscent of the Miḥna letters: a gate of salvation and repository of divine wisdom, which came into materialization not only in the Miḥna but also in the translation of ancient knowledge into Arabic and in his missionary and military activities throughout his reign. However, the caliph died prematurely, with most of his initiatives incomplete, and he left huge tasks for his successors.

Conclusion

Modern scholars are largely indebted to Nu'aym b. Ḥammād for illuminating the apocalyptic and messianic dimension of early Islamic history. Without his work, we would still know much about it, but we would not have such substantial evidence of its significance and impact. Traditionally, historical studies neglect the value of messianic beliefs as either popular misconstructions of, or subjective beliefs with no bearing on, historical reality, except in slogans and battle cries to rally popular support. While recent scholarship on early 'Abbāsid history appears well beyond this simplistic and positivistic outlook, the use of prophecies to understand mentality and worldview remains limited to studies on sectarian groups and opposition movements, even though the spectrum of messianic beliefs is much larger. What type of worldview, mentality, and outlook can be found in the prophecies about the 'Abbāsid civil war and the reign of al-Ma'mūn? Does this suggest some conclusions on the broader applications of prophecies in historical studies?

It must be pointed out that in the context of medieval Islam, messianic beliefs belonged primarily not to popular religiosity but to lettered tradition. They were produced, disseminated, written down, and transmitted by the learned elite. In fact many prophecies complain about the absence of scholars, burning of libraries and books, punishment of scholars, and diminishing knowledge as portents of declining society. Despite their manifest religious character, messianic beliefs are actually this-worldly and very pragmatic. They talk exclusively about this world, seek to change it, and act and react against its circumstances. Messianic beliefs rarely show interest in otherworldly judgment and punishment; they demand resolution here and now. They criticize the existing social and political order and the way that power is distributed in society, and demand an overhaul of society. Because they aspire to reestablishing the Golden Age of the past or hastening the future millennium, messianic beliefs find no satisfaction in the existing order. Happiness belongs in either the past or the future; hence the disillusionment with the present and the constant effort to transcend it. The future appears frequently imminent. Either it involves the awaited era of felicity, the millennium in which dreams are fulfilled, or the final confrontation or calamity that will terminate an epoch, the end of the world as we know it, and in extreme cases the termination of worldly life. However, not all apocalyptic beliefs entail the end of the world. Often the conclusion of an era and the dawn of a new one appear as the overriding concerns in prophecies—the best illustration in the context of this book is the prediction of the demise of the ʿAbbāsids. It is true that prophecies do not generally provide factual accounts of events, but they do reflect the mentalities of their time and how peoples perceived their realities. With their emphasis on perception and reaction and with their unambiguous stance on sociocultural and political matters, they add a valuable dimension to understanding historical events not necessarily readily visible in historiographical narratives.

Prophecies generally have a long life, but the Qur'ānic text did make it easier for its audience to refer to Qur'ānic exhortations to justify the end-of-time scenarios in subsequent centuries. Thus the Qur'ān insists on the approaching Hour, yet it does not specify a time for it nor does it mention a messianic figure. Although one cannot attribute medieval Islamic apocalyptic visions to the Qur'ānic discourse alone, it seems fair to argue that the Qur'ānic discourse partially inspired apocalyptic and, to a lesser extent, messianic ideas. Similarly the resurgence of biblical prophecies in the Umayyad and ʿAbbāsid milieu should not be underestimated. Non-Muslim inhabitants of the caliphate had already inherited a rich tradition of messianic and apocalyptic beliefs, on which they built new ones after the rise of Islam. Responsible for bringing much of the biblical apocalyptic lore into the context of the caliphate through oral and textual transmission, Middle East communities that were predominantly Christian, Zoroastrian, and Jewish exercised certain defensive and assimilative functions in linking the rise of Islam to pre-Islamic and biblical prophecies. These communities experienced their own anxieties during the rise of Islam, eventually arriving at a modus vivendi with their Muslim neighbors. Differences in confession were overshadowed by the similarity in sociopolitical norms and behavior as fittingly illustrated in imagining the ʿAbbāsid civil war as an apocalyptic and messianic event.

The prophecies of apocalyptic battles, *fitan* and *malāḥim*, before and during the civil war conveyed a double message of pessimism and of the need for change, and framed sociopolitical developments in an inescapably messianic light. The fear of *fitna*—the warnings against it and against participating in it—was counterbalanced by an equally powerful demand for action. The complexity of responses is certainly much deeper than what any type of binarism might suggest. On the one hand, the attitude toward *fitna* reveals the ambivalence of the observers, a mind and conscience torn between submission and resistance. On the other hand, it exemplifies a common thread of messianic thought across cultures: the rift between being resolved to one's fate or participation in its creation—in short, quietism or activism. The implications of the quietist position of some of the prophecies aside, the activist tendency in prophecies reveals militant attitudes vis-à-vis existing order ranging from arbitrary and destructive violence to organized and strategically planned action, such as conquests. The Mahdī is divinely guided, and his mission is for and in this world. He will go against all injustices and establish a paradise on earth.

Activism involves not only political, military, and social demands but also a militant propagation and implementation of faith, which emerges in prophecies in a clear, simple, manifest, and straightforward manner. There is no creedal ambiguity, particularly so because the Mahdī is the arbiter of what is right and wrong, admissible and inadmissible. However, this does not translate into a vulgar and simplistic faith for the consumption of the masses. On the contrary, the defense of a particular sectarian and theological position appears as a frequent means to describe the orthodox form of faith. What is ultimately demanded in prophecies is the restoration of the pristine form and the original clarity of faith. The Mahdī will eliminate historical disagreements, the fine but divisive theological details, and restore religious harmony and unity. Those who do not recognize his mission will by default be deviant, heretical, and unfaithful.

This radical stance within Islamic religiosity to identify the correct faith is contrasted with an accommodating tone in matters related to other monotheistic faiths. The fact that biblical materials constitute a frequent source of many Muslim prophecies shows the interconfessional dimension of messianic beliefs and the diverse trends that they represent. It is true that there is a strong inclination to oppose what the originators and transmitters of prophecies perceive as morally corrupt and culturally inferior, including religious minorities, ethnic and linguistic groups, and sects. However, views range from stricter and more exclusivist attitudes on faith and faith communities to perfectly accommodating and tolerant perspectives on the "People of the Book." Similarly the propagation of Islam is an important dimension of many prophecies. No doubt jihad is encouraged assertively, but for territorial expansion. Individuals and faith communities, on the other hand, appear to have been allowed to choose to convert voluntarily. Prophecies forecast the discovery of authentic religious scriptures to verify Islam's validity and to eliminate any disagreements among the Abrahamic faiths, in a sense making the final triumph of Islam a shared victory for all.

The evolution of the social and political dimensions of messianic and apocalyptic beliefs in the early Islamic period ultimately involved a negotiation between the Qur'ānic message, existing traditions in the region, and the Muslim community's experience under the caliphate. The appeal of this evolving discourse produced powerful movements right from the beginning and led to recurring episodes of charismatic interruptions, constructive or otherwise, in the social and political life during early Islam. What made this phenomenon a remarkable aspect of medieval Islamic history was the fact that messianic and apocalyptic beliefs did not show up only in opposition movements; they did so also in the central government itself since Umayyad times. Although the

Umayyads seem to have failed by and large to convince their opposition in their claims, the ʿAbbāsids succeeded in projecting an image of divinely guided rulers and approached messianic beliefs as an ideological resource to generate an imperial vision based on the promotion of such beliefs, rather than competing against them. Such an attitude might be explained as an all too familiar pragmatic utilization of messianic beliefs for shoring up popular support, but the fact is that what prophecies offered was politically relevant, religiously cogent, and practically feasible if the caliphs wanted to realize their agendas.

In a two-century-long evolution, Muslim society and polity produced a remarkable body of ideas, prophecies, and expectations, whose uses would sustain colorful messianic movements throughout Islamic history. Provoked by actual historical events or genuine prophecies, new or recycled, this body of ideas generated enduring normative principles and prescriptions for social and political action. Yet, as noted earlier, messianic sentiment did not function in a vacuum. Rather it took shape in a social and cultural context and adopted the concerns and values (even if it wanted to change these values) of the society in which it existed at the time (Shīʿī Mahdī, ʿAbbāsid Mahdī, the Sufyānī). This contextual flexibility kept the beliefs relevant to the concerns of society and made them an appealing perspective from which to approach social and political life. At the same time, this flexibility allowed prophecies to function not only during crises but also in the aftermath and during transitions to a more stable social and political stage.

In the case of the ʿAbbāsid civil war, Muslim and non-Muslim apocalyptic evidence, exegesis, court and panegyric poetry, *ḥadīth* compilations, and historiographical sources illustrate vividly how the witnesses to the civil war perceived the unfolding events in an unmistakable messianic context. In fact the civil war became an arena for the clash of prophecies, though what remains is largely anti-ʿAbbāsid. In particular the approach of the year 200 A.H. provoked a range of prophecies with direct bearing on caliphal politics, announcing the expectation that the ʿAbbāsid caliphate would soon collapse, and magnified the role of multiple religio-political movements (Shīʿī and non-Shīʿī) with messianic overtones in what was seen as an imminent millennium. The intellectual and sociopolitical developments inside and outside ʿAbbāsid society inspired the emphasis on the function of the Mahdī as a source of militant reform and renewal. Obviously the chronological relation of the Mahdī to the end of time and his sectarian and genealogical affiliation did certainly display flexibility, which encouraged a wide range of aspirants to lay claim to this title. Circulating prophecies focused their demands on three major changes the Muslim messianic ruler would initiate, the chief of which involved the universal messianic idea of social and political justice. Prophecies also advocated missionary and military activities inside and outside the Muslim community to make God's will universal. Finally prophecies called for the purification of faith from doctrinal and social residues so that the "real" word of God could manifest itself fully. Numerous prophecies insisted on restoring Islam to its pristine form under Prophet Muḥammad and called for a universal polity that would shelter all monotheistic faiths under the Mahdī's authority. A remarkable concentration of prophecies at the dawn of the third Islamic century elevated the 'Abbāsid political crisis to a cosmically preordained encounter between good and evil, and justified the birth of what Islamic tradition would call *mujaddid*, religious renewer.

The death of the 'Abbāsid caliph Hārūn al-Rashīd in 809 proved disastrous for the 'Abbāsid caliphate, as it triggered a civil war between his two sons that left one dead and the other's position precarious. It was also a seminal point in the history of the 'Abbāsids as it facilitated a reconfiguration of the caliphate. In this process of realignment, al-Ma'mūn seems to have aligned his actions with existing messianic expectations to reshape the caliphate in order to reflect more actively his religio-political goals. His revolt against his brother, and particularly his victory on the battlefield, won the soon-to-be caliph an evident legitimacy that rested on divine arbitration. The caliphate was not delegated to him through succession, rather by divine will. Therefore he could feel less attached to the political and religious legacy of his ancestors, whose policies he did not totally reject but reconsidered, altered, revised, and reoriented to fit his new agenda. Then he embarked on changes he deemed appropriate.

Within this context I have attempted to explain how al-Ma'mūn identified his movement as the "second summons" and framed it against the 'Abbāsid family in Baghdad. Granted that the tension between the 'Abbāsid center and the Khurāsānī periphery over social and political privileges underlined the conflict in the civil war. Al-Ma'mūn also aligned himself to the dynamics of this tension by defending the periphery against Baghdad. My argument has been that the cultural, ideological, and cognitive context of al-Ma'mūn would dictate how he would perceive the conflict and his role, and how to articulate his demands and goals. That he acted out of ideological conviction, which sometimes went clearly against pragmatic goals, was acutely displayed in the appointment of 'Alī al-Riḍā and later in the Miḥna. In Baghdad as well, al-Ma'mūn followed policies not necessarily loyal to traditional 'Abbāsid political values and religious positions. The far-reaching administrative and coinage reforms, his missionary activities in the eastern frontiers of the caliphate, his relentless push against Byzantium in the West, and his religious and intellectual activities to create and define an imperial culture derived their vigor from an acquired—not inherited—legitimacy and from the available messianic discourse of his time, as suggested in the competing modes of authority contained in his titles: imam, the leader of guidance, and God's caliph.

Like many rulers before and after him, al-Ma'mūn's challenge was how to bridge the gap between his broad aspirations and the day-to-day details of actual rule. How was he going to reconcile revolutionary fervor with imperial policies that needed stability? The caliph seems to have experienced ambivalence at certain junctures as how best to put his ideals into practice. In several significant incidents, this ambivalence led to what might appear arbitrary policy shifts during the caliph's relatively long rule. Nonetheless, he reacted against the routinized authority of his predecessors and against the central political and religious establishment that defined the ʿAbbāsid caliphate preceding him. It did not matter much to him if he reversed some of his decisions; he proved unequivocally that he could go against traditional norms, break with ʿAbbāsid conventions, and challenge established symbols.

He was not alone. Since al-Manṣūr's time the caliphs had tried to forge a symbiosis between revolutionary charisma and imperial demands. They sought and asserted a salvific role for themselves, but mostly within the limits of the practical demands of their realm. Al-Ma'mūn faced the same problem; however, instead of executing policies to normalize political life, he preferred a continuance of the revolutionary fervor and his charismatic authority. In many ways his position resembled that of al-Manṣūr but differed from that of his successors. Both al-Manṣūr and al-Ma'mūn came to power as a result, and in the wake, of a large revolt, and both had to deal with the revolutionary fervor that brought them to power. Whereas al-Manṣūr's successors gradually introduced policies to curb the revolutionary fervor, al-Ma'mūn actively maintained it; whereas al-Manṣūr's successors cooperated with the proto-Sunni jurists to institute orthodoxy to counterbalance the extremist revolutionaries, al-Ma'mūn challenged them and reasserted his authority; whereas al-Manṣūr's successors protected the *abnā'* and their privileges, al-Ma'mūn alienated them. In short, al-Ma'mūn, unlike al-Manṣūr's successors, insisted that the revolutionary charisma continue at full speed.

This study has been about illuminating a dimension of ʿAbbāsid politics from the perspective of prophecies. I hope to have made a case for messianic beliefs as a modality other than realpolitik to explain political action and change. Whether the main argument of the book is tenable is up to the reader; what is more significant is the prospect of more and better use of messianic and apocalyptic prophecies in specific historical studies.

Abbreviations

BSOAS	*Bulletin of the School of Oriental and African Studies*
EI	*Encyclopedia of Islam*, 1st ed.
EI(r)	*Encyclopedia Iranica*
EI(2e)	*Encyclopedia of Islam*, 2nd ed., electronic version
IJMES	*International Journal of Middle East Studies*
IQ	*Islamic Quarterly*
JAOS	*Journal of the American Oriental Society*
JESHO	*Journal of Economic and Social History of the Orient*
JNES	*Journal of Near Eastern Studies*
JRAS	*Journal of the Royal Asiatic Society*
JSAI	*Jerusalem Studies in Arabic and Islam*
JSS	*Journal of Semitic Studies*
MW	*Muslim World*
RSO	*Revisti degli Studi Orientali*
SI	*Studia Islamica*
ZDMG	*Zeitschrift der Deutschen Morgenländischen Gesellschaft Bibliography*

Notes

Introduction

1. Casanova, *Mohammed et la fin du monde,* 3 ff., 12 ff.; Crone and Cook, *Hagarism*, 5 ff., 21 ff.

2. Arjomand, "Islamic Apocalypticism," 239–48; Donner, "La Question de Messianisme," 17–27; Cook, *Studies,* 270 ff.

3. Clearly many were skeptical of and even ridiculed the authority of monotheistic scriptures in matters of future knowledge. See Nu'aym, *Kitāb al-Fitan,* 229–30. Ibn Abī Shayba, *Kitāb al-Muṣannaf,* 7:465: From Abū Usāma on the authority of Ibn 'Awn from Ibn Sīrīn, who said, "Muḥammad b. Abī Ḥudhayfa was with Ka'b [al-Aḥbār] on a ship one day when he asked him [the following]: O Ka'b do you [really] come across this [prophecy] in the Torah? How is this happening [teasing him], and how [this] and how [that]? Ka'b told him not to ridicule the Torah, [because] 'it is a book of God, it contains truth.'"

4. For several other reports, see Nu'aym, *Kitāb al-Fitan,* 230, 231.

5. Court poetry in particular confers the epithet Mahdī on later Umayyad rulers, most famously Sulaymān b. 'Abd al-Malik (r. 96–99/715–17) and 'Umar II (r. 99–101/717–20). Al-Farazdaq, *Diwān,* 1:264, 2:9; Jarīr, *Diwān,* 1:124–25. See also Ibn Abī Shayba, *Kitāb al-Muṣannaf,* 7:509, 514; *EI*[(2e)], Mahdī (Madelung). For further examples, see Crone and Hinds, *God's Caliph,* 34–36; Cook, *Studies,* 36 ff.

6. Abū Dāwūd, *Al-Sunan,* 5:35.

7. Al-Mas'ūdī, *Tanbīh,* 33. For further details, see *EI*[(2e)], Kharīṭa (S. Maqbul Ahmad); Johns and Savage-Smith, "Book of Curiosities"; Karamustafa, "Introduction to Islamic Maps."

8. Ḥamāda, *Al-Wathā'iq al-Siyāsiyya wa al-Idāriyya al-'Ā'ida,* 2:319. His remark deals with Muḥammad's prophecy.

9. For more information, see Yücesoy, "Between Nationalism and the Social Sciences."

10. The theory of rational action conceives rational behavior as the result of a conscious choice by a self-interest-pursuing actor who chooses the alternative with the highest expected utility. More broadly, the theory came also to mean utility maximization, pursuit of material self-interests, and purposive and goal-directed behavior. For an assessment and critique of the theory, see Coleman and Fararo, *Rational Choice Theory;* Jerolmack and Porpora, "Religion, Rationality, and Experience," 140 ff.

11. For an elegant articulation of this view, see Hodgson, *Venture of Islam,* 1:478, 479, 480, 481; Crone and Hinds, *God's Caliph,* 94–96; *EI*[(2e)] Miḥna (M. Hinds). Most recently, El-Hibri offered a sharp account of al-Ma'mūn from this perspective. See El-Hibri, *Reinterpreting,* 95 ff., 143 ff.

12. For a similar methodological issues in Ottoman history, see Fleischer, *Bureaucrat and Intellectual*, 4.

13. Lewis, "Regnal Titles," 19. See Nagel, *Staat und Glaubensgemeinschaft*, 170. He sees the reign of al-Ma'mūn as a fulfillment of Ibn al-Muqaffa''s absolutist views. Lewis, "Regnal Titles," 19. Cf. al-Dūrī, "Al-Fikra al-Mahdīyya," 123 ff. Also note *EI*$^{(2e)}$, Iran (A.K.S. Lambton), for a similar view: 'Abbāsids "quickly abandoned any messianic or extremist tendencies they may have entertained before their victory over the Umayyads. There was, it is true, alongside the 'conservative' tendency of society and government a messianic tendency, but its manifestations were usually fleeting."

14. Schwartz, "End of the Beginning."

15. Mannheim, *Ideology and Utopia*, esp. chaps. 2 and 4.

16. See Weber, *Theory of Social and Economic Organization*, 324 ff.

17. Cohn, *The Pursuit of the Millennium*, esp. foreword and introduction.

18. For a theoretical treatment of apocalyptic and messianic ideologies and movements, see McGinn et al., *Encyclopedia of Apocalypticism*; Bull, *Apocalypse Theory*.

19. McGinn, *Visions of the End*, 28–36; Talmon, "Millenarian Movements," 159–200.

20. McGinn, *Visions of the End*, 29.

21. Lerner, *Power of Prophecy*, 195–96.

22. I refer the readers to Cook, *Studies*, 31–33, for modern scholarship on Muslim apocalyptic thought.

23. See the work of Sachedina, Arjomand, Bashear, Bacharach, Blichfeldt, D. Cook, al-Dūrī, Geddes, Helperin, Jenkinson, Lewis, Madelung, Sharon, Tucker, Wasserstrom, van Vloten, and Zaman included in the bibliography.

24. Aguadé, *Messianismus;* Madelung, "New Documents"; El-Hibri, *Reign*.

25. Alexander, "Medieval," 997 ff.

26. Zaman, *Religion and Politics*.

27. Cooperson, *Classical*, 25 ff.; Cooperson, *Makers of Islam: Al-Ma'mūn*.

28. Nawas, "Psychoanalitic View."

29. Miskawayh, *Al-Ḥikma al-Khālida*, 124.

30. On this level, this is a case meriting evaluation within the context of cognitive dissonance. See Festinger, *Theory of Cognitive Dissonance*.

31. El-Hibri, *Reinterpreting*, esp. chaps. 3–5; cf. Radke, "Towards a Topology."

32. Al-Ṭabarī, *Tārīkh*, 8:573, 32:92; Ibn A'tham, *Kitāb al-Futūḥ*, 8:323–24. This account is one of several other eclipses, which are also correctly recorded in al-Ṭabarī, *Tārīkh*.

33. Verbelen, *Ancient Astronomy*, and his previous e-mail correspondence with me. Julian day number with decimals: 2020373.83/ DeltaT: 2427/ Year: 819/ Month: Jun/ Day: 26/ Maximum Eclipse on Earth (Universal Time): 7h 58m/ Hemispheric location: North/ Type of Solar eclipse: central annular/ Saros: 98/ Inex: 48. I am indebted to Felix Verbelen, the president of the Public Observatory MIRA (Belgium), for sharing these technical details.

34. Robinson, *Islamic Historiography*, 35–36.

35. For a recent evaluation of early Islamic historiography and the contemporary debates about it, see Donner, *Narratives*.

36. For an analysis of biographical sources on al-Ma'mūn and 'Alī al-Riḍā, see Cooperson, *Classical*, 24–107. See also Radke, "Towards a Topology," 1 ff.

37. El-Hibri, *Reinterpreting,* 59 ff., 95 ff.; El-Hibri, "Regicide," 334 ff.; Cooperson, *Classical,* 67–69.

38. See Bacharach, "Al-Amīn's Designated Successor."

39. Aguadé, "Messianismus," 209.

40. For his biography, see Aguadé, "Messianismus," 8 ff.; *EI*[(2e)], Nu'aym b. Ḥammād, (Ch. Pellat).

41. Aguadé, "Messianismus," 43–44.

42. Generally the prophecies in Nu'aym b. Ḥammād's work consist of a chain of authorities from whom the report is taken followed by a prophecy, mostly in a short anecdotal format, but at times relatively longer.

43. Nu'aym, *Kitāb al-Fitan,* 166, 168.

44. Nu'aym, *Kitāb al-Fitan,* 235–36.

45. Nu'aym, *Kitāb al-Fitan,* 223, 237, 238, 245, 249; al-Ṣan'ānī, *Al-Muṣannaf,* 11:388.

46. Nu'aym, *Kitāb al-Fitan,* 237. For further details about al-Qaḥṭānī, see Madelung, "Apocalyptic Prophecies," 149–56.

47. Nu'aym, *Kitāb al-Fitan,* 238.

48. Lerner, *Power,* 8.

49. Lerner, *Power,* 8.

50. Nu'aym, *Kitāb al-Fitan,* 180. The prophecy continues with the commencement of an apocalyptic battle in Palestine in which the seventh of the seven rises victorious. See the references to al-Ma'mūn as the seventh of the 'Abbāsids in Ibn A'tham, *Kitāb al-Futūḥ,* 8:327; al-Azdī, *Tārīkh Mawṣil,* 370–71; al-Mas'ūdī, *Murūj al-Dhahab,* 4:326.

51. Nu'aym, *Kitāb al-Fitan,* 123.

52. See Nu'aym, *Kitāb al-Fitan,* 52, 64, 67, 247–48, 271; Ibn Abī Shayba, *Kitāb al-Muṣannaf,* 7:513; al-Balādhurī, *Ansāb,* 3:47, 48; *EI*[(2e)], Mahdī.

53. The earliest reference is in Ibn Ḥibbān, *Al-Majrūḥīn,* 1:136–37.

54. Classical sources give conflicting accounts of his life. He is confused with 'Abd al-'Azīz b. Abbān and the above account attributed both to Ismā'īl and 'Abd al-'Azīz. Such controversies, which need a separate examination, notwithstanding, he is discredited as a liar and plagiarizer by the *ḥadīth*-transmitters. For his biography, see Ibn Abī Ḥātim, *Al-Jarḥ wa al-Ta'dīl,* 2:160; Ibn Ḥibbān, *Al-Majrūḥīn,* 1:136–37; al-Dhahabī, *Mīzān al-I'tidāl,* 1:211–12.

Chapter 1: Messianic Claims and Institutionalization

1. Al-Ṭabarī, *Tārīkh,* 3:200–201. See also Ibn Sa'd, *Al-Ṭabaqāt al-Kubrā,* 2:266–67. Arjomand has already suggested a similar view. See "Islamic Apocalypticism," 245–47. Crone and Cook discard this account as pointless. See *Hagarism,* 154, n. 24.

2. Khoury, *'Abdallāh b. Lahī'a (97–174/715–790),* 259 (*ḥadīth* #95) (henceforth cited as Ibn Lahī'a); al-Ṣan'ānī, *Al-Muṣannaf,* 11:375; Ibn Ḥanbal, *Musnad,* #1594; Abū Dāwūd, *Sunan,* #3712.

3. Naṣr b. Muzāḥim, *Waq'atu Ṣiffīn,* 200 (for 'Uthmān), 381 (for 'Alī: "*waj'alhu hādī ummatin mahdīyyan*"); al-Ṭabarī, *Tārīkh,* 5:589. The poet Hassān b. Thābit described Muḥammad as the Mahdī. Sulaymān b. Ṣurad (65/684–685), of the Tawwābūn movement, referred to al-Ḥusayn as the Mahdī, son of the Mahdī. *EI*[(2e)], al-Mahdī. Holt, "Islamic Millenarianism," 337 ff., maintains that the Mahdī belief in

Islam was first used among the Shīʿīs as an honorific title gradually evolving into a full-fledged eschatological concept.

4. *EI*[(2e)], al-Mahdī.

5. See Crone, *God's Rule,* 75.

6. Crone, *God's Rule,* 77.

7. Madelung, "ʿAbdallāh b. al-Zubayr," 291 ff.

8. Al-Ṣanʿānī, *Al-Muṣannaf,* 11:375; Nuʿaym, *Kitāb al-Fitan,* 390, 421; Ibn Abī Shayba, *Kitāb al-Muṣannaf,* 7:461; Ibn Ḥanbal, *Musnad,* #3523, 3570, 4088, 7968, 7969, 8300, 9407; Abū Dāwūd, *Sunan,* #3712. Predictions were taken seriously. When one of the transmitters was accused of spreading false traditions about the end of time as the year 70 A.H. elapsed and nothing of the sort he was predicting happened, he defended himself by claiming that others told lies about him while in fact what he had reported was that "there would be disasters and grave occurrences in the year 70." See Nuʿaym, *Kitāb al-Fitan,* 390.

9. Geddes, "Messiah in South Arabia," 311 ff.; Madelung, "Apocalyptic Prophecies," 141 ff.

10. See al-Ṣanʿānī, *Al-Muṣannaf,* 11:388; Nuʿaym, *Kitāb al-Fitan,* 66–67; al-Bukhārī, *Saḥīh,* #3256, 6584; Muslim, *Saḥīḥ,* #5182.

11. *EI*[(2e)], Mahdī; Geddes, "Messiah in South Arabia," 315–16; Madelung, "Apocalyptic Prophecies," 157–58. For al-Manṣūr, see Ḥusayn ʿAṭwān, *Al-Daʿwa al-ʿAbbāsiyya,* 174 (from al-Balādhurī, *Ansāb al-Ashrāf,* 2:22 manuscript); Ibn Qutayba, *Al-Maʿārif,* 385; al-Ṭabarī, *Tārīkh,* 8:582.

12. Ibn Saʿd, *Al-Ṭabaqāt,* 5:333: "Muḥammad b. ʿAlī said, the prophet is from among us, and the Mahdī is from the progeny of Banū ʿAbd al-Shams. We do not know him to be anyone other than ʿUmar b. ʿAbd al-ʿAzīz. He [Muḥammad b. ʿAlī] said this during the caliphate of ʿUmar b. ʿAbd al-ʿAzīz." See also Nuʿaym, *Kitāb al-Fitan,* 57–58, 67–68, 75, 222, 230; Crone and Hinds, *God's Caliph,* 114; *EI*[(2e)] Mahdī; Donner, "Question."

13. Ibn al-Mubārak, *Kitāb al-Jihād,* 190, 192, 193; al-Ṣanʿānī, *Al-Muṣannaf,* 11:373–74; Ibn Abī Shayba, *Kitāb al-Muṣannaf,* 7:509; Nuʿaym, *Kitāb al-Fitan,* 136–37, 149–50.

14. See Madelung, "Sufyānī," 8 ff.

15. For the Sufyānī legend, see Madelung, "Sufyānī," 5 ff.; Lammens, "Sofiani," 391 ff.; Hartmann, "Sufyānī," 141 ff.; ʿAbbās, *Tārīkh Bilād al-Shām,* 53–61; Aguadé, "Messianismus," 148 ff.; Cobb, *White Banners,* 55 ff.

16. Al-Balādhurī, *Ansāb,* 3:170. Nagel does not see him a figure associated with apocalyptic prophesies. See Nagel, *Rechtleitung,* 256.

17. Ibn Abī Shayba, *Kitāb al-Muṣannaf,* 7:514.

18. Ibn Aʿtham, *Kitāb al-Futūḥ,* 8:159.

19. Al-Balādhurī, *Ansāb,* 3:82; al-Ṭabarī, *Tārīkh,* 7:421, *History,* tr: 27:148. The anonymous author of *Akhbār al-Dawla al-ʿAbbāsiyya* relates a similar report that Muḥammad b. ʿAlī al-Imām instructed his followers to wait until the year 100 had passed; see *Akhbār al-Dawla al-ʿAbbāsiyya,* 193. See also al-Dīnawarī, *Al-Akhbār,* 332.

20. See al-Ṣanʿānī, *Al-Muṣannaf,* 11:366; Nuʿaym, *Kitāb al-Fitan,* 110–14.

21. Al-Ṣanʿānī, *Al-Muṣannaf,* 11:352, 395–96; Nuʿaym, *Kitāb al-Fitan,* 419.

22. Nuʿaym, *Kitāb al-Fitan,* 419. See similar predictions in Nuʿaym, *Kitāb al-Fitan,* 418 ff.

23. Nu'aym, *Kitāb al-Fitan*, 118, 121; Lewis, "Apocalyptic Vision," 314.

24. Akbash, literally head ram. Could this imply the Qur'ānic and biblical Golden Calf of the Israelites? For the image of the Golden Calf in the Bible and the Qur'ān, see Rubin, "Traditions in Transformations," 201 ff.

25. Nu'aym, *Kitāb al-Fitan*, 118 (on the authority of Sa'īd Abū 'Uthmān from Jābir al-Ju'fī from Abī Ja'far). The account continues to foretell briefly the collapse of the 'Abbāsids, the appearance of a comet (*dhū al-dhanab*), and dissension among them. The final section seems to be a later addition to an earlier account.

26. "Bahman Yast," *Pahlavī Texts*, 202. See also Hoyland, *Seeing*, 321–23.

27. Pāzand, *Jāmāspi*, 117.

28. Sharon argues that the 'Abbāsids began to gain serious support only after the murder of Zayd b. 'Alī and his son Yaḥyā by Naṣr b. Sayyār; i.e., after 125/743 A.H. See Sharon, *Black Banners*, 45, 75.

29. See Nu'aym, *Kitāb al-Fitan*, 115: "Al-Walīd b. Muslim from Abī 'Abdallāh from 'Abd al-Karīm b. Umayya from Muḥammad b. al-Ḥanafiyya: There will come forth a black banner from the direction of Khurāsān"; 118: "'Abdallāh b. Marwān from Arṭa' b. al-Mundhir from Tabī' from Ka'b: The days will not end until the black banners of the 'Abbāsids come forth from the East." See also Aḥmad b. Ḥanbal, *Musnad*, #21353; Ibn Māja, *Sunan*, #4074, 4078; *Akhbār al-Dawla al-'Abbāsiyya*, 199, 207, 245–47, for reports on the East, the black banners, Khurāsān, and the year 130. For further information, see the always useful study of van Vloten, *Recherches sur la domination Arabe*, 38 ff., 55 ff., esp. 62 ff.; 'Umar, *Buḥūth*, 198 ff. For the historical background of black banners, see Athamina, "Black Banners," 307 ff.; Sharon, *Revolt*, 79 ff.; *EI*(2e), Musawwida (C. E. Bosworth).

30. Al-Azdī, *Tārīkh Mawṣil*, 125 (al-Qā'im); *Akhbār al-Dawla al-'Abbāsiyya*, 238 (al-Qā'im al-Mahdī); Ibn A'tham, *Kitāb al-Futūḥ*, 8:197 (Mahdī). See also al-Balādhurī, *Ansāb*, 3:47, 162, 178.

31. Nu'aym, *Kitāb al-Fitan*, 230.

32. Nu'aym, *Kitāb al-Fitan*, 64–65, 66; al-Ya'qūbī, *Tārīkh*, 2:297; al-Balādhurī, *Ansāb*, 3:82; al-Ṭabarī, *Tārīkh*, 27:149, 7:421. See also al-Dūrī, "Al-Fikra al-Mahdīyya," 126 ff.

33. Al-Ṭabarī, *Tārīkh*, 7:421, *History*, 27:147; al-Ya'qūbī, *Tārīkh*, 2:297, 332, 342; al-Balādhuri, *Ansāb*, 3:82–86, 122, 178; *Akhbār al-Dawla al-'Abbāsiyya*, 139, 169, 201.

34. See al-Dūrī, "Al-Fikra al-Mahdīyya," 124. He cites an epigraph tablet fixed on the walls of the minaret of the mosque of Ṣan'a dated to 136/753: "*amara al-mahdī 'Abdallāh 'Abdallāh amīr al-mu'minīn . . . aẓẓama allāh ajr al-mahdī wa taqabbala 'amalahu.*"

35. For a comprehensive treatment of the sect and its development, see al-Qādī, *Al-Kaysāniyya*, 168 ff. See also al-Ash'arī, *Maqālāt*, 1:16 ff.

36. *EI*(2e), Kaysāniyya (Madelung).

37. Ibn Sa'd, *Al-Ṭabaqāt*, 5:101, 117, 162; Blichfeldt, *Early Mahdism*, 105 ff.

38. Al-Qādī, *Al-Kaysāniyya*, 168 ff.

39. Al-Ash'arī, *Maqālāt*, 1:17; al-Nāshī al-Akbar (Pseudo), *Masā'il al-Imāma*, 26–27; al-Shahrastānī, *Muslim Sects*, 128.

40. For a brief exposition of how some of the branches of the Kaysāniyya evolved into Imāmī Shī'ī messianic movements, see Sachedina, *Islamic Messianism*, 3 ff.

41. For fuller information, see Sharon, *Black Banners*, 103 ff.

42. *EI*(2e), Kaysāniyya. See also Madelung, "Hāshimiyyāt of al-Kumayt," 5–26; Sachedina, *Islamic Messianism*, 9–11; al-Ash'arī, *Maqālāt*, 1:19.

43. *Akhbār al-Dawla al-'Abbāsiyya*, 184–85. Ibn A'tham also relates a report that depicts Muḥammad b. 'Alī predicting the future of the 'Abbāsids. Ibn A'tham, *Kitāb al-Futūḥ*, 8:154–55. For an analysis of the color yellow, see Fierro, "Al-Aṣfar," 169 ff.

44. See Lassner, *Islamic Revolution*, 65–71; Shacklady, "'Abbāsid Movement," 98 ff. Sharon dismisses any association between the year 100 and the beginning of the 'Abbāsid propaganda but inclines to accept that 'Abbāsid revolutionaries adopted the twelve deputies and seventy missionaries as a prophetic model, *Sunna*, to organize their movement. See Sharon, *Black Banners*, 190–91. A similar model would also be adopted by al-Ma'mūn in the civil war.

45. *EI*(2e), Bayān b. Sam'ān (Hodgson); Tucker, "Bayān b. Sam'ān," 241–53; al-Ash'arī, *Maqālāt*, 1:5.

46. Al-Shahrastānī, *Muslim Sects*, 130; al-Baghdādī, *Al-Farq*, 47–48; al-Ash'arī, *Maqālāt*, 1:6.

47. *EI*(2e), Khidāsh (M. Sharon).

48. *EI*(2e), Kaysāniyya. For Khidāsh and his movement, see also Sharon, *Black Banners*, 165–73, 183–86.

49. Al-Ash'arī, *Maqālāt*, 1:5–6.

50. For a treatment of him, see Tucker, "'Abdallāh b. Mu'āwiya," 39–57.

51. Al-Ash'arī, *Maqālāt*, 1:20.

52. Al-Ash'arī, *Maqālāt*, 1:20.

53. Al-Ash'arī, *Maqālāt*, 1:20; al-Nāshī al-Akbar, *Masā'il*, 32.

54. Al-Ash'arī, *Maqālāt*, 1:19.

55. See *EI*(2), Sunbadh, (Madelung).

56. *EI*(2), Mukanna' (Editor).

57. Al-Ash'arī, *Maqālāt*, 1:6–8, 21. See also Wasserstrom, "Moving Finger Writes," 1–29.

58. Tucker, "Rebels and Gnostics," 33–47; *EI*(2e), Mughīriyya (Madelung). See also al-Baghdādī, *Al-Farq*, 42, 58.

59. Al-Azdī, *Tārīkh*, 182; *EI*(2e), Mahdī; Omar, *'Abbāsid Caliphate*, 223 ff.; al-Iṣfahānī, *Maqātil al-Ṭālibiyyīn*, 162, and for controversial views about him, 160–65 and 166 ff.

60. Omar, *'Abbāsid Caliphate*, 240 ff.

61. Al-Shahrastānī, *Muslim Sects*, 142; al-Baghdādī, *Moslim Schism*, 64–65; Sachedina, *Islamic Messianism*, 11–12.

62. See Büyükkara, "Schism," 78 ff.

63. Al-Shahrastānī, *Muslim Divisions*, 144.

64. See Nu'aym, *Kitāb al-Fitan*, 52, 64, 67, 247–48, 271; Ibn Abī Shayba, *Kitāb al-Muṣannaf*, 7:513; al-Balādhurī, *Ansāb*, 3:47, 48; *EI*(2e), Mahdī.

65. Al-Balādhurī, *Ansāb*, 3:198. Al-Suyūṭī has a small treatise on the merits of the 'Abbāsid caliphs, which includes similar traditions. Al-Suyūṭī, *Al-Asās*.

66. See al-Dūrī, "Al-Fikra al-Mahdīyya," 131–32.

67. Bacharach, "Laqab for a Future Caliph," 271–74; see 'Umar, *Buḥūth*, 213–14; *EI*(2e), Mahdī.

68. Al-Iṣfahānī, *Maqātil*, 162. See also al-Dūrī, "Al-Fikra al-Mahdīyya," 128–32.

69. Al-Ṭabarī, *Tārīkh*, 8:16.

70. Bates, "Khurāsānī Revolutionaries," 279–317.

71. See ʿUmar, *Buḥūth*, 214–18, for further examples.

72. See Ḥassūrī, "On the Ephitets," 111 ff.

73. Ibn al-Muqaffaʿ, *Conseilleur du Calife* [*Risāla fī al-Ṣaḥāba*], 25.

74. See Lewis, "Regnal Titles," 19; *EI*(2e), Iran (A. K. S. Lambton); Crone, *God's Rule*, 79; Zaman, "Routinization of Revolutionary Charisma"; Cook, *Studies*, 145–46; Omar, "Politics and Problem of Succession," esp. 41, where he maintains that the ʿAbbāsids promoted themselves as deliverers in order "to satisfy the hopes of the masses who were disappointed with the new regime and to dissuade them from joining other messianic opposition movements." See also Zaman, "Early ʿAbbāsid Response," 236 ff., for a similar argument.

75. Hoyland, *Seeing*, 257. For Ṣābiʿan communities, see Rosenthal, "Prophecies," 220 ff.

76. See Reinink, "Beginnings of Syriac," 165 ff.; Drijvers, "Gospel of the Twelve Apostles," 189 ff.

77. Hoyland, *Seeing*, 69 ff.

78. Hoyland, *Seeing*, 534–35.

79. Hoyland, *Seeing*, 260–63.

80. Hoyland, *Seeing*, 279–82.

81. *Bahman Yast*, 201 ff., 232–33. See also Hoyland, *Seeing*, 321–23.

82. *Bahman Yast*, 201–2.

83. *Dīnkard* was composed initially by a high priest, Ādur-farnbag Farrukhzādān, during the reign of al-Ma'mūn and completed later by another high priest, Adurbād-i E'me'tān. See Hoyland, *Seeing*, 326–27; Olsson, "Apocalyptic Activity." See also *Dīnkard*, Book 7, Part V, Marvels of Zoroastrianism, 94 ff.; Aturpatī, *The Wisdom of the Sasanian Sages* (*Denkard VI*), introduction, x.

84. See *Pāzānd Jāmāspi*, 117, 121–22; Hultgard, "Iranian Apocalypticism," 387 ff., 406.

85. Bashear, "Apocalyptic and Other Material."

86. See a review of such fears during the Umayyad period in Bashear, *Arabs and Others*, 94–111.

87. Hoyland, *Seeing*, 268–70; Drijvers, "Gospel," 199–208.

88. McCormick, "Imperial Edge," 17 ff.

89. For a study of the circulation of products and people, and the accompanying cosmopolitan outlook in the Near East and the Mediterranean, see Lombard, *Golden Age*, 15 ff.; Cahen, "Commercial Relations," 1–25.

90. See Dols, "Plagues," 371 ff.

91. For the extent of interregional trade and a critique of the Pirenne thesis from the perspective of archaeological evidence, see Hodges and Whitehouse, *Mohammed*.

92. Eyice, "İstanbul'da Abbasi Saraylarının," 79–104; Ricci, "Road from Baghdād," 131–49.

93. Vryonis, "Byzantium and Islam," 205 ff.

94. Koutrakou, "Image of the Arabs," 213 ff.; Gero, "Early Contacts," 125–32.

95. Cited in Papadakis, "Iconoclasm," 62.

96. For Iconoclasm and the reactions to it, see Vasiliev, *History*, 1:234 ff., esp. 251; Crone, "Islam, Judeo-Christianity," 59 ff.; Grégoire, "Byzantine Church," 105 ff.

97. Papadakis, "Iconoclasm," 60.

98. Choksy, *Conflict and Cooperation*, 59.

99. Brock, *Studies in Syriac Christianity*, 2:57, 71–72, 7:17 ff., for an informative discussion of Syriac sources.

100. Hoyland, *Seeing*, 195–97.

101. Hoyland, *Seeing*, 57.

102. See Hoyland, *Seeing*, 308–12, 317; Lewis, "Apocalyptic," 303, 312–13; Peters, *Jerusalem and Mecca*, 93; Silver, *History of Messianic Speculation*, 43–44.

103. Hoyland, *Seeing*, 316–17.

104. Wasserstrom, "'Īsāwiyya Revisited," 57 ff.; Silver, *History of Messianic Speculation*, 55–56.

105. For al-Manṣūriyya, see Tucker, "Al-Manṣūr al-'Ijlī," 66–76.

106. *EI*(2e), 'Īsāwiyya (Pines).

107. See the Synods of George I, the metropolitan of Arbela, in 676 in Hoyland, *Seeing*, 193–94.

108. This apocalypse was probably written around 700 (the range of proposed dates of composition fluctuates between 697 to 744 C.E.) or slightly earlier. Martinez, "Eastern," 261 ff., 501; Hoyland, *Seeing*, 282–83.

109. Paulus Alvaris Cordubensis, "Alvari Cordubensis Opera," 274.

110. Ibn Abī Shayba, *Kitāb al-Muṣannaf*, 7:479.

111. See Rubin, *Between Bible and Qur'ān*, 11–52.

112. Al-Farazdaq, *Diwān*, 1:264. For additional information on interconfessional exchange in reference to prophecies, see Cook, "Early Islamic," 25–29; and Cook, "Heraclian Dynasty," 3–23, where he also suggests a reworking and translation of what might have once been a Christian apocalypse.

113. Ibn Isḥāq's (d. 150/767), *Sīrat Rasūlallāh*, has reached us through copies dating to the second half of the second Islamic century. The most complete version appears to be that of Ibn Hishām. The account in question is most probably much earlier than the third Islamic century.

114. Ibn Hishām, *Life of Muḥammad*, 256–57 (with small modifications for clarity); al-Ya'qūbī, *Tārīkh*, 2:51.

115. Nu'aym, *Kitāb al-Fitan*, 18–19. For reports of this sort, see Nu'aym, *Kitāb al-Fitan*, 18–19, 63–64, 68, 113–14.

116. Cook, *Studies*, 2–3.

117. Alexander, "Medieval Legend," 1 ff.

118. Reeves, "Development of Apocalyptic," 45. See also Reinink, "Pseudo-Methodius," 82 ff.; McGinn, *Visions*, 70–76.

119. See Martinez, "King of Rūm," 247 ff.

120. Choksy, *Conflict and Cooperation*, 54 ff.

121. Cf. Palmer, "Messiah," 45 ff., 78–79. Palmer suspects that the honorific was intended for irony rather than recognition of the caliph as such.

122. See Caspar, "Les Versions Arabes," 152, 153; Mingana, *Christian Documents*, 52, 55, 59, 60, 81, 83–84.

123. Tartar, *Dialogue Islamo-Chrétien*, 234.

Chapter 2: Shaping Up a Messianic Discourse

1. Qur'ān, 22:7. Also in 42:17. I have adopted the following sources for translation: Arberry, *Koran Interpreted*; Pickthall, *Meaning of the Glorious Koran*.

2. Qur'ān, 21:1.

3. Qur'ān, 45:32. See also 25:11, 20:15, 54:1.

4. Qur'ān, 7:187. See also 33:63, 79:42–44, 72:25. Suliman Bashear deals with the concept of the Hour in the Qur'ān and exegesis in "Muslim Apocalypses and the Hour," 80 ff. See also Cook, *Studies,* 270 ff.

5. Qur'ān, 47:18. Also in 43:66.

6. Qur'ān, 16:77.

7. Qur'ān, 22:1.

8. Qur'ān, 27:87. See also 74:8, 50:20, 23:101, 44:10.

9. Qur'ān, 27:82.

10. Qur'ān, 18:94–99. Also 21:96.

11. Qur'ān,8:28. Also in this sense 7:155 and 2:102.

12. Qur'ān,3:7.

13. Qur'ān,7:27.

14. Qur'ān,8:73.

15. Qur'ān,9:47–48.

16. Qur'ān,2:191.

17. Qur'ān,2:217. Similarly 8:25, 8:39, 2:193.

18. For a treatment of the ephitet, "the seal of the prophet," *khatam al-nabiyyīn,* see Friedmann, "Finality of Prophethood," 177–215.

19. See Wansbrough, *Qur'ānic Studies,* 64–65.

20. Qur'ān,61:6. For a discussion of the term *Aḥmad,* see Watt, *Early Islam,* 43 ff.; Watt, *Muslim-Christian Encounters,* 9 ff., 33–37; *EI*[(2e)], Aḥmad (J. Schacht).

21. Mālik b. Anas, *Al-Muwaṭṭa, ḥadīth* #1594. This tradition figures rather prominently in later *ḥadīth* collections with some indicative additions. See Ibn Ḥanbal, *Al-Musnad,* #16134, 16148, 16169, 16170; al-Bukhārī, *Ṣaḥīḥ,* #3268, 4517; Muslim, *Ṣaḥīḥ,* #4342, 4343; Tirmidhī, *Sunan,* #2766; Dārimī, *Sunan,* #2656. Ibn Kathīr gives another tradition from Abū Dāwūd al-Ṭayālisī that similarly includes "and the messenger of . . . the apocalyptic battle, *malḥama*" (*wa nabī . . . al-malḥama*). See his exegesis of the verse in *The Holy Qur'ān* (Sakhr). See also Casanova, *Mohammed,* 1:92–95.

22. Al-Ṭabarī, *Tārīkh,* 3:178–79.

23. Ibn Qutayba, *Ta'wīl Mukhtalaf al-Ḥadīth,* 172–73.

24. Jesus' death is left inconclusive, provoking widely differing interpretations: "Behold! God said: O Jesus! I will take thee (*mutawaffīka*) and raise thee to myself and clear thee of those who blaspheme"(3:55). The following verse (4:157), however, denies that Jesus was killed: "And for their saying, We slew the Messiah, Jesus son of Mary, the Messenger of God—yet they did not slay him, neither crucified him, only a likeness of that was shown to them." Cf. *EI*[(2e)], Masīḥ (A. J. Wensick [C. E. Bosworth]): "One can assume with reasonable certainty that *al-Masīḥ* is a title of Jesus in the Qur'ān, but not a messianic one; clearly, no eschatological interpretation of Christ's mission could have been known in Arabia."

25. Qur'ān,4:159.

26. Arberry prefers the pronoun "it."

27. Qur'ān,43:61. For further discussion, see Casanova, *Mohammed,* 1:87–91.

28. See Crone and Cook, *Hagarism,* 11; Nau, "Lettre de Jacques d'Edesse," 518–23 ff.; Hoyland, *Seeing Islam,* 166.

29. Sahas, *John of Damascus,* 133.

30. Mujāhid b. Jabr, *Tafsīr,* 583.

31. In other prophecies the place is identified as ʿAqabat Afīq, Thaniyyat Afīq in Jordan.

32. Muqātil b. Sulaymān, *Tafsīr,* 1:421, 3:800.

33. Nuʿaym, *Kitāb al-Fitan,* 349.

34. Ibn Abī Shayba, *Kitāb al-Muṣannaf,* 7:514: "The Mahdī will not appear until al-Nafs al-Zakiyya, the Pure Soul, is killed, and the ones in the sky and on earth are angry at them [the members of the community?]. Then the Mahdī will appear to the people, who will ornament him as if they were adorning [a bride] for her husband. He will fill the earth with justice. The earth will give forth its plants, and the sky will pour down its rain. And my community will prosper to an extent that it has not seen before."

35. Ibn Abī Shayba, *Kitāb al-Muṣannaf,* 7:513; Nuʿaym, *Kitāb al-Fitan,* 230, 232. Or "The hour will not arrive until 'Jesus the son of Mary' descends as a just and righteous imam. He will break the cross, kill the swine, and institute the Jizya. Wealth will become so abundant that no one will accept it." Ibn Abī Shayba, *Kitāb al-Muṣannaf,* 7:494; al-Ḥumaydī (d. 219), *Al-Musnad,* 2:468–69.

36. Nuʿaym, *Kitāb al-Fitan,* 348.

37. Nuʿaym, *Kitāb al-Fitan,* 229–30.

38. *Ibn Lahīʿa,* 259. For traditions placing Jesus with the Mahdī as the end of time ruler, see Al-Ṣanʿānī, *Al-Muṣannaf,* 11:399 ff.

39. Abū Dāwūd's prophecy predicts not al-Ḥ ārith b. Surayj himself but instead a man leading his troops as the Manṣūr, who would pave the way for the expected one from the family of the Prophet. See Abū Dāwūd, *Sunan,* #3739: On the authority of Hārūn from ʿAmr b. Abī Qays from Muṭarrif b. Ṭarīf from Abī al-Ḥasan from Hilāl b. ʿAmr from ʿAlī from the Prophet: "A man from the Transoxiana who is called al-Ḥārith b. al-Ḥarrāth will rise. There will be a man called 'al-Manṣūr' in his vanguard."

40. Al-Ṭabarī, *Tārīkh,* 7:332, *History,* 27:32.

41. See Arjomand, "Islamic Apocalypticism," 270. Tübingen collection, inventory #94–33–1: The coin reads, "for the Manṣūr and justice." Ibn Surayj apparently made use of a large repertoire of epithets, including the "holder of the black banners," to characterize his uprising.

42. Al-Ṭabarī, *Tārīkh,* 7:331, *History,* 27:30. See Athamina, "Black Banners," 309.

43. Ibn Abī Shayba, *Kitāb al-Muṣannaf,* 7:513.

44. Nuʿaym, *Kitāb al-Fitan,* 212.

45. Nuʿaym, *Kitāb al-Fitan,* 224. For further traditions of this sort, see 211–14.

46. Nuʿaym, *Kitāb al-Fitan,* 229, 230. A similar tradition is also recorded in Ibn Abī Shayba, *Kitāb al-Muṣannaf,* 7:513.

47. Ibn Abī Shayba, *Kitāb al-Muṣannaf,* 7:513.

48. Ibn Abī Shayba, *Kitāb al-Muṣannaf,* 7:513. Also Al-Ṣanʿānī, *Al-Muṣannaf,* 11:371.

49. Ibn Abī Shayba, *Kitāb al-Muṣannaf,* 7:513; Nuʿaym, *Kitāb al-Fitan,* 226–27.

50. Nuʿaym, *Kitāb al-Fitan,* 231.

51. Nuʿaym, *Kitāb al-Fitan,* 225; al-Ṣanʿānī, *Al-Muṣannaf,* 11:372.

52. His age varied greatly: fifty-one to fifty-two years old, forty years old, youth, eighteen years old, around thirty to forty years old, sixty years old, twenty-four years old. See Nuʿaym, *Kitāb al-Fitan,* 225, 226, 234.

53. He will rule or remain for forty, thirty-nine, nine, eight, or seven years. See Nu'aym, *Kitāb al-Fitan,* 232, 233, 234.

54. Nu'aym, *Kitāb al-Fitan,* 226.

55. Nu'aym, *Kitāb al-Fitan,* 229, 231. This prediction, attributed to Muḥammad b. al-Ḥanafiyya, expects the Mahdī to be from Banū 'Abd al-Shams: "If there will be such a person, he will be from Banū 'Abd al-Shams." Similarly, what may be an account from 'Umar II's time predicts two Mahdīs from Banū 'Abd al-Shams, one of whom is 'Umar II himself. Nu'aym, *Kitāb al-Fitan,* 231.

56. Nu'aym, *Kitāb al-Fitan,* 231.

57. Nu'aym, *Kitāb al-Fitan,* 208: "There will be a *fitna* in which the people will be slaughtered. They will not recover from it until a 'voice from the sky' instructs them to follow a certain person."

58. Nu'aym, *Kitāb al-Fitan,* 209.

59. Nu'aym, *Kitāb al-Fitan,* 208.

60. Al-Ṣan'ānī, *Al-Muṣannaf,* 11:371–72.

61. Nu'aym, *Kitāb al-Fitan,* 208, 228–29, 230–31.

62. *Ibn Lahī'a,* 257. The relevant part of the tradition is quoted here.

63. Nu'aym, *Kitāb al-Fitan,* 246: "A caliph from Banū Hāshim will come to Jerusalem. He will fill the earth with justice and restore Jerusalem like it has never been seen before." For a Fatimid Mahdī, see Nu'aym, *Kitāb al-Fitan,* 228, 230, 231: "The Mahdī will be from the progeny of Fāṭima." The Fāṭimid Mahdī is also highlighted in the following delightful prophecy: "God will send a Fāṭimī, who will pull out his sword and carry it eight months. He will kill his enemies and extinguish the *fitna*. He will fight until the people start complaining about him saying 'what kind of Fāṭimī is this? What is he doing? If he were her [Fāṭima's] son he would have had mercy for us. God deceived him with the 'Abbāsids and the Umayyads.'" Nu'aym, *Kitāb al-Fitan,* 216.

64. Ibn Abī Shayba, *Kitāb al-Muṣannaf,* 7:527.

65. Nu'aym, *Kitāb al-Fitan,* 208. Note the editorial discretions in the tradition to reorient the prophecy as explained earlier.

66. *Ibn Lahī'a,* 248.

67. Ibn Abī Shayba, *Kitāb al-Muṣannaf,* 7:513.

68. Ibn Abī Shayba, *Kitāb al-Muṣannaf,* 7:513.

69. Nu'aym, *Kitāb al-Fitan,* 228, 229.

70. Nu'aym, *Kitāb al-Fitan,* 222. The following should be considered a commentary on the tradition and not a part of it: Al-Walīd said, "It has been narrated to me that Ka'b said, 'The Mahdī of welfare will rise after the Sufyānī.'"

71. D. Cook, *Studies,* 137 ff., overlooks two significant dimensions of the Mahdī, which I think deserve more attention, in his cyclical model. One, implicit in the messianic ideology itself and explicit in a myriad of prophecies, is commencing universal social justice. The second may be defined as religious renewal as the Mahdī is also given not only political but also religious authority, as many prophecies attest.

72. Nu'aym, *Kitāb al-Fitan,* 221.

73. Nu'aym, *Kitāb al-Fitan,* 220, 221, 222.

74. Ibn Abī Shayba, *Kitāb al-Muṣannaf,* 7:513.

75. Nu'aym, *Kitāb al-Fitan,* 221–24; al-Ṣan'ānī, *Al-Muṣannaf,* 11:372–73.

76. Nu'aym, *Kitāb al-Fitan,* 221.

77. Al-Ṣan'ānī, *Al-Muṣannaf,* 11:400–401, 402; *Ibn Lahī'a,* 303–4.

78. Nu'aym, *Kitāb al-Fitan,* 222–23; Ibn Abī Shayba, *Kitāb al-Muṣannaf,* 7:527. For similar predictions, see Al-Ṣan'ānī, *Al-Muṣannaf,* 11:372, 373, 399 ff.

79. Al-Ṣan'ānī, *Al-Muṣannaf,* 400–402; Nu'aym, *Kitāb al-Fitan,* 346–47, 348, 350, 351–52.

80. D. Cook, *Studies,* 170–71; al-Ṭabarānī, *Musnad al-Shāmiyyīn,* 1:386. Although al-Ṭabarānī is a relatively later source, the prophecy must date to late Umayyad or perhaps early 'Abbāsid times.

81. See Vasiliev, "Medieval Ideas," 463–67, 471–76.

82. *Ibn Lahī'a,* 249, 250; al-Ṣan'ānī, *Al-Muṣannaf,* 11:386–87; Ibn Abī Shayba, *Kitāb al-Muṣannaf,* 7:458–59, 491, 494.

83. For a more detailed account of apocalyptic prophecies concerning the Umayyad-'Abbāsid/Byzantine wars and the conquest of Constantinople, see Bashear, "Apocalyptic and Other Materials," 173 ff.

84. Nu'aym, *Kitāb al-Fitan* 257 ff.; *Ibn Lahī'a,* 301.

85. *Ibn Lahī'a,* 249, 250. For similar predictions, see Ibn Abī Shayba, *Kitāb al-Muṣannaf,* 7:458–59, 491, 494; Ibn Ḥanbal, *Musnad,* 3:71–72.

86. Nu'aym, *Kitāb al-Fitan,* 290, 307. Also *Ibn Lahī'a,* 302: "Persia, Rome (al-Rūm) and the Hour."

87. Zakkār's reading in the introduction to Nu'aym b. Ḥammād's *Kitāb al-Fitan,* 287. Cook, "Heraclian," 4, reads it "*qad yamliku.*"

88. Zakkār's reading, 287.

89. Cook's reading, "Heraclian," 3.

90. Nu'aym, *Kitāb al-Fitan,* 287, also 302–3, 305, 306. See Cook, "Heraclian," 8–9 ff.; see also Nu'aym, *Kitāb al-Fitan,* 292, 300, 301, 303, 305, 306, for the variants of the same prophecy. Cook, "Heraclian," suggests that the prophecy and its variant date somewhere between 122/740 and 158/775.

91. Some accounts include the conquest of Rome as well. See Nu'aym, *Kitāb al-Fitan,* 290 ff., 295, 307.

92. Nu'aym, *Kitāb al-Fitan,* 246. For the figure of the Antichrist, see Helperin, "Ibn Ṣayyād Traditions," 213 ff.; Jenkinson, "Moslem Anti-Christ," 50–55.

93. Al-Ṣan'ānī, *Al-Muṣannaf,* 11:388.

94. Nu'aym, *Kitāb al-Fitan,* 216.

95. For the word *Aṣfar,* see Fierro, "Aṣfar."

96. Alexander, *Byzantine,* 63–64, 69–70, 163.

97. *Ibn Lahī'a,* 303–4.

98. Al-Ṣan'ānī, *Al-Muṣannaf,* 11:387–88.

99. Al-Ṣan'ānī, *Al-Muṣannaf,* 11:399–400.

100. Al-Ṣan'ānī, *Al-Muṣannaf,* 11:400–401, 402.

101. Nu'aym, *Kitāb al-Fitan,* 221, 222.

102. Nu'aym, *Kitāb al-Fitan,* 220.

103. Al-Ṣan'ānī, *Al-Muṣannaf,* 11:372.

104. Nu'aym, *Kitāb al-Fitan,* 288.

105. The term *Mahdī* is interpreted to refer to the action of unearthing because he leads or guides to a hidden thing. Al-Ṣan'ānī, *Al-Muṣannaf,* 11:372; Nu'aym, *Kitāb al-Fitan,* 220, 221, also "from mountains of Damascus," 221.

106. Al-Ṣan'ānī, *Tafsīr,* 1:100–101, notes that *al-sakīna* means "spirit from God."

107. Nu'aym, *Kitāb al-Fitan,* 223; *Ibn Lahī'a,* 302–3.

108. Nu'aym, *Kitāb al-Fitan,* 420.

109. Nu'aym, *Kitāb al-Fitan,* 395, 423.

110. Nu'aym, *Kitāb al-Fitan,* 421. Also in 389 and Ibn Ḥanbal, *Musnad,* #1385–1386; Abū Dāwūd, #3785–3786. Some later calculations, which incorporated earlier ones with necessary chronological modifications, can be found in al-Hindī, *Al-Burhān,* 145–46, 184 ff., 199, 201; al-Hindī, *Kanz al-'Ummāl,* 14:211, 250–51, 572; al-Maqdisī, *Al-Bad',* 2:150 ff.; al-Haytamī, *Al-Qawl al-Mukhtaṣ,* 67–68, 70, 75; Ibn Kathīr, *Kitāb al-Nihāya,* 1:12–16; Ibn Khaldūn, *Kitāb al-'Ibar,* 1:596, 604 ff.

111. There is some confusion in the text.

112. There is apparently an omission of a name or pronoun since the sentence suddenly switches to miracles of Jesus.

113. Nu'aym, *Kitāb al-Fitan,* 429–32.

114. Al-Ṭabarī, *History,* 1:171–83.

115. Al-Ṭabarī, *History,* 1:183.

116. These included Muḥammad b. Ḥumayd (d. 248/862), Yaḥyā b. Ya'qūb (ca. early third/ninth century since he was an authority of al-Bukhārī), Ḥammād b. Abī Sulaymān (d. 119 or 120/737 or 738), Abū Hishām al-Rifā'ī (d. 248/862), Mu'āwiya b. Hishām (d. 204 or 205/819 or 820), Sufyān al-Thawrī (d. 161/777–778), Muḥammad b. Sahl al-'Askar (d. 251/865), Wahb b. Munabbih (d. ca. 106–19/725–737), Muḥammad b. Bashshār (d. 252/866), and many others who date to the early and middle third Islamic century. See a brief note on each in Rosenthal, "Prophecies," footnotes, 171–83.

117. Al-Ṭabarī, *History,* 1:184–86.

118. Landes, "Lest," 186: "Countdowns to the 7th millennium AM continued to show up where Carolingian domination made limited inroads."

119. Landes, "Lest," 191–92.

120. Williams, "Purpose," 217; McGinn, *Visions,* 77–78. Also Landes, "Lest," 193–94.

121. Ruggles, "Representation," 81; Reeves, "Development of Apocalyptic Thought," 44–45.

122. Quoted in Williams, "*Purpose,*" 224.

123. Williams, "*Purpose,*" 223–24.

124. Ruggles, "*Representation,*" 79–80, 89.

125. See Aguadé's introduction to Ibn Ḥabīb, *Kitāb al-Tārīkh,* 15 ff. See also *EI*(2e), Ibn Ḥabīb (A. Huici-Miranda); Pellat, "Origin and Development," 19:118. Pellat and Huici-Miranda consider this work a prehistoriographical product exactly because it discusses subjects such as these.

126. Ibn Ḥabīb, *Tārīkh,* 25–26.

127. Ibn Ḥabīb, *Tārīkh,* 73.

128. Ibn Ḥabīb, *Tārīkh,* 25. For a discussion of the number seven and numbers in general in mythology and religion, see *Encyclopedia of Religion and Ethics,* 9:406–17; Conrad, "Seven and Tasbī'," 42–73; *EI*(2e), Sab', Sab'a (A. M. Schimmel).

129. Landes, "Lest," 144. See also Vasilev, "Medieval Ideas," for an informed account of medieval chiliasm.

130. Nu'aym, *Kitāb al-Fitan,* 418.

131. Nu'aym, *Kitāb al-Fitan,* 389. See also two separate reports on 373.

132. Ibn Abī Shayba, *Kitāb al-Muṣannaf,* 7:502. For similar accounts, see 7:503. Ibn Abī Shayba provides a different *isnād* for the same account and adds to it a comment by Jābir: "Yazīd from Sulaymān al-Taymī from 'Abd al-Raḥmān Ṣāḥib al- Siqāya from Jābir. 'Jābir explained [this account] as shortening of life.'"

133. Al-Ṣan'ānī, *Al-Muṣannaf,* 11:395–96. Nu'aym b. Ḥammād also cites the same prediction on the authority of al-Ṣan'ānī. Nu'aym, *Kitāb al-Fitan,* 391–92.

134. Chavannes, *Documents,* 204–5.

135. Ibn Ḥanbal, *Musnad,* #676, 1126, 5360, 5755, 5873; Bukhārī, *Ṣaḥīḥ,* #113; Muslim, *Saḥīḥ,* #4605; al-Tirmidhī, *Sunan,* 2177; Abū Dāwūd, *Sunan,* 3784; al-Hindī, *Kanz,* 14:250, 259, 579–80, 625; Ibn Qutayba, *Ta'wīl,* 105–6. For an evaluation of such traditions, see Bashear, "Muslim Apocalypses," 87–92.

136. For a collection of major prophecies focusing on the year 200 A.H., see D. Cook, "Apocalyptic."

137. For numerous prophecies of this sort, see Nu'aym, *Kitāb al-Fitan,* 318–434.

138. It may refer to the extermination of the Umayyads or the revolt led by Sharīk b. Shaykh in Khurāsān. See al-Ṭabarī, *History,* 27:196–97.

139. Evidently there was a revolt in Khurāsān led by Ustādhsīs. See al-Ṭabarī, *History,* 29:44 ff.

140. One questions whether this prophecy refers to the fire of Baghdad or the revolts of Yūsuf b. Ibrāhīm al-Barm (al-Ṭabarī, *History,* 29:180–81) and 'Abd al-Salām al-Khārijī (al-Ṭabarī, *History,* 29:193). Another prophecy points to the year 160 and the events preceding it. It warns of the swallowing up of earth, metamorphosis, massive death, and tremors to be seen. Ibn Abī Shayba, *Kitāb al-Muṣannaf,* 7:462. For the year 136, see Ibn Abī Shayba, *Kitāb al-Muṣannaf,* 7:467; Nu'aym, *Kitāb al-Fitan,* 36.

141. Nu'aym, *Kitāb al-Fitan,* 422. A variant is on 422–23.

142. The text here reads *faraḥ wa maraḥ,* happiness and joy, which seems to be a textual corruption or editorial discretion as it does not fit the context and is followed by what would normally be stated, turmoil and bloodshed. Other versions read *harj wa marj,* turmoil and bloodshed.

143. Nu'aym, *Kitāb al-Fitan,* 427. The portion of the prophecy dealing with the year 210 A.H. is also cited in another location, where it reads: "the swallowing up [by earth] and metamorphosis in my community in 210." Nu'aym, *Kitāb al-Fitan,* 376.

144. Later comments delay the date even further to 220 A.H., when death befalls to people, and to 300, when the sun rises up from the west. See Nu'aym, *Kitāb al-Fitan,* 376, 395, 427.

145. Ibn Māja's prophecy predicts five ages ending in 200: "My community is composed of five generations [he mentions the generations each of forty years up to the year 160] . . . then killing, killing, refuge, refuge." Ibn Māja, *Sunan,* #4048.

146. The tradition reads, "Their kingdom will last nine multiplied by seven [years]."

147. Nu'aym, *Kitāb al-Fitan,* 120. See Nu'aym, *Kitāb al-Fitan,* 419:"Two men will rule, a man and his sons from Banū Hāshim, for 72 years." For similar accounts, see 124, 132, 134, 135, 165. For calculations based on months, see Nu'aym, *Kitāb al-Fitan,* 419. See also 125: nine hundred months, i.e., seventy-five years, which brings the time to 207 A.H. Aguadé, *Messianismus,* 118 ff.

148. Nu'aym, *Kitāb al-Fitan,* 205. For prophecies pointing to the year 200, see 395, 419, 422–23, 427, 432; Ibn Māja, *Sunan,* #4048.

149. Nu'aym, *Kitāb al-Fitan*, 419. See also Ibn Kathīr, *Kitāb al-Nihāya*, 1:12.

150. Al-Majlisī, *Biḥār*, 52:183–84.

Chapter 3: Prophecies and the Fourth Civil War

1. A detailed narrative of the years 193–95/809–12 and various aspects of it is contained in al-Ṭabarī, *Tārīkh*, 8:365–405. See also Ibn A'tham, *Kitāb al-Futūḥ*, 8:286 ff.; Samadi, "Struggle," 99–112; El-Hibri, "Reign," chap. 2; *EI*(2e), al-Ma'mūn (M. Rekaya); Nawas, *Al-Ma'mūn*, 15–24; Kennedy, *Prophet*, 145–52.

2. See El-Hibri, "Reign," 1–22. The circumstances in Khurāsān are also dealt with in Daniel, *Political*, 125 ff., 175; *EI*(2e), Khurāsān (C. E. Bosworth); *EI*(2e), 'Abbāsids (Bernard Lewis).

3. For some of the arguments about the reasons of the civil war, see Gabrieli, "Successione"; al-Dūrī, *Al-'Aṣr al-'Abbāsī*, 141 ff.; El-Hibri, "Reign," esp. chaps. 2, 5; Samadi, "Struggle," 99 ff.

4. Kennedy, *Prophet and the Age of the Caliphates*, 145–46.

5. The author of the *Al-Imāma wa al-Siyāsa* claims that al-Rashīd designated al-Ma'mūn rather than al-Amīn as his heir-apparent. See *Al-Imāma wa al-Siyāsa*, 345–46. Further information and studies are provided in Kimber, "Hārūn al-Rashīd," 55 ff.; Chejne, *Succession*, 89 ff., 109 ff.

6. El-Hibri, "Hārūn al-Rashīd," 461 ff.

7. Nu'aym, *Kitāb al-Fitan*, 123. Several other versions are listed in 123–24. For a prophecy of this nature, see also al-Majlisī, *Biḥār*, 52:210. The prophecy names the 'Abbāsids *Banū Fulān*, the sons of that individual. In another place al-Majlisī uses the same term to refer to the 'Abbāsids. The context ('Alī al-Riḍā, the years 195–200) does not allow any other possibility (al-Majlisī, *Biḥār*, 52:183–84). For the same information, see *Ibn Lahī'a*, 303–4. Al-Kulaynī, *Al-Uṣūl min al-Kāfī*, 8:209, also uses the same phrase for the 'Abbāsids in the context of the Sufyānī and the disagreement of Banū Fulān. Non-Muslim apocalypses, too, do not show an awareness of anything beyond double designation. See Young and Ebied, "Unrecorded," 297–301.

8. *Ahilla*, sacred lunar months leading up to the pilgrimage. See Qur'ān, al-Baqara, 2:189, for a reference to it.

9. Al-Mas'ūdī, *Murūj*, 4:272.

10. Bacharach, "Al-Amīn's," 108 ff.; al-Ṭabarī, *Tārīkh*, 8:389–90.

11. Abū Yūsuf, *Kitāb al-Kharāj*, 82–83. See Crone, *God's Rule*, 272–75; Yücesoy, *Taṭawwur*, 105, 160–61.

12. Al-Shāfi'ī, *Al-Risāla*, 419–20.

13. Al-Dīnawarī, *Al-Akhbār*, 390; al-Ṭabarī, *Tārīkh*, 8:404. Ibn Ṭiqṭaqa, *Al-Fakhrī*, 304–5, reports in a legendary anecdote that al-Faḍl b. Sahl had noticed al-Ma'mūn's moral qualities even when he was a prince and, consulting his horoscope, predicted that al-Ma'mūn would become a caliph.

14. See Ibn Ṭāwūs, *Faraj al-Mahmūm*, 132–33, 135–37. See also Pingree, *Thousands*, 93 ff.; Pingree, "Historical Horoscopes," 487 ff.; Pingree, "Fragments of the Works of Ya'qūb b. Ṭāriq," 97 ff.; Pingree, "Fragments of the Works of al-Fāzārī," 103 ff. In Spain, the Umayyads had had an official astrologer since the caliphate of al-Ḥakam I (796–822). 'Abd al-Raḥmān II (822–52) also was known for his interests in astrology. For additional details, see Samsó, *Islamic Astronomy*, 1, 79, 228–29.

15. Gutas, *Greek*, 33.

16. Al-Maqdisī also notes the fascination of al-Ma'mūn with ancient knowledge, astrology, astronomy, and philosophy. See al-Maqdisī, *Al-Bad'*, 6:112.

17. Al-Ya'qūbī, *Mushākalat*, 27–28. See Arjomand, "Islamic Apocalypticism," 265–66, who maintains that 'Abbāsid astrology was related to the civil war.

18. See Sezgin, *Geschichte*, 6:136–37; *EI*$^{(2e),}$ Banū Munajjim (M. Fleischhammer); Bar Hebraeus, *Tārīkh Mukhtaṣar*, 236–37. Ibn Khaldūn relates that Ya'qūb b. Isḥāq served al-Rashīd and al-Ma'mūn as their astrologer and wrote a book on the celestial conjunctions. Ibn Khaldūn, *Tārīkh*, 1:608–9. Al-Majlisī notes that al-Ma'mūn was a devoted believer in astrology. Al-Majlisī, *Biḥār*, 58:246. Yaḥyā b. Abū Manṣūr was one of the astronomers or astrologers assigned to testing Ptolemy's observations. His studies resulted in his famous *Zīj-i Mumtaḥan*. Sezgin, *Geschichte*, 6:136–37. See the facsimile copy of the work, Yaḥyā b. Abī Manṣūr, *Al-Zīj al-Ma'mūnī*. Muḥammad b. Jahm al-Barmakī, on the other hand, drafted a treatise for al-Ma'mūn on astrology based specifically on eastern cosmogonic doctrines. *EI*$^{(2e),}$ Muḥammad b. Jahm al-Barmakī (G. Lecomte). For another account of the caliph's interest in astronomy, see Langermann, "Book of Bodies," 108 ff.

19. *Fī al-Qirānāt wa al-Adyān wa al-Milal* (*On Conjunctions, Religions, and Sects*) and *Fī Qiyām al-Khulafā wa Ma'rifat Qiyām Kull Malik* (*On the Accession of Caliphs and Knowledge of the Accession of Each King*) are the most significant of his known work in political astrology. See *EI*$^{(2e),}$ Māshā'allāh (J. Samso).

20. Kennedy and Pingree, *Astrological*, v–vi.

21. See a detailed study and translation in Kennedy and Pingree, *Astrological*, 129 ff.

22. *EI*$^{(2e),}$ Khawārizmī (J. Vernet).

23. *EI*$^{(2e),}$ Khawārizmī.

24. Kennedy and Pingree, *Astrological*, 56–57, 113; Kennedy, *Studies in Islamic*, 362. For Mashā'allāh's cast, see Kennedy and Pingree, *Astrological*, vii;, *EI*$^{(2e),}$ Māshā'allāh. For a brief synopsis of major astronomers during the reign of al-Ma'mūn and a nice anecdote of one of the astrological gatherings in the court of al-Ma'mūn, see Bar Hebraeus, *Tārīkh*, 236–38. Ibn Khaldūn relates that the king of Zabūlistān sent to al-Ma'mūn his physician (*ḥakīmuhu*), who predicted the outcome of the civil war and the appointment of Ṭāhir to lead his army, up until the Selçuk migration. Ibn Khaldūn, *Tārīkh*, 1:606–7.

25. For accounts depicting celestial events as portents and, more important, encouraging the observation of celestial movements, see Nu'aym, *Kitāb al-Fitan*, 130, 132–33.

26. Hoffmann, "Al-Amīn," 27 ff.

27. For the composition of al-Amīn's army and the tension brought about by various ethnicities in the conflict, see Ayalon, "Military," 1:4 ff.

28. *EI*$^{(2)}$, Tahir b. al-Ḥusayn (C. E. Bosworth).

29. For the complex formation of the "Turkish" troops, see Ismail, "Mu'taṣim," 12–24; Ayalon, "Military," 1:1–39; Gordon, *Breaking*, 15–46.

30. Al-Ṭabarī, *Tārīkh*, 8:391–423.

31. Al-Ṭabarī, *Tārīkh*, 8:410–12, 416.

32. Al-Ṭabarī, *History*, 31:81.

33. Ibn 'Asākir, *Tārīkh Madinat Dimashq*, 56:228–29.

34. Al-Ṭabarī, *Tārīkh*, 8:428–32; Khalīfa, *Tārīkh*, 467.

35. Ibn Qutayba, *Al-Ma'ārif*, 385.

36. Nu'aym, *Kitāb al-Fitan,* 206.

37. Al-Ṭabarī, *Tārīkh,* 8:432 ff.

38. Al-Ṭabarī, *Tārīkh,* 8:415, 441, 456, 471, 473, 527; Khalīfa, *Tārīkh,* 467. See also Geddes, "Al-Ma'mūn's Shī'ite Policy," 100–107.

39. Al-Ṭabarī, *Tārīkh,* 8:439–40, 441, 444.

40. *EI*(2), Harthama b. A'yan (Ch. Pellat).

41. For historiographical challenges, see El-Hibri, "Regicide," 334 ff.; El-Hibri, *Reinterpreting,* 59 ff.

42. I part from David Cook on translating al-Zawrā' as the twisted city. See Cook, *Studies,* 262.

43. It is narrated on the authority of 'Alī b. Abī Ṭālib on Muḥammad. See al-Baghdādī, *Tārīkh,* 1:39, for this and similar reports. See also Nu'aym, *Kitāb al-Fitan,* 184–85.

44. Al-Majlisī, *Biḥār,* 52:183–84.

45. For a treatment of this subject, see Lapidus, "Separation"; Madelung, "Vigilante"; El-Hibri, "Reign," 110 ff.; van Ess, *Theologie und Gesellschaft,* 3:173–75; Cooperson, *The Makers of Islam: Al-Ma'mūn,* 66–68.

46. Khalīfa, *Tārīkh,* 470; al-Ṭabarī, *Tārīkh,* 8:557.

47. Al-Ṭabarī, *Tārīkh,* 8:562–64.

48. "*La ṭā'ata li-al-makhlūq fī ma'ṣiyat al-khāliq*/no obedience to the creature in disobedience of the creator." Lapidus, "Separation," 379. See also Ayalon, "Military Reforms, 1:4 ff.

49. Lapidus, "Separation," 375 ff.

50. Madelung, "Vigilante," 331 ff.

51. Al-Ṭabarī, *History,* 32:77.

52. Madelung, "Vigilante."

53. Al-Ṭabarī, *Tārīkh,* 8:527. According to al-Ṭabarī, many riffraff and Bedouins joined his revolt.

54. See al-Iṣfahānī, *Maqātil,* 347–50.

55. Muḥammad b. Ja'far al-Ṣādiq, known as al-Dībāj. Al-Iṣfahānī, *Maqātil,* 358–59. Cf. Khalīfa, *Tārīkh,* 469–70, who says he revolted in al-Baṣra, and al-Mas'ūdī, *Murūj,* 4:322–23. Al-Ḥasan al-Afṭas revolted in Mecca in 200, Khalīfa, *Tārīkh,* 469–70.

56. Al-Ṭabarī, *Tārīkh,* 8:535–36. Ibrāhīm b. Ja'far's revolt.

57. Al-Ṭabarī, *Tārīkh,* 8:528; al-Iṣfahānī, *Maqātil,* 348. This tradition predicts the uprising of Abū al-Sarāyā. Even the date is given, 10 Jumādā I, 199. A variant of it is given on p. 348. Al-Azdī, *Tārīkh,* 334; Khalīfa, *Tārīkh,* 469; Ibn Qutayba, *Al-Ma'ārif,* 387–88; al-Mas'ūdī, *Murūj,* 4:322.

58. He used the slogan "Yā Fāṭimī yā Manṣūr." Al-Iṣfahānī, *Maqātil,* 353.

59. Al-Ṭabarī, *Tārīkh,* 8:530.

60. Al-Fasawī, *Al-Ma'rifa,* 1:189, 190–91. See also the brief accounts of 'Alid revolts in Khalīfa, *Tārīkh,* 468–70.

61. Al-Iṣfahānī, *Maqātil,* 358–59. Note how the prophecy conveys the idea that a person may be uncertain of his own messianic identity and looks for signs to verify his feelings.

62. Al-Ṭabarī, *Tārīkh,* 8:540, *History,* 32:36–37.

63. The transmitter adds the following remarks to the prophecy: "Walīd b. 'Ayyāsh said, 'The civil war in Medina was that of Ṭalḥa and al-Zubayr, that in Mecca was Ibn

al-Zubayr's, the civil discord of Yemen was that of Najda, the *fitna* of Damascus is that of the Umayyads and the *fitna* from the East is that of those people [the 'Abbāsids?].'" Nu'aym, *Kitāb al-Fitan,* 28.

64. See, for instance, Al-Ṣan'ānī, *Al-Muṣannaf,* 11:349–71; Ibn Abī Shayba, *Kitāb al-Muṣannaf,* 7:446–88. The fact that the *Kitāb al-Fitan* of Nu'aym includes an extensive number of accounts is an excellent indication of the fear of *fitna* that had developed during the first two centuries of Islam. For a good coverage of relevant prophecies, see Cook, *Studies,* esp. 80 ff., 120 ff., 182 ff.

65. Nu'aym, *Kitāb al-Fitan,* 15, 20.

66. Nu'aym, *Kitāb al-Fitan,* 385. The assumption is, clearly, that the day ends with the sunset.

67. Nu'aym, *Kitāb al-Fitan,* 385.

68. For instance, see Al-Ṣan'ānī, *Al-Muṣannaf,* 11:378: swallowing up [in earth] in the east, one in the west, one in the Bedouin Ḥijāz, *Ḥijāz al-'arab,* the Antichrist, Jesus, the Beast, smoke, Gog and Magog, pleasant wind which takes the souls of believers smoothly, the sun rising from the west. Ibn Abī Shayba, *Kitāb al-Muṣannaf,* 7:500–501, with slight changes and addition of fire from Aden. See also Ibn Abī Shayba, *Kitāb al-Muṣannaf,* 7:467–68, 493–94, 506; al-Ṣan'ānī, *Al-Muṣannaf,* 11:390–92, 397–98; al-Ḥumaydī, *Al-Musnad,* 1:178–79, 2:337, 365, 368.

69. Al-Ṣan'ānī, *Al-Muṣannaf,* 11:374. Al-Sindī, the compiler of the *Musnad* of al-Shāfi'ī, attributes to al-Shāfi'ī the prediction that the rivers will dry up at the end of times. See al-Sindī, *Tartīb,* 2:182–83; Nu'aym, *Kitāb al-Fitan,* 205.

70. Al-Ṣan'ānī, *Al-Muṣannaf,* 11:377–78. A substantial number of similar reports are contained in Nu'aym, *Kitāb al-Fitan,* 362 ff., 396 ff; Ibn Abī Shayba, *Kitāb al-Muṣannaf,* 7:458–59, 467, 491 ff., 500.

71. Nu'aym, *Kitāb al-Fitan,* 386. The same incident is also narrated as happening to the Prophet himself. Nu'aym, *Kitāb al-Fitan,* 387, 389, 390, 392; Ibn Abī Shayba, *Kitāb al-Muṣannaf,* 7:501–2.

72. Nu'aym, *Kitāb al-Fitan,* 387; Qur'ān, 79:43–44.

73. Ibn Ḥanbal, *Musnad,* 3:216–18 (print edition).

74. For further references, see Nu'aym, *Kitāb al-Fitan,* 227; Cook, *Studies,* 140–41.

75. Al-Ṭabarī, *Tārīkh,* 8:364, *History,* 30:334. For additional information, see al-Baghdādī, *Tārīkh Baghdād,* 3:339.

76. Al-Ṭabarī, *Tārīkh,* 8:496. For similar information, see al-Baghdādī, *Tārīkh Baghdād,* 3:341.

77. Al-Ṭabarī, *Tārīkh,* 8:501.

78. Al-Ṭabarī, *Tārīkh,* 8:500, *History,* 31:213. The idea of return seems to be used in a messianic sense as it occurs in the poem of one of al-Ma'mūn's sympathizers.

79. Al-Ṭabarī, *Tārīkh,* 8:418–23.

80. Nu'aym, *Kitāb al-Fitan,* 118 (appearance of a comet and dissension among themselves), 123, 124.

81. Al-Azdī, *Tārīkh,* 324.

82. Nu'aym, *Kitāb al-Fitan,* 125–26; Madelung, "Sufyānī," 43–44.

83. Balādhurī, *Ansāb,* 3:169–70; al-Ya'qūbī, *Tārīkh,* 2:354. Al-Ṭabarī, *Tārīkh,* 7:444, talks about the Sufyānī who revolted during the caliphate of al-Saffāḥ in 133/751.

84. Ibn 'Asākir, *Tārīkh,* 33:485. Ibn 'Asākir relates an account that suggests that his revolt was a result of simple joke played on him. Abū al-'Amayṭir had been asked to

revolt multiple times, but he refused. One day, Khaṭṭāb al-Dimashqī and his friends came to his house secretly and dug a hole underneath it. At night they slipped into the hole and called to Abū al-'Amayṭir, "Rise, time has come for you!" He thought the voice was the devil's. The next night they came again, and he started to wonder about himself. The third night they repeated the same trick. When it was the morning, he decided to revolt. Ibn 'Asākir, *Tārīkh*, 43:27.

85. Cobb, *White Banners*, 56.

86. Ibn 'Asākir, *Tārīkh*, 43:26; Ibn Khaldūn, *Tārīkh*, 1:499–501. For further references, see Cobb, *White Banners*, 56–57, 59.

87. Al-Ṭabarī, *Tārīkh*, 8:415, 31:88; al-Azdī, *Tārīkh*, 323; al-Balādhurī, *Ansāb*, 1:317; al-Maqdisī, *Al-Bad'*, 6:110; al-Dhahabī, *Kitāb al-'Ibar*, 1:317–18; Ibn Khaldūn, *Tārīkh*, 3:499–500; Ibn al-Athīr, *Al-Kāmil*, 6:250.

88. See 'Abbās, *Tārīkh*, 56.

89. 'Abbās, *Tārīkh*, 54, 55–56; Cobb, *White Banners*, 58.

90. Nu'aym, *Kitāb al-Fitan*, 165.

91. In today's northern Jordan, east of the Jordan River.

92. Nu'aym, *Kitāb al-Fitan*, 166; for a similar tradition, see 168.

93. Nu'aym, *Kitāb al-Fitan*, 165, 166.

94. Al-Majlisī, *Biḥār*, 47:297.

95. Al-Kulaynī, *Al-Kāfī*, 8:209.

96. Nu'aym, *Kitāb al-Fitan*, 181; Nagel, *Rechleitung* 255–56; Madelung, "Sufyānī," 42–43; 'Umar, *Buḥūth*, 224–25.

97. The root verb to describe the ascension is *w-l-y*. The actual word used is *y-w-l-y*, which can be constructed as either *yuwalli* (he will appoint), *tawalla* (he ascended to), or *yuwalla* (he will be appointed to). The other verbs used in the prediction are all third-person active present tense (e.g., he will receive, etc.). If we follow the pattern in the text, we need to construct the sentence in the following manner: "al-Rashīd will designate his son." Otherwise, the sentence would simply mean, his son ascended [the throne].

98. Nu'aym, *Kitāb al-Fitan*, 124. A variant on p. 178. See also Madelung, "Sufyānī," 44–45.

99. Nu'aym, *Kitāb al-Fitan*, 205 (Abū Yūsuf from Fiṭr b. Khalīfa from al-Ḥasan b. 'Abd al-Raḥmān al-'Uklī from Abū Hurayra); Madelung, "Sufyānī," 13.

100. Al-Majlisī, *Biḥār*, 52:234–35.

101. Ibn 'Asākir, *Tārīkh*, 53:259; Ibn Khaldūn, *Tārīkh*, 1:500–501; Cobb, *White Banners*, 60–62.

102. Al-Ṭabarī has only one short paragraph dealing with him. Ihṣān 'Abbās and recently Paul Cobb have made us aware of the substantial material contained in Ibn 'Asākir's *Tārīkh* concerning Abū al-'Amayṭir. For traditions about him, see Ibn 'Asākir, *Tārīkh*, 43:26–29.

103. Nu'aym, *Kitāb al-Fitan*, 123–24. One prediction pauses after noting the following: "when they disagree with each other three banners will be raised in Damascus," 124. See also Nu'aym, *Kitāb al-Fitan*, 180–82, 425: "His [al-Sufyānī] appearance [will be with] the appearance of the Mahdī. There will be no other authority between them." See also pp. 189, 192, 197. Cf. Al-Majlisī, *Biḥār*, 52:210, where the prediction makes the Yamānī victorious.

104. Hoyland, *Seeing*, 436.

105. Mistranslation by the author. It should read: because of the (oppression of the) one who is called al-Amīn.

106. At this point, the vision continues to describe murder, social, moral, religious, and institutional decay among Christians and Muslims.

107. Young and Ebied, "Unrecorded," 279 ff., 297–301.

108. Young and Ebied, "Unrecorded," 285. Even though the editors of the Leeds manuscript date the copy to the late eighteenth century, the content of the prophecy favors a date of composition sometime before the civil war ended.

109. The editors have mistaken the meaning of "*wa tabkī Sūriyya min dhālika al-wāḥid alladhi yud'a Amīnan.*" The sentence clearly expresses how people of Syria suffered under "the one who is called Amīn."

110. Abel, "Changements politiques," 29–30.

111. Possibly the two with one name are al-Saffāḥ and al-Manṣūr ('Abdallāh); the one with two names could be Muḥammad al-Mahdī; the two mentioned in the law are al-Hādī and al-Rashīd (Mūsā and Hārūn); the name with three letters might be Muḥammad al-Amīn (m ḥ-m-d, counting the 'm" only once or a-m-n); and the name with seven letters is al-Ma'mūn ('Abdallāh). Obviously this suggestion is inconclusive.

112. Gottheil, "Christian," 226. For the whole study, see *Zeitschrift für Assyriology* 13 (1898), 15 (1990), 17 (1903). For a more recent study, see Griffith, "Muḥammad," 146–74.

113. In Griffith, "yellow." However, it should be "green" as Hoyland suggests. In the Arabic version it is "*akhḍar,*" and in the Latin version it is "*viridis.*" Hoyland, *Seeing Islam,* 272.

114. Gottheil, "Christian," 229–30.

115. Abel, "Changements," 29–30.

116. Ibn Abī Shayba, *Kitāb al-Muṣannaf,* 7:508, and 469, with some differences. A comparable view is also given in Al-Ṣan'ānī, *Al-Muṣannaf,* 11:357–58, 368; Ibn Ḥanbal, *Musnad,* #5125, 5432, where he contrasts the war against the unbelievers with the "fight for kingship." See also al-Bukhārī, Saḥīḥ #4284. The best illustration of the idea of dissent is found in the traditions of commanding good and forbidding evil. See the detailed study of Cook, *Commanding Good.*

117. Ibn Abī Shayba, *Kitāb al-Muṣannaf,* 7:513. Nu'aym, *Kitāb al-Fitan,* 228, 229 predicts an 'Abbāsid Mahdī who would arise at the end of times and hand over the supreme political leadership, imamate, to Jesus. Also al-Mas'ūdī, *Murūj,* 4:272.

Chapter 4: Second Black Banners from the East

1. For al-Ma'mūn's biography, see the following studies, from which I draw the main outline: *EI*(2e), Ma'mūn (Rekaya); Nawas, *Al-Ma'mūn,* 15–24; Kennedy, *Prophet,* 145–57; El-Hibri, *Reinterpreting,* 95 ff. A lucid biography of al-Ma'mūn has recently been provided in Cooperson, *The Makers of Islam: Al-Ma'mūn.*

2. See *EI*(2e), Ustadhsīs (Madelung); Madelung, "Was the Caliph al-Ma'mūn?"

3. When al-Ma'mūn was eighteen years old, he married his cousin, Umm 'Īsā, the daughter of Mūsā al-Hādī, who bore him two sons, Muḥammad al-Asghar and 'Abdallāh. He also had numerous concubines.

4. Ibn 'Asākir, *Tārīkh,* 33:384.

5. Carter, "Arabic Grammar," 120–25.

6. Carter, "Arabic Grammar," 124.

7. Ibn 'Asākir, *Tārīkh*, 33:384; al-Ṭabarī, *Tārīkh*, 8:662–63; Ibn A'tham, *Kitāb al-Futūḥ*, 8:340, 326–27; al-Mas'ūdī, *Tanbīh*, 351; al-Mas'ūdī, *Murūj*, 4:314–15, 326; al-Ṣābī, *Rusūm*, 52–55; al-Subkī, *Ṭabaqāt*, 2:56.

8. Ibn 'Asākir, *Tārīkh*, 33:288; 290 mentions that al-Ma'mūn transmitted *ḥadīth*.

9. *EI*(2e), Yaḥyā b. Aktham (C. E. Bosworth).

10. Abramsky-Bligh, "Judicary," 195–201.

11. El-Hibri, *Reinterpreting*, 23.

12. Katib Çelebi, *Kashf al-Ẓunūn*, 1:631. See *Al-'Uyūn wa al-Ḥadā'iq*, 321, where al-Faḍl b. Sahl encouraged al-Ma'mūn that he was more deserving and more likely to win because he had studied the Qur'ān and the *ḥadīth*, and became knowledgeable about religion. For alternative views on al-Ma'mūn's attitude toward *ḥadīth* and jurisprudence, see Cooperson, *The Makers of Islam: Al-Ma'mūn*, 27, 33–36.

13. Miles, *Numismatic*, 96, 97, 98.

14. Al-Dīnawarī, *Al-Akhbār*, 276; al-Ṭabarī, *Tārīkh*, 8:381–82.

15. Cf. El-Hibri's explanation of al-Ma'mūn's successful mobilization of the Khurāsānīs in El-Hibri, "Reign," 153 ff., where he emphasizes family ties or kinship with al-Ma'mūn.

16. Al-Jahshiyārī, *Kitāb al-Wuzarā'*, 292; *Al-'Uyūn wa al-Ḥadā'iq*, 321, 322, and 331, where al-Ma'mūn is cited for his good conduct, competence, thruthfulness, and reliability.

17. Al-Ṭabarī, *Tārīkh*, 8:372, *History*, 31:17. I modified the translation slightly. See also Ibn A'tham, *Kitāb al-Futūḥ*, 8:342–43.

18. Al-Azdī, *Tārīkh*, 318.

19. Ibn A'tham, *Kitāb al-Futūḥ*, 8:296; al-Ṭabarī, *Tārīkh*, 8:375, 386, also mentions a similar sympathy for al-Ma'mūn.

20. Gabrieli, "La Successione"; Gabrieli, *Al-Ma'mūn e gli 'Alidi*.

21. Al-Dūrī, *Al-'Aṣr al-'Abbāsī*.

22. For a recent study on the composition of al-Ma'mūn's army going against the general view that his army was mainly Persian, see Elad, "Mawali," 278 ff.

23. Hodgson, *Venture*, 1:299–300; Zahniser, "Insights," 8 ff. Geddes, "Al-Ma'mūn's Shī'īte Policy," suggests a change of policy toward the Shī'ītes after 207 A.H.

24. Tor argues that al-Ma'mūn was too weak and pliable to have any meaningful effect in his court. The vacuum created by his absence was filled with his vizier and other factions in and around the court. See Tor, "Historiographical Re-Examination."

25. *EI*(2e), Harthama b. A'yan (Ch. Pellat).

26. See Cooperson, *Classical*, 32 ff. Tor, "Historiographical Re-Examination," 111–12, also hints at this possibility.

27. Nu'aym, *Kitāb al-Fitan*, 124. The tradition is also mentioned in Aguadé, "Messianismus," 123–24. A variant will be mentioned in another context as well. The prophecy suffers from mistakes, additions, and other discretions. In one case, the seventh of the 'Abbāsids calls to justice, in another to unbelief, and yet in another to battle (*'arak*). The last section of the account, which I have not included above, reads: "Then a man from among his family from Banū Hāshim will kill him. When they attack him [kill him], they will disagree with each other. And he mentioned a prolonged disagreement until the Sufyānī appears." The variant reads, "Then he kills several people from his family. And they disagree among themselves. At that time a man from Banū Fahr will appear and gather men among the Berbers until he occupies the

pulpits of Egypt. Then a man from the progeny of Abū Sufyān will come forth. If his rise coincides with that of the Banū Fahr, they will split into three groups."

28. Al-Ṭabarī, *Tārīkh*, 8:387, *History*, 31:44

29. Miles, *Numismatic*, 93, #95D Muḥammadiyya. Shamma, *Aḥdāth*, 575, #504, reads the Bukhārā Dirham as "*al-imām al-ma'mūn waliyyu 'ahd al-muslimīn*" and dates it to 193/809. I am grateful to Bates, Ilish, Kimber, and Nawas for their useful comments and suggestions on this issue. See also Poole, *Coins*, 88, 90, "*al-imām al-ma'mūn waliyy 'ahd al-muslimīn 'abdallāh b. amīr al-mu'minīn*," on mints from 194–95/810–11. See *EI*(2e), Sikka (R. E. Darley-Doran). For the challenges caliphal titles on coinage pose in this particular period, see Bacharach, "Al-Amīn's Designated," 108 ff.

30. The first to use it was the caliph al-Mahdī.

31. See al-Ṭabarī, *Tārīkh*, 8:376. The report contains a remarkable discussion between al-'Abbās b. Mūsā, the envoy of al-Amīn, and al-Faḍl b. Sahl about the title *al-imām*. When al-'Abbās objects to its use by al-Ma'mūn al-Faḍl b. Sahl asserts that "he [al-Ma'mūn] may well become the imam of a mosque and of a tribe. If you keep faith he will not hurt you; but, if you betray, that's it." This report may show the early reluctance of al-Ma'mūn to press forward or back down to the demands of al-Amīn. It may very well be a forgery as well, as it speaks of betrayal, presumably alluding to designation stipulations.

32. Al-Ṭabarī, *Tārīkh*, 31:27, 8:377; El-Hibri, "Reign," 39.

33. See al-Ḥumaydī, *Al-Musnad*, 2:468–69; al-Ṣan'ānī, *Al-Muṣannaf*, 11:372, 399, 400, 401; *Ibn Lahī'a*, 258, 260; Ibn Abī Shayba, *Kitāb al-Muṣannaf*, 7:490, 493, 494, 513; Nu'aym, *Kitāb al-Fitan*, 209, 212, 213, 221, 224, 346 ff.

34. Al-Ṭabarī, *Tārīkh*, 8:389, 390; Ṣafwat, *Jamharat*, 3:332, where al-Ma'mūn is described as *imām hudā* in *Risālat al-Khamīs*.

35. Al-Ṭabarī, *Tārīkh*, 8:411, *History*, 31:83. See also other instances of the use of *imām al-hudā* for al-Ma'mūn; Ṭayfūr, *Baghdād*, 172; al-Ṭabarī, *Tārīkh*, 8:663, and 8:411 (*imām al-hudā*); Ibn 'Abd Rabbih, *Al-'Iqd*, 5:368; Baghdādī, *Tārīkh*, 10:189.

36. For the same reason he criticized the "weeds," *nābita*, for using it for al-Amīn. See Ṭayfūr, *Baghdād*, 109.

37. Artuk and Artuk, *Arkeoloji Müzeleri*, 1:82, 87, 91. For further use of this title on coins, see also Shamma, *Aḥdāth*, 306, 322, 324, 413, 416–17, 420, 443, 456, 465, 467, 480–81, 483, 488, 494–95, 575, 577–79, 586–88, 590, 591–94, 596–97, 641, 689–702. For further references on the use of *imām* and *imām al-hudā*, see Crone and Hinds, *God's Caliph*, 34–35, 80–81; Nagel, *Rechleitung*, 145 ff.

38. Prophecies vary in naming the Khurāsānī troops in the civil war: second black banners, small black banners, another black banner, and black banner from Khurāsān. Nu'aym, *Kitāb al-Fitan*, 188, 189, 190, 191.

39. Nu'aym, *Kitāb al-Fitan*, 122, 125.

40. Nu'aym, *Kitāb al-Fitan*, 190; Madelung "Sufyānī," 23–24.

41. A messianic ephitet of a historical figure whose identity remains obscure to me.

42. Nu'aym, *Kitāb al-Fitan*, 191.

43. Nu'aym, *Kitāb al-Fitan*, 190.

44. Al-Majlisī, *Biḥār*, 49:160.

45. Sharon, *Black Banners*, 190–91.

46. Al-Rifāʿī, *ʿAṣr al-Maʾmūn*, 3:28–29, 30. Such was his strategy against al-Amīn as he saw it.

47. Al-Rifāʿī, *ʿAṣr al-Maʾmūn*, 3:31.

48. Al-Rifāʿī, *ʿAṣr al-Maʾmūn*, 3:31. The text of the letter is provided in al-Rifāʿī's *Aṣr al-Maʾmūn*.

49. Cf. Arazi and El'ad, "L'Épitre Armée," 66 (1987): 27ff., and esp. 67 (1968), 39ff; Nawas, "Miḥna," 17; El-Hibri, "Reign," 34–36.

50. Al-Ṭabarī, *Tārīkh*, 8:546, 549.

51. Cooperson, too, rightly questions the wisdom that al-Maʾmūn simply appointed ʿAlī al-Riḍā as heir-apparent and then disposed of him for purely pragmatic political reasons. Cooperson, *Classical*, 28–32, 70 ff., 193–96. Tor maintains that al-Maʾmūn was not in control of his court in the first place to be able to eliminate al-Riḍā. Tor, "Historiographical," 112, 122–28.

52. For an assessment of sources and their limitations, see Tor, "Historiographical," 112, 122–28; Büyükkara, "Speculations," 65 ff.

53. Nuʿaym, *Kitāb al-Fitan*, 206–7: "ʿAlī said: There will be strife, and there will be a group of people around a man from my family who has no disagreement [?] with God; he will be killed or die. Then the Mahdī will rise." It seems to be referring to ʿAlī al-Riḍā.

54. See Cooperson, *Classical*, 29.

55. For the most comprehensive treatment of the letter, see Bayhom-Daou, "Al-Maʾmūn's Alleged Apocalyptic Beliefs." I thank Bayhom-Daou for providing me a draft of her research and Michael Cooperson for informing me the existence of the forthcoming article.

56. Gabrieli, "Successione"; Gabrieli, *Al-Maʾmūn*; Sourdel, "La Politique religieuse," 38–48; Sourdel, *Medieval Islam*, 77–79; Sourdel, *La Vizirat*, 1:183–242; Sourdel, "ʿAbbāsid Caliphate," 123–24; Faḍl b. Rabīʿ and Faḍl b. Sahl *EI*$^{(2e)}$, (D. Sourdel); ʿUmar, *Al-Khilāfa al-ʿAbbāsiyya*, 34–35, 40–41; ʿUmar, *Tārīkh al-ʿIrāq*, 121–22; Zahniser, "Insights," 8 ff.; Tor, "Historiographical"; Bayhom-Daou, "Al-Maʾmūn's." Geddes, "Al-Maʾmūn's Shīʿīte Policy in Yemen," suggests a change of policy toward the Shīʿītes after 207 A.H.

57. Madelung, "New Documents," 345–46. See also El-Hibri, "Reign," 137–39, where he states that "this was the official and public propaganda that he [al-Maʾmūn] used in the course of nomination," although this was something different from his true purpose and his personal conviction. Madelung argues elsewhere that al-Maʾmūn's appointment of ʿAlī al-Riḍā reflected his "hopes of dampening the strong Shīʿite revolutionary fervour in Iraq." Madelung, "Vigilante Movement," 335. For a similar view, see Arjomand, "Crisis of the Imāmate," 491 ff., esp. 495–96.

58. Ibn Khaldūn notes that *Kitāb al-Dawla* was one of the sources of apocalyptic battles, *malāḥim*, literature known to al-Maʾmūn. Ibn Khaldūn, *Tārīkh*, 1:608–9.

59. Madelung, "New Documents," 343; al-Majlisī, *Biḥār*, 49:212.

60. Jayyusi-Lehn argues convincingly that al-Maʾmūn did not appoint any successor at his death. See Jayyusi-Lehn, "Caliph al-Muʿtaṣim." I am grateful to Jayyusi-Lehn for referring me to the relevant chapter in her study.

61. Bayhom-Daou argues that the passage is a later forgery attached to otherwise authentic letter, which I also argued previously in my doctoral dissertation. See Yücesoy, "Seventh of the ʿAbbāsids," 197 ff.

62. See al-Mas'ūdī (pseudo), *Ithbāt al-Waṣiyya*, 179. Obviously al-Ma'mūn would be the twentieth caliph.

63. Ibn Bābawayh al-Qummī, *Kamāl al-Dīn*, 370; al-Khābushānī, *Musnad al-Imām*, 1:421, 425.

64. In fact, the crux of the debate before the Islamic revolution in Iran in 1979 among the Shī'ī clerics was whether one should withdraw from politics until the Mahdī's appearance or prepare the world for his coming. Needless to say that the latter camp won the day. For the nature of activist apocalyptic movements, see Rinehart, *Revolution*, 17 ff.

65. See *EI*(2e), Sikka (R. E. Darley-Doran); El-Hibri, "Reign," 47–48. "With God is the Decision in the past and in the future; on that day the Faithful shall rejoice in the help of God" (Qur'ān, 30:4–5).

66. See his letter to the 'Abbāsids in Al-Majlisī, *Biḥār*, 49:213.

67. El-Hibri, "Reign," 151, on al-Qalqashandī, *Ma'āthir*, 2:332–37. Later in the letter, al-Riḍā expresses his uncertainty about the future of his designation, stating that he accepted the position against the predictions of occult knowledge. This is perhaps a later insertion to an earlier and shorter letter.

68. Madelung, "New Documents," 342.

69. Madelung, "New Documents," 340.

70. Qur'ān, 43:22; Madelung, "New Documents," 344.

71. Al-Majlisī, *Biḥār*, 49:213; Madelung, "New Documents," 343.

72. See Crone, "On the Meaning." For a study of 'Alī al-Riḍā's depiction in biographical sources, see Cooperson, *Classical*, 70 ff., 193–96.

73. Ibn 'Abd Rabbih, *Al-'Iqd*, 2:385–86.

74. See, Miles, *Numismatic*, 103–6. For the use of this title in conjunction with or without 'Alī al-Riḍā, see Shamma, *Aḥdāth*, 683–85, 710, 713, 715, 716, 717, 718; see also Crone and Hinds, *God's Caliph*, 94–95; Artuk and Artuk, *Arkeoloji Müzeleri*, 1:88, where 'Alī al-Riḍā's coin refers to him as Commander 'Alī al-Riḍā heir-apparent of the Muslims (*amīr 'Alī al-Riḍā waliyyu 'ahd al-muslimīn*).

75. Al-Ṭabarī, *Tārīkh*, 8:554, *History*, 32:61. See also Ibn A'tham, *Kitāb al-Futūḥ*, 8:322–23; al-Iṣfahānī, *Maqātil*, 375; Ibn Ṭiqṭaqā, *Al-Fakhrī*, 299 (*aṣlah, arwa', afḍal, adyan*); Ḥamāda, *Al-Wathā'iq al-Siyāsiyya wa al-Idāriyya al-'Ā'ida*, 2:321; al-Azdī, *Tārīkh*, 341.

76. For a discussion of al-Jāḥiẓ's al'Uthmāniyya and the *afḍaliyya* debate, see Zahniser, "Insights," 8–17. See also van Ess, *Das Kitāb an-Nakt*, 22 ff.; Sourdel, "La politique religieuse," 34 ff.; Sourdel, "'Abbāsid Caliphate," 1:121; Crone, *God's Rule*, 93–94, 101 ff. An excellent discussion of the *afḍaliyya* debate in early Islam is found in Afsaruddin, *Excellence and Precedence*.

77. See al-Nāshī al-Akbar, *Masā'il*, 51–53, 65–66.

78. Ibn Qutayba, *Al-Ikhtilāf*, 41–43.

79. See al-Jāḥiẓ, *Al-'Uthmāniyya*. It seems that the debate was so intense that al-Jāḥiẓ was compelled to write the following treatises to cover the controversy and explain his views. See Pellat, "Risāla fī al-Ḥakamayn," 517 ff.; "Maqālāt al-Zaydīyya wa al-Rāfiḍa," in *Rasā'il al-Jāḥiẓ*, 4:211 ff.; "Istiḥqāq al-Imāma," in *Rasā'il al-Jāḥiẓ*, 4:207; "Al-Jawābāt fī al-Imāma," in *Rasā'il al-Jāḥiẓ*, 4:285.

Chapter 5: Al-Ma'mūn in Baghdad

1. Al-Ṭabarī, *Tārīkh*, 8:573, 32:92; Ibn A'tham, *Kitāb al-Futūḥ*, 8:323–24. The solar eclipse of 26 June 819. See Verbelen, *Ancient*.

2. *Al-'Uyūn wa al-Ḥadā'iq*, 358.

3. d. 174/790.

4. d. 128/745.

5. Nu'aym, *Kitāb al-Fitan*, 206. For similar accounts, see Nu'aym, *Kitāb al-Fitan*, 165; al-Haytamī, *Al-Qawl al-Mukhtaṣṣ*, 67–68, 70, 75; al-Hindī, *Al-Burhān*, 201, also adds one thousand. What appears to be Ibn Lahī'a's comment, "Ibn Lahī'a said, this is according to the reckoning of the Persians, not that of the Arabs," is clearly a later addition made in an attempt to dissociate al-Ma'mūn from this date. Even though Madelung contends that Ibn Lahī'a intentionally obscured this account in order to protect his reputation in the future, and M. Cook sees in Ibn Lahī'a's comment an editorial attempt to extend the date of the Mahdī's appearance to 209/825 (see Madelung, "Sufyānī," 34; Cook, "Eschatology," 27), the context makes it highly improbable that the comment comes from Ibn Lahī'a. Ibn Ḥammād himself, or someone whose name was dropped from the chain of transmission, is more likely to be the source of this addition. Ibn Ḥammād was in no position to see al-Ma'mūn as the Mahdī. See Ibn Ḥajar al-'Asqalānī, *Tahdhīb*, 10:460.

6. See Ibn A'tham, *Kitāb al-Futūḥ*, 8:325; al-Ṭabarī, *Tārīkh*, 8:574; al-Dīnawarī, *Al-Akhbār*, 278–79; Abū al-Fidā, *Kitāb al-Mukhtaṣar*, 1:34; *Al-'Uyūn wa al-Ḥadā'iq*, 358.

7. Ṭayfūr, *Baghdād*, 6; al-Azdī, *Tārīkh*, 354. Another welcome speech by a "man from among the *mawālī*" is recorded in Ibn 'Asākir, *Tārīkh*, 33:287–88.

8. Ṭayfūr, *Baghdād*, 4–5.

9. Ibn al-Nadīm, *Al-Fihrist*, 74.

10. *EI*(2e), Aḥmad b. Abī Khālīd al-Aḥwal (D. Sourdel).

11. Al-Ṭabarī, *Tārīkh*, 8:575, *History*, 32:97; Ibn A'tham, *Kitāb al-Futūḥ*, 8:325.

12. Ibn al-Ṭiqṭaqā, *Al-Fakhrī*, 304.

13. Al-Ya'qūbī gives a long list of al-Ma'mūn's royal pardons. Al-Ya'qūbī, *Mushākalat*, 28–29; Ibn A'tham, *Kitāb al-Futūḥ*, 8:342; Ibn 'Abd Rabbih, *Al-'Iqd*, 1:28, where an ordinary woman praises al-Ma'mūn: "O the best of forgivers who is guided by righteousness."

14. El-Hibri, "Reign," 239.

15. Al-Baghdādī, *Tārīkh*, 10:188; al-Suyūṭī, *Tārīkh*, 378.

16. 19:214: "And admonish thy nearest kinsmen."

17. Al-Ya'qūbī, *Mushākalat*, 29–30; al-Ṭabarī, *Tārīkh*, 8:347, 652–53; Ibn Qutayba, *Al-Ma'ārif*, 390. See also al-Maqdisī, *Al-Bad'*, 6:112, where he adds: "he [al-Ma'mūn] presided over court hearings, and took upon himself [the performance of] the prayer and the Friday sermon." Al-Suyūṭī adds that al-Ma'mūn presided over the court of cases of injustice every Sunday after he arrived at Baghdad. Al-Suyūṭī, *Tārīkh*, 381.

18. Ibn Khallikān, *Wafayāt al-A'yān*, 1:86.

19. The letter is found in Ṭayfūr's *Akhbār al-Manẓūm wa al-Manthūr*, which is reproduced in full in Al-Rifā'ī, *'Aṣr*, 3:39

20. Al-Majlisī, *Biḥār,* 36:260

21. See, for instance, Nu'aym, *Kitāb al-Fitan,* 124, 125, 126, 182; al-Majlisī, *Biḥār,* 47:297; Ibn A'tham, *Kitāb al-Futūḥ,* 8:327. It is also repeated in Ṭayfūr, *Baghdād,* 102, 112; and al-Ṭabarī, *Tārīkh,* 8:606, *History,* 32:152. The verses are Ibrāhīm b. al-Mahdī's; al-Azdī, *Tārīkh,* 370–71; al-Mas'ūdī, *Murūj,* 4:326.

22. Literally, deputyship or caliphate, but the context justifies this translation.

23. Al-Ṭabarī, *Tārīkh,* 8:606, *History,* 32:152; Ibn A'tham, *Kitāb al-Futūḥ,* 8:327.

24. For further information, see *Encyclopedia of Religion and Ethics,* 9:406–17; Hopper, *Medieval Number Symbolism.*

25. See Schimmel, *Mystery of Numbers,* 126–55; Conrad, "Seven and the Tasbī'," 42–73.

26. Nu'aym, *Kitāb al-Fitan,* 124, 182.

27. Ṭayfūr, *Baghdād,* 152; al-Ṭabarī, *Tārīkh,* 8:655.

28. See the biblical verse, "The wolf shall live with the lamb." *Cambridge Annotated Study Bible,* Isaiah 11:6, 65:25. For the symbolism of lamb and lion in literature and iconography, see Alexander, *Byzantine Apocalyptic,* 70; Klein, "Apocalypse"; Kinney, "Early Christian," 201 ff.

29. El-Hibri, "Coinage," 77.

30. See Waines, "Third Century," 286; Lassner, *Shaping,* 281.

31. Al-Ṭabarī, *Tārīkh,* 8:568, 32:85; al-Balādhurī, *Futūḥ,* 320. A strange account of a tax increase on the farmers of Qum in 210/825 does not seem to be credible. See al-Ṭabarī, *Tārīkh,* 8:614. Al-Azdī, *Tārīkh,* 368, does not mention a tax increase.

32. Al-Ya'qūbī, *Kitāb al-Buldān,* 92.

33. Note the difference between al-Ṭabarī's report (10 makkūks) and Ṭayfūr's (8 makkūks).

34. A measure of capacity. Its value varied regionally and chronologically. In the fourth/tenth century, the bridled Qafīz equaled 48.2 kg of wheat in Baghdad and al-Kūfa but only 24.1 kg in al-Wāsiṭ and al-Baṣra. In another place it equaled 10 kg. See *EI*(2e), Mawāzin (E. Ashtor).

35. Ṭayfūr, *Baghdād,* 12.

36. A measure of capacity; 6.025 kg during the times of the caliphs. It was bigger in the period of the Crusades, 14.91 kg of wheat. See *EI*(2e), Mawāzin.

37. Al-Ṭabarī, *Tārīkh,* 8:576, *History,* 32:98; see also Ṭayfūr, *Baghdād,* 12. Al-Azdī, *Tārīkh,* 353, mentions the *muqāsama*-tax reduction.

38. El-Hibri, "Coinage," 58 ff., 72–73; El-Hibri, "Reign," 232–36.

39. *EI*(2e), Sikka (G. S. P. Freeman-Greenville); El-Hibri, "Reign," 254–59; El-Hibri, "Coinage," 65–68.

40. Bates, "'Abbāsid Coinage System."

41. See El-Hibri, "Reign," 214 ff.

42. Al-Ṭabarī, *Tārīkh,* 8:614; al-Azdī, *Tārīkh,* 368.

43. See *EI*(2e), Khurramiyya, 5:63–65 (Madelung).

44. Al-Ṭabarī, *Tārīkh,* 8:339.

45. See *EI*(2e), Bābak, (D. Sourdel).

46. Al-Ṭabarī, *Tārīkh,* 8:556; al-Azdī, *Tārīkh,* 342. Al-Mas'ūdī dates Bābāk's uprising to 204/819. Al-Mas'ūdī, *Murūj,* 4:325.

47. Hultgard, "Iranian Apocalypticism," 406; see also Olsson, "Apocalyptic Activity," 31 ff.

48. Al-Ṭabarī, *Tārīkh*, 8:576, 580, 581, 601, 619, 622; al-Azdī, *Tārīkh*, 386; al-Dīnawarī, *Al-Akhbār*, 402–6.

49. Al-Ṭabarī, *Tārīkh*, 8:649.

50. Al-Kindī, *Wulāt Miṣr*, 186 ff. Aguadé discusses the image of this group in apocalyptic traditions. See Aguadé, "Messianismus," 147–49.

51. For a detailed political history of Egypt in the *fitna* period, see Dunn, "Struggle," 47 ff. Vasilev, *Byzance et les Arabes*, 1:49–55, treats this incident when he discusses the conquest of Crete. See a brief account of the developments after the Spaniards arrived at Crete in Jenkins, *Byzantium*, 144–45.

52. See Al-Ṭabarī, *Tārīkh*, 8:610 ff., for the details of his march to Egypt.

53. *EI*(2e), Ikrītish (R. Mantran).

54. *EI*(2e), Ḳibṭ (A. S. Atiya).

55. Ibn A'tham, *Kitāb al-Futūḥ*, 8:337; al-Kindī, *Wulāt*, 214–15, 216. See El-Hibri, "Reign," 288–89.

56. Al-Kindī, *Wulāt*, 216.

57. See Dunn, "Struggle," 77 ff.

58. Al-Ṭabarī, *Tārīkh*, 8:627.

59. Ibn el-Muqaffa', Severus, *Historia*, 278–79.

60. *EI*(2e), Ḳibṭ.

61. Ibn al-Muqaffa', Severus, *Historia*, 278–79.

62. Ibn al-Muqaffa', Severus, *Historia*, 248–49.

63. Al-Ṭabarī, *Tārīkh*, 8:613, *History*, 32:165.

64. Al-Kindī, *Wulāt*, 206. I have previously noted how prophecies allowed multiple readings and applications to fit diverse situations, for which they were not intended initially. This prophecy identifies 'Abdallāh b. Ṭāhir b. al-Ḥusayn as being "from among the sons of al-Ḥusayn." There is a good chance that the prophecy quoted in this report, which is in fact a variant of several traditions in Ibn Ḥammād's work, had been intended for an 'Alid-Ḥusaynid candidate, but not for a Ṭāhirid. Yet this did not prevent its application to another person when circumstances allowed.

65. Cf. El-Hibri, *Reinterpretation*, 131.

66. Al-Ṭabarī, *Tārīkh*, 8:556, *History*, 32:64. The translator of al-Ṭabarī notes that al-Ṭabarī alleges the poet was Salm al-Khāsir, who actually died fifteen years before this event took place during the reign of al-Ma'mūn.

67. Al-Balādhurī, *Futūḥ*, 430.

68. Al-Azraqī, *Akhbār Makka* 1:225–26; Grabar, *Formation*, 57–58.

69. Al-Azraqī, *Akhbār Makka*, 1:242–44.

70. Grabar, *Formation*, 57.

71. See al-Ma'mūn's concerns with the Islamization of Transoxiana, in al-Balādhurī, *Futūḥ*, 431.

72. Ibn Hāshim Khālidī, *Kitāb al-Tuḥaf*, 159–65. See also Dunlop, "Diplomatic Exchange."

73. Bulliet, *Conversion to Islam*, 23, 51–52, 57.

74. Al-Azraqī, *Akhbār Makka*, 2:120, 170–71, 231–32.

75. Grabar, *Shape of the Holy*, 60, 64.

76. This amendment seems to have been made in 216/831 along with some other decorative additions and alterations. See Creswell, *Early Muslim Architecture*, 72.

77. Rosen-Ayalon, *Early Islamic Monuments*, 12, n. 3.

78. Creswell, *Early Muslim Architecture,* 72.

79. Creswell, *Early Muslim Architecture,* 65. This idea is found in one of the poems of ʿUmar b. Abī Rabīʿa (b. 23/643–644 A.H.), which shows that Jerusalem had already come to be regarded as the place whence Muḥammad had made his famous journey, *Miʿrāj,* to heaven. For another view, see Grabar, *Formation,* 59; Rosen-Ayalon, *Early Islamic Monuments,* 67.

80. Grabar, *Formation,* 53–56, 58 ff.; *EI*(2e), Ḳubbat al-Ṣakhra (Oleg Grabar).

81. Grabar, *Formation,* 61; Grabar, *Shape of the Holy,* 162.

82. Rosen-Ayalon, *Early Islamic Monuments,* 59 ff. A yet more radical thesis, that the Dome of the Rock was considered a portion, the nucleus of, and even one of the paradises itself, is put forward by Tamari, *Iconotextual Studies,* esp. 63 ff.

83. Nuʿaym, *Kitāb al-Fitan,* 344.

84. Nuʿaym, *Kitāb al-Fitan,* 344.

85. See Bonner, *Aristocratic Violence,* 43 ff.

86. See Bashear, "Apocalyptic," 173 ff.; Bonner, *Aristocratic,* 106 ff.

87. Cf. Bonner, *Aristocratic,* 148: "At the end of his life, Ma'mūn thus assumed the role of *ghāzī*-caliph which his father Rashīd played before him. His reasons were probably similar."

88. Ḥamāda, *Al-Watha'iq al-Siyāsiyya wa al-Idāriyya fī al-Andalus,* 1:147.

89. Ḥamāda, *Al-Watha'iq al-Siyāsiyya wa al-Idāriyya fī al-Andalus,* 1:148.

90. Vasiliev, *History,* 1:237.

91. Alexander, *Byzantine,* 20–21, 38–39, 68–69, 72–73, 101–4.

92. See El-Hibri, *Reinterpretation,* 129; Ibn al-Nadīm, *Fihrist,* 2:254. Ibn al-Murtaḍa claims that al-Ma'mūn had written numerous treatises encouraging rulers to convert to Islam. Ibn al-Murtaḍa, *Ṭabaqāt al-Muʿtazila,* 122–23.

93. Vasiliev, *Byzance,* 21 ff.; Vasiliev, *History,* 1:274–75. See Michel le Syrien, *Chronique,* 3:37.

94. Bonner, *Aristocratic,* 148.

95. Al-Hindī, *Kanz,* 14:268. I quoted this prophecy in the preface.

96. Al-Ṭabarī, *Tārīkh,* 8:651; al-Maqdisī, *Al-Bad',* 6:112; al-Baghdādī, *Tārīkh Baghdād,* 3:184. See also Nuʿaym, *Kitāb al-Fitan,* 246, 271.

97. Treadgold, *Byzantine Revival,* 268, 272–73; Vasiliev, *Byzance,* 98–103.

98. Al-Ṭabarī, *Tārīkh,* 8:623, *History,* 32:185; Ibn Aʿtham, *Kitāb al-Futūḥ,* 8:333–34; al-Fasawī, *Al-Maʿrifa,* 1:199; al-Azdī, *Tārīkh,* 399. Ṭayfūr mentions al-Ma'mūn's route to Ṭarsūs as the following: Shammāsiyya-Burdan-Tikrīt-Mawṣil-Nisibīn-Ḥarrān-al-Ruhā-Manbij-Dābiq-Anṭākya-Maṣīṣa-Ṭarsūṣ-Arḍ al-Rūm. Ṭayfūr, *Baghdād,* 144.

99. El-Hibri, "Reign," 290.

100. Treadgold, *Byzantine,* 275; Vasiliev, *Byzance,* 103–4.

101. Treadgold, *Byzantine,* 275–76.

102. Al-Ṭabarī, *Tārīkh,* 8:625–26, 32:187–88; Ibn Aʿtham, *Kitāb al-Futūḥ,* 8:336–37; al-Azdī, *Tārīkh,* 405; Ṭayfūr, *Baghdād,* 145.

103. Genesios, *Reigns of the Emperors,* 58, maintains that al-Ma'mūn accepted the Byzantine peace offer. The chronology of the ʿAbbāsid-Byzantine relations remains confused. He mentions the embassy of John the Grammarian when he reports on the raids of al-Muʿtaṣim. For this and other problems with Genesios's account, see xxiv–xxviii.

104. Al-Ṭabarī, *Tārīkh,* 8:628, *History,* 32:194; Ibn Aʿtham, *Kitāb al-Futūḥ,*

8:337–38; al-Azdī, *Tārīkh*, 408; Treadgold, *Byzantine*, 277–79; Vasiliev, *Byzance*, 114 ff. Vasiliev depends mostly on 'Abbāsid historiography in recounting events.

105. Al-Ṭabarī's chronology of Byzantine rulers is approximate, but not accurate. Al-Ṭabarī, *Tārīkh*, 8:387, 388, 545, 601.

106. Al-Ṭabarī, *History*, 32:196–97.

107. Al-Ṭabarī, *Tārīkh*, 8:631, *History*, 32:198–99; al-Azdī, *Tārīkh*, 412.

108. Treadgold, *Byzantine*, 279–81.

109. Al-Mas'ūdī reports that the Byzantine emperor offered to pay a sum of money to free the war captives and to restore the Muslim-populated town, which the Byzantines had destroyed, if al-Ma'mūn would stop his advance. But al-Ma'mūn refused this offer. Al-Mas'ūdī, *Murūj*, 4:339–40.

110. Ibn A'tham, *Kitāb al-Futūḥ*, 8:336, 338.

111. Al-Ṭabarī, *Tārīkh*, 8:623–625, 628–30; al-Ya'qūbī, *Tārīkh* 2:567–568, 570, 573; Abū al-Fidā, *Kitāb al-Mukhtaṣar*, 1:40. There is a grave in Tarsus in modern Turkey reputed to be al-Ma'mūn's. It is located within the sanctuary of the Ulu Cami. With no archaeological/documentary evidence, however, one cannot verify whether the grave is actually his. Michael Cooperson has already published a report about the grave, "Grave of al-Ma'mūn in Tarsus," 47 ff. My own investigation on the site in the summer of 2004 verified only the absence of evidence.

112. Al-Ṭabarī, *Tārīkh*, 8:630, *History*, 32:196–97.

113. Jeffrey, *Foreign Vocabulary*, 112 ff.; Faris and Glidder, "Development," 1–2; Gündüz, *Knowledge*, 21; Bell, "Who Were the Ḥanīfs?" 120–25.

114. Qur'ān, 10:105, 30:43, 22:31, 98:5, 4:123.

115. Qur'ān, 30:130.

116. Qur'ān, 3:95, 4:79, 162, 10:105, 16:121–24.

117. Qur'ān, 2:136, 3:66.

118. Hilmi Ömer Bey, "Some Considerations," 73–75; Faris and Glidder, "Development," 4–5.

119. Al-Ṣan'ānī, *Tafsīr*, 1:177, 2:198.

120. Al-Ṭabarī, *Jāmi' al -Bayān*, 9:379 ff.

121. See Donner, "From Believers to Muslims," 9–53; Peters, *Muhammad*, 31 ff., 105 ff., 191 ff.; *EI*(2e), Naṣāra (J. M. Fiey); *EI*(2e), Ḥanīf (M. Watt). For a detailed textual analysis of the Medina Charter, see Lecker, *Constitution of Medina*. Unfortunately Lecker does not pay any attention to the socially and politically transformative impact of the charter.

122. Qur'ān, 3:64.

123. Qur'ān, 5:69

124. Al-Ṣan'ānī, *Al-Muṣannaf*, 11:388.

125. Nu'aym, *Kitāb al-Fitan*, 220.

126. Nu'aym, *Kitāb al-Fitan*, 216.

127. Bashear, "Apocalyptic and Other Material."

Chapter 6: God's Caliph as *Mujaddid*

1. This romanticized image of *Bayt al-Ḥikma* was shattered by Gutas. The House of Wisdom was a small library, not an independently funded center or institution of any kind. For an excellent evaluation of the House of Wisdom, see Gutas, *Greek Thought*, 53 ff.

2. "To the best imam, risen from the best lineage; to the most excellent person who ever ascended the boards of a pulpit; to the inheritor of the ancients' knowledge, *'ilm al-awwalīn,* and understanding; to the king al-Ma'mūn, from Umm Ja'far." Al-Ṭabarī, *Tārīkh,* 8:506, *History,* 31:221; Ibn A'tham, *Kitāb al-Futūḥ* 8:309. The poem was composed by Khuzayma b. al-Ḥasan as a lament for al-Amīn through the words of the mother of al-Amīn. If authentic, it must date after the murder of al-Amīn, when the translation activities of al-Ma'mūn were perhaps in their infancy.

3. See, for instance, al-Dīnawarī, *Al-Akhbār,* 401; al-Ya'qūbī, *Mushākalat,* 27–28; Ibn al-Nadīm, *Al-Fihrist,* ed. Rida-Tajaddud, 129.

4. Al-Dīnawarī, *Al-Akhbār,* 401; al-Ya'qūbī, *Tārīkh,* 2:501, 542; al-Mas'ūdī, *Al-Tanbīh,* 351; Ibn Ṭiqṭaqā, *Al-Fakhrī,* 297; Ibn al-Murtaḍa, *Tabaqāt al-Mu'tazila,* 123.

5. Al-Ṭabarī, *Tārīkh,* 8:577–78; al-Azdī, *Tārīkh,* 360–61; Ibn 'Abd Rabbih, *Al-'Iqd,* 2:407–8; al-Maqdisī, *Al-Bad',* 6:112; Burton, *Plain and Literal Translation,* 4:185; Ibn al-Murtaḍa, *Ṭabaqāt al-Mu'tazila,* 122–23.

6. Al-Ya'qūbī, *Mushākalat,* 27–28; Ibn Ṭiqaṭaqā, *Al-Fakhrī,* 297, 298–99. For similar descriptions, see al-Suyūṭī, *Tārīkh,* 362; al-Dhahabī, *'Ibar,* 375.

7. Al-Dīnawarī, *Al-Akhbār,* 400–401.

8. Langermann, "Book of Bodies." This incident took place in 828; Cooperson, *The Makers of Islam: Al-Ma'mūn,* 88–91.

9. Gutas, *Greek Thought,* 75 ff.; Saliba, *Islamic Science,* 1–25; Sabra, "Appropriation," 236–37. Al-Jābirī sees a battle against Gnosticism and Manichaeism in the translation movement. Al-Jābirī, *Takwīn,* 222–25. For a detailed analysis of Ibn al-Nawbakht's justification of sciences, the reader should consult Gutas, Saliba, and van Bladel.

10. By which I mean the practical knowledge accessible and in use in architecture, metal work, and computation methods involving tax surveys and collection.

11. Ibn al-Nawbakht's negative attitude toward Alexander notwithstanding, by the time of al-Ma'mūn, his image seems to have been elevated to a world conqueror, even a monotheist sage tutored by Aristotle. An interesting expedition commissioned by the caliph al-Wāthiq (r. 842–47) to Central Asia under the leadership of Sallām the interpreter to find out the whereabouts of the Qur'ānic wall of iron and brass built by *Dhū al-Qarnayn* against Gog and Magog testifies to a rectified image of Alexander in the 'Abbāsid court. For the caliph to send an expedition for the specific purpose of finding the wall, one would assume that a serious discussion of the legend had been taking place prior to the attempt. See al-Ya'qūbī, *Tārīkh,* 1:142–45 (identified as the Qur'ānic Dhū al-Qarnayn); al-Dīnawarī, *Al-Akhbār,* 29 ff. (both monotheist and Dhū al-Qarnayn). See also Bosworth, *Arabs,* xiii, 22–23; Wilson, "Wall of Alexander." For Alexander as the tutor of Aristotle, see Stoneman, "Alexander the Great," 15–16.

12. Ibn al-Nadīm, *Fihrist al Ibn al-Nadīm,* 2:574–75. Quotations are from Gutas, *Greek,* 39–40.

13. *Al-Fihrist,* 238 (Flugel edition).

14. Gutas, van Bladel, and Saliba have already pointed out the significance of Ibn al-Nawbakht's role in the transmission of ancient sciences into the 'Abbāsid world, but they took no note of the fact that Ibn al-Nawbakht refered to the earliest people in connection with ancient sciences. Gutas, *Greek,* 38 ff.; Saliba, *Islamic,* 31 ff.; van Bladel, "Hermes," 36 ff. I owe the reference to van Bladel to James E. Montgomery.

15. *Al-Fihrist*, 238 (Flugel edition). Dodge notes that he was "Jamshīd b. Tahmuras b. Hushang (Awijhan)." Ibn al-Nadīm, *Fihrist al Ibn al-Nadīm*, 2:572, n. 5.

16. Al-Dīnawarī, *Al-Akhbār*, 1–2.

17. Al-Ṭabarī, *History*, 1:325–27, 341–42, 344–45, 348 ff.

18. Gutas, *Greek*, 34, 43. Note that Ibn al-Nawbakht made Zoroaster "their prophet."

19. Ibn al-Nadīm, *Fihrist of Ibn al-Nadīm*, 2:575; Gutas, *Greek*, 46.

20. See Montgomery, "Al-Gāḥiẓ and Hellenizing Philosophy," where Montgomery clarifies in the specific instance of al-Jāḥiẓ's treatise, *Kitāb al-Tarbīʿ wa al-Tadwīr*, the process by which both Hellenic philosophy and Hellenizing philosophy were situated within Islamic worldviews. I am indebted to the author for making a draft of his study available to me.

21. *The Book of Treasures*, which documents the available sciences for learning and instruction in the early-ninth-century ʿAbbāsid Baghdad, shows which secular sciences were known to ʿAbbāsid literati. Mingana, *Encyclopaedia of Philosophical*. See also Kraus, *Jābir Ibn Ḥayyān*, 2:276 ff.

22. See Pingree, *Thousands*, 11; Gutas, *Greek*, 46 ff.

23. Qurʾān, 20:133.

24. Qurʾān, 87:18–19.

25. Qurʾān, 54:52.

26. Qurʾān, 80:13–16.

27. Qurʾān, 74:52.

28. Ibn Saʿd, *Al-Tabaqāt*, 5:543.

29. Ibn al-Nadīm, *Fihrist of Ibn al-Nadīm*, 1:41 ff. He gives additional examples about the scholarly and popular interest in ancient scriptures since the time of al-Rashīd.

30. Qurʾān, 18:60–85.

31. Al-Ṣanʿānī, *Al-Muṣannaf*, 2:407; Qur'ān, 18:82.

32. Al-Ṭabarī, *Jāmiʿ al-Bayān*, 16:5–6. He attributes this view to al-Ḥasan al-Baṣrī.

33. Nuʿaym, *Kitāb al-Fitan*, 18–19. For reports of this sort, see Nuʿaym, *Kitāb al-Fitan*, 18–19, 63–64, 68, 113–14.

34. Ibn ʿAbd al-Barr, *Al-Istīʿāb*, 3:1287.

35. Al-Ṣanʿānī, *Al-Muṣannaf*, 11:372. The same prophecy with a different chain of transmission is in Nuʿaym, *Kitāb al-Fitan*, 220.

36. Nuʿaym, *Kitāb al-Fitan*, 221.

37. Nuʿaym, *Kitāb al-Fitan*, 246, 295; *Ibn Lahīʿa*, 303, variant ending "it [treasure?] will be entrusted to a youth from Yaman." For a comparison between the biblical and Islamic narratives of the Ark of the Covenant, see Rubin, "Tradition and Transformation," 198 ff., 209 ff.

38. Nuʿaym, *Kitāb al-Fitan*, 223; *Ibn Lahīʿa*, 302–3.

39. Nuʿaym, *Kitāb al-Fitan*, 288.

40. Ibn al-Nadīm, *Fihrist of Ibn al-Nadīm*, 2:573–75. For a detailed discussion of Persian Hermetica and its transmission to Arabic, see van Bladel, "Hermes," 27 ff.

41. Ibn al-Nadīm, *Fihrist of Ibn al-Nadīm*, 2:575; Dorotheus Sidonius, *Carmen Astrologicum*, 161, 224. For a discussion of Ibn al-Nawbakht and the Hermes legend, see van Bladel, "Hermes," 140 ff.

42. See Kennedy and Pingree, *Astrological History*, 1 (f214v, line 13), translation, 39; van Bladel, "Hermes," 18, 44.

43. Van Bladel, "Hermes," 34, 45.

44. Stoneman, "Alexander."

45. See Kraus, *Jābir Ibn Ḥayyān*, 2:275–80.

46. Ṭayfūr, *Baghdād*, 36. Translation from Gutas, *Greek*, 101.

47. "And Ukhnukh, his name in the Torah, Hebrew; and its interpretation in Arabic is Idrīs, and he is Idrīs peace be upon him. And Ukhnukh, his name is Syriac" ("*Wa Ukhnukh ismuhu fī al-Tawrāt 'Ibrānī, wa tafsīruhu bi al-'Arabī Idrīs wa huwa Idrīs 'alayhi al-salām wa Ukhnukh ismuhu Suryānī*"), Khouri, *Wahb b. Munabbih*, 1:216–17 and 230, 294, 315

48. Al-Jāḥiẓ, *Le Kitāb at-ṭarbī'*, 45 (paragraph, 83).

49. Al-Jāḥiẓ, *Le Kitāb at-ṭarbī'*, 26 (paragraph, 40).

50. As early as the eighth century Idrīs was thought to be alive, but only taken to heaven, similar to Jesus. See Mujāhid b. Jabr, *Tafsīr*, 387.

51. In Arabic, because the legend of the three Hermeses is not Abū Ma'shar's invention as van Bladel demonstrated. The younger contemporary of Abū Ma'shar, the Greek George Synkellos, cites an earlier authority, Manetho's *Book of Sothis*, concerning Hermes in which three Hermeses are identified. Although the attribution of the *Book of Sothis* to Manetho is false, for the purposes of the origins of the idea of three Hermeses, the argument remains valid. See van Bladel, "Hermes," 145 ff.

52. Pingree, *Thousands*, 14–15; Pingree, "Sabians of Harran," 25–26; Plessner, "Hermes Trismegistos," 51.

53. Plessner, "Hermes," 50–51.

54. *Ghāyat al-Ḥakīm* mentions that Egyptian Copts claimed that the first Hermes was the builder of the cities along the Nile. The author of the *Ghāyat al-Ḥakīm* credits the Copts with the ability to decipher the ancient Egyptian script. See Pseudo al-Majrīṭī, *Das Ziel des Weisen*, 310–11.

55. For further elaboration on Abū Ma'shar's theory of the three Hermeses, see van Bladel, "Hermes," 129 ff. Van Bladel's suggestion that Abū Ma'shar constructed his theory of the three Hermeses by stringing together already existing legends concerning the identity of Hermes and that the figure of antediluvian Hermes was the earliest seems very plausible.

56. Pingree, *Thousands*, 11.

57. Al-Ṭabarī, *History*, 1:105.

58. For a thoughtful evaluation of the dream, see Gutas, *Greek*, 97–98, 101–2. As Gutas has suggested, the first version of the dream (Ibn al-Nadīm's version) seems to belong to a period of time most probably after al-Ma'mūn, and was used to lend legitimacy to the translation movement and philosophical inquiry. The second version (Ibn Nubāta's version), on the other hand, is more in accord with the intellectual concerns of al-Ma'mūn's time, particularly the debate between personal judgment and religious law and between the Mu'tazilīs and Ḥanafites and the people of *ḥadīth* and the colleagues of al-Shāfi'ī (d. 820). Ibn al-Nadīm, *Fihrist of Ibn al-Nadīm*, 2:583–84.

59. Gutas, *Greek*, 97, 101–102.

60. It is useful to remember that Muḥammad himself received revelation sometimes in his dream and that the Qur'ān is full of dream narratives. See the stories of Abraham and Joseph, which have an explicit revelatory aspect.

61. For an analogous incident reflecting al-Ma'mūn's premonition power, see al-Baghdādī, *Tārīkh Baghdād*, 10:188.

62. Al-Jāḥiẓ appears as the transmitter of the report on the authority of al-Ḥasan b. Sahl via al-Wāqidī (d. 823), which makes the story more difficult to rule out as a later fantasy.

63. Miskawayh, *Tajārib al-Umam,* 19–21. See also Pingree, *Thousands,* 1.

64. For whether the attribution of this treatise to al-Ma'mūn's vizier's brother al-Ḥasan b. Sahl is accurate, see Arberry, "Jāvidān Khiradh," 145.

65. For various examples, see al-Ḥimyarī, *Rawḍ al-Mi'ṭar,* 16 ff.; Graefe, "Das Pyramidenkapitel," 8 ff. The author of *Ghāyat al-Ḥakīm* similarly notes the connection between Hermes and the key to the secrets of Creation. See Pseudo al-Majrītī, *Das Ziel des Weisen,* 187–88.

66. The excavation in the Pyramids has been most recently dealt with in an excellent article by Cooperson, "Al-Ma'mūn, the Pyramids." I am grateful to the author for letting me use the draft of his study.

67. See Yāqūt al-Ḥamawī, *Mu'jam,* 5:402; al-Idrīsī, *Anwār 'Ulwiy,* 34–35.

68. Al-Idrīsī, *Anwār 'Ulwiy,* 60–61. The translation is from Cooperson, "Al-Ma'mūn, the Pyramids," with slight modifications.

69. We should dismiss medieval accounts claiming that al-Ma'mūn intended to demolish the pyramids out of religious zeal, or to take up an ancient challenge that no one could demolish them, or even to find a way of excavating the precious treasure buried within them. See al-Ḥimyarī, *Rawḍ al-Mi'ṭar,* 16–17; Graefe, "Das Pyramidenkapitel," 8–9, 36.

70. Al-Idrīsī, *Anwār Ulwiy,* 60–61.

71. Fodor, "Origins," 335–63.

72. See Fodor, "Origins," 346–52.

73. Graefe, "Das Pyramidenkapitel," 8–9.

74. See Fodor, "Origins," 335; Ibn al-Qifṭī, *Ikhbār al-'Ulamā',* 2–3; Graefe, "Das Pyramidenkapitel," 18, 42.

75. Van Reeth, "Caliph al-Ma'mūn," 229, 234.

76. Van Reeth, "Caliph al-Ma'mūn," 221–23, 230.

77. As argued by Plessner, "Hermes," 48–49, 55; Cooperson, "Al-Ma'mūn, the Pyramids." For the Arabic transmission of the Emerald Tablet and associated literature, see Ruska, *Tabula Smaragdina.*

78. Van Reeth, "Caliph al-Ma'mūn," 229, 234.

79. Translated into Latin in 1140 as *Tabula Smaragdina.* See Ruska, *Tabula Smaragdina.*

80. See Kraus, *Jābir Ibn Ḥayyān,* 2:270 ff., 275–80.

81. For a more detailed study of the translation activities and al-Ma'mūn's role, see my forthcoming article "Translation as Self-Consciousness: The 'Abbāsid Translation Movement, Ancient Sciences, and Antediluvian Wisdom."

82. See Collins, *Charlemagne,* 141 ff.; Halphen, *Charlemagne,* 85.

83. See Halphen, *Charlemagne,* 88, 158, 161–62; Jonas, Ninth-Century Political Tract for such universalistic aspirations and for a description of a model Christian king, esp. chaps. 1–7.

84. Al-Ṭabarī, *Tārīkh,* 8:618–19; al-Mas'ūdī, *Murūj,* 4:338–39; al-Dhahabī, *'Ibar,* 1:359; Ibn A'tham, *Kitāb al-Futūḥ,* 8:321; al-Suyūṭī, *Tārīkh,* 364; Ibn 'Abd Rabbih, *Al-'Iqd,* 5:92–101; Ṭayfūr, *Baghdād,* 50; Abū al-Fidā, *Kitāb al-Mukhtaṣar,* 1:39.

85. See Pellat, "Le culte de Mu'āwiya," 10:53 ff.

86. *EI*(2e), Fadak (L. Veccia Vaglieri).

87. Al-Ya'qūbī, *Tārīkh*, 2:571; al-Balādhurī, *Futūḥ*, 29–33.

88. Al-Balādhurī, *Futūḥ*, 33; *EI*(2e), Fadak.

89. Al-Balādhurī, *Futūḥ*, 32–33.

90. Al-Subkī, *Ṭabaqāt*, 2:57.

91. See, *EI*(2e), Mut'a (Heffening).

92. Nu'aym, *Kitāb al-Fitan*, 221; Ibn Abī Shayba, *Kitāb al-Muṣannaf*, 7:513. The text reads *akhbar* instead of *akhyar*, which is evidently a mistake.

93. Al-Ṭabarī, *Tārīkh*, 8:626 (on his deathbed al-Ma'mūn repeated this demand [648]), *History*, 32:189; al-Azdī, *Tārīkh*, 405. Ṭayfūr, *Baghdād*, 145.

94. See al-Ṭabarī, *Tārīkh*, 8:619 (when al-Ma'mūn made his view concerning the Qur'ān public in 212), 631 ff. He initiated the *Miḥna* in 218/833; see also Abū al-Fidā, *Kitāb al-Mukhtaṣar*, 1:39, 40.

95. An outline of the major events of the *Miḥna is* given in *EI*(2e), *Miḥna* (M. Hinds).

96. Yücesoy, "Between Nationalism," from which the following is largely drawn.

97. Patton, *Aḥmad Ibn Ḥanbal*, 2, 3, 52, 126–27. For similar views, see Muir, *Caliphate*, 489, 496–97, 501; 'Umar, *Al-Khilāfa al-'Abbāsiyya*, 34–35, 40–41; 'Umar, *Tārīkh al-'Irāq*, 121–22; Makdisi, "Authority in the Islamic Community," 121; Makdisi, *Rise of Humanism*, 5.

98. Sourdel, "La Politique religieuse," 38–48; Sourdel, *Medieval Islam*, 77–79; Sourdel, *La Vizirat*, 1:183–242; Sourdel, "'Abbāsid Caliphate," 123–24; *EI*(2e) Faḍl b. Rabī' and Faḍl b. Sahl, (D. Sourdel).

99. Watt, *Islamic Philosophy*, 34–35, 135; Watt, *Islamic Political Thought*, 85–89; Watt, *Formative*, 175–79.

100. Gibb, "An Interpretation of Islamic History," 11–12.

101. Hodgson, *Venture*, 1:478, 479, 480, 481. For a similar view, see Zahniser, "Insights," 8, 15–16; Geddes, "Al-Ma'mūn's Shī'īte Policy."

102. Crone and Hinds, *God's Caliph*, 94–96; *EI*(2e) Miḥna. Their arguments came against the background set by Watt, Sourdel, and Lapidus. See Lapidus, "Separation," 379. Cf. Madelung, "Vigilante," 331 ff.

103. Jad'ān, *Al-Miḥna*, 79 ff., 85, 189 ff., 280, 284, 293 ff., 352–53; van Ess, *Theologie und Gesellschaft*, 3:446, 451–52, 455 ff.; Bulliet, *Islam*, 118–20, 121; Nawas, "Reexamination," 615–24; Nawas, "Miḥna," 698–708, esp. 698–99, 704–8.

104. Zaman, *Religion and Politics*, 105, 106–7, 110, 113, 114, 209. See also Zaman, "Caliphs," 1 ff.

105. See *EI*(2e), Dja'd b. Dirham (G. Vajda), Jahm b. Ṣafwān (W. Montgomery Watt), Kalām (L. Gardet).

106. Al-Jurjānī, *Al-Kāmil fī Ḍu'afā' al-Rijāl*, 1:313: Ismā'īl b. Ḥammād b. Abī Ḥanīfa used to remark that "the Qur'ān is created. This is my belief, and the belief of my father and grandfather." For the controversies regarding the issue of the createdness of the Qur'ān, see Madelung, "Origins," 504 ff; van Ess, "Ibn Kullāb und die Miḥna"; Jad'ān, *Al-Miḥna*, 65 ff., 79 ff.; *EI*(2e) Miḥna; Nawas, "Reexamination," 616–17; Nawas, "Miḥna."

107. Daiber, *Das Theologisch-Philosophische System*, 169 ff. See also al-Jāḥiẓ, "Risāla fī Khalq al-Qur'ān," 3:289.

108. See Jad'ān, al-Miḥna, 65 ff.; *EI*(2e) Miḥna; Nawas, "Reexamination," 616–17.

109. See Nagel, *Rechleitung*, 439 ff.; van Ess, *Theologie und Gesellschaft*, 3:449, 459; *EI*(2e), *Miḥna*.

110. Al-Ṭabarī, *Tārīkh*, 8:635, 636, 637, 638. See also *EI*(2e), Miḥna.

111. Such as "God has made incumbent upon the imams and caliphs of the Muslims that they should be zealous in establishing God's religion." Al-Ṭabarī, *Tārīkh*, 8:631, 634.

112. Once, to be more accurate, he mentioned the name of a caliph in passing, when he criticized Yaḥyā b. 'Abd al-Raḥmān al-'Umarī that if he was indeed from the progeny of 'Umar b. al-Khāṭṭāb, he would know how to answer the question whether the Qur'ān was created. Al-Ṭabarī, *History*, 32:219.

113. Zaman, *Religion*, 105–10, 113–14, 209.

114. Nawas, "Reexamination," 615–24; Nawas, "Miḥna," 698–708.

115. On the authority of Sulaymān b. Dāwūd al-Mahrī (253/867) on 'Abdallāh b. Wahb (197/813) from Sa'īd b. Abī Ayyūb (161/778) from Shuraḥbīl b. Yazīd al-Ma'āfirī from Abī 'Alqama from Abū Hurayra from the Prophet. Abū Dāwūd, *Kitāb al-Sunan*, 4:109, #4291. It is most probably intended for rulers as it is included in the chapter on the *fitan*. The tradition is contained in a later source, Abū Dāwūd, but it certainly dates back to the late second or early third Islamic century. Van Donzel maintains that Ibn Sa'd (225/240) himself used the same designation for 'Umar b. 'Abd al-'Azīz. See *EI*(2e), *Mudjaddid*. However, there is no reference in Ibn Sa'd that supports his claim. He is described as the Mahdī, which is apparently taken by Donzel also to mean *mujaddid*.

116. Landau-Tasseron, "Cyclical Reform," 79 ff. Landau-Tasseron argues that the tradition was invented by al-Shāfi'ī's pupils, who wanted to legitimize his teachings, which were new at that time, and that the application of the tradition in the following centuries mostly to Shāfi'ite scholars shows, indeed, that the tradition was a Shāfi'ite invention. Landau-Tasseron ignores the currency of this tradition among medieval Muslim rulers, which is essential to properly evaluate the history of this tradition. For instance, this epithet is attributed to Ghazān Khān, Shahrūkh, Uzun Hasan, Selim I, Süleyman I, and Shaybānī Khān up to the sixteenth century. See Fleischer, "Lawgiver as Messiah," 151, 163, 165, for citations from sources and relevant literature.

117. Nu'aym, *Kitāb al-Fitan*, 188.

118. A similar understanding appears to be in circulation during al-Ma'mūn's time. In a casual conversation, according to al-Baghdādī, between two poets about what happened in the court of al-Ma'mūn between one of them and the caliph, the title of *imām al-hudā* is mentioned. Having heard that al-Ma'mūn was endowed with an outstanding memory of poetry, the poet Ibn Abī Ḥafṣa was exited to read in front of the caliph, anticipating that he would read a portion of the poem and then the caliph would complete it. He read the following lines: "The leader of guidance, *imām al-hudā*, continues to occupy himself with religion while people are preoccupied with the world." The caliph remained dead silent. The poet was surprised and disappointed. His colleague 'Amāra b. 'Aqīl then teasingly commented about what might have happened: "You almost made him an old lady sitting in the mosque counting her rosary beads. Who is going to watch over the affairs of the world if he were distracted from

it?" He then commented that Ibn Abī Ḥafṣa should have read something from Jarīr emphasizing how the caliph embraced piety, worldly affairs, and pleasures at once. Al-Baghdādī, *Tārīkh*, 10:189.

119. Al-Ṭabarī, *Tārīkh*, 8:631–32, 634 ff.

120. Quoted in al-Rifāʿī, *ʿAṣr*, appendix to book 3:41 (*naqtadī bi hudāhu wa naʿshū bi nūrihi fī dīninā*).

121. Al-Ṭabarī, *History*, 32:199–200.

122. Al-Ṭabarī, *Tārīkh*, 8:631–33, *History*, 32:200–204.

123. Al-Ṭabarī, *Tārīkh*, 3:634, *History*, 32:205–6.

124. Al-Ṭabarī, *History*, 32:205–6.

125. Ibn ʿAbd Rabbih, *Al-ʿIqd*, 2:100–101 (*lā-dīna illā bi-ka wa lā dunyā illa maʿaka*).

Bibliography

Primary Sources

Abū Dāwūd, Sulaymān b. Ash'ath. *Kitāb al-Sunan*. Ed. Muḥammad 'Awwāma. Jidda: Dār al-Qibla, Mu'assasat al-Rayyān, al-Maktaba al-Makkiyya, 1998.

———. *Al-Sunan*. In *Mawsū'at al-Ḥadīth al-Sharīf*, [computer file]. Cairo: Sharikat Ṣakhr li-al-Ḥāsūb, version 1.1, 1997.

Abū al-Fidā, 'Imād al-Dīn Ismā'īl. *Kitāb al-Mukhtaṣar fī Akhbār al-Bashar.* Beirut: Dār al-Fikr and Dār al-Biḥār, 1956.

Abū Yūsuf, Ya'qūb b. Ibrāhīm. *Kitāb al-Kharāj*. Ed. Iḥsān 'Abbās. Beirut: Dār al-Shurūq, 1985.

Abū Zur'a al-Dimashqī, 'Abd al-Raḥmān b. 'Amr. *Tārīkh Abī Zur'a al-Dimashqī*. Ed. Shukrī Ni'mat Allāh al-Qawjānī. Damascus: Majma' al-Lugha al-'Arabiyya bi-Dimashq, 1980.

Akhbār al-Dawla al-'Abbāsiyya wa fīhi Akhbār al-'Abbās wa Wildihi, (Anonymous). Ed. 'Abd al-'Azīz al-Dūrī and A. J. al-Muṭṭalibī. Beirut: Dār al-Ṭalī'a, 1971.

Arberry, Arthur John. *The Koran Interpreted: A Translation*. London: Allen and Unwin, 1955.

Al-Ash'arī, Abū Ḥasan 'Alī b. al-Ḥusayn. *Maqālāt al-Islamiyyīn*. İstanbul: Istanbul: Darülfünûn, Devlet Matbaası, 1927.

Al-Azdī, Yazīd b. Muḥammad. *Tārīkh Mawṣil*. Ed. 'Alī Ḥabībah. Cairo: Lajnat al-Iḥyā al-Turāth al-'Arabī, 1967.

Al-Azraqī, Abū al-Walīd Muḥammad b. 'Abdallāh. *Akhbār Makka wa mā Jā'a fīhā min al-Āthār.* Ed. Rushdī Ṣālih Malḥas. Beirut: Dār al-Andalus, 1983.

Al-Baghdādī, Aḥmad b. 'Alī al-Khaṭīb. *Tārīkh Baghdād aw Madinat al-Salām*. Ed. Muḥammad Amīn al-Khānjī. Beirut: Dār al-Kutub al-'Ilmiyya, n.d.

Al-Baghdādī, 'Abd al-Qāhir b. Ṭāhir. *Al-Farq bayna al-Firaq*. Ed. Muḥammad 'Uthmān al-Khisht. Cairo: Maktabat Ibn Sīnā, 1988.

———. *Moslim Schism and Sects.* Tr. Kate Chambers Seelye. New York: Columbia University Press, 1919.

"Bahman Yast or Zand-i Vohûman Yasno." In *The Sacred Books of the East*, Vol. 5, *Pahlavi Texts.* Tr. E. W. West; ed. F. Max Müller. Oxford: Clarendon Press, 1880.

Al-Balādhurī, Aḥmad b. Yaḥyā. *Ansāb al-Ashrāf*, Vol. 3. Ed. 'Abd al-'Azīz al-Dūrī. Weisbaden: Franz Steiner Verlag, 1978.

———. *Futūḥ al-Buldān*. Ed. M. J. DeGoeje. Leiden: E. J. Brill, 1866.

Bar Hebraeus, Ibn al-'Ibrī Abū al-Faraj. *Tārīkh Mukhtaṣar al-Duwal*. Ed. Anṭūn Ṣāliḥānī al-Yasū'ī. Beirut: Al-Maṭba'a al-Kāthūlikiyya, 1890.

———. *The Chronography of Gregory Abū'l Faraj the Son of Aaron, the Hebrew Physician Commonly Known as Bar Hebraeus Being the First Part of His Political History of the World*. Tr. from the Syriac by Ernest A. Wallis Budge. London: Oxford University Press, 1932.

Al-Bukhārī, Muḥammad b. Ismā'īl. *Ṣaḥīḥ al-Bukhārī*. In *Mawsū'at al-Ḥadīth al-Sharīf*, [computer file]. Cairo: Sharikat Ṣakhr li-al-Ḥāsūb, version 1.1, 1997.

The Cambridge Annotated Study Bible: New Revised Standard Version. Notes and references by Howard Clark Kee. Cambridge: Cambridge University Press, 1989.

Al-Dārimī, 'Abdallāh b. 'Abd al-Raḥmān. *Sunan*. In *Mawsū'at al-Ḥadīth al-Sharīf*, [computer file]. Cairo: Sharikat Ṣakhr li-al-Ḥāsūb, version 1.1, 1997.

Al-Dhahabī, Muḥammad b. Aḥmad. *Kitāb al-'Ibar min Khabar man Ghabar*. Ed. Ṣalāḥ al-Dīn al-Munajjid. Kuwait: Dā'irat al-Maṭbū'āt wa al-Nashr, 1960.

———. *Mīzān al-I'tidāl fī Naqd al-Rijāl*. Ed. 'Alī Muḥammad 'al-Bajāwī. Beirut: Dār al-Ma'rifa, 1963.

Al-Dīnawarī, Aḥmad b. Dāwūd. *Al-Akhbār al-Ṭiwāl*. Ed. 'Abd al-Mun'im 'Āmir and Jamāl al-Dīn al-Shayyāl. Cairo: Dār Iḥyā al-Kutub al-'Arabiyya, 1960.

"*Dīnkard* Book 7." In *The Sacred Books of the East*. Tr. W. E. West. Oxford: Clarendon Press, 1897.

Dorotheus Sidonius. *Carmen Astrologicum*. Ed. David Pingree. Leipzig: BSB B. G. Teubner, 1976.

Al-Farazdaq. *Diwān al-Farazdaq*. Ed. Karam al-Bustānī. Beirut: Dār Ṣādir, 1966.

Al-Fasawī, Ya'qūb b. Sufyān. *Al-Ma'rifa wa al-Ta'rīkh*. Ed. Akram Ḍiyā' al-'Umarī. Baghdād: Maṭba'at al-Irshād, 1974.

Genesios. *On the Reigns of the Emperors*. Tr. and commentary, Anthony Kaldellis. Canberra: National University of Australia, 1998.

Al-Haytamī, Ibn Ḥajar. *Al-Qawl al-Mukhtaṣ fī 'Alāmāt al-Mahdī al-Muntaẓar*. Ed. Muḥammad Zīnuhum and Muḥammad 'Azb. Cairo: Dār al-Saḥwa, 1986.

Al-Ḥimyarī, Muḥammad 'Abd al-Mun'im. *Rawḍ al-Mi'ṭār fī Khabar al-Aqṭār*. Ed. Iḥsān 'Abbās. Beirut: Maktabat Lubnān, 1984.

Al-Hindī, 'Alā' al-Dīn 'Alī b. Ḥusām al-Dīn al-Muttaqī. *Al-Burhān fī 'Alāmāt Mahdī Ākhir al-Zamān*. Ed. 'Alī Akbar al-Ghifārī. Qum, Iran: Maṭba'at al-Khayyām, 1979.

———. *Kanz al-'Ummāl fī Sunan al-Aqwāl wa al-Af'āl*. Ed. Bakrī Ḥayyānī et al. Beirut: Mu'assasat al-Risāla, 1989.

Al-Ḥumaydī, Abū Bakr 'Abdallāh b. al-Zubayr. *Al-Musnad*. Ed. Ḥabīb al-Raḥmān al-A'ẓamī. Karachi: Al-Majlis al-'Ilmī, 1963.

Ibn, 'Abd al-Barr, Yūsuf b. 'Abdallāh b. Muḥammad. *Al-Istī'āb fī Ma'rifat al-Aṣḥāb*. Ed. 'Alī Muḥammad al-Bajawī. Beirut: Dār al-Jīl, 1992.

Ibn 'Abd Rabbih, Aḥmad b. Muḥammad. *Al-'Iqd al-Farīd*. Ed. Aḥmad Amīn, Ibrāhīm al-Abyārī, and 'Abd al-Salām Hārūn. Cairo: Lajnat al-Ta'līf wa al-Tarjuma wa al-Nashr, 1940–53.

Ibn Abī Ḥātim, 'Abd al-Raḥmān. *Al-Jarḥ wa al-Ta'dīl*. Beirut: Dār Iḥyā' al-Turāth, 1952.

Ibn Abī Shayba, 'Abdallāh b. Muḥammad. *Kitāb al-Muṣannaf fī al-Aḥādīth wa al-Āthār*. Ed. Kamāl Yūsuf al-Ḥūt. Beirut: Dār al-Tāj, 1989.

Ibn 'Asākir, 'Alī b. al-Ḥasan. *Tārīkh Madinat Dimashq*. Ed. Ṣalāḥ al-Dīn al-Munajjid et al. Damascus: Majma' al-Lughā al-'Arabiyya, 1951– .

Ibn A'tham al-Kūfī, Abū Muḥammad Aḥmad. *Kitāb al-Futūḥ*. Ed. Muḥammad 'Abd al-Mu'īd Khān et al. Hyderabad, India: Osmania Oriental Publications Bureau, 1968–75.

Ibn al-Athīr, 'Alī b. Abī al-Karam. *Al-Kāmil fī al-Tārīkh*. Ed. Carolus Johannes Tornberg. Leiden: E. J. Brill, 1867. Reprint, Beirut: Dār Ṣadir and Dār Bayrūt, 1965–67.

Ibn Bābawayh, Muḥammad b. 'Alī b. al- Ḥusayn al-Qummī. *Kamāl al-Dīn wa Tamām al-Ni'ma*. Ed. 'Alī Akbar al-Ghifārī. Tehran: Dār al-Kutub al-Islāmiyya, 1975.

Ibn Ḥabīb, 'Abd al-Malik. *Kitāb al-Tārīkh*. Ed. Jorge Aguadé. Madrid: Consejo Superior de Investigaciones Cientificas Instituto de Cooperación con el Mundo Árabe, 1991.

Ibn Ḥajar al-'Asqalānī. *Tahdhīb al-Tahdhīb*. Beirut: Dar Ṣādir, 1968.

Ibn Ḥamdūn, Bahā al-Dīn Muḥammad b. Ḥasan. *Al-Tadhkira al-Ḥamdūniyya*. Ed. Iḥsān 'Abbās. Beirut: Ma'had al-Inmā' al-'Arabī, 1983.

Ibn Ḥanbal, Aḥmad. *Musnad*. Ed. Aḥmad Muḥammad Shākir et al. Cairo: Dār al-Ma'ārif, 1955–85.

———. *Musnad*. In *Mawsū'at al-Ḥadīth al-Sharīf*, [computer file]. Cairo: Sharikat Ṣakhr li-al-Ḥāsūb, version 1.1, 1997.

Ibn Hāshim al-Khālidī, Muḥammad. *Kitāb al-Tuḥaf wa al-Hadāyā*. Ed. Sa'īd b. Khalafān Khalīlī and Sāmī Dahhān. Cairo: Dār al-Ma'ārif, 1956.

Ibn Ḥibbān, Muḥammad b. Ḥibbān b. Aḥmad. *Al-Majrūḥīn min al-Muḥaddithīn*. Ed. Ḥamdī 'Abd al-Majīd al-Salafī. Riyad, Saudi Arabia: Dār al-Ṣamāy'ī, 2000.

Ibn Hishām, 'Abd al-Malik. *The Life of Muḥammad: A Translation of Ibn Isḥāq's Sīrat Rasūl Allāh*. Ed. and tr. Alfred Guillaume. Oxford: Oxford University Press, 2000.

Ibn Kathīr, Ismā'īl b. 'Umar. *Kitāb al-Nihāya aw Kitāb al-Fitan wa al-Malāḥim*. Ed. Ṭāhā Muḥammad al-Zaynī. Cairo: Dār al-Kutub al-Ḥadītha, 1969.

———. *Tafsīr Ibn Kathīr*. In *al-Qur'ān al-Karīm* [computer file]. Cairo: Sharikat Ṣakhr li-al-Ḥāsūb, version 6.3, 1991–96.

Ibn Khaldūn, 'Abd al-Raḥmān. *Kitāb al-'Ibar wa Diwān al-Mubtada' wa al-Khabar fī Ayyām al-'Arab wa al-'Ajam wa al-Barbar wa mā 'Āṣarahum min Dhawī al-Sulṭān al-Akbar*. Beirut: Dār al-Kitāb al-Lubnānī, 1957.

Ibn Khallikān, Aḥmad b. Muḥammad. *Wafayāt al-A'yān wa Anbā' Abnā' al-Zamān*. Ed. Iḥsan 'Abbās. Beirut: Dār al-Thaqāfa, 1968.

Ibn Lahī'a, 'Abdallāh. *'Abdallāh b. Lahī'a (97–174/715–790) Juge et grand maître de L'École Égyptienne: Avec édition critique de l'unique rouleau de papyrus arabe conservé à Heidelberg*. Ed. and tr. Raif G. Khoury. Weisbaden: Otto Harrassowitz, 1986.

Ibn Māja, Muḥammad b. Yazīd. *Sunan*. In *Mawsū'at al-Ḥadīth al-Sharīf*, [computer file]. Cairo: Sharikat Ṣakhr li-al-Ḥāsūb, version 1.1, 1997.

Ibn al-Mubārak, 'Abdallāh. *Kitāb al-Jihād*. Ed. Nazīh Ḥammād. Cairo: Majma' al-Buḥūth al-Islāmiyya, 1978.

Ibn al-Muqaffa', 'Abdallāh. *Conseilleur du Calife* [*Risāla fī al-Ṣaḥāba*]. Ed. Charles Pellat. Paris: University of Paris-Sorbonne, 1976.

Ibn el- Muqaffa', Severus (Ben El-Moqaffa'). *Historia Patriarcharum Alexandrinorum*, Tomus 1, Fasciculus 1, *Corpus Scriptorum Orientalum: Scriptores Arabici*, Textus Series 3, Tomus 9. Ed. Chr. Fred Seybold. Paris: Otto Harrassowitz, 1894.

Ibn al-Murtaḍa, Aḥmad b. Yaḥyā. *Ṭabaqāt al-Mu'tazila*. Ed. Susanna Diwald-Wilzer. Beirut: Al-Ḥayāt Library, 1980.

Ibn al-Nadīm, Muḥammad b. Isḥāq. *Al-Fihrist*. Ed. Gustav Flugel. Alle: 1876. Reprint, Beirut: Maktabat Khayyāṭ, 1966.

———. *Al-Fihrist*. Ed. Riḍā-Tajaddud. Tehran: Dānishgāh-i Tehrān, 1971.

———. *The Fihrist of Ibn al-Nadīm*. Tr. Bayard Dodge. New York: Columbia University Press, 1970.

Ibn al-Qifṭī, Jamāl al-Dīn 'Alī b. Yūsuf. *Ikhbār al-'Ulamā' bi Akhbār al-Ḥukamā.'* Ed. J. Lippert. Leipzig: Dieterische Verlagsbuchhandlung, 1903.

Ibn Quṭayba, 'Abdallāh b. Muslim. *Ta'wīl Mukhtalaf al-Ḥadīth.* Ed. 'Abd al-Qādir Aḥmad 'Atā. Cairo: Dār al-Kutub al-Islāmiyya, 1981.

———. *'Uyūn al-Akhbār.* Cairo: Al-Mu'assasa al-Miṣriyya al-'Āmma, 1964.

———. *Al-Ikhtilāf fī al-Lafḍ wa al-Radd 'ala al-Jahmiyya wa al-Mu'tazila.* Beirut: Dār al-Kutub al-'Ilmiyya, 1985.

———. *Al-Ma'ārif.* Ed. Tharwat 'Ukkāsha. Cairo: Dār al-Ma'ārif, 1969.

Ibn Sa'd, Muḥammad. *Al-Ṭabaqāt al-Kubrā.* Beirut: Dār Ṣādir, 1968.

Ibn Ṭāwūs, 'Alī b. Mūsā b. Ja'far b. Muḥammad. *Faraj al-Mahmūm fī Tārīkh 'Ulamā al-Nujūm.* Najaf: Al-Maṭba'a al-Ḥaydariyya, 1368 AH (1949).

Ibn al-Ṭiqṭaqa, Muḥammad b. 'Alī. *Al-Fakhrī fī al-Ādāb al-Sulṭāniyya wa al-Duwal al-Islāmiyya.* Ed. Hartwig Derenbourg. Paris: Librairie Émile Boullion, 1895.

Al-Idrīsī, Abū Ja'far Muḥammad b. 'Abd al-'Azīz. *Anwar 'Ulwiy al-Ajrām fī Kashf 'an Asrār al-Ahrām (Das Pyramidenbuch des Abu Ga'far al-Idrīsī (st. 649/1251).* Ed. and tr. Ulrich Haarmann. Beirut: Franz Steiner, 1991.

Al-Imāma wa al-Siyāsa (mistakenly ascribed to Ibn Qutayba al-Dīnawarī). Ed. Khalīl al-Manṣūr. Beirut: Dār al-Kutub al-'Ilmiyya, 1997.

Iṣfahānī, Abū al-Faraj. *Maqātil al-Ṭālibiyyīn.* Ed. Kāẓim al-Muẓaffar. Najaf: Maktabat al-Ḥaydariyya, 1965.

al-Jāḥiẓ, Abū 'Uthmān 'Amr b. Baḥr. *Al-'Uthmāniyya.* Ed. 'Abd al-Salām Hārūn. Cairo: Maktabat al-Khanjī bi-Miṣr and Maktabat al-Muthanna bi-Baghdād, 1955.

———. "Risāla fī al-Ḥakamayn wa Taṣwīb Amīr al-Mu'minīn 'Alī b. Abī Ṭālib." Ed. Charles Pellat. *Majallat al-Mashriq* 4–5 (1952–58).

———. *Rasā'il al-Jāḥiẓ.* Ed. Muḥammad 'Abd al-Salām Hārūn. Cairo: Maktabat al-Khānjī, 1979.

———. *Le Kitāb at-tarbī' wa-t-tadwīr de Gāḥiẓ.* Ed. and tr. Francesco Gabrieli. Damascus: Institut de Français de Damas, 1955.

Al-Jahshiyārī, Muḥammad b. 'Abdūs. *Kitāb al-Wuzarā' wa al-Kuttāb.* Ed. Musṭafā al-Saqqā et al. Cairo: Musṭafā al-Bābī al-Ḥalabī wa Awlāduhu, 1980.

Jarīr b. 'Aṭiyya. *Diwān Jarīr b. 'Aṭiyya.* Cairo: Al-Maṭba'a al-'Ilmiyya, 1313 (1896).

Al-Jurjānī, 'Abdallāh b. 'Adī b. 'Abdallāh. *Al-Kāmil fī Ḍu'afā' al-Rijāl.* Ed. Yaḥyā Mukhtār Ghazzāwī. Beirut: Dār al-Fikr, 1988.

Katib Çelebi, Mustafa b. Abdullah Ḥajjī Khalīfa. *Kashf al-Ẓunūn 'an Asāmī al-Kutub wa al-Funūn.* Ed. Şerefeddin Yaltkaya and Rıfat Bilge. Istanbul: Maarif Matbaası, 1941, 1943. Reprint, İstanbul: Milli Eğitim, 1971.

Al-Khābushānī, 'Azīzallāh al-'Utārīdī. *Musnad al-Imām al-Riḍā.* Beirut: Mu'assasat al-Wafā', 1983.

Khalīfa b. Khayyāṭ. *Tārīkh Khalīfa b. Khayyāṭ.* Ed. Akram Ḍiyā' al-'Umarī. Damascus and Beirut: Dār al-Qalam and Mu'assasat al-Risāla, 1977.

Al-Kindī, Muḥammad b. Yūsuf. *Wulāt Miṣr.* Beirut: Dār Bayrūt and Dār Ṣādir, 1965.

Al-Kulaynī, Muḥammad b. Ya'qūb. *Al-Uṣūl min al-Kāfī.* Beirut: Dār Ṣa'b, Dār al-Ta'āruf, 1401/1980–81.

Al-Majlisī, Muḥammad Bāqir b. Muḥammad. *Biḥār al-Anwār.* Tehran: Al-Maktaba al-Islāmiyya, 1956– .

(Pseudo) Al-Majrītī. *Das Ziel der Weisen (Ghāyat al-Ḥakīm wa Aḥaqq al-Natijatayn bi al-Taqdīm).* Ed. Helmut Ritter. Leipzig: B. G. Teubner, 1933.

Mālik b. Anas. *Al-Muwaṭṭā*. In *Mawsū'at al-Ḥadīth al-Sharīf*, [computer file]. Cairo: Sharikat Ṣakhr li-al-Ḥāsūb, version 1.1, 1997.

Al-Ma'mūn, 'Abdallāh b. Hārūn al-Rashīd, (attributed). *Kitāb al-Qur'a al-Ma'mūniyya fī Istikhrāj al-Fāl wa al-Ḍamīr.* Manuscript in Dār al-Kutub al-Miṣriyya, #9548.

Al-Mannāwī, Muḥammad 'Abd al-Ra'ūf. *Fayḍ al-Qadīr Sharḥ Jāmi' al-Ṣaghīr.* Ed. Nukhba min al-'Ulamā'. Beirut: Dār al-Ma'rifa, n.d.

Al-Maqdisī, Muṭahhar b. Ṭāhir. *Al-Bad' wa al-Tārīkh*. Ed. M. C. L. Huart. Paris: L' École des Langues Orientales Vivantes, 1901.

Al-Mas'ūdī, 'Alī b. Al-Ḥusay. *Murūj al-Dhahab wa Ma'ādin al-Jawhar.* Ed. Barbier de Meynard and Pavet de Courteille. Reviewed and corrected by Charles Pellat. Beirut: Lebanese University, 1973.

———. *Al-Tanbīh wa al-Ishrāf, Biblioteca Geographorum Arabicorum*, Vol. 8. Ed. V. R. Baron Rosen. Leiden: E. J. Brill, 1967.

———, (Pseudo). *Ithbāt al-Waṣiyya li-al-Imām 'Alī b. Abī Ṭālib 'Alayhī al-Salām.* Qum, Iran: Al-Maktaba al-Murtaḍawiyya, 1404/1984.

Mawsū'at al-Ḥadīth al-Sharīf, [computer file]. Cairo: Sharikat Ṣakhr li-al-Ḥāsūb, version 1.1, 1997.

Michel le Syrien. *Chronique de Michel le Syrien*. Ed. and tr. J. B. Chabot. Paris: Ernest Leroux, 1899–1910.

Miskawayh, Aḥmad b. Muḥammad. *Tajārib al-Umam*. Ed. De Goeje and P. D. Young. Leiden: E. J. Brill, 1871.

———. *Al-Ḥikma al-Khālida (Jāvidān Khirad)*. Ed. 'Abd al-Raḥmān Badawī. Cairo: Maktabat al-Nahḍa al-Miṣriyya, 1925.

Mujāhid b. Jabr. *Tafsīr.* Ed. 'Abd al-Raḥmān al-Ṭāhir al-Sūratī. Beirut: Al-Manshūrāt al-'Ilmiyyya, n.d.

Muqātil b. Sulaymān. *Tafsīr.* Ed. 'Abdallāh Maḥmūd Shahāta. Cairo: Al-Hay'a al-Miṣriyya al-'Āmma li-al-Kitāb, 1988.

Muslim b. Ḥajjāj. *Saḥīḥ*. In *Mawsū'at al-Ḥadīth al-Sharīf*, [computer file]. Cairo: Sharikat Ṣakhr li-al-Ḥāsūb, version 1.1, 1997.

Al-Nasā'ī, Aḥmad b. Shu'ayb. *Sunan*. In *Mawsū'at al-Ḥadīth al-Sharīf*, [computer file]. Cairo: Sharikat Ṣakhr li-al-Ḥāsūb, version 1.1, 1997.

Al-Nāshī al-Akbar (Pseudo). *Masā'il al-Imāma: Frühe Mu'tazilische Häresiographie.* Ed. Josef van Ess. Beirut: Franz Steiner Verlag, 1971.

Naṣr b. Muzāḥim. *Waq'atu Ṣiffīn*. Ed. 'Abd al-Salām Muḥammad Hārūn. Qum, Iran: Maktabat Āyatallāh al-'Uẓma al-Mar'ashī al-Najafī, 1962.

Nu'aym b. Ḥammād al-Khuzā'ī. *Kitāb al-Fitan*. Ed. Suhayl Zakkār. Beirut: Dār al-Fikr, 1993.

———. *Kitāb al-Fitan*. British Museum ms. no. or. 9449 [a microfilm reproduction at the University of Chicago JRL ms. no. 79].

Paulus Alvaris Cordubensis. "Alvari Cordubensis Opera: Indiculus Luminosus." In *España Sagrada: Theatro Geografico-Historico de la Iglesia España* ed. F. Henrique Florez. Madrid: Oficina de Pedro Marin, XI, 1753.

Pāzand Jāmāspi (Pahlavi Translations, Part III, Jāmāspi). Tr. Jivanji Jamshedji Modi. Bombay: Bombay Education Society, 1903.

Pickthall, M. M. *The Meaning of the Glorious Koran: An Explanatory Translation*. New York: New American Library, 1932.

Al-Qalqashandī, Aḥmad b. 'Alī. *Ma'āthir al-Ināqa fī Ma'ālim al-Khilāfa*. Ed. A. A. Farrāj. Kuwait: n.p., 1964.

Al-Qur'ān al-Karīm, [computer file]. Cairo: Sharikat Ṣakhr li-al-Ḥāsūb, version 6.3, 1991–96.

Al-Ṣābī, al-Hilāl b. al-Muḥassin. *Rusūm Dār al-Khilāfa*. Ed. Mikhā'īl 'Awad. Baghdād: Maṭba'at al-'Ānī, 1964.

Al-Sahmī, Ḥamza b. Yūsuf. *Tārīkh Jurjān aw Kitāb Ma'rifat 'Ulamā Ahl Jurjān*. Ed. M. A. Mu'īd Khān. Hyderabad, India: Osmania Publication Bureau, 1967.

Al-Ṣan'ānī, 'Abd al-Razzāq b. Hammām. *Al-Muṣannaf*. Ed. Ḥabīb al-Raḥmān al-A'zamī. Beirut: Al-Majlis al-'Ilmī, 1970.

———. *Tafsīr al-Qur'ān li-al-Imām 'Abd al-Razzāq ibn Hammām al-Ṣan'ānī*. Ed. Musṭafa Muslim Muḥammad. Riyad: Maktabat al-Rushd, 1989.

Al-Shāfi'ī, Muḥammad b. Idrīs. *Al-Risāla*. Ed. Aḥmad Muḥammad Shākir. Cairo: Maktabat Ibn Taymiyya, 1940.

Al-Shahrastānī, Muḥammad b. 'Abd al-Karīm. *Muslim Sects and Divisions*. Tr. A. K. Kazi and J. G. Flynn. London: Kegan Paul International, 1984.

Al-Shaybānī, Muḥammad b. Ḥasan. *Kitāb al-Kasb*. Ed. Suhayl Zakkār. Damascus: 'Abd al-Qādir Ḥarsūnī, 1980.

Al-Sindī, Muḥammad 'Abīd. *Tartīb Musnad al-Imām al-Mu'aẓẓam wa al-Mujtahid al-Muqaddam Abī 'Abdallāh Muḥammad b. Idrīs al-Shāfi'ī*. Ed. Muḥammad Zāhid b. al-Ḥasan al-Kawtharī. Beirut: Dār al-Kutub al-'Ilmiyya, 1951.

Al-Subkī, 'Abd al-Wahhāb b. 'Alī. *Ṭabaqāt al-Shāfi'īyya al-Kubrā*. Ed. Maḥmūd Muḥammad al-Tunahī and 'Abd al-Fattāḥ Muḥammad al-Ḥilū. Cairo: Dar Iḥyā' al-Kutub al-'Arabiyya, n.d.

Al-Sulamī, Yūsuf b. Yaḥyā. *Al-'Iqd al-Durar fī Akhbār al-Muntaẓar*. Ed. 'Abd al-Fattāḥ Muḥammad al-Ḥilū. Cairo: Maktabat 'Ālam al-Fikr, 1979.

Al-Suyūṭī, 'Abd al-Raḥmān b. Abī Bakr. *Tārīkh al-Khulafā*. Ed. Ibrāhīm Ṣāliḥ. Beirut: Dār Ṣādir, 1997.

———. *Al-Asās fī Manāqib Banī al-'Abbās*. Ms. Dār al-Kutub al-Miṣriyya #1420 Ḥadīth.

Al-Tabarānī, Sulaymān b. Aḥmad. *Musnad al-Shāmiyyīn*. Ed. Ḥamdī b. 'Abd al-Majīd al-Salafī. Beirut: Mu'assasat al-Risāla, 1984.

Al-Ṭabarī, Muḥammad b. Jarīr. *Tārīkh al-Rusul wa al-Mulūk*. Ed. Muḥammad Abū al-Faḍl Muḥammad Ibrāhīm. Cairo: Dār al-Ma'ārif, 1968. Translated as *The History of al-Ṭabarī*, Ihsan Yarshater, general editor. 38 vols. Albany: SUNY Press, 1985–99.

———. *Jāmi' al-Bayān 'an Ta'wīl al-Qur'ān*. Ed. Maḥmūd Muḥammad Shākir and Aḥmad Muḥammad Shākir. Cairo: Dār Maṭba'at wa Mu'assasat Musṭafā al-Bābī al-Ḥalabī wa Awlāduhu, 1968.

Ṭayfūr, Aḥmad b. Abī Ṭāhir al-Kātib. *Baghdād fī Tārīkh al-Khilāfa al-'Abbāsiyya*. Cairo: n.p., 1968.

Al-Tirmidhī, Muḥammad b. 'Īsā. *Sunan*. In *Mawsū'at al-Ḥadīth al-Sharīf*, [computer file]. Cairo: Sharikat Ṣakhr li-al-Ḥāsūb, version 1.1, 1997.

Al-'Uyūn wa al-Ḥadā'iq fī Akhbār al-Ḥaqā'iq (Fragmenta Historicorum Arabicorum). Ed. M. J. De Goeje. Leiden: E. J. Brill, 1871.

Wahb b. Munabbih. Ed. Raif Georges Khoury. Wiesbaden: O. Harrassowitz, 1972.

Yaḥyā b. Abī Manṣūr. *Al-Zīj al-Ma'mūnī al-Mumtaḥan*. Facs. ed. by Fuat Sezgin.

Frankfurt: Institute for the History of Arabic-Islamic Science at the Johann Wolfgang Goethe University, 1986.

Al-Ya'qūbī, Aḥmad b. Abī Ya'qūb b. Wāḍih. *Tārīkh al-Ya'qūbī*. Ed. M. Th. Houtsma. Leiden: E. J. Brill, 1969.

———. *Mushākalat al-Nās lī Zamānihim*. Ed. William Millward. Beirut: New York Publishing House, 1962.

———. *Kitāb al-Buldān*. Ed. T. G. J. Juynboll. Leiden: E. J. Brill, 1861.

Yāqūt al-Ḥamawī, Shihāb al-Dīn Abī 'Abdallāh. *Mu'jam al-Buldān*. Beirut: Dār Ṣādir, 1984.

Scholarship

'Abbās, Iḥṣān. *Tārīkh Bilād al-Shām fī al-'Aṣr al-'Abbāsī 132–255/750–870*. Amman: Al-Jāmi'a al-Urduniyya and Jāmi'at al-Yarmūk, 1992.

Abbott, Nabia. *Two Queens of Baghdad*. Chicago: University of Chicago Press, 1946.

Abel, Armand. "Changements politiques et littérature eschatologique dans le Monde Musulman." *SI* 2 (1954).

Abramsky-Bligh, Irit. "The Judicary (Qāḍīs) as a Governmental-Administrative Tool in Early Islam." In *The Formation of Islamic Law*, ed. Wael B. Halla. Hants, U.K.: Ashgate, 2004.

Afsaruddin, Asma. *Excellence and Precedence: Medieval Islamic Discourse on Legitimate Leadership*. Leiden: E. J. Brill, 2002.

Aguadé, Jorge. *Messianismus zur Zeit der frühen 'Abbāsiden: Das Kitāb des Nu'aym Ibn Ḥammād*. Ph.D. diss., University of Tübingen, 1979.

———. "Algunos hadices sobre la ocupación de Alejandria por un grupo de Hispano-Musulmanes." *Boletín de la Asociación Espan ola de Orientalistas* 12 (1976).

Alexander, Paul. *Religious and Political History and Thought in the Byzantine Empire*. London: Variorum, 1978.

———. *The Byzantine Apocalyptic Tradition*. Ed. Dorothy de F Abrahamse. Berkeley: University of California Press, 1985.

————. "The Medieval Legend of the Last Roman Emperor and Its Messianic Origin." *Warburg Institute Journal* 41 (1978).

————. "Medieval Apocalypses as Historical Sources," *American Historical Review* 73 (1968).

Arazi, Albert, and 'Amikam Elad. "L'Épitre Armée al-Ma'mūn et la Seconde *Da'wa*." *SI* 66 (1987), 67 (1988).

Arberry, Arthur John. "Jāvidān Khiradh." *JSS* 8 (1963).

Arjomand, Said Amir. *The Shadow of God and the Hidden Imām*. Chicago: Chicago University Press, 1984.

———. "Islamic Apocalypticism in the Classical Period." In *Apocalypticism: Apocalypticism in Western History and Culture*, ed. Bernard McGinn. New York: Continuum, 1998.

————. "The Crisis of the Imāmate and the Institution of Occultation in Twelver Shī'īsm: A Sociohistorical Perspective." *IJMES* 28 (1996).

Artuk, Ibrahim, and Cevriye Artuk. *Arkeoloji Müzeleri Teşhirdeki İslami Sikkeler Kataloğu*. İstanbul: Milli Eğitim Basımevi, 1971.

Athamina, Khalil. "The Black Banners and the Socio-Political Significance of Flags and Slogans in Medieval Islam." *Arabica* 36 (1989).

'Aṭwān, Ḥusayn. *Al-Da'wa al-'Abbāsiyya: Mabādi' wa Asālīb.* Beirut: Dār al-Jīl, 1984.

Ayalon, David. "The Military Reforms of Caliph al-Mu'taṣim: Their Background and Consequences." In *Islam and the Abode of War: Military Slaves and Islamic Adversaries.* Hampshire, U.K.: Variorum, 1994.

Bacharach, Jere L. "Laqab for a Future Caliph: The Case of the 'Abbāsid Mahdī." *JAOS* 113 (1993).

———. "Al-Amīn's Designated Successor: The Limitations of Numismatic Evidence." *JAOS* 116 (1996).

Bashear, Suliman. "Apocalyptic and Other Material on Early Muslim-Byzantine Wars: A Review of Arabic Sources." *JRAS* 1 (1991).

———. *Arabs and Others in Early Islam.* Princeton, N.J.: Darwin Press, 1997.

———. "Muslim Apocalypses and the Hour: A Case Study in Traditional Interpretation." *IOS* 13 (1993).

Bates, Michael L. "Khurāsānī Revolutionaries and al-Mahdī's Title." In *Culture and Memory in Medieval Islam: Essays in Honor of Wilferd Madelung,* ed. Farhad Daftary and Joseph W. Meri. London: I. B. Tauris, 2003.

———. "The 'Abbāsid Coinage System, 833–946." Paper presented at the annual meeting of the Middle East Studies Association (1996).

Bayhom-Daou, Tamima. "Al-Ma'mūn's Alleged Apocalyptic Beliefs: A Reconsideration of the Evidence." *SOAS* (forthcoming).

Blichfeldt, Jan-Olaf. *Early Mahdīsm: Politics and Religion in the Formative Period of Islam.* Leiden: E. J. Brill, 1985.

Bonner, Michael. *Aristocratic Violence and Civil War: Studies in the Jihād and the Arab Byzantine Frontier.* New Haven, Conn.: American Oriental Society, 1996.

Bosworth, C. E. "An Early Arabic Mirror for Princes: Ṭāhir Dhu al-Yamīnain's Epistle to His Son 'Abdallāh (206/821)." *JNES* 29 (1970).

———. *The Arabs, Byzantium and Iran: Studies in Early Islamic History and Culture.* Brookfield, Vt.: Ashate-Variorum, 1996.

Boyce, Mary. *Textual Sources for the Study of Zoroastrianism.* Chicago: University of Chicago Press, 1990.

Brock, Sebastian. *Studies in Syriac Christianity.* Hampshire, U.K.: Variorum, 1992.

———. *Syriac Perspectives on Late Antiquity.* London: Variorum, 1984.

Bull, Malcolm, ed. *Apocalypse Theory and the End of the World.* Oxford: Blackwell, 1995.

Bulliet, Richard. *Islam: The View from the Edge.* New York: Columbia University Press, 1994.

———. *Conversion to Islam in the Medieval Period: An Essay in Quantitative History.* Cambridge, Mass.: Harvard University Press, 1979.

Burton, Richard F. *Plain and Literal Translation of the Arabian Nights' Entertainments Now Entitled the Book of the Thousand Nights and a Night.* N.p.: Burton Club, 1885.

Büyükkara, M. Ali. "The Schism in the Party of Mūsa al-Kāẓim and the Emergence of the Wāqifa." *Arabica* 47 (2000).

———. "The Speculations about the Death of Imām 'Alī al-Riḍā." *Islamic Culture* 76/4 (2002).

Cahen, Claude. "Commercial Relations between the Near East and Western Europe from the VIIth to the XIth Century." In *Islam and the Medieval West: Aspects of Intercultural Relations,* ed. Khalil I. Semaan. Albany: SUNY Press, 1980.

Cameron, Averil, and Lawrence Conrad, eds. *The Byzantine and Early Islamic Near East I: Problems in the Literary Source Material.* Princeton, N.J.: Darwin Press, 1992.

Carter, M. G. "Arabic Grammar." In *Religion, Learning and Science in the 'Abbāsid Period,* ed. M. J. L Young, J. D. Latham, and R. B. Serjeant. Cambridge: Cambridge University Press, 1990.

Casanova, Paul. *Mohammed et la fin du monde: Étude critique sur l'Islam primitif.* Paris: Libraire Paul Geuthner, 1911–24.

Caspar, Robert. "Les Versions Arabes du Dialogue entre le Catholicos Timothée I et le Calife al-Mahdī (IIe/VIIe siècle): 'Mohammed a suivi la voie des prophètes' (Introduction, édition Critique du texte Arabe et la Traduction." *Isamochristiana* 3 (1977).

Chavannes, Edouard. *Documents sur les Tou-kiue occidentaux: Recueillis et comments suivi de notes additionelles.* Paris: Librairie d'Amérique et de Orient, 1942.

Chejne, Anwar. *The Succession to Rule in Islam with a Special Reference to the Early 'Abbāsid Period.* Lahore, Pakistan: Ashraf, 1960.

Choksy, Jamsheed K. *Conflict and Cooperation: Zoroastrian Subalterns and Muslim Elites in Medieval Iranian Society.* New York: Columbia University Press, 1997.

Cobb, Paul M. *White Banners: Contention in 'Abbāsid Syria, 750–880.* Albany: SUNY Press, 2001.

Cohn, Norman. *The Pursuit of the Millennium.* New York: Oxford University Press, 1970.

Coleman, J. S., and T. Fararo, eds. *Rational Choice Theory: Advocacy and Critique.* Newbury Park, Calif.: Sage, 1992.

Collins, John J. *The Apocalyptic Imagination.* New York: Crossroad, 1984.

Collins, Roger. *Charlemagne.* Toronto: University of Toronto Press, 1998.

Conrad, L. "Seven and the Tasbī': On the Implications of Numerical Symbolism for the Study of Medieval Islamic History." *JESHO* 31 (1988).

Cook, David. *Studies in Muslim Apocalyptic.* Princeton, N.J.: Darwin Press, 2002.

———. "The Apocalyptic Year 200/815–16 and the Events Surrounding It." In *Apocalyptic Time,* ed. Albert I. Baumgaten. Leiden: E. J. Brill, 2000.

———. "Messianism and Astronomical Events during the First Four Centuries of Islam." *Monde Musulman et de la Méditerranée* 91 (2000).

Cook, Michael. "An Early Islamic Apocalyptic Chronicle." *JNES* 52 (1993).

———. *Commanding Good and Forbidding Wrong in Islamic Thought.* Cambridge: Cambridge University Press, 2001.

———. "The Heraclian Dynasty in Muslim Eschatology." *Al-Qantara* 13 (1992).

———. "Eschatology and the Dating of Traditions." *Princeton Papers in Near Eastern Studies* 1 (1992).

Cooperson, Michael David. *Classical Arabic Biography: The Heirs of the Prophets in the Age of al-Ma'mūn.* Cambridge: Cambridge University Press, 2000.

———. "Al-Ma'mūn, the Pyramids, and the Hieroglyphs," *'Abbāsid Studies II. Occasional Papers of the School of 'Abbāsid Studies Leuven, 28 June–1 July, 2004.* Orientalia Loveniensia Analecta Series, 177. Leuven: Peeters, 2009.

———. "The Grave of al-Ma'mūn in Tarsus: A Preliminary Report." In *'Abbāsid Studies: Occasional Papers of the School of 'Abbāsid Studies, Cambridge, 6–10 July 2002, School of 'Abbāsid Studies, Orientalia Lovaniensia Analecta,* 135, ed. James E. Montgomery. Leiden: Peeters, 2004.

———. "The Heirs of the Prophets in Classical Arabic Biography." Ph. diss., Harvard University, 1994.

———. *Makers of Islam: Al-Ma'mūn*. London: Oneworld, 2005.

Creswell, K. A. C. *Early Muslim Architecture.* Oxford: Oxford University Press, 1969.

Crone, Patricia. *God's Rule: Government and Islam*. New York: Columbia University Press, 2004.

———. "On the Meaning of the 'Abbāsid Call to al-Riḍā." In *The Islamic World from Classical to Modern Times: Essays in Honor of Bernard Lewis,* ed. Clifford Edmund et al. Princeton, N.J.: Darwin Press, 1991.

———. "Islam Judeo-Christianity and Byzantine Iconoclasm." *JSAI* 2 (1980).

Crone, Patricia, and Michael Cook. *Hagarism: The Making of the Islamic World.* Cambridge: Cambridge University Press, 1977.

Crone, Patricia, and Martin Hinds. *God's Caliph: Religious Authority in the First Centuries of Islam.* Cambridge: Cambridge University Press, 1986.

Dagron, Gilber. "Juifs et Chrétiens dans l'Orient du VIIe siècle." *Travaux et Mémoires* 11 (1991).

Daiber, Hans. *Das theologisch-philosophische System des Mu'ammar Ibn 'Abbād as-Sulamī (gest. 830 n. Chr.)*. Beirut: Der Deutschen Morgenländischen Gesellschaft, 1975.

Daniel, Elton. *Political and Social History of Khurāsān under 'Abbāsid Rule 747–820.* Minneapolis: Bibliotheca Islamica, 1979.

Darmesteter, James. *The Mahdī: Past and Present.* London: T. Fisher Unwin, 1885.

Dols, Michael. "Plagues in Early Islamic History." *JAOS* 94 (1974).

Donner, Fred M. "Was Early Islam an Apocalyptic Movement?" Draft of the lecture presented at the Medieval Institute of Notre Dame, 26 February 1998.

———. *Narratives of Islamic Origins: The Beginnings of Islamic Historical Writing.* Princeton, N.J.: Darwin Press, 1998.

———. "La Question de Messianisme dans l'Islam primitif." *Révue du Monde Musulman et de la Méditerranée* 91 (2000).

———. "From Believers to Muslims: Confessional Self-Identity in the Early Islamic Community." *Al-Abḥāth* 50–51 (2002–3).

Dozy, R. *L'Historie de l'Islamisme.* Tr. Victor Chauvin. Leiden: E. J. Brill, 1879.

Drijvers, Han J. W. "The Gospel of the Twelve Apostles: A Syriac Apocalypse from the Early Islamic Period." In *The Byzantine and Early Islamic Near East,* ed. Averil Cameron and Lawrence E. Conrad. Princeton, N.J.: Darwin Press, 1992.

Dunlop, D. M. "A Diplomatic Exchange between al-Ma'mūn and an Indian King." In *Medieval and Middle Eastern Studies in Honor of Aziz Suryal Atiyya,* ed. Sami Hanna. Leiden: E. J. Brill, 1972.

Dunn, Michael Collins. "The Struggle for 'Abbāsid Egypt." Ph.D. diss., Georgetown University, 1975.

Al-Dūrī, 'Abd al-'Azīz. *Al-'Aṣr al-'Abbāsī al-Awwal.* 1945. Reprint, Beirut: Dār al-Ṭalī'a, 1988.

———. "Al-Fikra al-Mahdīyya bayna al-Da'wa al-'Abbāsīyya wa al-'Aṣr al-'Abbāsī al-Awwal." *Studia Arabica and Islamica Festschrift for Iḥsān 'Abbās.* Beirut: American University of Beirut, 1981.

———. *Baḥth fī Nash'at 'Ilm al-Tārīkh 'inda al-'Arab.* Beirut: Dār al-Mashriq, 1983.

Elad, Amikam. "Mawali in the Composition of al-Ma'mūn's Army: A Non-Arab

Takeover?" In *Patronate and Patronage in Early and Classical Islam*, ed. Monique Bernards and John Abdallah Nawas. Leiden: E. J. Brill, 2005.

Faris, Nabih and Harold W. W. Glidder. "The Development of the Meaning of the Koranic Ḥanīf." *Journal of the Palestine Oriental Society* 19 (1946).

El-Hibri, Tayeb. *The Reign of the 'Abbāsid Caliph al-Ma'mūn (811–833): The Quest for Power and the Crisis of Legitimacy.* Ph.D. diss., Columbia University, 1994.

———. *Reinterpreting Islamic Historiography: Hārūn al-Rashīd and the Narrative of the 'Abbāsid Caliphate.* Cambridge: Cambridge University Press, 1999.

———. "Hārūn al-Rashīd and the Mecca Protocol of 802: A Plan for Division or Succession?" *IJMES* 24 (1992).

———. "The Regicide of the Caliph al-Amīn and the Challenge of Representation in Medieval Islamic Historiography." *Arabica* 42 (1995).

———. "Coinage Reform under the 'Abbāsid Caliph al-Ma'mūn." *JESHO* 36 (1993).

Emetan, Aturpat-i. *The Wisdom of the Sasanian Sages (Denkard VI)*. Tr. Shaul Shaked. Boulder, Colo.: Westview Press, 1979.

Encyclopedia Iranica. Ed. Ihsan Yarshater. Boston: Routledge and Kegan Paul, 1983– .

Encyclopedia of Islam. 4 vols. and Supplement. Leiden: E. J. Brill, 1913–38.

Encyclopedia of Islam, new edition, electronic version. Leiden: E. J. Brill, 1958–2004.

Encyclopedia of Religion and Ethics. Ed. James Hasting. New York: Charles Scribner's Sons, 1917.

Eyice, Semavi. "İstanbul'da Abbasi Saraylarının Benzeri Olarak Yapılan bir Bizans Sarayı: Bryas Sarayı." *Belleten* 23 (1959).

Festinger, Leon. *A Theory of Cognitive Dissonance.* Evanston, Ill: Row Peterson, 1957.

Fierro, Maribel. "Al-Aṣfar." *SI* 77 (1993).

Fleischer, Cornell. "The Lawgiver as Messiah: The Making of the Imperial Image in the Reign of Süleymân." In *Süleyman the Magnificent and His Time: Act of Parisian Conference Galeries Nationales du Grand Palais 7–10 March 1990*, ed. Gilles Veinstein. Paris: École de Hautes Études en Sciences Sociales, 1992.

———. *Bureaucrat and Intellectual in the Ottoman Empire: The Historian Mustafa 'Ālī (1561–1600)*. Princeton, N.J.: Princeton University Press, 1986.

Fodor, A. "The Origins of the Arabic Legends of the Pyramids." *Acta Orientalia Academiae Scientarum Hungaricae*, vol. 23 (3).

Fowden, Garth. *From Empire to Commonwealth: Consequences of Monotheism in Late Antiquity.* Princeton, N.J.: Princeton University Press, 1993.

———. *The Egyptian Hermes: A Historical Approach to the Late Pagan Mind.* Princeton, N.J.: Princeton University Press, 1993.

Friedmann, Yohannan. "Finality of Prophethood in Sunnī Islam." *JSAI* 7 (1986).

Gabrieli, Francesco. "La Successione di Hārūn al-Rashīd e la guerra fra al-Amīn e al-Ma'mūn: Studio Storico su un Periodo del Califfato 'Abbāside." *RSO* 11 (1926–28).

———. *Al-Ma'mūn e gli 'Alidi.* Leipzig: Verlag von Eduard Pfeiffer, 1929.

Geddes, C. L. "Al-Ma'mūn's Shī'ite Policy in Yemen." *Weiner Zeitschrift für die Kunde des Morgenlandes* 59–60 (1963–64).

———. "The Messiah in South Arabia." *MW* 57 (1967).

Gero, S. "Early Contacts between Byzantium and the Arab Empire: Some Considerations." In *Proceedings of the Second Symposium on the History of Bilād al-Shām*, ed. Muḥammad 'Adnān al-Bakhīt. Amman: Jordan University, 1987.

Gibb, H. A. R. *Studies on the Civilization of Islam.* Ed. Stanford Shaw and William R. Polk. Boston: Beacon Press, 1962.

Gilman, Arthur. *The History of the Saracens from the Earliest Times to the Fall of Baghdād.* New York: G. P. Putman's Sons, 1887.

Goldziher, I. *Muslim Studies.* Ed. S. M. Stern; tr. C. R. Barber and S. M. Stern. Chicago–New York: Aldine-Atherton, 1971.

———. *Introduction to Islamic Theology and Law.* Tr. Andras Hamori and Ruth Hamori. Princeton, N.J.: Princeton University Press, 1981.

Gordon, Matthew S. *The Breaking of a Thousand Swords: A History of the Turkish Community of Samarra (200–275/815–889 CE).* New York: SUNY, 2001.

Gottheil, R. "A Christian Bahira Legend." *Zeitschrift für Assyriologie* 14 (1899).

Grabar, Oleg. *The Formation of Islamic Art.* New Haven, Conn.: Yale University Press, 1973.

———, with contributions by Muḥammad al-Asad, Abeer Audeh, and Said Nusseibeh. *The Shape of the Holy: Early Islamic Jerusalem.* Princeton, N.J.: Princeton University Press, 1996.

Graefe, Eric. "Das Pyramidenkapitel in al-Maqrizi's Khiṭaṭ'." *Leipziger Semitischen Studien* 5 (1968).

Green, Tamara M. *The City of the Moon God.* Leiden: E. J. Brill, 1992.

Grégoire, Henri. "The Byzantine Church." In *Byzantium: An Introduction to East Roman Civilization,* ed. N. H. Baynes and H. St. L. B. Moss. Oxford: Oxford University Press, 1961.

Griffith, Sidney. "Muḥammad and the Monk Baḥīra: Reflections on a Syriac and Arabic Text from Early 'Abbāsid Times." *Oriens Christianus* 79 (1995).

Gündüz, Şinasi. *The Knowledge of Life: The Origins and Early History of the Mandaeans and Their Relation to the Sabians of the Qur'ān and to the Harranians.* Oxford: Oxford University Press on behalf of the University of Manchester, 1994.

Gutas, Dimitri. *Greek Thought, Arabic Culture: The Graeco-Arabic Translation Movement in Baghdād and Early 'Abbāsid Society (2nd–4th/8th–10th centuries).* London: Routledge, 1998.

Halphen, Louis. *Charlemagne and the Carolingian Empire.* New York: North Holland, 1977.

Ḥamāda, Muḥammad Māhir. *Al-Wathā'iq al-Siyāsiyya wa al-Idāriyya al-'Ā'ida li-al-'Āṣr al-'Abbāsī al-Awwal.* Beirut: Mu'assasat al-Risāla, 1979.

———. *Al-Wathā'iq al-Siyāsiyya wa al-Idāriyya fī al-Andalus wa Shimālī Afrīqiyya: 64–897 AH-783–1492, Dirāsa wa Nuṣūs.* Beirut: Mu'assasat al-Risāla, 1986.

Ḥaṣṣūrī, 'Alī. "On the Ephitets of the 'Abbāsid Caliphs." *Der Islam* 59 (1982).

Hanson, Paul D., ed. *Visionaries and Their Apocalypses.* Philadelphia: Fortress Press, 1983.

Hartmann, Richard. "Der Sufyānī." In *Studia Orientalia Ioanni Pedersen Septuagenario A.D. VII 10 Nov. Anno MCMLIII Collegis Discipulis Amicis Dicata.* Hauniae, Denmark: Einar Munksgard, 1953.

Hellholm, David, ed. *Apocalypticism in the Mediterranean World and the Near East: Proceedings of the International Colloquium on Apocalypticism Uppsala, August 12–17, 1979.* Tubingen: J. C. B. Mohr (Paul Siebeck), 1983.

Helperin, David. "Ibn Ṣayyād Traditions and the Legend of al-Dajjāl." *JAOS* 96 (1976).

Hilmi Ömer Bey. "Some Considerations with Regard to the Ḥanīf Question." *MW* 22 (1932).

Hodges, Richard, and David Whitehouse. *Mohammed, Charlemagne and the Origins of Europe: Archeology and the Pirenne Thesis.* Ithaca, N.Y.: Cornell University Press, 1983.

Hodgson, Marshall G. S. *The Venture of Islam.* Chicago: University of Chicago Press, 1974.

Hoffmann, Von Gerhard. "Al-Amīn, al-Ma'mūn und der 'Pöbel' von Baghdād in den Jahren 812/813." *ZDMG* 143 (1993).

Holt, P. M. "Islamic Millennarianism and the Fulfillment of Prophecy: A Case Study." In *Prophecy and Millennarianism: Essays in Honour of Majorie Reeves,* ed. Ann Williams. Essex: Longman, 1980.

Hopper, Vincent Foster. *Medieval Number Symbolism: Its Sources, Meaning, and Influence on Thought and Expression.* Mineola, N.Y.: Dover, 2000.

Hoyland, Robert. *Seeing Islam as Others Saw It.* Princeton, N.J.: Darwin Press, 1997.

Hultgard, Anders. "Forms and Origins of Iranian Apocalypticism." In *Apocalypticism in the Mediterranean World and the Near East: Proceedings of the International Colloquium on Apocalypticism Uppsala, August 12–17, 1979,* ed. David Hellholm. Tubingen: J. C. B. Mohr (Paul Siebeck), 1983.

Hurgronje, C. Snouck. *Selected Works of C. Snouck Hurgronje,* ed. G. H. Bousquet and Joseph Schacht. Leiden: E. J. Brill, 1957.

———. *Verspreide Geschriften.* Bonn: Kurt Schoeder, 1923.

Innes, Matthew, and Rosamond McKitterick. "The Writing of History." In *Carolingian Culture,* ed. Rosamond McKitterick. Cambridge: Cambridge University Press, 1994.

İslam Ansiklopedisi. Istanbul: Türk Diyanet Vakfi İslam Araştırmaları Merkezi, 1988– .

Ismail, Osman S. A. "Mu'taṣim and the Turks." *BSOAS* (1966).

Al-Jābirī, Muḥammad Ābid. *Takwīn al-'Aql al-'Arabī.* Beirut: Markaz Dirāsāt al-Waḥda al-'Arabiyya, 1988.

Jad'ān, Fahmī. *Al-Miḥna: Baḥth fī Jadaliyyat al-Dīnī wa al-Siyāsī fī al-Islām.* Amman: Dār al-Shurūq, 1989.

Jayyusi-Lehn, Ghada. *The Life and the Career of the Caliph al-Mu'taṣim: A Problem in Historiography.* Ph.D. diss., University of Toronto, 2008.

Jeffrey, Arthur. *The Foreign Vocabulary of the Qur'ān.* Leiden: E. J. Brill, 2006.

Jenkins, Romilly. *Byzantium: The Imperial Centuries AD 610–1071.* Toronto: University of Toronto Press, 1987.

Jenkinson, E. J. "The Moslem Anti-Christ Legend." *MW* 20 (1930).

Jerolmack, Colin, and Douglas, Porpora. "Religion, Rationality, and Experience: A Response to the New Rational Choice Theory of Religion." *Sociological Theory* 22 (2004).

Johns, Jeremy, and Emilie Savage-Smith. "The Book of Curiosities: A Newly Discovered Series of Islamic Maps." *Imago Mundi* 55 (2003).

Jonas, Bishop of Orléans. *A Ninth-Century Political Tract: The Institutione Regia of Jonas of Orleans.* Tr. R. W. Dyson. Smithtown, N.Y.: Exposition Press, 1983.

Kaegi, Walter. *Army, Society and Religion in Byzantium.* London: Variorum, 1982.

Karamustafa, Ahmet T. "Introduction to Islamic Maps." In *The History of Cartography: Cartography in the Traditional Islamic and South Asian Societies,* ed. David Woodward. Vol. 2, Book 1. Chicago: University of Chicago Press, 1992.

Kennedy, E. S., and D. Pingree. *The Astrological History of Māshā'allāh.* Cambridge, Mass.: Harvard University Press, 1971.

———. *Studies in Islamic Exact Sciences.* Ed. David A. King and Mary Helen Kennedy. Beirut: American University of Beirut, 1983.

Kennedy, Hugh. *The Prophet and the Age of the Caliphates: The Islamic Near East from the Sixth to the Eleventh Century.* London: Longman, 1986.

Kieckhefer, Richard. *Magic in the Middle Ages.* Cambridge: Cambdrige University Press, 1989.

Kimber, R. A. "Hārūn al-Rashīd's Meccan Settlement of AH 186 / AD 802." *Occasional Papers of the School of 'Abbāsid Studies* 1–4 (1986–92).

Kinney, Dale. "Early Christian Monumental Decoration." In *The Apocalypse in the Middle Ages,* ed. Richard K. Emerson and Bernard McGinn. Ithaca, N.Y.: Cornell University Press, 1992.

Kister, M. J. "A Booth Like the Booth of Moses." *BSOAS* 25 (1962).

Klein, Peter K. "The Apocalypse in Medieval Art." In *The Apocalypse in the Middle Ages,* ed. Richard K. Emmerson and Bernard McGinn. Ithaca, N.Y.: Cornell University Press, 1992.

Koutrakou, N. A. "The Image of the Arabs in the Middle-Byzantine Politics: A Study in the Enemy Principle (8th–10th Centuries)." In *Languages of Power in Islamic Spain,* ed. Ross Brann and David I. Owen. Occasional Publications of the Department of Near Eastern Studies and the Program of Jewish Studies Cornell University, No. 3. Bethesda, Md.: Cornell University, 1997.

Kraus, Paul. *Jābir Ibn Ḥayyān: Contribution à l'histoire des idées scientifiques dans l'Islam: Jabir et la science grecque.* Paris: Les Belles Lettres, 1986.

Lambton, A. K. S. "Justice in the Medieval Persian Theory of Kingship." *SI* 17 (1962).

Lammens, Henri. "Le 'Sofiani': Héros national des Arabes Syriens." In *Études sur le siècle des Omayyades.* Beirut: Imprimeire Catholique, 1930.

Lamoreaux, John. "Early Eastern Christian Responses to Islam." In *Medieval Christian Perceptions of Islam: A Book of Essays,* ed. John Victor Tolan. New York: Garland, 1996.

Landau-Tasseron, Ella. "The 'Cyclical Reform:' A Study of the *Mujaddid* Tradition." *SI* 70 (1989).

Landes, Richard. "Lest the Millennium Be Fulfilled: Apocalyptic Expectations and the Pattern of Western Chronography 100–800 CE." In *Use and Abuse of Eschatology,* ed. Werner Verbeke, Daniel Verhelst, and Andries Welkenhuysen. Louvain: Louvain University Press, 1988.

Langermann, Y. Tzvi. "The Book of Bodies and Distances of Ḥabash al-Ḥāsib." *Centaurus* 28 (1985).

Lapidus, Ira M. "Separation of State and Religion in the Early Islamic Society." *IJMES* 6 (1975).

Lassner, Jacob. *Islamic Revolution and Historical Memory: An Inquiry into the Art of 'Abbāsid Apologetics.* New Haven, Conn.: American Oriental Society, 1986.

———. *Shaping of 'Abbāsid Rule.* Princeton, N.J.: Princeton University Press, 1980.

Lecker, Michael. *The "Constitution of Medina": Muḥammad's First Legal Document.* Princeton, N.J.: Darwin Press, 2004.

———. "An Apocalyptic Vision of Islamic History." *BSOAS* 13 (1950).

Lerner, Robert E. *The Power of Prophecy: The Cedar of Lebanon Vision from the Mongol Onslaught to the Dawn of the Enlightenment.* Berkeley: University of California Press, 1983.

Lewis, Bernard. "The Regnal Titles of the First 'Abbāsid Caliphs." In *Dr. M. Husayn Presentation Volume.* New Delhi, 1968.

Lombard, Maurice. *The Golden Age of Islam.* Tr. Joan Spencer. New York: North-Holland, 1975.

Madelung, Wilferd. *Religious and Ethnic Movements in Medieval Islam.* Hampshire, U.K.: Variorum, 1992.

———. "The Origins of the Controversy Concerning the Creation of the Koran." In *Orientalia Hispanica sive Studia F.M. Pareja Octogenario Dictata,* ed. J. M. Baral. Leiden: E. J. Brill, 1974.

———. "The Vigilante Movement of Sahl b. Salāma al-Khurāsānī and the Origins of Ḥanbalism Reconsidered." *Journal of Turkish Studies* 14 (1990).

———. "'Abdallāh b. al-Zubayr and the Mahdī." *JNES* 40 (1981).

———. "Apocalyptic Prophecies in Ḥims in the Umayyad Age." *JSS* 31 (1986).

———. "The Sufyānī between Tradition and History." *SI* 63 (1986).

———. "New Documents Concerning al-Faḍl b. Sahl and 'Alī al-Riḍā." In *Studia Arabica and Islamica: Festschrift for Iḥsān 'Abbās,* ed. Wadad Qadi. Beirut: American University of Beirut, 1981.

———. "The Hāshimiyyāt of al-Kumayt and the Hāshimī Shī'ism." *SI* 70 (1989).

———. "Was the Caliph al-Ma'mūn a Grandson of the Sectarian Leader Ustadhsīs?" In *Studies in Arabic and Islam: Proceedings of the 19th Congress, Union Européenne des Arabisants et Islamisants, Halle 1998,* ed. S. Leder et al. *Orientalia Lovaniensia Analecta,* 108. Louvain: Peeters, 2002.

Makdisi, George. "Authority in the Islamic Community." In *La Notion d'authorité au Moyen Age: Islam, Byzance, Occident Colloques internationaux de la Napoule,* ed. George Makdisi, Dominique Sourdel, and Janine Sourdel-Thomine. Paris: Presses Universitaires de France, 1982.

———. *The Rise of Humanism in Classical Islam and the Christian West.* Edinburgh: Edinburgh University Press, 1990.

———. *Religion, Law and Learning in Classical Islam.* Hampshire, U.K.: Variorum, 1991.

Mannheim, Karl. *Ideology and Utopia: An Introduction to the Sociology of Knowledge.* Tr. Louis Wirth and Edward Shils. 1936. Reprint, New York: Harcourt, Brace and World, 1968.

Martinez, Francisco Javier. "Eastern Christian Apocalyptic in the Early Muslim Period: Pseudo-Methodius and Pseudo-Anastasius." Ph.D. diss., Catholic University of America, 1985.

———. "The Apocalyptic Genre in Syriac: The World of Pseudo-Methodius." In *IV. Symposium Syriacum 1984: Literary Genres in Syriac Literature (Groningen-Oosterhesselen 10–12 September),* ed. H. J. W. Drijvers et al. Rome: Pont. Institutum Studiorum Orientalum, 1987.

———. "The King of Rūm and the King of Ethiopia in Medieval Apocalyptic Texts from Egypt." In *Coptic Studies: Acts of the Third International Congress of Coptic Studies, Warsow, 20–25 August 1984,* ed. Wlodzimiers Godlewski. Warsaw: PWN, 1990.

Massignon, Louis. "Inventaire de la littérature hermétique arabe." In *Opera Minora.* Paris: Universitaires de France, 1969.

McCormick, Michael. "The Imperial Edge: Italo-Byzantine Identity, Movement and Integration, A.D. 650–950." In *Studies on the Internal Diaspora of the Byzantine*

Empire, ed. Hélène Ahrweiler and Angeliki E. Laiou. Washington, D.C.: Dumbarton Oaks, 1998.

McGinn, Bernard. *Visions of the End: Apocalyptic Traditions in the Middle Ages.* New York: Columbia University Press, 1979.

McGinn, John, Joseph Collins, and Stephen J. Stein. *The Encyclopedia of Apocalypticism*. New York: Continuum, 1998.

Meynard, M. C. Barbier de. "Ibrāhīm fils de Mehdi: Fragments historiques, scènes de la vie d'artiste au III siècle de l'Hégire (778–839 de Notre Ére)." *Journal Asiatique* (1869).

Miles, George C. *The Numismatic History of Rayy: Numismatic Studies No. 2*. New York: American Numismatic Society, 1938.

Mingana, A. *Christian Documents in Syriac, Arabic and Garshūnī, Edited and Translated with Critical Apparatus, Timothy's Apology for Christianity.* Woodbrooke Studies, Vol. 2, Part 1. Cambridge: W. Heffer and Sons, 1928.

———. *Encyclopaedia of Philosophical and Natural Sciences as Taught in Baghdād About A.D. 817 or Book of Treasures by Job of Edessa.* Cambridge: W. Heffer and Sons, 1935.

Montgomery, James. "Al-Gāḥiẓ and Hellenizing Philosophy." D'Ancona Costa, Christina, ed. The Libraries of the Neoplatonists, Proceedings of the meeting of the European Science Foundation Network "Late Antiquity and Arabic Thought: Patterns in the Constitution of European Culture," Strasbourg, March 12–14, 2004. *Philosophia Antiqua*, v. 107. (Leiden and Boston: Brill, 2007).

Muir, Sir William. *The Caliphate: Its Rise, Decline and Fall.* 1898. Reprint, Beirut: Khayāṭ, 1963.

Nau, F. "Lettre de Jacques d'Edesse sur la généalogie de la sainte Vierge." *Revue de l'Orient Chrétien* (1901).

Nagel, Tilman. *Untersuchungen zur Entstehung des 'Abbāsidischen Kalifates.* Bonn: Bonn University, 1972.

———. *Staat und Glaubensgemeinschaft im Islam: Geschichte der politischen Ordnungsvorstellungen der Muslime.* Munich: Artemis Verlag, 1981.

———. *Rechtleitung und Kalifat.* Bonn: Orientalische Seminare der Universität, 1975.

Nawas, John A. *Al-Ma'mūn: Miḥna and the Caliphate.* Nijmegen, 1992.

———."A Reexamination of Three Current Explanations for al-Ma'mūn's Introduction of the Miḥna." *IJMES* 26 (1994).

———. "The Miḥna of 218 A.H. / 833 A.D. Revisited." *JAOS* 116/4 (1996).

———. "A Psychoanalitic View of Some Oddities in the Bahavior of the 'Abbāsid Caliph al-Ma'mūn." *Sharqiyyat* 8 (1996).

Olsson, Tord. "The Apocalyptic Activity: The Case of Jamasp Namak." In *Apocalypticism in the Mediterranean World and the Near East: Proceedings of the International Colloquium on Apocalypticism Uppsala, August 12–17, 1979,* ed. David Hellholm. Tubingen: J. C. B. Mohr (Paul Siebeck), 1983.

Oppolzer, Theodor von. *Canon der Finsternisse.* New York: Dover Books, 1962.

Palmer, Andrew. "The Messiah and the Mahdī: History Presented as the Writing on the Wall." In *Polyphonia Byzantina: Studies in Honour of Willem J. Aerts,* ed. Hero Hokwerda et al. Groningen: Egberg Forsten, 1993.

Papadakis, Aristeides. "Iconoclasm: A Study of the Hagiographical Evidence." Ph.D. diss., Fordham University, 1968.

Patton, Walter M. *Aḥmad Ibn Ḥanbal and the Miḥna: A Biography of the Imām Including an Account of the Mohammedan Inquisition Called the Miḥna 218–234 AH*. Leiden: E. J. Brill, 1897.

Pellat, Charles. "The Origin and Development of Historiography in Muslim Spain." In *Etudes sur l'Histoire socio-culturelle de l'Islam (VIIe-Xve s)*. London: Variorum, 1976.

———. "Le culte de Muawiya au IIIe siècle de l'Hégire." In *Études sur l'histoire socio-culturelle de l'Islam (VIIe-Xve s)*. London: Variorum, 1976.

Peters, F. E. *Jerusalem and Mecca*. New York: New York University Press, 1986.

———. *Muhammad and the Origins of Islam*. New York: SUNY Press, 1994.

Pickthall, M. M. *The Meaning of the Glorious Koran: An Explanatory Translation*. New York: New American Library, 1932.

Pingree, David. *Thousands of Abū Ma'shar*. London: Warburg Institute, 1968.

———. "Historical Horoscopes." *JAOS* 82 (1962).

———. "The Fragments of the Works of Ya'qūb b. Ṭāriq." *JNES* 27 (1968).

———. "The Fragments of the Works of al-Fāzārī." *JNES* 29 (1970).

———. "The Sabians of Harran and the Classical Tradition." *International Journal of the Classical Tradition* 9 (2002).

Plessner, M. "Hermes Trismegistos and Arab Science." *SI* 2 (1954).

Poole, Stanley Lane. *The Coins of Eastern Khaleefehs in the British Museum*. London: Longmans, 1875.

Price, Major David. *Mahommedan History: From the Death of the Arabian Legislator to the Accession of the Emperor Akbar and the Establishment of the Moghul Empire in Hindustaun—From Original Persian Authorities*. New Delhi: Inter India, 1812.

Al-Qādī, Wadād. *Al-Kaysāniyya fī al-Tārīkh wa al-Adab*. Beirut: Dār al-Thaqāfa, 1974.

Radke, Bernard. "Towards a Topology of 'Abbāsid Universal Chronicles." *Occasional Papers of the School of 'Abbāsid Studies* 3 (1990).

Ricci, Alessandra. "The Road from Baghdād to Byzantium and the Case of the Bryas Palace in Istanbul." In *Byzantium in the Ninth Century: Dead or Alive?* ed. L. Brubaker. London: Ashgate-Variorum, 1998.

Al-Rifā'ī, Aḥmad Farīd. *'Aṣr al-Ma'mūn*. Cairo: Maktabat Dār al-Kutub al-Miṣriyya, 1927.

Reeves, Marjorie. "The Development of Apocalyptic Thought: Medieval Attitudes." In *The Apocalypse in the English Renaissance Thought and Literature*, ed. C. A. Patrides and Joseph Wittreich. Manchester: Manchester University Press, 1984.

Reinink, G. J. "The Beginnings of Syriac Apologetic Literature in Response to Islam." *Oriens Christianus* 77 (1993).

———. "Pseudo-Methodius und die Legende vom römischen Endkaiser." In *The Use and Abuse of Eschatology in the Middle Ages*, ed. Werner Berke et al. Louvain: Louvain University Press, 1988.

Rinehart, James. *Revolution and the Millennium*. Westport, Conn.: Praeger, 1997.

Robinson, Chase F. *Islamic Historiography*. Cambridge: Cambride University Press, 2003.

Rosen-Ayalon, Myriam. *The Early Islamic Monuments of al-Ḥaram al-Sharīf: An Iconographic Study*. Jerusalem: Hebrew University, 1989.

Rosenthal, F. "The Prophecies of Bābā the Ḥarrānian." In *A Locust's Leg: Studies in*

Honour of S. H. Taqizade, ed. W. B. Henning and E. Yarshater. London: Percy Lund, Humphries, 1962.

Rubin, Uri. *Between Bible and Qur'ān: The Children of Israel and the Islamic Self-Image.* Princeton, N.J.: Darwin Press, 1999.

———. "Traditions in Transformations: The Ark of the Covenant and the Golden Calf in Biblical and Islamic Historiography." *Oriens* 36 (2001).

Ruggles, D. F. "Representation and Identity in Medieval Spain: Beatus Manuscripts and the Mudejar Churches of Teruel." *Occasional Publications of the Department of Near Eastern Studies and the Program of Jewish Studies Cornell University*, No. 3, ed. Ross Brann and David I. Owen. 1997.

Ruska, Julius. *Tabula Smaragdina: Ein Beitrag zur Geschichte der Hermetischen Literatur.* Heidelberg: Carl Winter's Universitätbuchhandlung, 1926.

Sabra, A. I. "The Appropriation and Subsequent Naturalization of Greek Science in Medieval Islam: A Preliminary Statement." *History of Science* 25 (1987).

Sachedina, Abdulaziz A. *Islamic Messianism: The Idea of the Mahdī in Twelver Shī'ism.* Albany: SUNY Press, 1981.

Ṣafwat, Aḥmad Zakī. *Jamharat Rasā'il al-'Arab.* Cairo: Maktabat Musṭafā al-Bābī al-Ḥalabī wa Awlādu bi Miṣr, 1971.

Sahas, Daniel J. *John of Damascus on Islam: The Heresy of the Ishmaelites.* Leiden: E. J. Brill, 1972.

Saliba, George. *Islamic Science and the Making of the European Renaissance.* Cambridge, Mass.: MIT Press, 2007.

Samadi, S. B. "The Struggle between the Two Brothers Al-Amīn and Al-Ma'mūn." *Islamic Culture* 31–32 (1957–58).

Samsó, Julio. *Islamic Astronomy and Medieval Spain.* Brookfield, Vt.: Variorum, 1994.

Schimmel, Annemarie. *The Mystery of Numbers.* New York: Oxford University Press, 1993.

Schmithals, Walter. *The Apocalypic Movement: Introduction and Interpretation.* Tr. John L. Steely. Nashville, Tn.: Abingdon Press, 1973.

Schwartz, Hillel. "The End of the Beginning." *Religious Studies Review* 2/3 (1976).

Sezgin, Fuat. *Geschichte des arabischen Schrifttums.* Leiden: E. J. Brill, 1971.

Shacklady, H. "The 'Abbāsid Movement in Khurāsān." *Occasional Papers of the School of 'Abbāsid Studies* 1 (1986).

Shamma, Samīr. *Aḥdāth 'Aṣr al-Ma'mūn Kamā Tarwihā al-Nuqūd.* Irbid, Jordan: Jāmi'at al-Yarmūk, 1995.

Sharon, Moshe. *Black Banners from the East.* Leiden: E. J. Brill, 1983.

————. *Revolt: The Social and Military Aspects of the 'Abbāsid Revolution.* Jerusalem: Hebrew University, 1990.

Silver, Abba Hillel. *A History of Messianic Speculation in Israel: From the First through the Seventeenth Centuries.* New York: Macmillan, 1927.

Sourdel, Dominique. "La politique religieuse du calife 'Abbāside Al-Ma'mūn." *Revue des études islamiques* 30 (1962).

———. *Medieval Islam.* London: Routledge and Kegan Paul, 1983.

———. *La Vizirat 'Abbāside de 749 a 936.* Damascus: Institut Français de Damas, 1959.

———. "'Abbāsid Caliphate." In *The Cambridge History of Islam*, ed. P. M. Holt, A. K. S. Lambton, and B. Lewis. Cambridge: Cambridge University Press, 1970.

Stoneman, Richard. "Alexander the Great in the Arabic Tradition." In *The Ancient Novel and Beyond*, ed. Stelios Panayotakis et al. Leiden: E. J. Brill, 2003.

Suermann, Harald. "Einige Bemerkungen zu syrischen Apokalypsen des 7. Jhds." In *IV. Symposium Syriacum 1984: Literary Genres in Syriac Literature (Groningen-Oosterhesselen 10–12 September)*, ed. H. J. W. Drijvers et al. Rome: Pont. Institutum Studiorum Orientalum, 1987.

———. "Muḥammad in Christian and Jewish Apocalyptic Expectations." *Islam and Christian-Muslim Relations* 5 (1994).

Talmon, Yonina. "Millenarian Movements." *Archives européenes de sociologie* 7 (1966).

Tamari, Shemuel. *Iconotextual Studies in the Muslim Vision of Paradise.* Weisbaden: Harrasovitz, 1999.

Tartar, Georges. *Dialogue Islamo-Chrétien sous le Calife al-Ma'mūn (813–834): Les épitres d'al-Hāshimī et d'al-Kindī*. Paris: Nouvelles Editions Latines, 1985.

Thrupp, Sylvia, ed. *Millennial Dreams in Action: Essays in Comparative Study.* The Hague: Mouton, 1962.

Tolan, John Victor, ed. *Medieval Christian Perceptions of Islam*. New York: Garland, 1996.

Tor, Deborah G. "An Historiographical Re-Examination of the Appointment and Death of ʻAlī al-Riḍā." *Der Islam* 78 (2001).

Treadgold, Warren. *The Byzantine Revival 780–842*. Stanford, Calif.: Stanford University Press, 1988.

Tucker, William F. "Al-Manṣūr al-ʻIjlī and the Manṣūriyya: A Study in Medieval Terrorism." *Der Islam* 54 (1977).

———. Bayān b. Samʻān and the Bayāniyya: Shīʻite Extremists of Umayyad Iraq." *MW* 65 (1975).

———. "ʻAbdallāh b. Muʻāwiya and the Janaḥiyya: Rebels and Ideologues of the Late Umayyad Period." *SI* 51 (1980).

———. "Rebels and Gnostics: Al-Mughīra ibn Saʻīd and the Mughīriyya." *Arabica* 22 (1975).

ʻUmar, Fārūq (Farouk Omar). *Al-Khilāfa al-ʻAbbāsiyya fī ʻAṣr al-Fawḍa al-ʻAskariyya: 861–947.* Baghdad: Dār al-Muthanna, 1977.

———. *Tārīkh al-Iraq fī ʻUṣūr al-Khilāfa al-ʻArabiyya al-Islāmiyya 35/656–622/1258.* Baghdad: Maktabat al-Nahḍa, 1988.

———. *Buḥūth fī al-Tārīkh al-ʻAbbāsī*. Beirut and Baghdad: Dār al-Qalam and Maktabat al-Nahḍa, 1977.

———. *The ʻAbbāsid Caliphate: 132/750–170/786*. Baghdad: n.p., 1969.

———. "Politics and Problem of Succession in the Early ʻAbbāsid Caliphate: 132/750–158/775." *IQ* 18 (1974).

van Bladel, Kevin. "Hermes Arabicus." Ph.D. diss., Yale University, 2004.

van Ess, Joseph. "Ibn Kullāb und die Miḥna." *Oriens* 18–19 (1967).

———. *Theologie und Gesellschaft im 2. und 3. Jahrhundert Hidschra: Eine Geschichte des religiösen Denkens im frühen Islam*. Berlin: Walter de Gruyter, 1992.

———. *Die Gedankenwelt des Ḥarit al-Muhāsibī: Anhand von Übersetzungen aus seinen Schriften dargestellt und erläutert*. Mainz: Bonn University, 1961.

———. *Das Kitāb an-Nakṭ des Naẓẓām und seine Rezeption im Kitāb al-Futyā de Gāḥiẓ: Eine Sammlung der Fragmente mit Übersetzung und Kommentar.* Gottingen: Vandenhoeck und Ruprecht, 1972.

van Reeth, J. M. F. "Caliph al-Ma'mūn and the Treasure of the Pyramids." *Orientalia Lovaniensia Periodica* 25 (1994).

van Vloten, G. *Recherches sur la domination arabe, le Chiitisme et les croyances messianiques sous le Khalifat des Omayyades.* Amsterdam: J. Müller, 1894.

Vasiliev, A. A. *History of the Byzantine Empire 324–1453*. Madison: University of Wisconsin Press, 1964.

———. "Medieval Ideas of the End of the World: West and East." *Byzantion* 16 (1944).

———. *Byzance et les Arabes.* Ed. Henri Grégoire et al. Brussels: Editions de l'Institut de Philologie et D'Histoire Orientales, 1935.

Verbelen, Felix. *Ancient Astronomy.* http://users.online.be/felixverbelen/catzeute.htm (accessed 10 February 2001).

Vryonis, Speros, Jr. "Byzantium and Islam: Seven-Seventeenth Century." In *Byzantium: Its Internal History and Relations with the Muslim World.* London: Variorum, 1971.

Waines, D. "The Third Century Internal Crisis of the 'Abbāsids." *JESHO* 20 (1977).

Wansbrough, John. *Qur'ānic Studies.* Oxford: Oxford University Press, 1977.

Wasserstrom, Steven. "The 'Īsāwiyya Revisited." *SI* 75 (1992).

———. "The Moving Finger Writes: Mughīra b. Sa'īd's Islamic Gnosis and the Myths of its Rejection." *History of Religions* 25 (1985–86).

Watt, Montgomery W. *Early Islam: Collected Articles.* Edinburgh: Edinburgh University Press, 1990.

———. *The Formative Period of Islamic Thought.* Edinburgh: Edinburgh University Press, 1973.

———. *Islamic Philosophy and Theology.* Edinburgh: Edinburgh University Press, 1992.

———. *Islamic Political Thought.* Edinburgh: Edinburgh University Press, 1980.

———. *Free Will and Predestination in Early Islam.* London: Luzac, 1948.

———. *Muslim-Christian Encounters: Perceptions and Misperceptions.* London: Routledge, 1991.

Weber, Max. *The Theory of Social and Economic Organization.* Tr. A. M. Henderson and Talcott Parsons. New York: Oxford University Press, 1947.

Weil, Gustav. *Geschichte der Chalifen.* Mannheim: Verlag von Friedrich Bafferman, 1848.

Wellhausen, J. *Das arabische Reich und sein Sturz.* Berlin: Verlag von Georg Reimer, 1902.

———. *The Arab Kingdom and its Fall.* Tr. Margaret Graham Weir. 1927. Reprint, Beirut: Khayyāṭ, 1927.

Williams, John. "Purpose and Imagery in the Apocalypse Commentary of Beatus of Liebana." In *The Apocalypse in the Middle Ages,* ed. Richard K. Emmerson and Bernard McGinn. Ithaca, N.Y.: Cornell University Press, 1992.

Wilson, C. E. "The Wall of Alexander Against Gog and Magog, and the Expedition Sent Out to Find it by the Khalif Wathiq in 842 A.D." In *Hirth* [*sic*] *Anniversary Volume (=Asia Major, introductory volume)*, ed. B. Schindler. London: Robsthain, 1922.

Woodward, David, ed. *The History of Cartography: Cartography in the Traditional Islamic and South Asian Societies,* Vol. 2, Book 1. Chicago: University of Chicago Press, 1992.

Young, M. J. L., and R. Y. Ebied. "An Unrecorded Arabic Version of a Sibylline Prophecy." *Orientalia Christiana Periodica* 43 (1977).

Yücesoy, Hayrettin. "Between Nationalism and the Social Sciences: A History of Modern Scholarship on the 'Abbāsid Civil War and the Reign of al-Ma'mūn." *Medieval Encounters* 8 (2002).

———. *Taṭawwur al-Fikr al-Siyāsī 'inda Ahl al-Sunna: Fatrat al-Takwīn*. Amman: Dār al-Bashīr, 1993.

———. "Translation as Self-Consciousness: The 'Abbāsid Translation Movement, Ancient Sciences, and Antediluvian Wisdom." *The Journal of World History* (forthcoming).

———. "The Seventh of the 'Abbāsids and the Millennium: A Study of the Fourth Civil War and the Reign of al-Ma'mūn (193–218 A.H. / 808–833 C.E.)." Ph.D. diss., University of Chicago, 2002.

Zahniser, Mathias. "Insights from the 'Uthmāniyya of al-Jāḥiẓ into the Religious Policy of al-Ma'mūn." *MW* 69 (1979).

Zaman, Muhammad Qasim. *Religion and Politics under the 'Abbāsids: The Emergence of the Proto-Sunni Elite.* Leiden: E. J. Brill, 1997.

———. "The Caliphs, the 'Ulamā', and the Law: Defining the Role and the Function of the Caliph in the Early 'Abbāsid Period." *Islamic Law and Society* 4/1 (1997).

———. "Early 'Abbāsid Response to Apocalyptic Propaganda: A Note." *Islamic Quarterly* 32 (1988).

———. "Routinization of Revolutionary Charisma: Notes on the 'Abbāsid Caliphs al-Manṣūr and al-Mahdī." *Islamic Studies* 29 (1990).

Zaydān, Jurjī. *Al-Amīn wa al-Ma'mūn.* N.p.: Dār al-Hilāl, 1965.

Index